LITERATURE AS SYSTEM

Literature as System

ESSAYS TOWARD THE

THEORY OF LITERARY HISTORY

CLAUDIO GUILLÉN

PRINCETON UNIVERSITY PRESS 1971

This book has been composed in Linotype Granjon

17429

Printed in the United States of America
by Princeton University Press, Princeton, New Jersey

para Stephen Gilman

ACKNOWLEDGMENTS

"The Aesthetics of Literary Influence" was first published in *Comparative Literature: Proceedings of the Second Congress of the International Comparative Literature Association*, edited by Werner P. Friederich (Chapel Hill, N.C., 1959), and is reprinted here by permission of the University of North Carolina Press.

Quotations from Antonio de Villegas, *El Abencerraje*, edited by Francisco López Estrada and translated by John Esten Keller (Chapel Hill, N.C., 1964), are included here with the permission of Professor Keller and the University of North Carolina Press.

"Toward a Definition of the Picaresque" first appeared in the *Proceedings of the IIId Congress of the International Comparative Literature Association*, edited by W. A. P. Smit (The Hague, 1962), and is reprinted here by permission of Mouton & Co.

"On the Concept and Metaphor of Perspective" was first published in *Comparatists at Work. Studies in Comparative Literature*, edited by Stephen G. Nichols, Jr., and Richard B. Vowles (Waltham, Mass., 1968), and is included here by permission of the Blaisdell Press.

"Literature as System" was published in *Comparative Literature* (Summer, 1970) and is reprinted here by permission of the editors of that journal.

"Second Thoughts on Literary Periods" was written for *The Disciplines of Criticism: Essays in Literary Theory, Interpretation, and History Honoring René Wellek on the Occasion of his Sixty-Fifth Birthday*, edited by Peter Demetz, Thomas Greene, and Lowry Nelson, Jr. (New Haven and London, 1968), and is reprinted here by permission of the Yale University Press.

"On the Object of Literary Change" first appeared in *The Yearbook of Comparative and General Literature* (1969) and is reprinted here by permission of the editors of that journal.

"The Cats of Rome," Julian Palley's translation of "Gatos de Roma," published in Jorge Guillén's *Affirmation. A Bilingual Anthology, 1919-1966* (Norman, Okla., 1968), is reprinted here with the permission of Professor Palley and the University of Oklahoma Press.

CONTENTS

LITERATURE AS SYSTEM

INTRODUCTION

I have gathered in this volume eleven essays that I venture to regard as—in a large degree—theoretical. The oldest, "Stylistics of Silence," was published in Spanish some dozen years ago; and I have both translated and, of course, rewritten it. The same applies to two other Spanish articles, and to portions of a few more. The remaining pieces were written originally in English. I have retouched them a bit—and perhaps translated them as well, if the term may be used to denote the passage from one stage of thought to another.

Only the first two essays deal explicitly with questions pertaining to the theory and practice of comparative literature. Yet no one who has labored in or for that discipline will fail to recognize that most of the following pages answer to the theoretical concerns of comparatists.

The oldest and most basic of these concerns—spanning the early decades of comparative studies, from the end of the nineteenth century to the years preceding World War II—has been the idea of literary influence, which I analyze in the first section of this book. Section II centers on the idea of genre, a focus which might be called characteristic of comparative studies in their mature phase. The essays in the final section move rather more boldly in the direction of the theory of literary history.

Today comparatists are being called upon more and more to fulfill the theoretical function without which no body of knowledge can emerge from the accomplishments of literary criticism. This function should not be confused with the preliminary and empirical aims of methodology; nor does it necessarily coincide with the overall—usually metahistorical—inquiry into either the aesthetics of the verbal work of art or the peculiarities of poetic language. As I understand it, the object of this theoretical effort—hence the difficulty and the fascination of the task—is literary history itself. And its role is comparable to that played by linguistic theory in a department of linguistics where a number of researchers are also engaged in the study of French, Japanese, and Guaraní; or even more, to that of anthropological theory in the teaching of a team of anthropologists who have completed their respective field trips and then tried to assimilate the results of their year-long observation of isolated communities in New Mexico, Brazil, or the South Seas. As far as literary history is concerned, each of us has known (and can or should return to) his own formative, unforgettable South Sea island: a particular language, a nation, a moment in history, perhaps even a single play or poem fully and decisively understood. Without the lessons drawn from such "field trips," literary theory would be bloodless indeed. Without subsequent theory, a lonely item of research remains a modest contribution to chaos. It is the movement not so much from the national to the international as from criticism to theory (a movement one is likely to reiterate, in both directions, time and time again) which is characteristic of comparative literature in its present phase.

My broadest intent has been to support a structural approach toward the fundamental units, terms, and problems of literary history. I have begun to show some of the ways in which literature presents itself or functions historically as a system—i.e., as an order (of interacting parts) and a cluster of orders, changing and yet enduring through the centuries.

The single poem or novel acts upon the reader as a unit, of course, on an aesthetic level; and no genuine literary critic will fail to observe with attention how the singularity of this experience reflects the poet's earlier attempt to shape and unify a complex of forms. But the aims of literary history are markedly different; and no real historian will fail to insert the isolated object of study into a larger pattern of events—into one of the constituent premises, alternatives, or designs of a particular society or civilization at a certain moment in its history. To behold and admire the Cathedral of Notre Dame is not to deny that it has been a functional part of Paris for a great many years, and that the relationship between Notre Dame and Paris has evolved from one epoch to another. The concern of the historian is with the fact that a poem or a novel has belonged to an organized whole considered as a historical occurrence and thus been brought into one of the "orders" that societies strive to build. Insofar as it did so belong, the individual work of art did not merely become an additional unit in a sum of separate units. It entered a structural whole, a system, among whose parts significant and reciprocal relations existed.

The inability to perceive these relations is what one might call the "atomistic fallacy" in literary studies. Section I of this book examines the idea of influence and its association with this fallacy during the nineteenth century. From the Renaissance to the Enlightenment, the integrity of literature had been assured by the normative impact and the remarkable continuity of poetics and rhetoric. This timeless whole was divided during the Romantic movement and conclusively shattered, as we all know, by the combined action of at least two prevailing trends: the rampant interest in individuality; and the historical imagination. The main consequence was a serial view of literature as a chronological succession of individual works and writers. To counteract this seriality and compensate for the loss of an independent focus found in poetics or poetry itself, literary historians were forced to form new alliances and seek outside means of support. The concept of the nation, regarded by definition as an organic whole, growing and developing in history, became the all-embracing principle of unity. I have tried to show that comparative literature in its early stages represented not only a politic compromise between the national and the universal but a clear expression of atomistic attitudes. The study of literary influences across international frontiers brought these attitudes into contact with a nearly biological obsession with origins, genesis, and growth, while respecting at the same time the sacrosanct notion of the organic unity of a national culture and a national literature.

I have also indicated that influence studies, as we look back on them today, yielded some positive results as well. They had the merit, in fact, of strangely highlighting (especially in their account of what was appropriately though unconsciously named "the fortunes of a writer," *la fortune d'un écrivain*) the contingency of our literary past as a historical process. In using the word "contingency," I should add that I have had in mind not Baruch Spinoza but Claude Lévi-Strauss and the literary structuralists, in inner dialogue with whom some parts of this book were written. Despite the vastness of the subject, and difficult though it is to describe it simply but not pompously, the central role of the idea of structure in our time may be ascribed to this: to the search for an "order" or a "sense" in a fast-changing, time-filled, historical world left to its own devices—bereft of any external or eternal source of meaning. Granted that such are the situation and the search, there are at least four procedures confronting the historian. One is the discovery of underlying designs, polarities, or "deep structures" beneath the actual tale of events and processes of which history is made. A second procedure singles out and concentrates on the individual event or object, the moment of intuition, liberation (in the case of literary history, through the lone masterpiece), or extasis, as the believer does, or the poet when he is, in Heidegger's words, "the shepherd of Being." A third consists in abstracting from history a final cause or concept, such as progress, ultimate redemption and judgment, or inevitable revolution. The fourth, finally, seeks to recognize enduring constructions and meaningful relations in history itself, actual structures and systems in the agelong career of existing civilizations— and thus to assist in healing, perhaps, the detachment, the reluctant encounter with historical time of those who do not easily countenance the remoteness of "deep structures" and promised salvations, or the waiting from one moment of truth to another.

I am not saying that any of these attitudes is incompatible with the rest. But my subject is a particular intellectual discipline and its contemporary viability, not the relationship between theory and praxis in the life of the historian. And it strikes me that the first three of these attitudes, insofar as they assume either the uselessness of history "as what actually happened" or its subordination to a cause, an article of faith, or the vision of what ought to happen, are not directly relevant to the efforts of the historian. It is only, I think, the fourth way, the interpretation of temporal orders or of struggles for order that have taken place in the past, which makes literary history *possible* today. To the general search for intrahistorical structures the literary historian has made and can continue to make important contributions: by means of the comparative study, for example, of imaginative constructions and past designs involving great poetic works, prevailing types or themes or styles, and literary genres traditionally arranged in the theoretical orders of poetics.

Section II addresses itself to the idea of genre. Its four essays, drawing nearer to practical criticism (and the chief opposition "picaresque-pastoral"), approach the organization of literary works in generic terms from several angles. "Toward a Definition of the Picaresque" grants the critic one of his traditional rights: the freedom to define, compare, arrange the available stories and forms into various groups, according to the criteria derived from the analysis of key novels. Since Romanticism and the breakdown of normative poetics, the tendency has been to view the description of particular genres as a topic for historical or critical scholarship. One can readily overlook the fact that poetic norms and models have composed historical constellations, lasting and yet constantly moving, ideal spaces with which the practicing writer had to come to terms. "On the Uses of Literary Genre" looks at the question from three points of view: the writer's, the critic's, and the theorist's. But an unavoidable consequence, besides, of the structural-historical approach is the contact between different provinces of history. The last two essays in this section, dealing with aspects of the picaresque, the Hispano-Moorish novel, and the pastoral within the dialectics of "genre and countergenre" and, in general, of the evolution of poetic systems, bring gradually into focus some of the relations existing between these literary designs and the structures of contemporary society.

The polarity of genre and countergenre echoes the dialectics of fiction and society. An "imperfect" fictional world like the picaresque can insinuate or connote, in the Hegelian sense, the very opposite of itself as a potentiality and a need. An imaginary picture of perfection such as the eclogue may act upon us like the antithesis and the disclosure of the inadequacies among which we live. In "Literature as Historical Contradiction" I discuss some of the ways in which the idyllic, expanding forms of the Moorish novel (the dream of friendship between Arabs and Christians) embraced and disputed the structures of contemporary society (the exclusion and finally the banning of the *moriscos* or descendants of the Moors) through the strategies of implication and allusion.

The nature of these allusive techniques and "expanding forms" is the subject of "Stylistics of Silence," which is based on a detailed formal analysis of a single poem by Antonio Machado. While writing this essay, which I first undertook as an exploration of both the limits of formal analysis and the limits of a single poem, it became clearer to me that the allusiveness of poetic language is not necessarily a kind of vagueness or omission, but is rather the exact effect of a poem's exceptional structural qualities. The curious alliance one finds in the "poetry of silence" between a principle of unity and a principle of expansion—between motion and emotion—is a function, oddly enough, of the high degree of structuration such poetry can offer. Thus the poem is a "little system" for very special reasons, which is what we sometimes mean when we prefer to speak not of its structure but of its form.

It seems to me today (more than a dozen years after my reading of Machado) that this "principle of expansion" is a close ally of that *referential* function which so many students of literature tend to underestimate. Some of the most acute interpreters of poetry—whether linguists like Roman Jakobson or writers and critics like Octavio Paz—have focused our attention in recent years on how poems essentially pursue a creative exploration of language for its own sake. In "Stylistics of Silence," I was also interested in showing how a poem, in my own terms, "transfers the qualities of system from the code to the message." Using Jakobson's terms, this is a point that I could now rephrase as follows: "the poem projects the qualities of system [one of which may be equivalence] from the axis of selection into the axis of combination." But I must immediately point out that "poem," not "poetic function," is used in this definition. In the case of the latter alone, it is indeed possible to speak of an exclusive concentration on the qualities of the "message." But where genuine poems are concerned, there is a final paradox to be confronted: that the strengthening and perfecting of the message itself, which, at one phase of the reading, narcissistically emphasizes its own felicitous form, strengthens and energizes ultimately the other aspects or functions of language as well—the referential, the conative, the emotive, the metalingual, etc. We are all aware of the powerful ways in which the poet's exploration of the possibilities of the verbal sign is capable of affecting, enriching, structuring, replacing, or destroying the object to which it refers. Jakobson has stated that "the supremacy of poetic function over referential function does not obliterate the reference but makes it ambiguous" ("Linguistics and Poetics," in

Style in Language, ed. Thomas A. Sebeok [Cambridge, Mass., 1960], p. 371). This idea should be studied and expanded. The effect of a metaphor is multifold not only for the poem itself but in a referential direction too. To multiply the power of the poetic function of words within the system of the poem is to heighten the conscious and active level of the referential function.

"On the Concept and Metaphor of Perspective" sustains some of the recurrent themes of this volume in a manner that I am perhaps not best qualified to judge. Suffice it to say here that the career of the metaphor of "perspective" brings out and exemplifies visibly some of the main issues which a theory of history must face, to wit: the extraordinary continuity of verbal discoveries; the clash and confrontation within a single time span of different cultural processes (the visual arts, literature, philosophy, among others); and the emergence of certain structures—in this case, the structure of a metaphor—through historical time only and as a precipitate of history.

In the three essays that follow (Section V), I have proceeded to examine more directly this complex of problems with particular regard not to the relationship between "literature" and "history" (an insoluble and unsound question) but to literary history itself, considered as a specific and original branch of history. "Literature as System," the first of these essays, identifies certain aspects in the career of literary structures—the old alliances with the designs of grammar, philosophy, or pedagogy; the impact of anthologies and canons of great writers; the durability of elemental structures—on the basis of examples chosen from the history of poetics. "Second Thoughts on Literary Periods" explores by means of the study of a representative polarity (literary period against literary current) an essential problem: the connections between artistic criticism and historical time. The resulting stress on the "multiplicity of time," on the co-presence in a single historical moment of a "cluster of durations," goes back to the poetic experience analyzed in "Stylistics of Silence," while relying also on two theoretical sources of support: Alfred North Whitehead's view of the world as an immense complex of events and processes, each destined to reach its own end and by the same token to serve as basis for the growth of still more processes; and the pluralistic conception of time implicit in Fernand Braudel's historical methodology (particularly the idea of *longue durée*). These questions are discussed further in "On the Object of Literary Change," where structures are envisaged as the necessary framework of historical discourse—not only for the sake of literature itself but as an approach to the difficult issue of the changing relations between literary and social or economic systems.

The word "system," reminiscent though it is of mechanical contraptions or, even worse, of dusty tomes of philosophical prose, has been usefully applied to the study of literary history by a number of critics and theorists, from Friedrich Schlegel to René Wellek. (I have tried to clarify these matters of terminology in the second part of "On the Object of Literary Change.") It has fulfilled, of course, a number of different functions. When the frame of reference is an individual poem and its analysis, as in "Stylistics of Silence," the relational effects of which poetic language is capable become so highly multiplied and transfigured that a term like "structure" or "system" takes on a very special force. Today I would prefer to restrict myself to "form" when speaking of the inner qualities of the work of art. "System," on the other hand, goes back for us to Ferdinand de Saussure and to the attempts to bring a linguistic model to bear on literature as a whole—entire groupings of works, styles, genres. These two areas were decisively linked from a structural point of view by Roman Jakobson, Yuriy Tynyanov, and other Russian formalists. As I understand these terms, "system" is the broader notion, while "structure" is more precise, closer to actualization. "Structure" designates especially the interrelations (of significant dependence) between constituent units; "system," the set which is held together by these relations or the larger configuration embracing one set after another in historical time. For example: French literature was a system in the 1870's, and the triad "poetry-prose poem-prose" was one of its structures. In most cases, detailed study shows that "system" as applied to historical wholes often stands for "tendency toward system" or structuration. This is why, I think, the use of these terms on more than one level is perhaps justified. As I indicate in the essay "Literature as System," the effectiveness of the structural links existing between the ancient designs of grammar, ethics, pedagogy, and poetics results largely from the fact that they all contribute to make "order" possible, to serve as principles of organization. The exceptional formal qualities of the verbal work of art appear less remote if only one views poetic "form" (the achievement of the writer as maker or "poet") as both a product and a creative process underlying this product—as form-making, that is, or formation; and a cultural structure, in a dynamic sense too, as structuration. "Forms," "structures," and "systems" are different manifestations—moving from the individual to the collective, from the manmade object to the social environment fashioned by successive generations—of a constructive struggle for order. A metaphor, a poem, and a system are like concentric spirals rising and tending toward meaningful order.

I have also proposed a simpler analogy in more than one passage of this book. It has seemed to me that a cultural whole or a literary system could be visualized, metaphorically speaking, as the verbal and imaginary equivalent of an ancient yet living, persistent yet profoundly changing *city*. The great cities we have all admired, merging stone with flowing water, monuments with gardens, humble streets with spacious plazas, Gothic churches with Baroque palaces, accomplish time and again the integration of a plurality of styles in an existing, growing environment. Who has not paused to feel and recognize this unity—the immediacy of an old building, the manner in which small things are granted a role or mediocre places vindicated, the peculiar atmosphere of the great city? As I remember those I myself have loved best—Seville, Paris, Cologne, Lisbon, Venice, and a few more —I venture to think that their "atmosphere" is like a silent sign of the presentness of the past. The freedom and vitality of the great city are such that they succeed in assembling not only a variety of styles and ways of life but series of historical moments, layers of historical time.

Civitas verbi: artistic wholes and literary systems are, like great cities, complex environments and areas of integration. They are there, all around us, real and available; though their fully franchised citizens, until now, have been far too few, and the literary scholar, vexed and divided as he is by the competing claims of his own dialectics (between theory and practice, the regional and the universal, the individual and the system, the artistic and the social), cannot easily overlook the relations of priority or of servitude he may discover between the cities of stone and brick and the cities of the mind.

Beyond what I have just suggested, however, this book does not itself offer a system, but rather a process of inquiry and personal growth.

My thanks, as I close these prefatory remarks, go above all to those who made the growth and the inquiry possible: the teachers with whom I studied, or who later became my colleagues and friends. I shall mention here but two literary historians and teachers, no longer living, among the eminent men I have been fortunate to know: Amado Alonso and Renato Poggioli. With his own very personal combination of rigor and familiarity, severity and charm, Amado Alonso introduced his students to the life of scholarship equally shared by all. (Don Amado was the first who taught me, *inter alia,* the Saussurian model on which the idea of literary system rests.) Renato Poggioli, while exercising his rare poetic sense and demonstrating his unique command of European culture, of the sources of his own sensibility as an admirably complete European, brought poetics to life and made manifest the need for a theory of literary history. I should like to express, through the remembrance of these two great teachers and critics, my gratitude to all the generous men from whom I learned at Williams College and Harvard University, and later, as I pursued my career, at the University of Cologne, the Middlebury Summer School, Princeton University, and the University of California at San Diego. I recall, finally, with special affection, the friends with whom I worked so closely at Princeton for a dozen years; and acknowledge gratefully the support of my battling and embattled colleagues in the University of California.

Málaga
February 1970

I

The Aesthetics of Literary Influence

A theoretical discussion such as this must confront, for better or for worse, a wealth of possibilities.[1] What Ferdinand Brunetière once called "the nearly infinite field of comparative literature"[2] requires, to be sure, the use not of one but of many methods, as the huge range of phenomena that it covers is submitted to more than one theoretical model. Does this diversity of both object and hypothesis reflect, as some scholars have thought, the nearness of the discipline to the texture and the winding course of literary history, i.e., to the very reluctance with which this species of history yields to a unitary theory?[3] I do not deny that such might be the case. But before the pluralism of comparative studies can be evaluated, it seems necessary that it be once more surveyed and understood.

Not long ago Henri Peyre called for a reappraisal of the notion of literary influence,[4] and I believe that an examina-

---

[1] The substance of this paper was presented at the Second Congress of the I.C.L.A., held in Chapel Hill, N.C., on September 8-12, 1958; and it was published under the title "The Aesthetics of Influence Studies in Comparative Literature" in *Comparative Literature. Proceedings of the Second Congress of the International Comparative Literature Association*, ed. Werner P. Friederich (Chapel Hill, N.C., 1959), I, 175-192. I have expanded it somewhat, mostly by adding certain passages from the article "Perspectivas de la literatura comparada," *Boletín del Seminario de Derecho Político*, no. 27 (August 1962), 252-266.

[2] Ferdinand Brunetière, "La littérature européenne," in *Variétés littéraires* (Paris, n.d.), p. 5: "le champ presque infini de la littérature comparée."

[3] Cf. Italo Siciliano, "Quelques remarques sur la littérature comparée," *Lettere italiane*, VIII (1956), 8; and especially Alexander Gillies, "Some Thoughts on Comparative Literature," *Yearbook of Comparative and General Literature*, I (1952), 17 (hereafter cited as *Yearbook*).

[4] Cf. Henri Peyre, "A Glance at Comparative Literature in America," *Yearbook*, I (1952), 7.

tion of this problem can provide us with a central approach to the area of comparative studies as a whole and a way of charting its several provinces. Thus, most of this essay will be devoted to the preliminary analysis of the concept of literary influence.

I

Any theory of influence implies an intuition, whether conscious or not, of the nature of the creative act in art. As we glance back at earlier periods in the history of comparative literature, so heavily reliant on the compilation of influences and sources, we cannot but ask ourselves what the aesthetic assumptions of our predecessors were. The question of course is very broad, and can be dealt with here only in a selective manner. I shall refer to certain ideas prevalent in France, and adopted elsewhere, during the last quarter of the nineteenth century, and use as starting point the following words by Luigi Foscolo Benedetto: "*Letteratura comparata, Storia generale della letteratura*: due aspirazioni romantiche rifiorite in un clima tainiano"[5] (two romantic aspirations that reflowered in a Tainian climate).

Benedetto's words could not be more appropriate: the discipline of comparative literary studies did indeed result from the adaptation of certain romantic aspirations to an intellectual climate of which the thought of Taine remains the most powerful and representative example. As for what the "due aspirazioni romantiche" actually were, I should like to interpret Benedetto's intent somewhat freely and go on to distinguish between two different, though obviously related, historical forces: a desire for system; and an internationalist or cosmopolitan spirit.

The yearning for system, synthesis or unity, is an aspect of the Romantic movement which is too often neglected or for-

---

[5] "La letteratura mondiale," *Il Ponte*, ii (1946), 129; reprinted in *Uomini e tempi* (Milan and Naples, 1953), p. 14.

gotten. Herder's conception of culture as a mosaic of national cultures led to the Romantic nationalism—in literary matters —with which we are so familiar. But it had its counterpart in a powerfully synthetic trend, rooted in a yearning for total experience, for the unitary vision of interconnections and interactions, for knowing, in Faust's words, "wie alles sich zum Ganzen webt": how all things are woven and joined into a whole. As far as the criteria of poetics were concerned, the writer could no longer believe that they composed a static and normative order, nor that a few great authorities continued to preside over an exquisite *Temple du goût*. With the advent of new critical theories the vast edifice of neoclassical norms had come tumbling down; and the whole of European poetry, as it were, had been shattered to pieces. Thus there were a number of reasons for reviving the durable dream of an artistic macrocosm. It appears, to put it very briefly, that a renewed vision of the integrity of literature—conceived not in normative but in historical terms—found support in three basic and parallel developments: the transcendent function attributed by many to the arts; the systematic mode of scrutiny and thought in the sciences and in philosophy; and the belief in progress.

Friedrich Schlegel, at one point, had defined art as the appearance of the kingdom of God on earth; and this enthusiastic position was of course widespread.[6] But in the *Athenäum* fragments (1798) he had also used the word "Sympoesie" and commented upon "progressive Universalpoesie"—while poking fun too, in an ironic moment, at the fact that synthesis seemed to be in fashion: "Uebersichten des Ganzen, wie sie jetzt Mode sind, entstehen, wenn einer alles einzelne übersieht, und dann summiert" (Surveys of the

---

[6] Cf. René Wellek, *A History of Modern Criticism: 1750-1950* (New Haven, 1955), II, 18, 349. Professor Wellek quotes the *Philosophische Vorlesungen*: "Die Kunst ist eine sichtbare Erscheinung des Reichs Gottes auf Erden."

whole, of the kind that are in fashion now, arise when someone overlooks all the single parts and then sums them up.)[7]
The tendency toward systematic thinking and writing had
been strengthened immeasurably by the trajectory of the natural sciences and of philosophy since Newton and Kant. A mechanical model of system was offered by physics, but there
were others as well. In the Kantian view, as Ernst Cassirer
explains, experience had ceased to be an empirical bundle of
sense perceptions. "Experience, declared Kant, is a system;
it is not a mere 'Rhapsodie von Wahrnehmungen.' Without
systematic unity there can be no experience and no science."[8]
The unified cosmos of the metaphysicians made possible various modes of unified rational response, as in Kant's *Archi-
tektonik*,[9] or later in Hegel's dialectical interpretation of the
indivisibility of the part from the whole. In the literary field,
however, an *organic* conception of system, based on the
widely accepted analogy—since Herder and Goethe—between the artistic work and the biological organism, was
found to be most effectual and convincing. René Wellek
stresses in the first two volumes of his *History of Modern
Criticism* the historical fruitfulness of this analogy, and how
the unity of all art was reconciled with an appreciation of its
single components by the comparison with the relationship
between a living body and its members, or between a biological order and its different species.

[7] Friedrich Schlegel, *Kritische Ausgabe*, ed. E. Behler (Munich,
Paderborn, Vienna, Zurich, 1967), I, *Athenäum* fragment no. 72, p.
175. Cf., on "progressive Universalpoesie," no. 116, pp. 182-183, and
on "Sympoesie," no. 125, pp. 185-186.

[8] Ernst Cassirer, "Structuralism in Modern Linguistics," *Word*, I
(1945), 117.

[9] Cf. José Ferrater Mora, "Filosofía y arquitectura," in *Cuestiones
disputadas* (Madrid, 1955), pp. 43-59. In linguistics, although the comparative scrutiny of national languages would generally predominate,
Wilhelm von Humboldt, in *Ueber die Verschiedenheit des menschlichen Sprachbaues* (1836), would recommend the study of not only
the particular "form" of each language but the universal form underlying all languages.

As for the idea of progress, it too fulfilled a unifying function. Its adaptation to literature, which goes back to the "Querelle des Anciens et des Modernes," and to the suspicion since the Renaissance that progress might not take place only in the sciences, was a distinctive feature of the eighteenth century. One of the first histories of world literature, published in Parma in 1782-1799 by an exiled Spanish Jesuit, Juan Andrés, was entitled *Dell'origine, de'progressi e dello stato attuale d'ogni letteratura*; and Condillac had written somewhat earlier in his *Traité des systèmes* that "les beaux-arts . . . paraissent précéder l'observation, et il faut qu'ils aient fait des progrès pour pouvoir être réduits en système."[10] The notion of literary progress reappears in Friedrich Schlegel's famous vision of "progressive Universalpoesie," and in numerous other instances of overlapping during the Romantic period (notably in Adam Müller's *Vorlesungen über die deutsche Wissenschaft und Literatur*, 1806) with the dominant organic or biological analogy.

That the organic analogy could be brought to bear not only on single works but on vast artistic wholes, on groups of works assembled in the memory of the critic, Goethe began to show on more than one occasion. I shall cite but the closing words of the Introduction to the *Propyläen*, published in 1798, when the impact of Napoleon's first Italian campaign (1796-1797) was still strong on the thoughts of the writer. How does the removal or the destruction of single artistic masterpieces—Goethe asks—affect our appreciation of art as a whole? What is happening to that great "art body" (*Kunstkörper*) that is Italy? What can replace it? We will be able to answer such questions, Goethe adds, only when we know more about that new "art body" that is being formed in Paris—and "what other nationalities should do, especially the German and the English, in this time of dispersion and loss, as citizens of the world in spirit, a spirit manifested perhaps most purely in the

---

[10] *Oeuvres philosophiques de Condillac*, ed. G. Le Roy (Paris, 1947), I, 215.

arts and the sciences, to make generally available the numerous art treasures which have been casually distributed in these countries and thus help to constitute an ideal body of art which may happily compensate in time for what the present moment tears apart, if not tears away" ("was andere Nationen, besonders Deutsche und Engländer thun sollten, um, in dieser Zeit der Zerstreuung und des Verlustes, mit einem wahren, weltbürgerlichen Sinne, der vielleicht nirgends reiner als bei Künsten und Wissenschaften stattfinden kann, die mannichfaltigen Kunstschätze, die bei ihnen zerstreut niedergelegt sind, allgemein brauchbar zu machen, und einen idealen Kunstkörper bilden zu helfen, der uns mit der Zeit, für das was uns der gegenwärtige Augenblick zerreisst, wo nicht entreisst, vielleicht glücklich zu entschädigen vermöchte"— *Werke*, Weimar edn. [1896], XLVII, 31). Historical and structural at once, these words anticipated the day when works of art would again compose "ideal" and supranational wholes.

The systematic impetus that I have just discussed has origins that are primarily philosophical, scientific, or literary. Our second "romantic aspiration," the cosmopolitan or internationalist tendency, on the other hand, regards literature as a *cause*—in more than one sense of the word. It presupposes the vitality of nationalism, and responds to a broader style of living, to the experiences of political or social man. Rooted in the eighteenth century, it inspired not only the contemporaries of Goethe and Mazzini but the European pioneers of comparative literature as an academic discipline, from the days of Joseph Texte (1865-1900) to those of Fernand Baldensperger (1871-1958). Texte's main book was called *Jean-Jacques Rousseau et les origines du cosmopolitisme littéraire* (1895); and it dealt with a topic that had attracted the interest of a number of his contemporaries. Brunetière had just written for the *Revue des Deux Mondes* a series of fighting articles on the idea of European literature. In 1890 Georg Brandes, as prestigious as he was controversial, had published the final volume of his lengthy history of European letters in the nineteenth century. The first volume bore the subtitle *Emigrant Literature* (*Emigrantliteraturen*), and Brandes underlined from the start (with reference to that cosmopolitan *malgré lui,* the political exile: Chateaubriand, Madame de Staël, Benjamin Constant, and others), that a principal feature of European life during the Romantic period was the growth of internationalism: the impact of cultural events, the quick dissemination of literary movements, and the wide-ranging consequences of political developments. It should be remembered that Marx and Engels used the term "Weltliteratur" in the *Communist Manifesto,* while stressing that the intellectual production of single nations was becoming the common patrimony of all.[11] In this sense the militant liberalism of the great Danish critic, like the antinationalism of Marx, was not as distant as one might think from the French academic attitudes that are my principal concern here. It became nearly a tradition for *comparatistes* to write of the brotherhood of nations, or of the need for a rebirth of "humanism." Joseph Texte had asked for "la formation, au point de vue littéraire, des Etats-Unis d'Europe," and had said, further: "ce ne sera pas trop peut-être, un jour ou l'autre, pour s'occuper d'histoire littéraire, d'avoir l'esprit international. Pour l'instant, il faut tâcher du moins d'avoir, suivant le mot de Mme. de Staël, dans notre étroite Europe, 'l'esprit européen.'"[12] And in 1921, not long after the close of World War I, Baldensperger inaugurated the *Revue de Littérature Comparée* with a ringing call for a new humanism

[11] Cf. Karl Marx and Friedrich Engels, *Werke* (Berlin, 1964), IV, 466: "Die geistigen Erzeugnisse der einzelnen Nationen werden Gemeingut. Die nationale Einseitigkeit und Beschränktheit wird mehr und mehr unmöglich, und aus den vielen nationalen und lokalen Literaturen bildet sich eine Weltliteratur."

[12] "L'histoire comparée des littératures," in *Etudes de littérature européenne* (Paris, 1898), pp. 13, 23.

based on the comparatist's search for universals beyond change and national differences, in order to "fournir à l'humanité disloquée un fonds moins précaire de valeurs communes."[13]

Let us now turn to Taine, very briefly, and to the intellectual environment of the early comparatists. It is apparent that Taine's conception of the creative act is not as explicit as his view of the nature of art in general or of the relationship between an artistic work and the people or the conditions that produced it. To indicate a starting point and an end result, a cause and a product, is not the same as to show how the distance between the two is eliminated, that is to say, as to question the process of creation itself. We know that in Taine's thought every work of art is determined by a cause and should be explained by it; but, again, to state that A controls B is not to show how the artist proceeded from A to B. Yet this very absence of emphasis reveals the belief that the intervention of the artist is not as radical or as inventive as the term "creation" might lead one to think. That a slender "coefficient of creation" is a corollary to Taine's theory is actually made clear by his inclination for the biological metaphor: artistic criticism, he writes, is "une sorte de botanique appliquée, non aux plantes, mais aux œuvres humaines."[14] Spiritual events are, like physical ones, based on the principle of the conservation of matter, that is, of the transmutation or reorganization of certain elements into differently structured products. Thus the creation of a poem or a painting is analogous to the process of chemical transformation that accounts for the growth of a plant.

Taine himself was so occupied with the nonartistic causes of art that he tended to underestimate the importance of those artistic causes that are usually called influences. Art

---

[13] "Littérature comparée. Le mot et la chose," *Revue de Littérature Comparée*, 1 (1921), 29.

[14] Hippolyte Taine, *Philosophie de l'art*, 8th edn., 1 (Paris, n.d.), 15.

imitates nature directly, and only art indirectly. When faced with a coherent group of artists such as the Flemish painters, Taine would rather point out the national forms of existence or the historical conditions which they shared as causes than observe the trajectory of strictly pictorial influences. Two of Taine's fundamental assumptions are operative in such cases, and cannot be divided: first, the idea of causality, as applied to the arts; and second, Taine's own formulation and refinement of the Romantic concept of the "character" or the "soul" of nations. For Taine a civilization is an organic system, which he defines in ways that are compatible with a modern anthropologist's "holistic" or "structural" approach to distinct cultures: "ici, comme partout, s'applique *la loi des dépendances mutuelles. Une civilisation fait corps, et ses parties se tiennent à la façon des parties d'un corps organique. . . . Dans une civilisation la religion, la philosophie, la forme de famille, la littérature, les arts composent un système où tout changement local entraîne un changement général. . . .*"[15] Thus in Taine the idea of cultural system and that of cultural causality do not necessarily clash, and the impact of one poet on another, indeed the dependence of one writer on another, simply demand to be inserted within a larger network of dependences. In what ways the *"loi des dépendances mutuelles"* did or could apply to the literatures of nations or to the processes of artistic creation was, of course, an arduous question for those contemporaries of Taine who were critics of art and, particularly, comparatists. Comparatists could scarcely refrain from seeking a reconciliation between, on the one hand, Taine's approach to the work of art as document and a more substantial concern with literature for its own sake; and, on the other, between his marked emphasis on national psychologies and the cosmopolitan or synthetic aspirations of the Romantic age. The contribution of Joseph Texte is clearly representative of this convergent phase.

---

[15] *Histoire de la littérature anglaise* (Paris, 1866), I, xl.

Joseph Texte's reliance on the idea of "le génie des peuples" and on the biological analogy dominated his thought on the subject of international influences when he published his *Jean-Jacques Rousseau et les origines du cosmopolitisme littéraire* (1895) and his *Etudes de littérature européenne* (1898). The later concentration of comparative literature on influences of one nation on another, while neglecting similar phenomena within a single country, was largely due to the early blending in such works of the romantic belief in national originalities and the evolutionary biology of the time. "Pour qu'il y ait lieu à des études du genre de celles dont nous parlons," explained Texte, "il faut en effet qu'une littérature soit conçue comme l'expression d'un état social déterminé, tribu, clan ou nation, dont elle représente les traditions, le génie et les espérances. . . . Il faut, en un mot, qu'elle constitue un *genre* bien déterminé dans la grande *espèce* de la littérature de l'humanité."[16] Thus each single literature was regarded as a sort of subspecies, and comparative literature as the study of the cross-fertilizations and contacts between these subspecies, and of their evolution and mutations: "C'est qu'en effet, pas plus qu'un organisme animal, une littérature ou une nation ne grandissent isolées des nations et des littératures voisines. L'étude d'un être vivant est, en grande partie, l'étude des relations qui l'unissent aux êtres voisins et des influences de tous genres qui nous enveloppent comme d'un réseau invisible."[17] Thus national and international attitudes were comfortably blended. Comparative literature, at this stage, was the fruit of a polite compromise.

Texte's biological and evolutionary approach led him to a concept of creation, although implicit, similar to Taine's. His gifts were, in fact, those of a psychological critic. And never is what one might call the "concept of transfer" as clear as when criticism tries to deal with both an author's states of

[16] Texte, "L'histoire comparée des littératures," p. 3.
[17] *Ibid.*, p. 14.

mind and his works, or to show how the substance of the former is incorporated in the latter. In his essay on Wordsworth, Texte is interested above all in asking how happy poetry could be written by any but a happy man; and in his essay on *Aurora Leigh*, in demonstrating how the author, Elizabeth Barrett Browning, "s'y est révélée tout entière."[18] The idea of transfer implied by such biographical criticism precludes the question which is central to this essay: When speaking of an influence on a writer, do we make a psychological or a literary statement? To which the psychological critic would have answered that states of mind and works of art are not only indivisible, but two stages of an uninterrupted process of formal reorganization; as the work of art, to recall Taine's definition, "a pour but de manifester quelque caractère essentiel ou saillant . . . , plus clairement et plus complètement que ne le font les objets réels, . . . en employant un ensemble de parties liées, *dont elle modifie systématiquement les rapports.*"[19]

The nineteenth-century idea of influence sprang from this notion of literature as the product of a direct reorganization of human experience into art. It was as if literary scholars selected their own targets without altering the view of the creative process which was expressed by historians and social philosophers. These scholars went about looking for literary causes instead of human ones—a natural thing to do, since the two kinds of phenomena were in their opinion practically interchangeable. One inspected the fact that literary works transmit not only the substance of experience, but that of previous literary works. The etymological image of flow (*fluere*) was taken to mean that an influence represents the undisturbed passage of certain elementary substances from one poem to another.

[18] Texte, "Elizabeth Browning et l'idéalisme," in *Etudes de littérature européenne,* p. 240.

[19] Taine, *Philosophie de l'art,* p. 47 (italics mine).

II

The aim of this essay being methodological, I do not propose to recall the vicissitudes of literary theory since the days of Taine and Texte. My examples are intended not to be exhaustive, but to serve for a theoretical discussion and a summary of a large section of contemporary criticism. It will suffice, then, simply to consider briefly a view that is representative and has the merit of providing us with a different approach to our problem.

Artistic creation, according to this view, may be found somewhere between two poles: the process of transfer and reorganization mentioned above; and at the other end, the religious concept of absolute creation. Both notions are incompatible with the peculiar nature of art. The former appears to be based on an unsatisfactory biological analogy. The emergence of a work of art is not comparable to the appearance of a new member of a species as only a variation of that species, or to the gradual unfolding of embryonic elements, or to a simple mutation of structure—implying a separation of "form" and "content." Life, or the biological, or what is not fully shaped or formed by man (or, if you wish, that total environment or locus of my life, which encloses so much that is man-invented but is not a unitary form), yields precisely where art begins, in order to give place to an inorganic entity or process endowed with formal qualities and expressive virtualities and thus capable of stimulating in turn a kind of experience that is vital (that is "life" too) but must be distinguished from other classes of experience. As for the other pole, total creation, it seems, in the artistic area, to be a requirement of the mind rather than a fact: a "limit-idea" to which other ideas of creation should be referred.[20] Creation is a term particularly adaptable to art insofar as one excludes

[20] Cf. José Ferrater Mora, *Diccionario de filosofía*, 4th edn. (Buenos Aires, 1958), p. 291.

from it both the extreme of *creatio ex nihilo* and the supposition that the creative process represents a passage from one thing to another within the same order of reality (the same "unity," that is to say) without a contrast, an effort, and a change of *kind*. The movement from one sort of experience to another (*not* from life to nonlife, or vice versa) is what the idea of creation can reasonably mean and what the artist is precisely able to achieve. For he makes possible the emergence of a form which is *sui generis,* not preexistent, yet entitled to a vital status of its own. The "un-formed" environment is separated from the completed artistic product by a difference of being or "ontological gap." From Kant to Croce, the premise of modern aesthetics has been that action, ethics, logic, art belong to different (though mutually dependent) orders of existence. Creation bridges this fundamental gap, then, and cannot be considered a sort of continuum. The poet does not merely deflect, refract, or contradict experience. He is able to displace or replace both un-formed life and previous works of art—for the sake of the reader as well as for his own sake. Negatively speaking, the poem is the result of a displaced process of experience. Positively speaking, it reveals the attempt to inform, shape, and conquer one's environment through a creative passage from one order of existence to another. Every truly great work of art, to the knowing observer, is still vibrant with this triumph—with a decisive energy, with an underlying process of "formation" and form-creation.

To circumscribe this process is an arduous task—and "would know no boundaries," as Goethe said to Eckermann (December 16, 1828) regarding literary influences on himself. It does not quite include the entire life of the writer, in the sense that a particular poem will be related to particular strata of experience or of personality, though the strata may run across the whole of the artist's experience. The genesis of a poem is, if not an endless process, an endlessly complex one—as extensive, within certain temporal limits, as our knowledge of the individual's inner life may be. Certain events or conditions are crucial in it, and others trivial; but of course no single event or condition controls, shapes, or elucidates the final dimensions of the work of art.

Our idea of influence would be relevant to the aesthetic context I have just indicated. It would define an influence as a recognizable and significant part of the genesis of a literary work of art. It would refer to poetry as entering the writer's experience (so that every *source* is a *source vécue*), and would distinguish between genuinely genetic conditions and the presence in the finished poem of those conventions and techniques which belong to the writer's equipment or to the possibilities of his medium handed down by way of tradition. The writer's life and his creative work develop, as I have just recalled, within two different orders of experience. Influences, since they develop strictly on one level, are individual experiences of a particular nature, for a number of reasons: because they represent a kind of intrusion into the writer's being or a modification of it or the occasion for such a change; because their starting point is previously existing poetry; and because the alteration they bring about, no matter how slight, has an indispensable effect on the subsequent stages of the *genesis* of the poem. They are forces that introduce themselves into the process of creation, so to speak, from the outside—*élans* and incitations which carry the genetic "movement" further, and allow the artist to pursue his elaboration of expressive forms. At the same time, then, influences make a poem possible and are transcended by it, as other experiences are. (Their effect often ceases or vanishes within the span of the writer's consciousness.) The poem, to repeat our terms, is also the product of a displaced series of influences. And the latter, precisely because they are displaced and make way for what is different from them, should be distinguished from the recognizable techniques which are present in the finished poem, and may or may not be comparable to the forms responsible for the original genetic incitations.[21]

If we now return to what I called the concept of transfer, the current deviation from it should be plainer. An influence, according to the old nineteenth-century idea, was the transfer and rearrangement of literary forms and themes from one work to another. I cannot dwell at length on the theoretical difficulties involved in this notion, though it seems evident that it is not only untenable from the viewpoint of modern aesthetics, but inimical to the very existence of aesthetics. Analogous difficulties are encountered by the analysis of persistent forms or themes. A form cannot be rearranged, by anyone's logic: it cannot be reformed or deformed and yet subsist. As for themes, as Benedetto Croce showed many years ago in his criticism of *Stoffgeschichte*,[22] they are conveniently misleading entities. Tirso de Molina's Don Juan does not exist outside of the *Burlador de Sevilla* anymore than Hamlet does beyond *Hamlet*, or than any form or poetic

[21] I do not mean to imply that influences take place only "in the mind," as may be suggested to some readers by Haskell Block's concise summary of my article "Literatura como sistema" in his essay "The Concept of Influence in Comparative Literature," *Yearbook*, vii (1958), 33: an influence would be "a part of the process by which works are created, hence located in the mind of the writer rather than in his work." My emphasis, as Professor Block also indicates, is on the fact that influences are a part of the "work in progress," and that they happen *to* the writer primarily—to the whole of his being. This may take place before actual work in the artist's medium has begun, and in such cases it is clear that the artistic product is affected indirectly. Fortunately, most significant influences appear to enter just such a part of the creative process. If actual work has started, our problem grows of course more complex, and I would be the first to recognize the difficulty of any attempt to single out the exact moment in which a work of art becomes independent of its creator and assumes an aesthetic vitality of its own. But the *existence* of such a moment must, for theoretical purposes, be accepted.

[22] Cf. "Storia di temi e storia letteraria," in *Problemi di estetica*, 6th edn. (Bari, 1966), pp. 77-91.

feature of the *Burlador de Sevilla* does. To call "theme" both the figure in the drama, where it is uniquely formed and expressive, and the bare plot or conceptual scheme we usually associate with themes, is to strain a single word beyond reason. These are entities that cannot be approached, as I have said elsewhere,[23] through the same process of definition. Don Juan is a dramatic character, the theme of Don Juan is a sequence of situations. The former only is literary, and only the latter is a theme. Because Don Juan is inseparable from a poetic form, he first must be perceived aesthetically, while the theme is a prepoetic outline which can be defined conceptually. Prepoetic outlines, of course, belong properly to the area of poetics and rhetoric, whether they are formal or thematic, as Ernst Robert Curtius demonstrated brilliantly with regard to those microthemes called *topoi* or *loci communes*.[24] Thus the study of themes acquires its real significance in the area of poetics.

As far as practice is concerned, the "concept of transfer" has three definite disadvantages:

1. It implies that an influence is an objective connection, a tangible affair, of which some material traces ought to remain after the work is finished. This precludes all subtler phenomena, genetic or psychological, of which the critic cannot find adequate objective proof. (In some cases the positivistic critic will be satisfied with locating the proof in evidence that is external to either the source or the influenced product, such as letters, or marginal notes on the writer's copy of a book,[25] as long as this *rapport de fait* can be counterchecked later against the work.)

---

[23] Cf. my article "Problemas de tematología: *Die verführte Unschuld* de H. Petriconi," *Romanische Forschungen*, LXVI (1955), 397-406.

[24] Cf. *Europäische Literatur und lateinisches Mittelalter* (Bern, 1948), Chaps. 5, 10.

[25] An example of this fallacy is discussed by Harry Levin, "La littérature comparée: Point de vue d'outre-Atlantique," *Revue de Littérature Comparée*, XXVII (1953), 20.

2. The idea of transfer ascribes to phenomena of influence, in many cases, a kind of importance, of necessity, of effectiveness as great and enviable as that of the artistic works themselves. As all influential elements are ultimately embodied in the finished poem, nothing is lost and all is well that ends well. The traditionally sanguine comparatist is not inclined to observe the arbitrariness, the absurdity, or what I should like to call the *contingency* of so many of these phenomena. He discovers and records with a light heart that, for example, the reputation of Cervantes was largely inferior for many years to those of several of his Spanish contemporaries; or that no Frenchman truly appreciated Dante before the nineteenth century;[26] or that Antonio de Guevara was translated into English from French, into German from Italian, into Hungarian from Latin, into Dutch and Swedish from German.[27] For this complacent attitude toward influences it is probable, I think, that the aesthetic theories just mentioned are responsible. Because they posit that influences are efficient, they overestimate the proximity of influences to art, or maintain them within the area in which genuine literature takes place and in which the critic is inclined to take pleasure.

3. The most remarkable consequence of this view is the persistent confusion between influences and textual similarities, or the refusal to scrutinize with some sharpness how these two groups of facts are related.[28] The notion of transfer,

[26] Cf. Carlo Pellegrini, "Relazioni fra la letteratura italiana e la letteratura francese," in *Letterature comparate*, ed. A. Viscardi et al. (Milan, 1948), p. 48.

[27] Cf. Carlos Clavería, *Estudios hispano-suecos* (Granada, 1954), p. 12.

[28] I refer the reader to some articles on the subject, which I cannot discuss within the limits of this paper (my differences with Professors Bateson and Stallman, besides, being quite clear): Louis Cazamian, "Goethe en Angleterre. Quelques réflexions sur les problèmes d'influence," *Revue Germanique*, XII (1921), 371-378; F. W. Bateson, "Editorial Commentary," *Essays in Criticism*, IV (1954), 436-440; Ihab

since it assumes that an influence leads to the presence in work B of elements in some manner comparable to others in A, as well as derived from them, is equivalent to the premise that influences and parallelisms are indivisible. Our assumption, on the contrary, is that genetic incitations are part and parcel of the writer's psychic experience, whereas textual similarities pertain to the order of literature. Hence the conviction, shared by numerous scholars in recent years,[29] that

---

B. Hassan, "The Problem of Influence in Literary History: Notes Toward a Definition," *Journal of Aesthetics and Art Criticism*, xiv (1955), 66-76; R. W. Stallman, "The Scholar's Net: Literary Sources," *College English*, xvii (1955), 20-27; and Haskell Block, "The Concept of Influence in Comparative Literature." I find myself in agreement, not only with Professor Block's criticism of the more mechanical practices of comparatists, but with his view of influences as real and indispensable to the understanding of literature itself. But when he writes that "substitution of terminology will not alter this need" (p. 37), and that "the movement of influence is not simply from writer to writer but from work to work" (p. 35), without further analysis or explanation, it seems to me that he is dealing with questions that are different from those I raise here. Surely we can all think of influences that are genuine and convincing. But we also recognize the existence of recurrent techniques and conventions, or of noninfluential echoes and parallelisms. And what is needed today is not an empirical, haphazard approach to these differences, but concepts that will account for them. I accept the statement "influences from work to work exist." But I think it calls for clarification.

[29] Cf., generally speaking, Henry W. Wells, *New Poets From Old* (New York, 1940), p. 25; Carlos Clavería, *Cinco estudios de literatura española moderna* (Salamanca, 1945), p. 7; Henri Peyre, "A Glance at Comparative Literature in America," p. 7: "an influence is almost never an imitation"; Harry Levin, "La littérature comparée: Point de vue d'outre-Atlantique," p. 25; René Wellek, "The Concept of Comparative Literature," *Yearbook*, ii (1953), 1-5; Amado Alonso, "Estilística de las fuentes literarias. Rubén Darío y Miguel Angel," in *Materia y forma en poesía* (Madrid, 1955); the practice of Mario Praz, "Rapporti tra la letteratura italiana e la letteratura inglese," in *Letteratura comparate*, pp. 145-196; and, finally, Kurt Wais, "Vergleichende Literaturbetrachtung," in *Forschungsprobleme der Vergleichenden Literaturgeschichte* (Tübingen, 1951), p. 11: "es empfiehlt sich überdies, zwischen Aufnahme und Einfluss zu unterscheiden und je nachdem

an influence need not assume the recognizable form of a parallelism, just as every parallelism does not proceed from an influence.

The former theory (best manifested by the equally liquid metaphor of "source," which is useless within any other perspective) had the advantage of being empirically manageable and simple. In other words, it made influence studies viable. The latter theory is fraught with difficulties, both theoretical and practical, inasmuch as it approaches the riddle of the creative act. For these reasons, it might be profitable to discuss an example.

We know that the process of creation often springs from, or is decisively stimulated by, a singularly favorable emotional state that may be described as an intense disposition of the will, an urgent need to write, or, most simply, a desire: the desire, whether joyful or not, to compose a work of which only the basic or vaguest lineaments can be perceived. This is the condition which Schiller described to Christian Gottfried Körner in a letter of May 25, 1792: "Ich glaube, es ist nicht immer die lebhafte Vorstellung seines Stoffes, sondern oft nur ein *Bedürfnis* nach Stoff, ein unbestimmter Drang nach Ergiessung strebender Gefühle, was Werke der Begeisterung erzeugt. Das Musikalische eines Gedichtes schwebt mir weit öfter vor der Seele, wenn ich mich hinsetze, es zu machen, als der klare Begriff von Inhalt, über den ich oft kaum mit mir einig bin" (I believe it is not always the vivid conception of a subject, but often rather the *need* for a subject, an undefined urge to allow one's driving feelings to pour out, that produces works of enthusiasm. The musical quality of a poem hovers much more often before my soul, before I sit down to write it, than the clear notion of a content, about

---

das Sprunghafte . . . oder das Kontinuierliche in der Art der Auswirkung festzustellen."

which I am not always so certain).[30] Such a disposition of the will may be connected, as Schiller records, with a vision of the poem's musical quality—its tone, rhythm, or structure. It is also well known that this mood can be set off or nourished by another work of art, and it seems clear that such external support, arriving at a crucial moment, deserves to be called an influence. The work in question, moreover, need not be literary. We have learned from such writers as Alfieri, Kleist, and Fray Luis de León that the creative mood can be profitably stimulated by a musical experience.

Thus Jorge Guillén explains the influence exerted on the final poem of his *Cántico,* "Cara a cara," by Ravel's "Boléro." The stubborn, unrelenting, obsessive quality of the latter's musical rhythm—only of its rhythm—fired the poet's initial desire to write his tenacious response to the more chaotic aspects of life. Would it be correct to seek here an objective parallelism? I doubt it, and not only because such a resemblance would be very vague; but rather because we would thereby be carrying over to Ravel's work the Spanish poet's highly personal interpretation of it. Or, to be more precise, we would be applying the poet's recollection of his original experience of the piece at the moment of *Stimmung* or desire. Our conclusion, should we persist in establishing a parallelism, would be based essentially on the evidence provided not by an analytical comparison of the two works of art, but by our acquaintance with the kind of psychic state on which the music acted. The effect of the "Boléro" on Jorge Guillén is representative of the sort of influence of which no objective echo can be *expected* (the mood being important insofar as it is connected with the dynamics of the writing or the intention of the poet, and as it prepares later emotions, releases forces preserved in the poet's sensibility, etc.), although of course such an echo may *also* be present. No one-to-one relationship exists, in other words, between the influential ele-

[30] Schiller, *Briefe,* ed. G. Fricke (Munich, 1955), p. 272.

ment and the final text. Of this the "mood" influence is an extreme example.

At the other extreme we find parallelisms which are not influences, that is to say, which play such a limited role in the genetic process that we cannot assign to them a name reserved for significant repercussions of one artistic work on another. I am not referring to fortuitous resemblances or coincidences, valid only insofar as they enter the reader's or the critic's experience; for these are not the source of our problem. Certain textual correspondences are not the products of chance, could only be encountered in the writings of a particular author, and yet are not connected with the central stream of genetic development to which influences necessarily belong. (This could apply to smaller or larger elements; their function, not their extent, is relevant.) It has been noted, to return to Jorge Guillén, that a line from the poem "La Florida,"

> Todas las rosas son la rosa
>
> (All roses are the rose)

reproduces almost exactly an *endecasílabo* by Juan Ramón Jiménez:

> Todas las rosas son la misma rosa
>
> (All roses are the same rose).

A textual comparison, again, would yield a scanty result, for we can be certain that even the meanings of these lines are different within their respective contexts. Once more the comparative method cannot provide us with a valid conclusion, as the absence of a similarity may conceal a genuine influence (which was the case with the "Boléro" and "Cara a cara"). It is much more informative to learn that this minute echo proceeds from an involuntary reminiscence, of which the author was not aware until several years after he had written the poem; and that Jorge Guillén's considerable debt to Juan Ramón is of the kind that affects only the initial "vocabulary" of a poet. (Juan Ramón shaped to a large extent the linguistic instrument which the poets of the following generation in Spain used perhaps more fully than he had.) This "vocabulary" is the sum of the elements preserved in the memory or the sensibility of the poet before the genesis of a particular poem begins, and which are available indifferently to all his later writing. It contains potential vehicles of sensibility, reminiscences, self-contradictions. And it includes also linguistic or formal procedures, preserved in the technical memory of the artist, and of the sort covered by the terms "conventions" and "techniques." These devices and verbal mores are conditions of the poet's production. They are the circumstances of his medium, the situation in which he finds himself linguistically. But they cannot be regarded as causes unless they touch directly the emergence of the poem. The fact is that no significant psychic state, within the limits of the genesis of "La Florida," linked "Todas las rosas son la rosa" with "Todas las rosas son la misma rosa."[31]

Thus one is led to recognize the following propositions:

1. The comparative method is insufficient in such cases. The question of the possible influence of A on B cannot be settled by a simple comparison between A and B. Every study of influences is initially a study of the genesis of a work of art, and should be predicated on the knowledge and interpretation of the components of that genesis.

2. To ascertain an *influence* is to make a value judgment, not to measure a fact. The critic is obliged to evaluate the function or the scope of the effect of A on the making of B,

---

[31] Cf. "Cara a cara" and "La Florida" in Jorge Guillén, *Cántico* (Buenos Aires, 1950), pp. 514-523, 352-353. Concerning the older poet's bilious reaction, cf. Enrique Díez-Canedo, *Juan Ramón Jiménez en su obra* (Mexico, 1944), p. 127.

for he is not listing the total amount of these effects, which are legion, but ordering them. Thus "influence" and "significant influence" are practically synonymous. (The decision and the final value judgment must be the critic's. Thus a term like "borrowing" is not very helpful, since it stresses unduly the poet's own awareness of the event.)

3. An influence study, when pursued to the full, contains two very different phases, just as it bridges the gap between the origin of the creative process and the poem itself. The first step consists, as we have seen, in interpreting genetic phenomena. It deals with the influence as such, or *impact*. The second step is textual and comparative, but entirely dependent on the first for its existence and value. It deals with *parallelisms* or *echoes*. Thus our method would first ascertain that an influence has been operative; and then evaluate the relevance or *genetic function* of that effect. Then one would consider the objective result which may have been a product of the influence, and define the latter's *textual function*. The genetic function controls the impact, and the textual function the echo or the parallelism.

4. The value of an influence is not aesthetic, but psychological. In evaluating an influence we are engaged in judging its genetic function. The added presence or absence of a parallelism is a different matter, for the order of the aesthetic —the area of the poem—is to be kept apart from the domain of influences (where function is psychological or biographical) also where values are concerned. Obviously the discovery of an influence does not modify our appreciation or evaluation of a poem (although conventions may), and the analysis of these phenomena has precious little to do with any absolute scale of aesthetic values or broad survey of literary achievements. Although the fundamental difference between *artistic value* and influential value, which I would rather call *effectiveness of impact*, seems quite simple in this context, it appears to be easily forgotten, curiously enough, when the

object of consideration is extended under the aegis of literary history. It is important that comparatists should keep this distinction in mind on a broad scale, too, and that the study of a topic such as, say, Dutch poetry be encouraged not for charitable but for poetic reasons. Influence and effectiveness of impact should not affect the choice of works that is sometimes termed *Weltliteratur*. The more sensible critics, following Goethe, never intended this term to signify a sort of literary *Who's Who*, but to stress the fruitfulness of literary relations, of what Guillermo de Torre calls "diálogo de literaturas." A compilation of influential works would turn out to be, like most snobbish endeavors, a *Temple du mauvais goût*; and one would be perpetuating the distasteful error of Brunetière, who regarded only those works or those literatures which had exercised an influence beyond their frontiers as worthy of being a part of "European literature."[32] The evaluation of a Dutch poet like Gerrit Achterberg should not suffer from the fact (though the actual study of his works may) that Manhattan Island was not permanently settled by his compatriots. Whenever students of influences overlook this point, they become ratifiers of success, colonialism, and international power—political historians in spite of themselves.[33]

5. The study of conventions and techniques (modes, genres, myths, themes, devices of style and structure) is distinct from the study of influences—and of parallelisms when these are viewed as related to the latter. The merit of influence studies may be that they point out how much of a writer's equipment is left untouched, in many cases, by the

---

[32] Cf. Brunetière, "La littérature européenne," p. 23: "les productions d'une grande littérature ne nous appartiennent qu'autant qu'elles sont entrées en contact avec d'autres littératures, et que, de ce contact ou de cette rencontre, on a vu résulter des conséquences."

[33] See Guillermo de Torre's distinction between "literatura universal" and "literatura cosmopolita" in *Las metamorfosis de Proteo* (Buenos Aires, 1956), p. 284.

truly valuable influences exerted upon him. As these investigations analyze the various strands which interweave in the genesis of a poem, they are able to distinguish between what is more conventional and what is centrally operative, or to discover what conventions become particularly operative. As for echoes and parallelisms alone, they evidently increase the harvest of the student of recurrences and conventions.

III

In closing, I have planned to glance at some of the fundamental areas and aims of comparative studies from the point of view of literary influences as discussed and defined here. Although a number of additional subdivisions could naturally be presented, I will limit myself here to four broad perspectives, theoretically distinct though they may often converge in practice.

These perspectives all assume or advance a historical view and a historical preoccupation. But there are important differences between them, and I should like to mention at this point four basic criteria that may help to clarify the differences. (1) It will be readily apparent that the first two perspectives, which have been characteristic of comparative literature in its early stages and of the so-called French school, center on influence studies and on their particular uses of the genetic method, as opposed to a direct concern with literary works as finished forms or with literary categories. (2) Only the last perspective is synchronic, while the others are above all diachronic. (3) It is also pertinent to distinguish between history as narrative (that is, as narrative of events and processes *in illo tempore*, as story of events in the making) and history as recapitulation (as an a posteriori review of the profile of events), if I may use terms that are reminiscent of Ramon Fernandez's memorable distinction, in the field of the novel, between *roman* and *récit*.[34] (4) One may also observe

---

[34] Cf. *Messages* (Paris, 1926), pp. 59-77.

the ways in which comparatists focus their attention on the individual (work, writer, process)—thus furthering some sort of *critica individualizzante*, to use Croce's term—as well as on the areas where they are likely to practice their concern with synthesis and system. It has of course been the position of Croce's followers that this dichotomy is meaningless, as the individual work of art embraces, expresses, or symbolizes, through its forms, not only universal values but those of history itself.[35] Why construct broader configurations, when this is just what the work of art accomplishes? Yet comparatists are likely to retort that the single work of art either fails to provide the critic-historian with a symbol of history as diachrony and as narrative, or obliges the critic, in order to rejoin the flow of process, of time passing and time past, to turn once more to the study of genetic and biographical phenomena.

The historical heritage of the comparatist, as I recalled earlier, is precisely the synthetic-systematic view, and the main challenge with which he is confronted is to make synthesis possible, or to draw out systems, on a genuinely literary level. "Literary history as a synthesis, literary history on a supernational scale," René Wellek and Austin Warren have said, "will have to be written again."[36] In other words, the problem is whether or how the systematic view can find within the order of literature itself the organizational principles that it requires.

Before I delineate briefly these perspectives, I should like to mention an additional kind of research, which provides the comparatist with many of the materials he needs.

Comparative studies use their own fact-finding agency, as it were, their own *Hilfswissenschaft*, whenever they rely on

---

[35] Cf. Benedetto Croce, *Nuovi saggi di estetica*, 4th edn. (Bari, 1958), p. 177; and Luigi Russo, *La critica letteraria contemporanea*, 3rd edn. (Bari, 1953), I, 100, 287.

[36] *Theory of Literature* (New York, 1949), p. 42.

the preliminary gathering of all manner of data that are not intended to have a function in the interpretation of a work of art or of a category, like a genre or a style, that is both literary and historical. These data are elementary and genetic, very much as what I called earlier an "impact" (the first stage of an influence study, dealing with genetic data) is. I am referring to miscellaneous information concerning, for example, travel, the teaching of foreign languages, dictionaries, newspaper coverage, personal intermediaries, and translations when they are not regarded, which is often the case here, either as literature or as a problem in poetic theory. This information has the advantage sometimes of rescuing from oblivion the second-rate writer who made possible the first-rate work, or of supplying the positivists with what Jean-Marie Carré called "rapports de fait."[37] Actually, its status is rather puzzling, and one wonders whether it is at all literary or historical. Surely, it does not compose a branch of literary history, understood as a history *of* literature, of its works and forms. But does it pertain to general history (i.e., the history of non-art)? Let us recall some of the numberless instances that come to mind: Cervantes or Goethe in Italy, Voltaire or Chateaubriand in London, Navagero in Granada, Hemingway or Montherlant in Madrid; César Oudin, Ambrosio de Salazar, and other interpreters or teachers of Spanish in seventeenth-century France; the use made by Manzoni, while revising his *Promessi Sposi*, of Cherubini's *Vocabolario milanese-italiano*; the very large part played by the press in the diffusion of Goethe's work in France, as Baldensperger proved in *Goethe en France* (1904); or, in our day, the anti-parochial effects of such literary magazines as *La Nouvelle Revue Française, Sur*, etc.; the crucial role played by "intermediaries" such as Charles de Villers (whose articles in the *Spectateur du Nord* in 1799 revealed German literature to

---

[37] "Avant-Propos" to M.-F. Guyard, *La Littérature comparée* (Paris, 1951), p. 5.

Madame de Staël), José María Blanco White (an essential link in the career of Spanish Romanticism), or the exiled European intellectuals in America during the second third of the twentieth century; the invitation to poetic discovery beyond ordinary frontiers offered in the work or the personal example of such critics as Charles Du Bos, Ernst Robert Curtius, Ricardo Baeza, Edmund Wilson; exact surveys of the translations of Dostoevsky, Rilke, Valéry, or Kafka; and so forth. The character of some of these data is reminiscent of biography, and the character of others, of bibliography, that is, of research concerning first editions, reprints, recovered manuscripts, and so on. One cannot say that these topics are pertinent to any of the central regions of general history. But they are relevant to what may be regarded as a special province of social history: the career of literary communications on an international scale. They clarify not art but the literary life and its function in society. In other words, they offer the comparatist an opportunity to contribute to historical sociology.

Comparative critics, to begin with, may concentrate on influence studies and thus interpret the genesis of individual works of art, and, beyond them, of a writer's whole production, a school, a movement, a tradition. Both the origin and the result of an influence can be seen as involving a group of writers or a movement or a period, so that their scope becomes quite extensive. But critics have usually preferred, under this first perspective, to broaden only one of the two basic terms. When a single author is either the origin of an influence or its receiver, the critic can gather more readily, as in a single sheaf, the numerous forces that he wishes to observe. Sometimes the single author is the transmitter: Montaigne and his influence in England (Charles Dédéyan); or he may be the receiver: Goethe and his experience of European culture (Fritz Strich); or influences may be followed in both directions: Shelley and France, and their reciprocal contacts (Henri Peyre).

For reasons well known to all of us,[38] this class of comparative study, usually associated with the so-called French school, appears less promising and stimulates less interest today than it once did. Contemporary critics are inclined to narrow their target and to examine, when influences attract their attention, contacts between single works and single authors. It seems clear that this kind of study is an example of *critica individualizzante,* and perhaps for the very same reasons that influence studies no longer conceal their psychological bias. In this sense, it seems natural that certain comparatists in the past should have been so fond of topics like national mirages, national reputations, and other instances of the *psychologie comparée des peuples*—usually a mediocre but operative truth—or of the impact and prestige not of great works but of great writers (the legend and charisma of Rousseau, Goethe, Nietzsche, J. R. Jiménez, Gide, Hemingway, etc.). Critics with an insight into the "soul" of nations may hope to emulate Sainte-Beuve on a large scale, while others still prefer the format of the *Causeries du Lundi.* Thus influence studies contribute, for good or ill, to various kinds of literary "psychology."

Comparative studies, secondly, have also stressed the global consideration of influences which French specialists call *fortune.* The term can be relied upon to evoke, in a nineteenth-century context, the bourgeois historian's appreciation of solid success. But a much earlier framework, that of the Latin goddess Fortuna, is rather more suggestive of the relations that a modern critic can hope to discover between influence studies and political or social history.

A traditional textbook, Paul Van Tieghem's *La Littérature comparée,* introduced this branch of comparative literature

---

[38] Cf. Wellek and Warren, *Theory of Literature,* p. 40.

with the following words: "on sait qu'il faut distinguer le *succès* d'un auteur dans un pays de son *influence* sur la littérature de ce pays. Le premier ne prouve nullement la seconde; mais il la favorise, il l'aide à naître et à s'exercer. D'ailleurs, dans la pratique, l'étude de l'influence d'un écrivain à l'étranger est si étroitement liée à celle de son appréciation ou de sa *fortune*—comme l'on dit maintenant de préférence—qu'il est le plus souvent impossible de les séparer l'une de l'autre. Nous pouvons appeler ce genre d'études *doxologie* (Gr. *doxa*, opinion, gloire), puisqu'il y est question de la réputation d'un auteur ou de plusieurs auteurs, et de l'opinion qu'on se forme à leur égard."[39] To return to the terms of this discussion, the notion of fortune, then, implies three things: that the student of influences chooses to underline their ultimate effectiveness as "echoes" or "parallelisms," rather than the preliminary stage of biographical or psychological "impact"; that he surveys broad or synthetic configurations, instead of analyzing individual parts; and, third, that he approaches history not as narrative (the "novelistic" narrative of events "under way") but as recapitulation (the "tale" of events "after the fact"). For as all literary historians are bound to remark, the patterns of literary history, indeed the shape and direction of literary history, are largely conditioned by the arbitrary sequence of events appropriately named *fortune*.

Poetry is *not* composed by unambitious writers in a peaceful universe where the greatest of literary accomplishments are freely and justly made available to the proper audience of enlightened men. Poetic phenomena do *not* unfold and disclose in history—i.e., as they become actualized in time—an ideal order of "structures" or of autonomous processes. Alexander Gillies recalled not long ago that both the influence of Shakespeare on Herder and the impact of Herder on the

---

[39] Paul Van Tieghem, *La Littérature comparée*, 4th edn. (Paris, 1951), p. 117.

Romantic movements in the Slavic countries—two crucial conjunctions—were based on the misreading of literary texts.[40] As no student or theorist of influences, including myself, denies that literature breeds literature, it seems apparent that the writing of new works is prepared for not only by misreadings, legends, mirages, mistranslations, and other verbal delusions or failures of communication, but by their conjunction with political and historical circumstances like exile or national conquest. The diffusion of literature demands translation or the knowledge of foreign languages, that is to say, either the most hazardous of creative efforts or a condition notoriously dependent on political or economic power.

Comparatists are in a better position to observe these vicissitudes than specialists in the so-called national literatures, particularly in countries still burdened with romantic mythologies concerning not only the "genius" but the "sense" of their respective literary traditions.[41] I have had the opportunity to notice that a most important link in the genesis of the modern novel, the success in seventeenth-century Europe of the Spanish picaresque genre, with its portrayal of squalor and corruption, was made possible by the pleasure with which these narratives were read by the enemies of Spain, who were legion, in the heyday of the Spanish empire. Even today there are a number of critics who think that the picaresque novel was prompted by the misery and the struggle for life that were characteristic of the land of the Inquisition (even though urban poverty and delinquency were the most general of phenomena in sixteenth-century Europe), rather than by the compassion or the sheer inventiveness of individual Spaniards (or of classes of Spaniards). I have even been tempted to postulate that national antagonisms necessarily

[40] Cf. Gillies, "Some Thoughts on Comparative Literature," pp. 17-24.

[41] Cf. Russo, *La critica letteraria contemporanea*, I, 102ff., II, 196ff.

result in an increased amount of literary influence on the part of the dominant nation (for example, that the landing of American troops in Lebanon would probably bring about a rash of Lebanese novels in the manner of Faulkner or of Hemingway). But this hypothesis is bluntly disproved by the fact—recently recalled by Alda Croce[42]—that the Spanish presence in Italy for several hundreds of years hindered rather than promoted Italian acceptance of the prose and poetry of the *Siglo de Oro*. Actually, the array of data collected by what I called a moment ago the comparatist's fact-finding agency is most useful insofar as it makes clear the precariousness of all literary relations, communications, and intermediary processes—the huge distance, as it were, normally separating the poetic work from the writer and the ordinary reader who were "born" to be inspired by it. Comparative literature, in short, highlights the *contingency* of our literary past and the contingent profile of literary history (though not of the single works of art). I realize of course that the term is arguable; but much more important, I also know that the concept is, i.e., that this is just the sort of argument which is likely to engage us in the theory of literary history.

Our subject now is not the usual elucidation of the connections between "history" and "literature"—as practiced, for example, by sociological criticism, *Geistesgeschichte*, the history of ideas. I am not referring here to the important and difficult area of literary theory that concerns the relations existing between historical experience and the literary work *before* it is written or completed. In this area one studies the passage from history to art. In terms of influences, the stage of "impact" would be involved, which is rather restricted and mostly psychological. The comparative study of *fortune* deals, instead, with a far more aleatory object, which is the

---

[42] Cf. "Relazioni della letteratura italiana con la letteratura spagnuola," in *Letterature comparate*, p. 110.

passage from art to history. It observes how poetry fares (to take a modest contemporary example: by way of the Nobel Prize)[43] in the arena of political, social, or economic history. A sociology of literature exists which, as José F. Montesinos reminded us recently,[44] considers how a *poem* (as it emerges from the writer's workshop) becomes a *book* (something that is forgotten or read, printed or reprinted, acclaimed or condemned, and, for good or ill, translated). Thus, our first perspective embraces the genesis of the poem, and our second, the career of the book. If literary creation, as I suggested earlier, bridges the "gap" between historical experience and the poem as between two different "orders" of the real, by a kind of displacement of experience, the career of the book represents, and is a function of, the replacement of the poem in history. This branch of comparative studies contributes significantly, I think, to the theory of literary history.

The third type of investigation is so predominant today that it is all around us, and I shall limit myself to pointing to its existence. It is diachronic without being basically genetic. As it does not rely on influences, indivisible as these are from biographical-historical factors, it can and primarily does consider the history of literature as an object, a process or an interpretative construction that is primarily literary. As we all know, comparative literature is the systematic study of literature in international terms. The numerous kinds of research that are subsumed under this third perspective have, besides, two essential traits in common: they postulate the integrity of literary study, and hence of comparative literature, as an inquiry entitled to establish its own procedures and goals (without claiming necessarily the "autonomy" of literature itself in any formalistic sense); and they regard this

[43] Cf. my review-article "The Problem of Juan Ramón Jiménez," *The New Republic*, December 16, 1957, pp. 17-18.

[44] Cf. *Introducción a una historia de la novela en España, en el siglo XIX* (Valencia, 1955).

study as a historical discipline. Obvious and fundamental though both objectives seem, their true reconciliation and joint development are continuing and demanding tasks for comparative scholarship.

Within the prevalent contemporary perspective, then, comparative studies remain historical while disengaging themselves from the automatic subservience to the nonliterary that was the burden of influence studies. The movement toward independence from other branches of history has been very clear in recent years. But whether this trend will develop such momentum as to sweep a number of critics away from or beyond history *tout court*, remains to be seen. The assumption of the third perspective is that it will not. Under the impact of Jungian psychology, or of Gaston Bachelard's anthropology of the imagination, there are gifted scholars who doubtless appear to strive for a vision of permanence and a critical neoclassicism. This is not surprising at a time when such poets, historians, art critics, anthropologists, or literary historians as Saint-John Perse, Toynbee, Malraux, Eliade, Ernst Robert Curtius, and Northrop Frye all share the very long and synthetic view. Yet the scholar usually stops short of quarreling with history, salutary though the consequences of the quarrel could be. In my opinion, the more formidable adversaries of comparative literature—that is, of its commitment to a historical humanism—are not the different versions of formalism, which have their place in literary criticism and can be assimilated by it, but such semi-temporal and elusive entelechies as the idea of "tradition" and the notion of "myth," that is, not the open rejection but the jaded, lukewarm, halfhearted exercise of the historical imagination.

It could be pointed out that comparatists investigate formal or thematic categories such as genres, modes, styles, metrics, motifs, images, types, archetypes, *topoi*; while they also examine, on the other hand, historical classes such as periods, movements, schools, generations. But this is hardly more than a practical distinction. Periods or movements are collective clusters into which critical insights become integrated. The trajectory of a genre like the pastoral or of a heroic type like Prometheus constitutes some sort of historical series. Comparative studies of this kind are not oriented basically toward other disciplines. In fact, they condition and mold literary history itself.

Finally, I should like to refer to a fourth perspective which has little practical value but is nevertheless a part of our theoretical scheme. This view questions the existence of synchronic orders in literature. Until now, every form of comparative research that I have discussed assumed a diachronic dimension, and in some cases a genetic one as well. Do literary configurations exist, we might now ask, that are neither diachronic nor genetic but merely synchronic? Moreover, I have recalled earlier the synthetic-systematic aspirations that are an essential legacy of comparative literature. These aims, one notices, are seldom realized in practice; a topic like the history of tragedy or the career of the figure of Ulysses is wide-ranging enough from a chronological point of view, but does it provide anyone with a qualitative basis for synthesis? Thus we are also led to ask: Are there literary groupings that are not merely synchronic but systematic? Though I do not possess the answers to these questions, I should like to indicate two of the levels on which one is likely to confront them. The first of these levels is historical. Following the terms of Ferdinand de Saussure, we may wish to inquire whether synchronic "states of literature" or "stages of literary development" can be profitably studied and described. Is the aesthetic organization of literature available to the cultured reader in the form of groupings or patterns? Is this what a "tradition," in T. S. Eliot's sense, really means? Or the idea of *Weltliteratur*? Is it what the concept of literary period (Renaissance, Baroque) or the notion of movement

(Romanticism, Symbolism) actually accomplishes? Secondly, I have suggested elsewhere that synchronic designs are known to all insofar as they enter the reading experience.[45] Formal and semantic relations play a part in the apprehension and evaluation of the individual literary work. Poems are recalled and organized into clusters by the reading of poems. In Saussure's terms, the *langue* of universal literature becomes, as we read, the *parole* of remembered systems; and the links created by this comparative aesthetic experience are similar to the interdependence of the semantic units of a single language, which Saussure called *valeur*. On this level, literary systems, like linguistic ones, possess a mental, mnemonic existence. The synchronic view highlights problems that pertain, in the final analysis, to the area of aesthetics.

[1958, 1962]

[45] Cf. my essay "Literatura como sistema," *Filologia Romanza*, IV (1957), 22-27.

A Note on Influences and Conventions

Scholars are embarrassed at times, as well as aroused, by the remembrance of things past.[1] Forty years ago Gustave Rudler was able to state with a great deal of plausibility: "la Littérature Comparée est un cas particulier de la critique d'influence."[2] Today, instead, the sway of influence studies seems to have come to an end. The specific field that they covered has been increasingly encroached upon by the survey, generally speaking, of traditions and conventions.

The facts of the case, nevertheless, will not vanish. Artistic influences continue to exist, or rather, to happen. The contacts between *Don Quixote* and *Tom Jones, Hérodiade* and *La Jeune Parque*, Haskell Block suggested not long ago, *are* influences of some sort, and ought to be studied as such.[3] One of our principal tasks today, with regard not only to methodology but to theory, consists in establishing the correct position of influences within the present coordinates of comparative literature. I should like to suggest that this may be done at the present time by examining the articulation between influences and the general area of conventions. For this is a polarity that appears to mirror cultural oppositions that have developed beyond the boundaries of any particular discipline.

[1] The core of this paper was read at the first meeting of the American Comparative Literature Association, held in New York on September 10 and 11, 1962, as part of a symposium on "The Concept of Influence in Comparative Literature"; and it was published in *Comparative Literature Studies*, 1 (1963), 149-151. The present version is considerably longer.

[2] *Les Techniques de la critique et de l'histoire littéraires* (Oxford, 1923), p. 160.

[3] Cf. "The Concept of Influence in Comparative Literature," *Yearbook of Comparative and General Literature*, VII (1958), 35-37.

Allow me, first of all, to touch upon some of the problematic aspects of influence studies by considering the historical trends they exemplify. These aspects may be reduced here to two: "genetic" and "atomistic." As for the other pole, the idea of convention, I shall discuss it briefly at the end of this essay.

I

The study of influences reflected for many decades the spirit, in the area of comparative studies, of what René Wellek has called "the genetically minded nineteenth century."[4] It was in the precise use of the genetic imagination, in the literal and sincere concern with how poetry is born and grows, that influence studies found their highest justification. One realizes that the stress, in this sense, was not on *what* passed from one writer to another, but on the fact that something *did* pass *from* one *to* the other and thus created a direct, nearly biological link between the two. Ultimately, an insight was gained into the very nature of this passage and of genesis in the literary field. An influence seemed to provide the student with a more concrete and vital introduction to a writer's workshop, to his full-fledged biography, than, for example, the intellectual order of discourse to which poetics belongs.

These insights echoed parallel discoveries in other fields. One need look no further than to the neighboring regions of folklore and linguistics. The nineteenth-century folklorist was absorbed in genealogy. In a characteristic and famous essay, "On the Migration of Fables" (1870), Max Müller inserted a genealogical tree in order to show that La Fontaine's "La Laitière et le Pot au lait" descended from an ancient beast fable of India (in the *Pañcatantra* and the *Hitopadeśa*); as part of a "literary caravan"—to repeat Müller's simile—the

---

[4] "The Concept of Comparative Literature," *Yearbook of Comparative and General Literature*, II (1953), 3.

fable would have traveled from India to Persia and then Arabia and finally to the nations of medieval Europe. Alessandro D'Ancona, to mention another example, maintained in his *Poesia popolare italiana* (1878) that the origin of all monostrophic Italian lyrics was Sicilian. A later critic like Michele Barbi would emphasize, instead, the lasting value of a folkloric tradition: rather than the reconstruction of ancient "originals," the continuity of a poetic effort.[5] As for nineteenth-century linguistics, the impact of its spectacular advances on philology and literary history is widely known. I am referring to the growth of comparative linguistics since the days of Rasmus Rask and Franz Bopp.

The family of Indo-European languages was identified, as the term "comparative linguistics" suggests, through the analysis of relations. These relations were found where none, in many cases, appeared to exist; and further, they were shown to proceed from a certain origin. The main goal of study, in other words, was linguistic kinship based on common ancestry. Jakob Grimm's discovery of the *Ablaut* or vowel shift was important because it made possible a number of genealogical inferences. The detection of morphological or phonetic similarities not due to common descent was considered not merely a trivial but a false reading of surface appearances. An instance of the need to subordinate resemblance to kinship can be seen in Holger Pedersen's discussion of the similarities between the inflection of nouns in Hungarian and in Turkish: "the agreements in phonology and morphology which are to be recognized as decisive for relationship must, however, be etymological, in that they point back to the original *identity* of the words and inflectional forms, not merely to *parallelism*."[6] A simple but classic exam-

[5] Cf. Luigi Russo, *La critica letteraria contemporanea*, 3rd edn. (Bari, 1953), I, 77.

[6] *The Discovery of Language. Linguistic Science in the Nineteenth Century*, tr. J. W. Spargo (Bloomington, 1962), p. 245.

ple of a fortuitous resemblance (since August Pott)[7] is Persian *bad* and English "bad," which apparently mean the same thing.

The challenge of this word is interesting, because it can be met in more than one way. Pedersen, in the tradition of nineteenth-century comparative linguistics, merely stresses that resemblance should disclose kinship. That is, synchrony must yield either to diachrony or to an earlier stage of synchrony. (Transferring the terms to comparative literature, this is the notion that textual or formal parallelisms are not significant unless there exists some kind of historical parentage, like a direct influence, a thematic current, a national premise.) But the contemporary linguist, faced with Persian and English *bad*, comes up with a different response. As far as structural linguistics is concerned, the isolated word or form should be inserted into the *system* to which it belongs. No part can be interpreted while overlooking the whole. (That is, the synchronic view is sufficient as long as it is systematic too. In terms of comparative literature, one might say that literary relations can be meaningful in a merely synchronic way insofar as they disclose a common system of conventions.)

Max Müller acknowledged more than once the crucial indebtedness of the comparative study of myths and religions to comparative linguistics. In our day the impact of the structural approach to language on anthropology and literary criticism has been increasingly visible, and there are good reasons for asking whether the invariant at work in these areas of research is not the continued prestige of a linguistic model.

Ernst Cassirer, in one of his last essays, published in 1945, suggested that the methods and goals of structural linguistics are representative of a general tendency of thought in modern scientific research. The emphasis on structure and system can also be found, he showed, in such fields as biology, psy-

[7] Cf. *The Discovery of Language*, p. 263.

chology, and philosophy.[8] One is inclined to agree: in the area of literature it seems clear that we live in a time characterized not by a genetic but by a synthetic-analytical frame of mind (simple chronology, to which the old concept of influence was wedded, is manipulated as freely by the literary historian as by the novelist). But Cassirer may help us to realize that it is not geneticism alone that is being surpassed: a certain "atomicism"—i.e., the isolation of the single parts of a system—is also under general attack. A number of distinguished linguists of the last third of the nineteenth century (Hermann Paul, Karl Brugmann, the Neo-Grammarians), and of psychologists as well (following Herbart's *Mechanik des Vorstellungslebens*), owed a great deal to the procedures of physics. As Cassirer points out, to understand a physical phenomenon was to construct a mechanical model of it. In the tradition of Newton and Lagrange, mechanics was a *Punkt-Mechanik,* the movement of material "points." Toward the end of the century, however, it was observed that certain electromagnetic occurrences could not be described in terms of matter. Matter had to be defined in terms of electricity. As the electromagnetic field is not an aggregate of material points, and the electron is not a single element within it, physics in such cases could not deal with movement in the traditional way. One had to recognize that particles are embedded in the structural conditions of a field, or that they are, in Hermann Weyl's words, an outgrowth of the field ("eine Ausgeburt des Felds") : "an electron is nothing but a part in which the electro-magnetic energy is condensed and assumes a peculiar strength."[9] In *Gestalt* psychology, a similar passage would take place from the observation of independent data to that of the field, the configuration, or the structure.

[8] Cf. Ernst Cassirer, "Structuralism in Modern Linguistics," *Word*, I (1945), 97-120.

[9] *Ibid.*, p. 101.

Now, I need not stress here once more the extent to which poetic influences are genetic or biographical processes. But I might suggest in passing that their study often exhibits, as in a kind of double exposure, disparate methods and aims. Genetic data are oddly interpreted by the nongenetic mind. A series of aberrations in our field can be ascribed to this basic maladjustment. Influences are recommended by some critics because they provide us with occasions for aesthetic analysis and understanding. Thus, we may compare Kafka to Dickens with no real concern for influence *qua* influence or genetic link, but with the peace of mind that may be derived from the knowledge that Kafka admired Dickens very much. It happens rather often that because a certain book reminds us of another, habit leads us to think of an influence rather than of traditions and conventions. Influences thus become perspectives for reading and fair game for the critic, despite the fact that an analysis of the product of an influence shows that no genuine distinction exists between the study of this product and the study of parallelisms or other synchronic groupings. Influences become contingent critical devices. In other words, it seems superfluous to keep them alive by equating them with conventions and techniques.

Ambiguities beset this most complex of terms, but I will recall only two of the more common usages. First, when I state "Kafka was influenced by Dickens," I probably ought to be saying "*Amerika* was influenced by *Martin Chuzzlewit*" (which is what one really knows). But I do not. The verb appears to imply or require a person, a human agent, and thus to make the ambiguity possible. There is greater clarity by far in the word "source"—so much so, actually, that the metaphor sounds simpleminded and positivistic. Thus one is likely to retain the equivocal "X was influenced by Y," where the genetic-psychological is commingled with the literary. ("Y influenced X" is possible too; but it is either shorthand for the other or chronological legerdemain. The passive character of influences is best served by the corresponding mode of the verb. This is one of the departures from the active, neoclassical "X imitated Y.") Secondly, the word "influence" often implies both a fact and a value judgment. One describes the effect of a certain work on another—while insinuating that the change, however slight, is not trivial. Things otherwise might have been different. The question is not simple, but one can make the best of it by admitting that "influence" is synonymous with "significant influence." And as these phenomena are truly innumerable, the need to organize or to structure them becomes very clear.

II

Turning now to those situations in which the atomistic position is no longer held, we might wish to identify some of the terms that we use. There are a number of them, of which perhaps two, "convention" and "tradition," may be considered representative. Let us suppose that A resembles B and C. We are confronted with parallelisms or relations. These may be thematically restricted, like motifs, or textually minute; or they may embrace the overall structure of a genre or mode. Let us assume that we are not examining these relations as independent data, but as parts of the literary equivalent of the scientist's "field" or system. Our framework is a larger area of observation in which A, B, and C become jointly meaningful, or, to paraphrase Cassirer's words concerning electromagnetic fields, where they seem to condense a certain energy and assume a peculiar strength. This effect takes place, we notice, whenever the observed relations reveal a common system of conventions, such as a motif or a plot or a formal dénouement in the novel, or an antithesis and a ringing final symmetry in a sonnet. The isolated relation conjures up, so to speak, the whole vehicle. In this context, one often hears today the term "tradition," but I suspect that its content is not truly distinct from the semantic province to which "convention" belongs. Traditions tend to be conventions laid out as sequences (conventions, one might say, with a past). When A occurs a reasonable number of years after B and C, we are inclined to state that we have encountered a tradition. Diachrony plays here, it seems to me, the most perfunctory of roles. In the case of either a convention or a tradition, what is at stake is not the unusual trait, the single impact, the inventive individual, or the concrete shape of a historical process, but a collective usage. "Whereas new movements," Harry Levin writes, "are propelled by individual talents, the vehicle of convention is tradition."[10] Conventions and traditions are "fields" or "systems" where the main unifying factor is accepted usage. The possible genetic link between A, B, and C is regarded either as irrelevant or as secondary to the existence of the field which this relation energetically condenses and reveals.

Where conventions (systematically speaking) are extensive, influences (genetic and individual) are intense. Significant influences are usually unmediated, one-to-one relationships—not distant kinships by association. Mallarmé and Rimbaud were crucial nourishment for the younger André Breton, just as the conversations with Vaché and the events of World War I must have been. These were positive incitements, not merely negative conditions "without which certain works could not have been written." But if a recent war novel reminds us of Homer, it is a common body of cultural premises and traditions, rather than the *tête-à-tête* of an influence, that comes into play. It would surely be inadequate to state that Virgil influenced Dante, when so many other elements stood by and what was operative was the total "field"—the authority and continuity of a tradition. It is true that one steals from single works, not traditions. But it is equally true that certain poems incarnate traditions, condense and vitalize

---

[10] "Notes on Convention," in *Perspectives of Criticism*, ed. H. Levin (Cambridge, Mass., 1950), p. 77.

systems of conventions, and symbolize other poems. Similarly, when influences spread and amalgamate, when they become common premises or usages—the common air that writers breathe at the same moment—then they ought to be called something like conventions. Who influences the contemporary novelist or the filmmaker who portrays aimless, alienated adolescents? How can these conventions be shared by a young Polish novelist like Marek Hlasko and a young Spanish novelist like Juan Goytisolo? Did a Renaissance poet have to read Petrarch in order to compose a Petrarchan sonnet? How many truly modern writers are not, in some fashion, the heirs of Mallarmé? In other words, literary conventions are not only technical prerequisites but broader fields or systems resulting from earlier, singular, genetic influences. The goal of the impact is transferred, as it were, from the writer to the vehicle.

A cluster of conventions determines the medium of a literary generation—the repertory of possibilities that a writer has in common with his living rivals. Traditions involve the competition of writers with their ancestors. These collective coordinates do not merely permit or regulate the writing of a work. They enter the reading experience and affect its meaning. The new work is both a deviant from the norm (as a crime is based on an attitude toward accepted social custom) and a process of communication referring to the norm. When individual influences seem to make the deviant possible, as opposed to the norm, they are furthest apart from conventions and least likely to be confused with them. Thus one can well understand why an ambitious young poet, groping for originality, will seek "an influence." For this could become for him an individual, hence an unconventional, matter. Although the origin of the influence may seem familiar, or even old hat, to another writer, it will fulfill the young poet's need if it acts upon him like a fresh discovery. At the moment, it cannot possibly coincide with a convention. The young writer may be battling, in a way, the logic of a medium and the coherence of a fabric of conventions.

Literary influences, then, may well continue to play a leading role in comparative studies. But it seems desirable that, whenever possible, they should not be miscast. Doubtless an influence *can* lead to literary analysis. Conventions *can* lead to insights into the creative process. Yet we know that in each case the opposite function is the most effective. Conventions and traditions unfold broad perspectives—fields and systems —more readily than influences do; and they show us the patterns that literature presents when we observe it from a primarily synchronic point of view. Influences do not "organize the chaos" of individual literary facts in as useful a manner. But they open, by means of the extensive examination of unmediated writer-to-writer or work-to-work contacts, more vigorously than traditions or conventions would, the doors of the writer's workshop and the endlessly complex process of artistic creation.

III

In a definitive article, to which I should like to refer my readers, Harry Levin has made clear the pertinence and significance of the concept of convention.[11] I should like at this point to note some of the broader aspects of the term. There is a great deal to be learned, first of all, from Professor Levin's survey of its history. A most important date is that of Madame de Staël's *De la Littérature* (1800), where the analogy between social and literary conventions, with regard to the stage, is forcibly expressed: "la nature de convention, au théâtre, est inséparable de l'aristocratie des rangs dans le gouvernement: vous ne pouvez soutenir l'une sans l'autre."[12] The central paradox we encounter is implicit in a historical fact: poetic conventions were fully recognized for the first

[11] Cf. the previous note.
[12] As quoted by Levin, "Notes on Convention," p. 64.

time by the cultural movement which had begun by estranging itself from them, namely the Romantic movement. Estrangement and revolt made possible, it seemed, a more profound understanding of the embattled institutions—such as literature itself. Political revolution had contributed to lay bare the conservative aspect of artistic structures; and the priority of the spontaneous, individual, unconventional, "natural" qualities, which had spread irresistibly since the days of Rousseau, appeared to question the premises of art itself. Professor Levin recalls that classical poetics, as codified by Longinus and others, had postulated the perfect correspondence between nature and art. Insofar as this had been true, there had been no need to distrust the conventionality of forms. But neoclassicism, since the seventeenth century, grossly overvalued those prescriptive conventions called rules, and as a consequence the Romantic movement "drew its heavy line between the artificial and the natural."[13]

But the idea of convention was found to be a double-edged sword. This essential ambiguity—it could be regarded as enwrapping all modern literature—was most sharply perceived not by such sociological critics as Madame de Staël and other pre-Romantics but by those writers who had gone on to acquire a command of their own experience as Romantics: in particular the "classical" German poets. Schiller's aesthetics was a constant attempt to establish meaningful relationships between the formal conditions of art and man's varying approaches to "nature." "In Schiller's conception," René Wellek sums up, "the artist is the mediator between man and nature, between intellect and sense, between the *Stoffrieb* (the urge to assimilate the world of senses) and the *Formtrieb* (the urge to subdue the world to the moral law)."[14] "Sentimental" rather than "naïve," the modern poet stands outside artificial

[13] *Ibid.*, p. 73.
[14] *A History of Modern Criticism: 1750-1950* (New Haven, 1950), I, 233.

society—"conventional" society—and is alienated from his age. The sentimental poet now seeks the "infinite," and surpasses the limits of "nature." In this sense, poetic form becomes for him a weapon against social convention. And in his later criticism Schiller went on to emphasize increasingly the stylized character of all art.[15] In the preface to *Die Braut von Messina* (1803), as Harry Levin points out, Schiller justified the use of the tragic chorus while praising the ability of the poet to bring about a liberation from the barriers of the real ("eine gewisse Befreiung von den Schranken des Wirklichen").[16] A year later, Goethe, in a review written for the *Jenaische Allgemeine Literaturzeitung* (April 16, 1804), praised the poems of Johann Heinrich Voss in such terms as these: "durch den entschiedenen, oben gepriesenen Sieg der Form über den Stoff, durch manches von äusserer Veranlassung völlig unabhängige Gedicht zeigt uns der Dichter, dass es ihm frei stehe, das Wirkliche zu verlassen und ins Mögliche zu gehen, das Nahe wegzuweisen und das Ferne zu ergreifen, das Eigene aufzugeben und das Fremde in sich aufzunehmen" (through the decisive victory of form over matter, praised earlier, through many a poem fully independent from any external cause, the poet shows us that he may freely choose to leave behind the real and go off into the possible, to dismiss what is near and apprehend what is far, to relinquish his own and take in the unfamiliar).

It could finally be observed and brought to light that poetry, considered as a triumph of the imagination, had no genuine quarrel with conventions, without which it would not be possible to draw the necessary line between the poetic and the natural. The revolt against conventions, in other words, had really been a reaction against neoclassical poetics. The rise of a new poetics stressing the power of the imagination

[15] Cf. *ibid.*, p. 249.

[16] As quoted by Levin, "Notes on Convention," p. 76. For the full text, see Schiller, *Gesammelte Werke*, ed. R. Netolitzky (Berlin, 1955), II, 527.

would alter completely the terms of the problem. As long as
one accepted the neoclassical equation of art with "nature,"
every formal convention could seem a hindrance. But if the
value of art consisted in a liberation from nature, or in an
enrichment and a formal transformation of it, then every
artistic convention could be turned into an ally.

Artistic conventions, in the final analysis, were not the true
target. The questions raised by the formal premises of literature actually pointed in another direction: that of the relationship between the artist and his experience, rather than
between the artist and his medium. The battleground of
much of modern poetics would be the writer's approach to
a "reality principle." Since Cervantes, the practitioners of a
certain "realism" had found it useful to overturn the conventions of previous "romances." In the history of the novel a
change of goals would seem to call for a change of means.
Unfortunately, the theorists of realism would often confuse
the latter with an absence of means—a rejection of form,
style, or symbol. It has become one of the skills of the twentieth-century critic to distinguish substance from shadow in
such cases, and not to take such pronouncements at face
value. One observes on the one hand the varying degrees of
necessary conventionality, distinctiveness, and freedom
(from the conventions of social life) in poetry and in the
novel, and on the other, the different approaches that may be
chosen toward experience. Photographic "realism" and "nat-
uralism" may prepare the ground in some cases for political
or social revolution, by portraying society in all its horror;
but as art, they are slavishly chained to the status quo of
familiar middle-class perspectives. Madame de Staël was
wrong, as the contemporary theater proves, when she failed
to perceive that social conventions and stage conventions belong to two separate orders of experience, so that the two can
be made not only to coincide, or to conflict by appearing to
overlap, but to clash. Literary conventions can mirror in

ironic ways the routines of social conformism. But they can also go far beyond them. Since the Romantic movement, modern art has rediscovered the paradox that without the struggle with strict forms and conventions, an important use of human freedom would disappear.

The metaphor of convention, then, like the metaphor of institution, assimilated and implied certain basic dimensions of social life: not only the restraints of contractual obligations but the exercise of freedom on the part of individuals and groups. It announced the future sway of the critical analogy between literature and society (literary studies and linguistics, literature and social institutions, poetic structures and social structures) and the decline of the analogy—which had prevailed during the late eighteenth century—between poetry and nature, artistic processes and cosmic processes. I am not referring, of course, to the earlier, naive notion of *l'imitation de la nature*, as in, say, the Abbé Batteux and other neo-classical critics, but to the emergence of natural and organic analogies from the days of Moses Mendelssohn—*Ueber die Hauptgrundsätze der schönen Künste und Wissenschaften* (1757)— or of Lessing to those of Kant and Goethe. An aphorism such as "every beautiful artistic whole is a reproduction on a small scale of the highest beauty in the vast whole of nature"— "Jedes schöne Ganze der Kunst ist im Kleinen ein Abdruck des höchsten Schönen im grossen Ganzen der Natur," in the "Grundlinien zu einer vollständigen Theorie der schönen Künste" by Karl Philipp Moritz (1789)—was only meaningful insofar as the idea of the autonomy of art had come fully into its own from Mendelssohn to Kant. The recognition of the special status of art was a previous condition for the development of significant comparisons with either nature or society.

Obviously the idea of convention can adapt itself to phenomena of the most varied scope. It may be applied to any part or dimension of an artistic whole, as long as it manifests in some fashion the conventionality of the work. In a medieval love poem the ideal of feminine beauty may appear as most conventional. Or the poet may evoke the fragrance of a daisy, which (as John Livingston Lowes explained) is odorless in real gardens. Or exotic plants and animals: Curtius observed how abundant olive trees and lions were in the medieval North.[17] He also noticed that they reappear in *As You Like It*. But he did not mention that even Victor Hugo could, in "Booz endormi," conventionally tame the great animal and lead him to water like a horse:

C'était l'heure tranquille où les lions vont boire. . . .

Nevertheless, it is the whole rather than the part that reveals the function of convention most effectively. The term brings into sharper focus, I think, the broad prerequisites and structural dimensions that are characteristic of a *vehicle* as a whole—a genre, a craft, a medium. It stresses the fundamental premises without which the writer, so to speak, cannot set pen to paper or even begin to conceive his work. The vehicle is such—both an invitation to the creative imagination and a series of tasks, of technical demands, of problems to solve—that it postulates the passage from experience to art, or rather, from one order of activity to another. In *Convention and Revolt in Poetry* (1919), John Livingston Lowes addressed himself admirably to the conventionality of the poetic medium as a whole. It is not only language that is a system of conventions, but its use as the basic material for a certain sort of formal fiction. The individual literary effort does not presuppose anyone's acceptance. The single poem does not assume a contractual relation with a given public.[18]

[17] Cf. *Europäische Literatur und lateinisches Mittelalter* (Bern, 1948), Chap. x, sec. 1.

[18] The concept of convention, like that of institution, is the extension of a legal analogy. On nineteenth-century interpretations of this analogy, particularly between language and law, cf. Augusto Gaudenzi, "Lingua e diritto nel loro sviluppo parallelo," *Archivio Giuridico*, xxxi (1883), 271-304; and Giovanni Nencioni, *Idealismo e realismo nella scienza del linguaggio* (Firenze, 1946), Chap. x, "L'istituzionalità della lingua."

But the poetic *medium* does. An isolated invention is incorporated into a vehicle or a medium only after a certain community and a potential audience have made it their own. Like folklore, the vehicle belongs to all and may be tampered with at any time. In Lowes's words: "convention, therefore, so far as art is concerned, represents concurrence in certain accepted methods of communication."[19] On such a level, as Harry Levin stresses, there is no need to differentiate between theme and form. The notion of medium as convention, or of vehicle or genre as convention, supersedes from the start any distinction between form and content.[20] It is a unifying, structural notion. And it encourages the literary critic who is confronted with a chaos of resemblances or relations between hopelessly scattered individual phenomena to try to recognize not merely the isolated or atomistic contacts between them, but the broader demands of a vehicle regarded as a system of conventional premises.[21]

[1962]

[19] John Livingston Lowes, *Convention and Revolt in Poetry* (Boston and New York, 1919), p. 3.

[20] Cf. Levin, "Notes on Convention," p. 57.

[21] I have preferred not to recall in this short discussion the evident but complex parallel between our subject and "conventionalism" in modern science, logic, and philosophy. Since the discovery of non-Euclidian geometries during the nineteenth century, and the mathematical theories of Henri Poincaré, it has been increasingly stressed that the procedures of science and of logical thought consist in elaborating the correct consequences of certain initial premises, models, or hypotheses. Literature, like logic or mathematics or physics, in this sense, is no mere empirical or inductive response to fact. It is based on a set of preliminary rules. I shall limit myself here to quoting Rudolf Carnap, *Der logische Aufbau der Welt*, 2nd edn. (Hamburg, 1961), p. 150: "die Logik (einschl. der Mathematik) besteht nur aus konventionellen Festsetzungen über den Gebrauch von Zeichen und aus Tautologien auf Grund dieser Festsetzungen." There is a useful presentation of the origins of conventionalism in the philosophy of mathematics in J.J.A. Mooij, *La philosophie des mathématiques de Henri Poincaré* (Paris-Louvain, 1966), Chap. 1.

II

Toward a Definition of the Picaresque

I enjoy a double advantage as I begin. The publication of various contemporary novels of more or less roguish character has proved, beyond any doubt, that to regard the picaresque as an event of the past *only* is a pedantic and erroneous view. The fact, besides, that this Congress has officially in mind the problems involved in "the preparation of a dictionary of literary terminology" excludes from the start any levity or roguery of method. To be sure, a full definition of the term "picaresque" cannot be attempted here.[1] I propose, rather, to sketch a way toward such a definition, which will lead us today in four separate but neighborly directions.

It may be useful to distinguish between the following: the picaresque genre, first of all; a group of novels, secondly, that deserve to be called picaresque in the strict sense—usually in agreement with the original Spanish pattern; another group of novels, thirdly, which may be considered picaresque in a broader sense of the term only; and finally, a picaresque myth: an essential situation or significant structure derived from the novels themselves.[2]

[1] This paper was read at the Third Congress of the I.C.L.A. held in Utrecht, Holland, on August 21-26, 1961, and published in the *Proceedings of the IIId Congress of the International Comparative Literature Association* (The Hague, 1962), pp. 252-266. It was expanded for lectures delivered soon afterwards at Wellesley College and the University of Puerto Rico.

[2] There is a very large bibliography on the subject. I shall mention some of the specialized studies I have found useful: Frank W. Chandler, *Romances of Roguery* (New York, 1899); Quintiliano Saldaña, "El pícaro en la literatura y en la vida española," *Nuestro Tiempo*, xxvi (1926), 193-218; Erich Jenisch, "Vom Abenteuer- zum Bildungsroman," *Germanisch-Romanische Monatsschrift*, xiv (1926), 339-351; F. Courtney Tarr, "Literary and Artistic Unity in the Lazarillo de Tormes," *PMLA*, xlii (1927), 404-421; Helmut Petriconi, "Zur

I

No work embodies completely the picaresque genre. The genre is not, of course, a novel any more than the equine species is a horse. A genre is a model—and a convenient model to boot: an invitation to the actual writing of a work, on the basis of certain principles of composition. From a historical point of view, the early existence of a picaresque genre is undeniable. Mateo Alemán seems to be aware of it as he opens his *Guzmán de Alfarache* (1599); and Cervantes

Chronologie und Verbreitung des spanischen Schelmenromans," *Volkstum und Kultur der Romanen*, I (1928), 324-342; Amado Alonso, "Lo picaresco de la picaresca," *Verbum*, Buenos Aires, 1929, 321-328; Marcel Bataillon, *Le Roman picaresque* (Paris, 1931), and the Preface to his edition of *Lazarillo de Tormes* (Paris, 1958); Leo Spitzer, "Zur Kunst Quevedos in seinem Buscón," in *Romanische Stil- und Literaturstudien*, II (Marburg, 1931); José F. Montesinos, "Gracián o la picaresca pura," *Cruz y Raya*, 1933, 39-63, reprinted in his *Ensayos y estudios de Literatura española*, ed. Joseph H. Silverman (Mexico, 1959); Américo Castro, "Perspectiva de la novela picaresca," *Rev. de la Bibl., Arch. y Museo*, XII (1935), 123-143, *La realidad histórica de España* (Mexico, 1954) and the essays printed in the later works, such as *Hacia Cervantes* (Madrid, 1957); Miguel Herrero García, "Nueva interpretación de la novela picaresca," *Revista de Filología Española*, XXIV (1937), 343-362; Manuel Muñoz Cortés, "Personalidad y contorno en la figura del *Lazarillo*," *Escorial*, X (1943), 112-120; Pedro Salinas, "El 'héroe' literario y la novela picaresca española," *Revista de la Universidad de Buenos Aires*, IV (1946), 75-84, reprinted in his *Ensayos de literatura hispánica* (Madrid, 1958); *La novela picaresca española*, ed. Angel Valbuena Prat (Madrid, 1946); José María de Cossío, Introduction to Camilo José Cela, *Nuevas andanzas y desventuras de Lazarillo de Tormes* (Madrid, 1948); Enrique Moreno Báez, *Lección y sentido de Guzmán de Alfarache* (Madrid, 1948); J. Frutos Gómez de las Cortinas, "El anti-héroe y su actitud vital (sentido de la novela picaresca)," *Cuadernos de Literatura*, VII (1950), 97-143; Robert Escarpit et al., "Le roman picaresque," *Bulletin, Centre d'études et discussions de littérature générale*, Bordeaux, I (1951-52), 1-18; Joaquín Casalduero, "Notas sobre *La ilustre fregona*," *Anales Cervantinos*, III (1953), 1-9; Oskar Seidlin, "Pikareske Züge im Werke Thomas Manns," *Germanisch-Romanische Monatsschrift*, XXXVI (1955), 22-40; and Carlos Blanco Aguinaga, "Cervantes y la picaresca. Notas sobre dos tipos de realismo," *Nueva Revista de Filología Hispánica*, XI (1957), 313-342.

alludes to it six years later in a famous sentence of the *Quixote*: "mal año para *Lazarillo de Tormes*, y para todos cuantos de aquel género se han escrito o escribieren" (a bad year it will be for *Lazarillo de Tormes* and all others of that sort that have been or will be written). Like any other genre, the picaresque model must be viewed in terms of its relevance not only to the contemporary historian but to the readers and writers of the sixteenth and seventeenth centuries. It is most useful to approach a genre, as Renato Poggioli suggests, from the perspective of the writer, as a "traditional model or conventional pattern" exerting an influence on the creation of a work in progress.[3] It belongs to a larger body of poetics, and affects poetry insofar as the actual poem is a dream more or less fulfilled.

The dream is generally, if not always, a combination in the memory of the artist of certain already existing prototypes. The picaresque novel-to-be begins (for it has a clear beginning, and I am not speaking of a metatemporal myth) with an overture in two movements: *La vida de Lazarillo de Tormes* (1554), the primitive of the form (in the sense that Giotto is a primitive), and the *Primera parte de Guzmán de Alfarache* (1599), which would become a best seller and the main target of imitation for many decades. Yet the latter did not entirely supersede the former, and Quevedo surely remembered both as he wrote his *Historia de la vida del Buscón* (1626). One could think of the picaresque genre as an ideal type blending, in varying degrees or fashions, *Lazarillo de Tormes* with *Guzmán de Alfarache* (each having its predominant tonality, technique, and goals), with the addition of other novels according to the case. A genre has stable features, but it also changes, as a precise influence on the work in progress, with the writer, the nation, and the period.

[3] Cf. Renato Poggioli, "Poetics and Metrics," in *Comparative Literature. Proceedings of the I.C.L.A. Congress in Chapel Hill, N.C.* (Chapel Hill, 1959), I, 192-204.

In the eighteenth century, for example, the Spanish models would usually be replaced, as an incitement to French or English storytellers, by Le Sage's *Gil Blas.* And a genre, of course, confronts certain "countergenres" (the picaresque opposing, for example, the pastoral or the Greek romance), with which it constitutes the "ideal spaces" in which writers dwell before they set pen to paper. It should be possible to write a history of the poetics of the picaresque, as distinct from a history of one of the novels properly speaking.

II

I shall name picaresque novels in the strict sense a group of works that fluctuate around a norm with respect to each of certain characteristics. This central tradition would spring from the main current of the Spanish *Siglo de Oro*, from *Lazarillo* to *Estebanillo González* (1646). It would gather a number of French, German, Dutch, and English narratives, too numerous to be reviewed here: whether servile imitations, like Oudin de Préfontaine's *Les aventures tragi-comiques du Chevalier de la Gaillardise* (1662), or creative ones, such as *Gil Blas* or Defoe's *Moll Flanders*—or, in our day, Thomas Mann's *Felix Krull*.

I should make clear at this point that I am not proposing an absolute norm, to which one might be tempted later to subordinate the actual works under study. On the contrary, my definition is entirely relative to its possible usefulness in two ways: as a procedure for ordering the continuum of individual literary facts; and as a critical perspective, perhaps fruitful at the moment of reading. I shall order my subject—the novels—by means of some distinctions. But the ordering is tentative and empirical. The target of this discussion is a series of literary works, not a definition. The definition itself, like every critical act, is merely a limited perspective.

Here the historian must decide what those "certain characteristics" are that control his critical perspective. His terms must attempt to embrace a large enough, yet limited, quantity of works. Any description is, of course, arbitrary insofar as it is a choice, a classification based on a number of outstanding features. Thus, I have singled out eight features of the picaresque. I shall dwell at some length upon the first characteristic, which is crucial, and sketch very briefly the other seven.

1. This first characteristic may be approached most simply by asking the question: How important is a definition of the *picaro*? Should one attempt a portrait of him, alone and with no background (as in Murillo's paintings of young ragamuffins)? My answer is that this definition is necessary but not by any means sufficient. The portrait of the *picaro* is not sufficient even for an understanding of the hero of picaresque novels, who—if by *picaro* we mean a type or a character—only *becomes* one at a certain point of his career, and afterwards often ceases to be a rogue at all.

The *picaro* as such (or if you wish, the hero when he is a *picaro*) can be distinguished readily enough from three older types: the wanderer, the jester, and the have-not. The wanderer (from Odysseus to the knight-errant) has deep roots in both the Greco-Roman and the Semitic cultures. The *picaro* (the rogue-errant) is only *partly* a wanderer, as we shall see later. The jester or fool is an important person in Renaissance art and life: he is related to Latin Comedy and *Le Roman de Renart*, the Italian *novella* and the Germanic *Schwänke*, Eulenspiegel and Rabelais.[4] Yet the reflective, introspective, changing *picaro* cannot be confused with the static, happy hero of jest-books. As for the have-not—the artistic depiction of a lower-class type—one should recall that only during the Renaissance did literature begin to show a saturation of low life comparable to society's. I allude to the numerous and often obscure works dealing with rogues, beggars, ruffians,

---

[4] There is also a relation with such folkloric figures as Scoggin, Pierre Faifeu, and Pedro de Urdemalas.

and criminals, which F. W. Chandler has called "anatomies of roguery." I shall presently show how sharply the picaresque novel ought to be distinguished from them. The *pícaro* both incorporates and transcends the wanderer, the jester, and the have-not. (Everyone knows another exceptional fictional creation of whom the same could be said: Falstaff.) He is not all *picardía*—the slyness of the trickster who lives on his wits, just short of delinquency if possibly he can. Guile and wile are only his offensive weapons. A stoical good humor is his defensive one. And a philosophical temper, in the wake of Diogenes, i.e., a cynical bent, his deeper vindication.

Let us recall for a moment the anatomies of roguery. I have in mind such pieces as the German *Liber Vagatorum: Der Bettler Orden* (1510); in England, criminal biographies, from Lodge to Defoe, conny-catching pamphlets, prison tracts like Thomas Dekker's;[5] in Spain, works by Cristóbal de Chaves and Carlos García;[6] the French seventeenth-century

[5] The first typical English presentation of beggar life or city thieves is John Awdeley's *Fraternitye of Vacabondes* (1561). Best known are the conny-catching pamphlets by Robert Greene, and Thomas Dekker's *The Bellman of London* (1608) and *Lanthorne and Candlelight* (1608). The latter's *The Seven Deadly Sins of London* is a prison tract, like Mynshul's *Essays and Characters of a Prison and Prisoners* (1618). Thomas Lodge, the author of pastorals, wrote also *The Life and Death of William Longbeard* (1593).

[6] To wit, C. de Chaves' *Relación de la cárcel de Sevilla*, written sometime after 1585 and connected with slang writings in the language of *germanía*; and C. García's *La desordenada codicia de bienes ajenos* (1619). In Spain these "anatomies" were rare, since they were superseded from the start by the picaresque novels, which use similar materials. Carlos García's book, a perfect example of the anatomy of roguery (with its concentration on two main themes, the classification of thieves and the brotherhood of rogues, which Cervantes' *Rinconete y Cortadillo* uses to build elaborate ironies), was written and published in France, under the influence of the French anatomies. In Spain the anatomy will *follow* the novel, through a process Montesinos has very rightly called "desnovelización": I refer especially to the pre-*costumbrista* works, from Vélez de Guevara's *Diablo Cojuelo* (obviously unpicaresque) to Zabaleta.

slang-books;[7] the Italian *Il vagabondo*; the Portuguese *Arte de furtar*.[8] Unlike the picaresque novels, none of these books focuses on the *interaction* between a growing individual and his environment. Criminal biographies and jest-books stress exclusively the deeds of the hero. The main subject of beggar-books, caveats against city thieves, prison tracts, gambling pamphlets, and sketches of manners is unfailingly a social milieu. My point is that the *pícaro* is not an independent hero who may be studied *in vacuo*. If the picaresque story could be effectively described through him, it would not be a sub-genre of what we call today the novel, or an integral stage in the emergence of the modern novel. The picaresque is based on a situation, or rather, a chain of situations. Its hero is involved from the start in what Henry James called, in the Preface to *The Portrait of a Lady*, a "tangle." This tangle is an economic and social predicament of the most immediate and pressing nature (not a confrontation with absolute forces), an entanglement with the relative and the contemporaneous; and it leads to further situations or "adventures." Our hero becomes a *pícaro* through the lessons he draws from his adventures. It must be stressed that the picaresque narrative, like most modern narratives, cannot be understood if one continues to rely on a neo-Aristotelian terminology, i.e., on the notion that literature presents "characters" or "men in action." Essentially, the novel deals with lives, with evolvement, with the unfolding in historical time

[7] Like the nearly picaresque *Vie généreuse des Gueux, mercelots et bohémiens* (1596) and *L'Histoire générale des Larrons* (1623). The French slang-books of the seventeenth century deserve serious study, as an example of "l'envers du siècle." D'Aubrincourt's *L'Histoire générale des Larrons*, with its continuation by F. de Calvi, the *Inventaire général de l'histoire des Larrons*, relegated by classical taste to a kind of literary "Cour des Miracles," was reprinted at least twelve times between 1623 and 1709.

[8] *Il vagabondo* (1627) was the work of a Dominican priest, Giacinto Nobili, who used the pen name of Rafaele Frianoro. *A arte de furtar* (1652) has been attributed to António Vieira.

of individual destinies. In Spanish, the key word is *vida*, which most often has a place in the titles of picaresque tales: *La vida de Lazarillo de Tormes, y de sus fortunas y adversidades*. The picaresque *novel*, then, offers a process of conflict between the individual and his environment, inwardness and experience, whereby one element is not to be perceived without the other.

This double articulation is fundamental, and its appropriateness is confirmed by the memory of two distinct kinds of excess which critics of the picaresque have incurred. The first of these was characteristic of the nineteenth century, and it rested on an exclusive and positivistic reading of the picaresque as reproduction of social fact—of vagabondage, destitution, and squalor in the Spain of Philip II.[9] The second approach consisted in a "Copernican" reversal of the first, and it focused on a moral or psychological analysis of the *pícaro* as a typical figure of his time, for example, as "Renaissance man."[10] The former view was wrong even in factual terms: from a sociological point of view, it was not legitimate to single out Spain (except through the circular argument that picaresque novels were written there), in view of the fact that vagabondage and crime were prevailing conditions in all the growing cities of sixteenth-century Europe; from a literary angle, it failed to recognize the crucial distinction, which I have just stressed, between the picaresque narrative and the "anatomy of roguery." We have seen that it is misleading to conceive of the *pícaro* as an isolated character or

[9] Cf., for example, Arvède Barine, "Les gueux d'Espagne," *Revue des Deux Mondes*, April 15, 1888, pp. 870-904; Alfred Morel-Fatio, *Etudes sur l'Espagne*, 1st series (Paris, 1888); Wilhelm Lauser, *Der erste Schelmenroman, Lazarillo von Tormes* (Stuttgart, 1889); and Albert Schultheiss, *Der Schelmenroman der Spanier und seine Nachbildungen* (Hamburg, 1893).

[10] Particularly during the 1930's: cf. an early interpretation by Américo Castro, "Perspectiva de la novela picaresca," *Rev. de la Bibl., Arch. y Museo*, XII (1935), 123-143; and José F. Montesinos, "Gracián o la picaresca pura."

type. Today it seems clear that the *pícaro* was a creative comment on sixteenth-century *vidas* in general—on how it felt to be a man among men (or rather to become one, against all economic and social odds), whether one was a beggar, a merchant, or a *hidalgo*, in post-Renaissance Europe.

Our first feature, then, is a dynamic psycho-sociological situation, or series of situations, which can only be described —however briefly—in narrative fashion. It is, in this sense, a "plot." The *pícaro* is, first of all, an orphan. In the history of narrative forms, *Lazarillo de Tormes* represents the first significant appearance of the myth of the orphan. All later picaresque novels will build on this same highly suggestive situation. A young *orphan*, then, faces early dishonor or want and is led to break all ties with his native city. He has an unusually precocious taste of solitude. (This experience of solitude is presented most purely, I think, and developed into a lasting detachment, by the author of *Robinson Crusoe* in *Moll Flanders*.) Left without a father, or a mother, or both, he is obliged to fend for himself ("buscarse la vida") in an environment *for which he is not prepared.* He is for the moment an insular, isolated being. He has not been adapted to ruling conventions or shaped into a social or a moral person. The family, in this sense, has not fulfilled its primary functions. The beginnings of knowledge are forced upon the young boy by the shock of premature experience.[11] All values must be rediscovered by him anew, as if by a godless Adam. Turning toward others, he finds himself unwanted or unin-

[11] It might be objected that the *pícaro*'s parents are already rogues in many cases, and that heredity is shown to be strong, as indeed it is. But the author as a rule lets the hero learn by himself (lets him experience in actuality and over a period of time) what he *might* have learned from his parents. Thus, Lazarillo's final choice ("yo determiné de arrimarme a los buenos") reproduces word for word his mother's early advice. Yet it took him the length of the novel to acquire truly what he had heard—to "erwerben," in Goethe's words, "was du ererbt von deinen Vätern hast. . . ."

vited. (Of the early days in the life of the hero of *Dead Souls*, Gogol writes: "life looked at him at first with sour inhospitality, as through a dim, snow-darkened window." In the words of Moll Flanders, " . . . I was, as it were, turned out of Door to the wide World." Or to quote Eichendorff's *Aus dem Leben eines Taugenichts*: "es ist, als wäre ich überall eben zu spät gekommen, als hätte die ganze Welt gar nicht auf mich gerechnet" [it seems that I had arrived everywhere just too late, that the whole world had not expected me]). Inwardly and outwardly alone, the young boy is wounded, hardened, and never quite assimilated by an adult society and its many scandals. At once fatherless and homeless—self-exiled, or, in the words of Tristan L'Hermite's *Le page disgracié* (1643), "dépaysé"—he will seek new cities, further replacements for the absent tutor, only to discover that the world can at best act like a cruel stepfather. He will remain, like Gil Blas, "un vieil adolescent." The author, of course, has tampered with the cards, so that hardship and bitter lesson conspire at every turn to shape the hero into an enemy of the social fabric, if not into an active foe. For the "unfortunate traveler" soon learns that there is no material survival outside of society, and no real refuge—no pastoral paradise—beyond it. Social role-playing is as ludicrous as it is indispensable. This is where the solution of "roguish" behavior is preferred. Now a *pícaro*, the hero chooses to compromise and live on the razor's edge between vagabondage and delinquency. He can, in short, *neither join nor actually reject his fellow men*. He becomes what I would like to call a "half-outsider." Hence the ambivalence of the final narrative situation, and the wealth of variations that it can inspire.

An obvious corollary of this process: the hero of the mainstream picaresque novel *does* grow, learn, and change. In this connection, I would like to lodge, in passing, a protest against a peculiar scholarly delusion. Although, of course, the *Bildungsroman* has a peculiar significance within German culture, it is utterly false to pretend, as some critics have, that only German picaresque novels are, in the broader sense of the term too, *Bildungsromane*.[12]

Other characteristics will be outlined quickly.

2. The picaresque novel is a pseudoautobiography. This use of the first-person tense is more than a formal frame. It means that not only are the hero and his actions picaresque, but everything *else* in the story is colored with the sensibility, or filtered through the mind, of the *pícaro*-narrator. Both the hero and the principal point of view are picaresque. Hence the particular consistency and self-saturation of the style. Life is at the same time revived and judged, presented and remembered.[13]

The first-person technique is profoundly relevant, besides, because our hero, as we have seen, is a "half-outsider." This amounts to a considerable split between what was once traditionally called the "inner man" and "outer man." Sometimes it is the *homo interior* who is radically estranged from his fellow man, while the *homo exterior* acts and appears to conform. But who tells the story? How does the storytelling half-outsider interpret his own active career and social roles? I shall soon return to this point. Let us notice, for the moment, that language in the picaresque tradition is the instrument of dissimulation or of irony, and the pseudoautobiographical

---

[12] For example, cf. Jenisch, "Vom Abenteuer- zum Bildungsroman," p. 339. In fact, the picaresque plot is based on a series of conventional "climaxes of change." No scene is more representative of these novels than the initial moment of truth, the turning point at which the boy loses his innocence or begins to do so: the prototype is the knocking of Lazarillo's head against the stone bull; more often, Guzmán's deception in an inn is imitated (by Quevedo, Espinel, Le Sage). This scene reappears in later novels of broader scope: such as Fabrice del Dongo's disillusionment (which begins also in an inn) at Waterloo in *La Chartreuse de Parme*.

[13] Cf., in the bibliography of note 2, the contributions by A. Alonso, J. M. de Cossío, Moreno Báez, O. Seidlin.

form, a way of inserting the entire tale into a double perspective of self-concealment and self-revelation.

3. The narrator's view is also partial and prejudiced. In this willful limitation are to be found some of the virtues and drawbacks of the form. It offers no synthesis of human life.

4. The total view of the *pícaro* is reflective, philosophical, critical on religious or moral grounds. As an autobiographer and an outsider, he collects broad conclusions—*il met le monde en question*. "Si je devais ériger mes vices en vertus," we hear in *Gil Blas*, "j'appellerais ma paresse une indolence philosophique." The *pícaro* as an "ongoing" philosopher, as a constant discoverer and rediscoverer, experimenter and doubter where every value or norm is concerned, never ceases to learn. Each person or action is for him a possible "example."

Exempla trahunt: There is an important current of writing during the sixteenth and seventeenth centuries in which the impact not of values as such but of exemplary, value-carrying individuals is stressed: the great men whose "imitation" Machiavelli recommended in Chapter 14 of *The Prince*, or the educators sought by Luis Vives, whose pedagogy would transform education into a personal matter between teacher and student.[14] (In the absence of a father, Lazarillo "goes to school" with the blind man—"el gran maestro el ciego.")

Most often these novels tend to be *romans à thèse*, or rather *à antithèse*, for they are often parodic. In this sense, as Carlos Blanco Aguinaga observes, the picaresque is a "closed" form.[15] This has led to a frequent insertion of discourse, essay, or sermon.

[14] Cf. Montaigne, *Essais*, I, Chap. 13: "c'est au demourant une tres utile science que la science de l'entregent. Elle est, comme la grace et la beauté, conciliatrice des premiers abords de la société et familiarité; et par consequent nous ouvre la porte à nous instruire par les exemples d'aultruy, et à exploicter et produire nostre exemple, s'il a quelque chose d'instruisant et communicable."

[15] Cf. Blanco Aguinaga, "Cervantes y la picaresca."

5. There is a general stress on the material level of existence or of subsistence, on sordid facts, hunger, money. "Comamos," says the hero of *Alonso, mozo de muchos amos* (1624-1626), "pues nosotros no somos espíritus, sino formados de carne y hueso, cuyo alimento ha de ser cotidiano, palpable, y no por obra de entendimiento" (Let us eat, since we are not spirits but men of flesh and bone, and our food has to be there before us every day, palpably so, and not merely in our minds). Hence a profusion of objects and details.[16] There are no *relicta circunstantia*—no topics, persons, or things unworthy of interest and compassion.[17]

6. The *pícaro* (though not always a servant of many masters) observes a number of collective conditions: social classes, professions, *caractères*, cities, and nations. This rogues' gallery has been a standing invitation to satire. And, of course, to comic effects (also for reasons implied before).

The place of satire, however, is not quite secure in the picaresque, and varies from work to work. As novelist, the picaresque author is more compassionate, more capable of presenting a variety of perspectives than one might sometimes expect, so that the portrayal of collective conditions and vices, which critics have tended to overestimate, is tempered with humor and the recognition of individual complexity. Moreover: How could a rogue fail to show some understanding toward other rogues? Let us not forget that the *pícaro* himself is the narrator and the satirist. As a "half-outsider," his moral credentials are equivocal, though not his

---

[16] To call this partial, highly stylized view "realism" is of course equivocal. On this problem, cf. Spitzer, "Zur Kunst Quevedos in seinem Buscón"; K. Vossler, "Realismus in der spanischen Dichtung der Blütezeit," in *Südliche Romania* (Munich and Berlin, 1940), p. 240; and Harry Levin, "What is Realism?" *Comparative Literature*, III (1951), 193-199.

[17] The *pícaro* himself is perhaps the first "low" character in literature who is not a supernumerary, but a hero or antihero: cf. Salinas, "El 'héroe' literario."

expert sense for fraud and deception. Students of satire have pointed out that the satirist often becomes contaminated by his own rectitude:[18] distance and the constant practice of denunciation slowly corrode his concern and inner passion. This process of self-righteous "dehumanization" can be encountered, I think, in a number of picaresque novels, from *Lazarillo de Tormes* to Günter Grass's *Die Blechtrommel*.

7. The *pícaro* in his odyssey moves horizontally through space and vertically through society (with these novels the wheel of Fortune begins to turn for the social climber), along the road and into the inn, the large city, the war camp. Thus we find a narrative of travel and adventure, sometimes genuinely cosmopolitan.[19] This international dimension is present already in Mateo Alemán's *Guzmán de Alfarache* (1599), the first of the Spanish novels whose hero is an unfortunate traveler in Italy. It is a well-known fact that Smollett and the English eighteenth-century novelists were the first to make the *pícaro* a good sailor. In our day the adventures of Felix Krull in Paris and Lisbon are a delightful example of the picaresque combination of social climbing and detachment from national ties.

8. The novel is loosely episodic, strung together like a freight train and *apparently* with no other common link than the hero. Since *Lazarillo*, however, other narrative devices have been superimposed on this basic structure.[20] The use of

[18] Cf. Alvin B. Kernan, *The Cankered Muse* (New Haven, 1959).

[19] For this point, and in general for an interesting description of the picaresque novel, see Max Rouche's contribution to the colloquium conducted in Bordeaux by Robert Escarpit, "Le roman picaresque."

[20] A representative example of the older view (insisting exclusively on the episodic structure of the picaresque) can be found in Petriconi, "Zur Chronologie und Verbreitung des spanischen Schelmenromans," p. 326. For the more modern view, cf. Tarr, "Literary and Artistic Unity in the *Lazarillo de Tormes*"; Professor Bataillon's Preface to his recent edition of *Lazarillo de Tormes* (Paris, 1958), which incorporates two earlier contributions to the subject; my own "La disposición temporal del *Lazarillo de Tormes*," *Hispanic Review*, xxv (1957), 264-

recurrent motifs, circular patterns, and incremental processes is particularly frequent in the picaresque. The first-person form supplies an additional framework. These various devices create an objective or a subjective order beneath or above the linear sequence of events. (In this connection, there is much to be learned from Edward E. Lowinsky's researches into the polyphonic music of the Renaissance and the secret system of *musica ficta*. As instances of "double meaning" in the Renaissance, not only in Biblical exegesis but in the arts, Lowinsky discusses dual images in paintings, such as the sixteenth-century "anamorphoses" created by illusion-producing perspectives.[21] Similarly, the picaresque structure has traditionally added to the "life-like," or biographical, sequence of occurrences a formal "melody line" of recurrences and crescendos.) This type of narrative allows for endless stories-within-the-story. It can have a sequel, or remain incomplete, or both (as in the cases of *Guzmán* and *Felix Krull*). The roguish novel is formally open, so to speak, and ideologically closed.[22]

I should now like to add a few words concerning the first two characteristics (the story of the orphan turned rogue, and the function of autobiography), which are especially relevant to the definition of the picaresque *stricto sensu*.

Obviously the theme of orphanhood was a discovery: it implied the *pícaro*'s detachment from the historical past or the presence of God, from an "essential" image of man. It

---

279; and R. S. Willis, "Lazarillo and the Pardoner: The Artistic Necessity of the Fifth *Tractado*," *Hispanic Review*, viii (1959), 267-279.

[21] Cf. Edward E. Lowinsky, *Secret Chromatic Art in the Netherlands Motet*, tr. C. Buchman (New York, 1946).

[22] The modern world did not have to wait for *Tom Jones* in order to discover the virtues of a good plot. The most wonderful plot that Spanish sixteenth-century story-tellers knew was, one suspects, Heliodorus' *Theagenes and Chariclea* (translated in 1554 and 1587). Cf. the Preface by Francisco López Estrada to the *Historia etiópica de los amores de Teágenes y Cariclea*, tr. Fernando de Mena (Madrid, 1954).

suggested the self-reliance and the "homelessness" of the hero
—*Obdachlosigkeit,* according to Lukács in his early *Theorie
des Romans.* The fatherless protagonist would be a choice
subject for the psychoanalyst of literature. (The asexual character, indeed the antifeminism, of many of the Spanish novels
is undeniable.) Before this theme is further interpreted, however, I suspect that the reader might wish me to supply some
additional facts. I know of no *pícaro* who outdoes, for that
matter, the central character in Castillo Solórzano's *Bachiller
Trapaza* (1637), whose father died before he was born; or
the hero of Alcalá Yáñez's *Alonso, mozo de muchos amos*
(1624-1626), who was orphaned twenty days after he saw the
light of day. This sudden deprivation of the hero is well presented, either humorously or tearfully, in English novels of the
eighteenth century. Moll Flanders is born in prison, abandoned at the age of eighteen months, passed from hand to
hand until she is three. One recalls Smollett's Roderick Ran-
dom, a "friendless orphan" whose mother died within a week
of his birth, thereby causing his father to lose his mind; at last
he is befriended by an uncle, a naval officer. Ferdinand
Count Fathom was "acknowledged by no mortal sire," though
several sergeants in the British Army were persuaded that
they had begotten him. (Here orphanhood is combined with
illegitimacy.) Fathom, besides, was born in a moving carriage—a wanderer and a cosmopolitan, so to speak, from the
very start: "he might be said," wrote Smollett, "to be literally a native of two different countries; for, though he first
saw the light in Holland, he was not born until the carriage
arrived in Flanders." Nevertheless, there are picaresque
novels in which the actual conditions of orphanhood are not
brought out too explicitly. The parents of Gil Blas do not die,
but he is educated by an uncle; and Le Sage stresses throughout the story the fact that his hero received little or no affection. This same equivocal situation is retained by contemporary novels of a relatively roguish nature. Engelbert Krull,

the father in Thomas Mann's *Felix Krull,* is dishonored and commits suicide; the family scatters to the four winds, though in this case the son Felix is no longer a boy. Who is to say, however, that godfather Schimmelpreester was not Felix's real progenitor? The father of Alfred Kern's *Le Clown* (1957) is killed by a carriage. The Black protagonist of *Juyungo* (1943), by the Ecuadorian writer Adalberto Ortiz, forsakes his quarrelsome father. When asked "¿Tienes padre?", he answers "Soy guácharo" (I am an orphan). In Joyce Cary's *The Horse's Mouth* (1944), Gulley Jimson reminisces: "when I was a kid my father died and I went to live with an uncle who used to try which was harder, his boot or my bottom." There are many instances, it appears, of the prominent role played by uncles in the picaresque. Karl Rossmann in Kafka's *Amerika* is separated from his family, crosses the Atlantic Ocean, and is placed upon his arrival in the hands of a demanding Uncle Jacob. Moreover, it would be pertinent to indicate the influences of "real" autobiographies on the picaresque, and vice versa. There are a number of examples of this during the eighteenth century: in the works of Torres Villarroel, for instance; and undoubtedly in the writings of Jean-Jacques Rousseau, who was actually brought up by two aunts and an Uncle Bernard, and later abandoned his own children and made orphans out of them. The first chapters of the *Confessions* read like a picaresque novel, and the last, one might add, like *Robinson Crusoe.*

The name of Rousseau brings to mind an important dimension of the theme of orphanhood: the possible passage from an innocence approximating nature to the corruption of an *état de société.* That life is an endless "learning situation," that it constitutes a process, that it should take the form of a moral ascent, the Christian world view had taught for many centuries. It had also been an axiom of faith that man's original link with his Creator—renewed time and again through the sacraments—provided him from the start with the appropriate spiritual status and the necessary foundation for his growth and amelioration. The rise of the picaresque represents a transition, generally speaking, between the Middle Ages and the Enlightenment. We have seen that the *pícaro*'s premature exposure to the world coincides with a state of "natural" ignorance, and that he proceeds to "discover" all values anew. Our orphan learns, to be sure, but he does not improve. He steals, dissimulates, hardens his heart to emotion, betters his lot at the expense of others. He is "corrupted by society" in the sense that the knowledge he gains is not transmitted to him by another person: the locus for cultural continuity has been shifted from the individual or the church to the community. Though it may be another individual who initiates the transfer (like the blind man in *Lazarillo*), the learning process begins abruptly with a crisis, or rite of passage, such as the knocking of the boy's head against the stone bull in *Lazarillo,* or in many other novels the treachery of an innkeeper. Sometimes the agent is clearly collective, like the regiment of soldiers who plunder and rape in the hero's household at the beginning of Grimmelshausen's *Simplicius Simplicissimus* (1668). *Lazarillo* is characteristic of the kind of picaresque narrative in which the protagonist gradually vanishes as an individual and dissolves into a role, a social status, a mask. There is still another tradition, going back to Alemán's *Guzmán de Alfarache,* where the hero is converted and triumphs finally as an exemplary Christian. The process leading to conversion—and to a final withdrawal from society —may be based, nevertheless, on the early "natural" state. Of this *Simplicissimus* is a classic instance: Grimmelshausen's rustic hero is little more than a young animal at first, who discovers the teachings of Christianity only after the disasters of war have forced him to flee to a hermit's retreat. There, he tells us, he learns quickly from the hermit, "because the smooth tablet of my mind was completely blank, and no images were etched on it that could hamper the addition of anything else" ("weil er die geschlichte Tafel meiner Seel ganz leer und ohn einzige zuvor hineingedruckte Bildnissen gefunden, so etwas anders hineinzubringen hätte hindern mögen"). Whether we are dealing with a conversion story or not, the initial ignorance of the orphan yields to the need for dissimulation, competitiveness, ambition, in ways reminiscent of the moral decay that Rousseau ascribes to civilization in the *Discours sur l'origine de l'inégalité parmi les hommes.*

"Il fallut, pour son avantage, se montrer," Rousseau writes, "autre que ce qu'on étoit en effet. Etre et paroître devinrent deux choses tout-à-fait différentes; et de cette distinction sortirent le faste imposant, la ruse trompeuse, et tous les vices qui en sont le cortège."[23] As I started to point out earlier, this distinction between being and appearance, or between "inner" and "outer" man, is especially relevant to the picaresque and to its highly inventive uses of the autobiographical form. While the *pícaro* becomes "socialized," while he assumes, quite lucidly, a social role, a process of "interiorization" is also taking place. An inner man (embracing all the richness and subtlety of one's private thoughts and judgments) affirms his independence from an outer man (the patterns of behavior, the simplicity of the social role). This profound division of the hero is, I think, one of the most significant achievements of the picaresque, and perhaps its most substantial contribution to the thematics of the modern novel (its shattering of the unity of "dual man," its concentration on the dreams and the thoughts of fictional beings, its unrealistic saturation with inwardness). This notion would demand a thorough historical investigation, and I shall limit myself here to a few representative instances.

Modern anthropologists have shown, in terms that do not contradict Rousseau's, that certain primitive peoples regard the world as a continuum, and do not experience "psychic distance." They live, as Maurice Leenhardt points out in his

---

[23] *Oeuvres de J. J. Rousseau* (Paris, 1823), IV, 273.

study of Melanesia, in a "cosmomorphic" world, where there is no need to distinguish between thought and speech, feeling and gesture.[24] In his commentary on Aristotle's *Poetics*, S. H. Butcher discusses a passage of the *Politics* from which it might be inferred that sculpture and painting are only capable of rendering the outward appearance of persons and things. But it would be an error to conceive of such a split in modern terms: "here, it might be thought, we are introduced to a type of art foreign to the mind of Greece, an art in which the inner qualities are shadowed forth in outward forms, with which they are conventionally associated but which suggest no obvious and immediate resemblance."[25] Facial expressions, gestures, external attitudes were assumed to be natural, not deliberate, signs of the movement of the spirit. In his *Physiognomy* (808b) Aristotle stressed that the reading of character by gesture and facial expression "rests on an assured harmony, not in the case of hearing only but of other organs of sense also, between the movements within and those without."[26] The art of European painting has depended for centuries on the ancillary skill of the physiognomist, i.e., on the visualization of the emotions or "passions." (This skill, like perspective, continued to play a part in an artist's academic training for many years after Giambattista Della Porta's *De humana physiognomonia* [1586] and Charles Le Brun's writings on *L'Expression des différents caractères des passions* [1667].) During the Middle Ages the dichotomy of man (*homo duplex*) was taken for granted, but it was also understood that the actions and the body of the outer man (*homo exterior*), which alone are *visible*, were fundamental signs of the inner man (*homo interior*). With regard to the medieval epic Leo Spitzer writes, with only a measure of exaggeration: "toute émotion se

[24] Cf. Pierre Francastel, *Peinture et société* (Lyon, 1951), p. 87.

[25] S. H. Butcher, *Aristotle's Theory of Poetry and Fine Art* (London, 1911), p. 133.

[26] *Ibid.*, p. 134.

trahit en geste, tout geste révèle une émotion; le geste est, je dirais, psychophysique."[27] Bernard of Clairvaux (1090-1153) explains in *The Steps of Humility (De Gradibus Humilitatis)* that in order to become humble, man must learn to know not only himself but his neighbor (Chap. 5)—to recognize, for example, the symptoms of curiosity:

"Primus itaque superbiae gradus est curiositas. Hanc autem talibus indiciis deprehendes. Si videris monachum, de quo prius bene confidebas, ubicumque stat, ambulat, sedet, oculis incipientem vagari, caput erectum, aures portare suspensas; e motibus exterioris hominis interiorem immutatum agnoscas. Vir quippe perversus annuit oculo, terit pede, digito loquitur; et ex insolenti corporis motu, recens animae morbus deprehenditur: quam, dum a sui circumspectione torpescit, incuria sui curiosam in alios facit."

(The first step of pride, then, is curiosity, and you may recognize it by these marks. If you shall see a monk, whom you formerly trusted confidently, beginning to roam with his eyes, hold his head erect, prick up his ears, wherever he is standing, walking, sitting; you may know the changed inner man from the movements of the outer. For a wicked man winketh with his eyes, speaketh with his feet, teacheth with his fingers; and the strange movement of the body reveals a new disease of the soul, which has tired of introspection and which neglect of self makes curious toward others.)[28]

During the sixteenth century, to be sure, these ideas persist.[29] But we also know of opposite trends that testify to a robust

---

[27] "Le vers 830 du Roland," *Romania*, LXVIII (1944-1945), 474. On this topic, see the valuable article by Lionel J. Friedman, "Occulta Cordis," *Romance Philology*, XI (1957-1958), 103-119.

[28] *The Steps of Humility*, ed. George B. Burch (Cambridge, Mass., 1950), pp. 180-181. The translation is Mr. Burch's.

[29] For example, cf. Alejo Vanegas, *Primera parte de las diferencias de libros que hay en el universo* (Toledo, 1540), Bk. IV , Chap. 7, "De las porciones superior e inferior del ánima."

distrust of all externals and a growing sympathy for the withdrawal of the self, the protection of inwardness, the exercise of dissimulation. We need only recall Machiavelli; Erasmus' praise of the "inner man" in the Fifth Rule of his *Enchiridion militis christiani* (and his stress on the "inner spiritual meaning" of the Bible, which must be distinguished from the letter or outer "flesh" of the holy text if one is to see more than "through a glass darkly"); the ways in which morality was internalized and personalized during the Reformation, while confidence was being lost in the existence of a single road to salvation or to knowledge, and while on the Catholic side interest grew in manifold interpretations of the Bible, *duplex veritas*, hidden meanings.[30] For, says Folly in Erasmus' *Praise of Folly*, "I do not feign one thing in my face while I hold something else in my heart." If such was the opinion of Folly, the judicious reader must have thought, what could possibly be the attitude of Wisdom? Montaigne's advice, though directed only to the intelligent, was to try and perceive the multiple, mobile, erratic inner man: "ce n'est pas tour d'entendement rassis, de nous juger simplement par nos actions du dehors; il fault sonder jusques au dedans, et veoir par quels ressorts se donne le bransle" (Bk. II, §1: "De l'inconstance de nos actions"). In this context, the place of the picaresque author is quite clear. His antihero is a lonely spirit, or a dissembler, or a hypocrite.[31] So is, of course, his narrator. The picaresque novel is, quite simply, the confession of a liar.

The practice of impersonation imposes certain restraints

[30] Cf. Lowinsky, *Secret Chromatic Art*, Chap. IX, "The Meaning of Double Meaning in the Sixteenth Century."

[31] The hero, explains Ortega y Gasset in his *Meditaciones del Quijote*, is essentially *one*: an undivided being, in whom no distinction between faith and behavior exists. The antihero, we would add, is multiple. In the seventeenth century, heroes can be found in Corneille's plays, in which "actions show the man"; cf. Robert J. Nelson, *Corneille: His Heroes and Their Worlds* (Philadelphia, 1963), p. 75.

on the *pícaro*-narrator; but it also liberates his imagination. In this sense, *Lazarillo de Tormes* remains, after five hundred years, the masterpiece of the genre. It presents the growth and alienation of an *homo interior,* and demonstrates his ability to consider with endless ambiguity the simplified career of the *homo exterior.* Lazarillo, sociologically speaking, represents the necessary dissimulation of the poor when obliged to give an account of themselves ("dar entera noticia de mi persona") to the rich and the powerful. Thematically speaking, he shows us the uses not of vision but of insight—through all externals—into the souls of men. Above all, he has learned from his master the blind man, who constantly outwitted him, that it is not the visible shell of man that matters. He has taught himself to "see" the world like a blind man forced to fend for himself in a cruel society. All later picaresque heroes will, in varying degrees, be disciples of Lazarillo's blind man.

III

We come to our next grouping: picaresque novels in the wider sense of the term. The question is naturally: How wide?

The picaresque novel *sensu lato* would fail to include each of the characteristics I have sketched earlier, and thus the total effect will be modified. However, it will not be a matter of indifference whether a novel displays this or that characteristic, if it is to qualify for our second concentric circle. Certain traits must be considered indispensable. A few examples may make this point clearer in a general way.

The absence of the first-person form prevents a story, I think, from being picaresque in the full sense. For instance: Salas Barbadillo's *La hija de Celestina* (1612), or Castillo Solórzano's *Bachiller Trapaza* (1637). The lack of an overall roguish coloration, in the manner that I have just discussed, alters the substance of the work too significantly. Yet such a narrative is surely picaresque in a less puritanical sense of the word. Similarly, Joyce Cary's very fine book *The Horse's Mouth* (1944) has all the qualifications of the picaresque, but is only so *lato sensu*, because of its durable cast of characters and tight form.

There are works, besides, which are even more distantly, or secondarily, related to the picaresque, and thus belong to still a third concentric circle. One notices, for example, that Scarron's influential *Roman comique* (1651-1657) contains certain picaresque elements, such as the stress on material necessity, the satirical gallery, the road. But no one would mistake it for one of our picaresque novels, even in the wider sense. It would be read ordinarily as burlesque, or as an actors' novel, or as a *roman bourgeois* like Furetière's. The technique is one of apparent improvisation, more akin to that of Sterne or Stendhal (or Diderot, Xavier de Maistre, Machado de Assis) than to Alemán. Most revealing is the antipicaresque reliance on *two* heroes, sentimentally united. Throughout Scarron's story there runs the thread of the everthwarted relationship between two young lovers, in the manner of the Greek or Byzantine romance.[32] It might have deserved a title linking two names, like *Theagenes and Chariclea* or *Persiles y Sigismunda*—whereas every roguish novel worthy of its salt could be described by a single name. For the same simple reason Cervantes' *Rinconete y Cortadillo* (placed within a framework based on the theme of friendship) is not picaresque at all, though it contains at the beginning a pair of minimal picaresque autobiographies, told (unlike the rest of the *novela*) in the first person by the two heroes.

The tradition of Sterne and Scarron, of improvisation and

[32] I refer to the Byzantine plot in a broad sense also. In that sense, one might consider as heirs of the same tradition Voltaire's *Candide*, Manzoni's *I Promessi Sposi* and the first series of Galdós' *Episodios nacionales*.

travel on the open road, of the gallery of satirical types, brings to mind, of course, Gogol's *Dead Souls* (1842), which some critics have regarded as partially picaresque.[33] In terms of our definition, the problem posed by this great work is perhaps insoluble. It is not only the absence of the auto-biographical form that is crucial in this case, but the dazzling uses of the third-person narrator, whose voice and presence are infinitely more compelling than Tchitchikov's. Tchitchikov, to be sure, is an itinerant near-swindler. As a boy he had been abandoned by his father and brought up by an old woman. But these facts concerning his childhood are contained in one of the fragments remaining from the loss of the second part of the novel. We shall never know how picaresque *Dead Souls* would have appeared as a whole, had we possessed both the beginning and the end of Tchitchikov's story. Following the pattern of *Guzmán de Alfarache* (and *Simplicissimus*), would the protagonist have turned out to be a regenerated *pícaro*? In fact, the narrator, who was the real hero, was able to tell the "wicked" but not the "penitent part" of his tale—to use Defoe's terms in *Moll Flanders*.

The elements that may be considered indispensable to the broader group are all contained in our first characteristic, which we can reduce to the following: the radical solitude of the orphan as a child or young man; and his lasting but ambiguous estrangement from society, "reality," or established beliefs and ideologies. (One could add roguish behavior—a moot point: but ordinarily such estrangement will lead to a break with conventional ethics.)

Espinel's *Marcos de Obregón* (1618) lacks this genuine distance from established social requirements and thus does not belong, despite its numerous picaresque elements, to the second group. There are a few moments of social tension in the novel (as in the bitterness of the *morisco* from Valencia); but

[33] Cf. Karl L. Selig, "Concerning Gogol's *Dead Souls* and *Lazarillo de Tormes*," *Symposium*, VIII (1954), 138-140.

on the whole the main perspective of the narrator is not that of the outsider or half-outsider, as Espinel's flattery of the powerful clearly demonstrates. Not only the social but the moral position of Espinel is ambivalent. The hero fluctuates between repentance and nonrepentance, humility and pride, just as his narrative oscillates between a past and a present that might have been phases of moral growth: the remembrance of things past could not be more satisfying. On this occasion, as George Haley has shown in his valuable book,[34] the picaresque becomes a vehicle for self-disguise—on the part of the real author—through the ambiguity of the first-person form. Thus the rogue's life story can be, as it were, doubly spurious. Certain contemporary novels are cases in point. I do not find any substantial tension between the hero and society in Camilo José Cela's travel narratives, tensely written as they are. The same applies, of course, to Raymond Queneau's articulate orphan Zazie, or to the innocent, lonely hero of his *Pierrot mon ami* (1942).

I shall end this characterization of the second group with an all-too-brief mention of three famous German works. Grimmelhausen's *Simplicissimus* portrays more rigorously than any comparable novel the passage of the orphan from absolute innocence to negative experience, as well as his ultimate conversion. But it would appear to be picaresque *lato sensu* insofar as the hero, the victim of war, only seldom and provisionally assumes the attitude of the rogue, of self-conscious guile and wile, of cynical behavior. We need only notice his affection for his friend Herzbruder. As I questioned earlier with regard to *Rinconete y Cortadillo,* can any true *pícaro* have a "heart brother"? Eichendorff's *Aus dem Leben eines Taugenichts* (1826) proves that it is possible to incorporate picaresque components, *mirabile dictu,* into a modern pastoral. Eichendorff's romantic vagabond is en-

---

[34] Cf. *Vicente Espinel and Marcos de Obregón: A Life and its Literary Representation* (Providence, R.I., 1959).

amored of nature and the free, easy life. He yearns for an infinite *locus amoenus*, far from the madding crowd. This does not signify that he inwardly excludes or despises the established values of society. Rather, he has been excluded by them from the start. His final surrender to the bourgeoisie might seem the most picaresque trait of the story—a reversal that reminds one, for example, of *Gil Blas*. But the pursuit of happiness has always been one of the conventions of the pastoral. The return to society does not imply here, as it does in the picaresque, a division between inner man and outer behavior—the tactics of dissimulation, the choice of a role. Basically, from the sixteenth century to this very day, the pastoral and the picaresque have represented two diametrically opposite attitudes toward the ills of the city: the pastoral attempt to flee the city and to replace it with nature and sentimental love; and the decision to live and survive in it, but not to fight or to "join" it, on the part of the "half-outsider." I can only mention, thirdly, Kafka's *Amerika*, perhaps the first important picaresque narrative of this century. Kafka employs in his own ways the solitude and the estrangement of the *pícaro*, his premature discovery of injustice, his submission to a series of masters, his horizontal pilgrimage in a strange land, his constantly renewed and constantly frustrated vertical ascensions, his lasting exile, his search for a new "native" city, a New World, an "America." There are other picaresque elements too: the wealth of concrete detail, the negative experience of sexuality, the gradual moral degradation of the hero. At the same time, *Amerika* lacks the first-person form (the order brought to one's life by the memory and narration of it) and a substantial amount of roguish behavior.

It could be said that my definition of the picaresque, in either the strict or the broad sense, is not historical enough; and the objection would be well founded. Mine is certainly an a posteriori description (as distinct from the historical notion of genre to which I alluded at the beginning of this essay) of a group of works as they appear and are available to the contemporary reader. However, it should also be said that no history of a literary form can be started without a pre-existing idea of what the form might be: there must be an object for the historian to write a history of. Within this circular movement, then, my definition belongs to the preliminary phase—the attempt to delineate as clearly as possible an object of study. It is sufficiently flexible, moreover, to allow for the fundamental alterations which the form underwent as it passed from Spain to France, Germany, Holland, and England during the seventeenth and eighteenth centuries. The *pícaro* can remain a *pícaro* while changing the ethical justification—the ideology—for his behavior. My fourth item, the "total view" of the *pícaro*, is a vacuum to be filled with many substances. Only a subclassification of historical nature could order this diversity. Initially the total view of the rogue arises in the framework of the Spanish seventeenth century, sometimes named Counter-Reformation or Baroque. It stresses the insufficiency of man. It presents the world as vanity, delusion, theatrical performance.[35] The *pícaro* acts immorally by virtue of the most exacting of ethics, and his realization that all men actually fail to be honest or truthful.[36] This somber Christian view will be no less uncompromising in the German Baroque. But the antics of the rogue will also give rise to a novel of manners bereft of a substantial religious dimension: the gay, though biting, portraiture of Le Sage. Satire, likewise, will take different directions and come into contact with various contemporary currents: burlesque, English humor, the bourgeois realism of Defoe and Smollett, etc.[37] The travel motif, basically unreligious in *Lazarillo*, becomes identified after Alemán with the Pauline view of life as pilgrimage or exile within the confusion, the ocean, the labyrinth of earthly

---

[35] Cf. Casalduero, "Notas sobre *La ilustre fregona*," p. 6.
[36] Cf. Montesinos, "Gracián o la picaresca pura," p. 49.
[37] Cf. Escarpit, "Le roman picaresque," pp. 6-7.

existence. These distinctions involve national structures of values, in Américo Castro's sense; individual techniques or aims; polar connections with other genres, like the pastoral, etc. No literary definition, if it avoids remaining simply formal, can do without literary history for very long.

IV

The greatest compliment that a literary historian can pay a mere story or plot is to call it a "myth." Whereby we say a number of things, even on the most elementary level. We may wish to stress that this story or plot is "already alive," and has been so for many centuries. We may mean that it has subtly changed through the years and experienced different reincarnations. We may also acknowledge that this particular figuration, so powerfully suggestive of meanings beyond the merely literal, has developed, even in purely secular or historical terms, into a kind of permanent temptation to the human mind. Sometimes this permanence attaches to a work that has never been successfully imitated, like *Hamlet*, and yet has become a conspicuous favorite with critics, spectators, and readers. In most of these cases, it seems to me, we refer to two things: to myth as a precipitate of cultural history, as that special recognition of the *déjà vu* that alludes not so much to considerations of genre or technique as to a simple narrative or dramatic theme, plot, or story, and to the pleasure one derives from reading or seeing it *once more*; and secondly, to the fact that this pleasure implies a reader who remembers and is "in the know." A literary myth (though not in the occult sense) assumes a certain cultural continuity and the participation of the reader in this continuity. (Sometimes this status or prestige—nearly as a way of life or an "ideal" —may influence the real author's, the living man's understanding of himself: I have already mentioned the *pícaro's* impact on such autobiographies as Tristan L'Hermite's, Rousseau's, and Torres Villarroel's.) Just as we approached the picaresque genre from the point of view of the writer—of poetics, of the work in progress—we may conceive of the picaresque myth as being connected particularly with the reader's or the critic's understanding of its larger significance —his ultimate appreciation, independent of any particular work, of the theme as a whole. It refers to a structure in the barest way, and at the same time interprets the various directions of meaning it has followed through the centuries.

I cannot begin to define such a myth here, and will limit myself to sketching two principal lines of inquiry. One would deal with the *pícaro* as "half-outsider." The other would seek to explain the near-absence of the picaresque theme from the nineteenth century.

Going back to the initial pattern of the picaresque novel, we have already seen how functional its ambiguity was. The wisdom of Guzmán de Alfarache was that of a Diogenes converted by Saint Thomas:[38] like the cynic, the *pícaro* first sacrifices family, homeland, wealth, and honor to self-sufficiency and freedom. This would-be freedom, however, is thwarted by fact. The maximum suppression of wishes is not viable. The *pícaro's* living must be extorted from a cruel society, beyond which there is no pastoral refuge. The pastoral hero's decision was so "unreal" that it could be self-consistent. The *pícaro*, instead, is the outsider that fails. Lazarillo makes a pact, finally, with the very same values he recognizes as empty. Guzmán's career is a chain of contradictions and reversals. Gil Blas at the end of his life lives in retirement from the world, but with a castle, a good cook, and letters of nobility.

The "outsider that fails" is of course what interested

[38] It has been said that Boileau thought of writing a *Life of Diogenes* "beaucoup plus plaisante et plus originale que celle de Lazarillo de Tormes et de Guzmán de Alfarache"—cf. *Bolaena* (Amsterdam, 1742), p. 552. Cervantes was not far off the mark when he identified his canine *pícaros* with dogs—speaking dogs—in his *Coloquio de los perros*, a literary jest critics have not taken seriously enough.

Cervantes and led him to introduce in some of his stories (like *La ilustre fregona*) his quixotic rogues: *pícaros* who—like Don Quixote—imitated literature, abandoned established society, tried to shape their lives anew under the guidance of an idea.

There is a historical correlative for the half-outsider, which Américo Castro has the merit of having brought out and interpreted in his studies of Spanish history: the situation of the Spanish New Christian. This is not the Jew, naturally, a genuine outsider in the sixteenth century, but the *converso*. Castro believes that the author of *Lazarillo* was a *converso*. We know for a fact that a Jewish forefather of Mateo Alemán was burned alive by the Inquisition. Several heroes of picaresque novels (as in *La pícara Justina*, *El Buscón*) are of Semitic origin. The family background of the hero of *Guzmán de Alfarache* is willfully obscure and ambiguous; his father appears to have been a Levantine who emigrated to Genoa and then to Seville, and the plot is based on the young boy's attempt to return to Genoa and claim his inheritance there, in search of nonexistent origins, and on his further travels in Italy (critics have pointed out the peculiar intensity of Alemán's description of Florence). We also know that Mateo Alemán, the author, was doubly a "half-outsider," since his mother was a Del Nero (from one of the merchant families constituting the powerful Florentine enclave in Seville), so that the plot of *Guzmán* reflects and transposes not only the author's status as a New Christian but his links with Italy.[39] The *pícaro*, in other words, is an orphan and a self-made man in social and religious terms. Alemán, as a descendant—rejected by his environment—of converts from Judaism, was able to envisage not only the society of his day, but the values of Christianity itself both from within and

[39] Cf. my article "Los pleitos extremeños de Mateo Alemán. I. El juez, 'Dios de la Tierra,'" *Archivo Hispalense*, nos. 103-104 (1960), 1-21.

from without. This was surely an important incitement to the picaresque author's discovery of the myth of the orphan and the type of the half-outsider.

In view of these facts, one is not surprised to find that not only Kafka but a number of contemporary Jewish-American authors, like Saul Bellow, reflect in some of their works the perplexities of the picaresque.

These ambiguities could be elaborated on several levels: a social level, first of all, as I have already stressed.[40] It could also have a moral or religious object: the oscillation, as in *Simplicissimus*, between earthly experience and asceticism; or, as in *Guzmán*, between belief and behavior. The Spanish-type *pícaro* asked himself not "What shall one believe?" but "How will I act?" With the seventeenth century, the connection between faith and action had become problematical. Man, halfway to the assumption of his own destiny, yet undeviating in his allegiance to his creed, found it increasingly difficult to translate belief into individual behavior. These moral and social ambiguities would remain operative within the framework of the picaresque through the eighteenth century, from Defoe to Le Sage and Smollett. But one could also detect in the ending of *Lazarillo* the seed of a metaphysical ambivalence: the will to hold reality, one might say, at a distance; or, if one prefers, the shock of birth, and later of adult living, as seen through the eyes of a child. This is the ground where the contemporary picaresque or near-picaresque will not fear to tread: Kafka, Mann, Cary, Alfred Kern (*Le Clown*, 1957), Günter Grass (*Die Blechtrommel*, 1959). In the latter the shock of birth is such that Oskar, the young hero, freely chooses to *remain* a child: Oskar, whose birth,

[40] Under conditions which Renato Poggioli has pointed out in his study of the pastoral: the decline of the ancient concept of the *polis*, of social man, of the communal structure of the Middle Ages; the rise of the modern metropolis, the bourgeoisie, shifting social classes. Cf. Poggioli, "The Oaten Flute," *Harvard Library Bulletin*, xi (1957), 147-184.

of course, is dubious (and hence his ethnic origins, precisely like those of Danzig and East Prussia), becomes a half-satirist, capable of shattering glass from a distance and yet of desiring or befriending from a distance too. The German uses of the picaresque come through strongly and clearly. Thomas Mann had masterfully stressed his hero's equivocal dissatisfaction with the real. Felix Krull, like Oskar, comes reluctantly into the world. He has, besides, a tendency to sleep. But will not his need for sleep, he asks, diminish together with his urge for living, his *Lebensdrang?* And he adds: "In dieser Zeit wurde die Neigung zur Weltflucht und Menschenscheu weiter ausgebildet, die von jeher meinem Charakterbilde angehaftet hatte und mit werbender An-hänglichkeit an Welt und Menschen so einträchtig Hand in Hand zu gehen vermag." (At that time my inclination to flee the world and shy away from other men was developed further, which had belonged to my character earlier and is able to go so amiably hand in hand with a spirited attachment to the world and to other human beings.) But Felix as half-outsider discovers the duplicity of his position on other levels as well. One notices, beneath the episodic form, the throbbing of a leitmotif: the "double image" (the handsome brother and sister in Frankfurt, Zouzou seduced with a drawing of the naked Zaza, etc.). With Felix the *picaro* has become the artist or creator of himself, to the degree that poetry (as Plato states in the *Republic*) is a species of impersonation, and art a kind of picaresque deception. But does this mean—fiction as a way of life—a fascination with variety? An untiring surrender to mutability, enumeration, succession? This is where Felix encounters his ultimate hesitation: he the lover of the Many, the Multiple, the Protean is suddenly entranced by the One—the resemblances beneath the series, the unity beyond plurality. Life irresistibly tends to gather into meaning. Even the will-to-multiplicity is rooted in an ancient myth. The life of fiction becomes a reincarnation, as Madame Houpflé half-guesses (*Felix Krull*, Part II, Chap. 9), of the "eternal" Hermes, the god of merchants, travelers, and thieves.

"I was stabbed alive!" exclaimed Gulley Jimson, in an image that fuses the pain and the enchantment of the rogue's life. Modern art will often lend a voice to this combination of rejection and surrender, nausea and attachment. We recognize in it the failure of total reproach, the half-outsider's inability to either accept or deny by means of ideas alone. I do not refer only to the novel. The picaresque myth will influence other arts, such as the film (the divided reporter in *La dolce vita*) or even the stage (*Mother Courage*). We need only recall French or Italian films of recent date: young students around Saint-Germain, wealthy adolescents on the Riviera, scattering gratuitous acts and practical jokes; toying with crime for intellectual reasons; trying to establish, beneath their indifference or their boredom, a relationship with the real through sexuality, money, or the nearness of death. Literate young men who have read Camus but remain half-"strangers."

The nineteenth century did not welcome the ambiguous outsider. We all recall, of course, some exceptions to this: there were picaresque echoes in Dickens's child-man—the vehicle of a social criticism not restricted to remote observation. I mentioned earlier the riddle of Gogol's *Dead Souls*. But I find most characteristic the fleeting appearance, in a story within a story, of Manoel, the roguish sergeant of Stendhal's *Lucien Leuwen*. When a *picaro* is introduced by Galdós, he soon yields to another dimension or a more spacious theme. By and large, the nineteenth century was the time for the full outsider, the dreamer and the bohemian, the revolutionary and the ideologist, the man of courage, the rebel against man and God. The *picaro* could not rival Prometheus or Robespierre. In Spain, the heroines of the two more important novels were orphans: Fortunata in *Fortu-*

nata y Jacinta by Galdós, and Ana de Ozores in Clarín's *La Regenta*; but the former was a symbol of humble living, and the latter was a dreamer. In America, the land of pioneering and self-made men, as well as of conservative tastes in literature, the *pícaro*, from Concolorcorvo and Lizardi to Mark Twain and Roberto J. Payró, was not forgotten. But why should the energy and the ambition of the Balzacian hero not sustain and inspire the self-made man?[41] The nineteenth-century novel developed under the sign of Cervantes and Fielding, not Alemán and Defoe. It made possible the huge syntheses of Balzac and Tolstoy. The picaresque novel prepares for or follows, apparently, periods of full novelistic bloom.

The picaresque would return during days of irony and discouragement—times less favorable than the nineteenth century to the plans of the bold individual. In the twentieth century, as in the Spain of Philip II and the Germany of the Thirty Years' War, the career of the rogue would once more disclose an awareness of civilization as oppression. This became especially clear after World War II. As far as irony is concerned, the genre itself serves as one of its objects: the traditions of the picaresque are humored and revived at the same time. From this ironic disposition, on the edge of parody, *Felix Krull* profits supremely. But there have been other instances of self-conscious imitation and literary fun. In more than one passage of *La vida inútil de Pito Pérez* (1938), the Mexican writer José Rubén Romero alludes to *Lazarillo de Tormes* and Lizardi's *Periquillo Sarniento*— while he winks at the knowing reader. Every chapter of Zunzunegui's *La vida como es* (1954) opens with an epi-

[41] William Dean Howells thought that the picaresque novel was the form of the future for America. With regard to *Lazarillo de Tormes,* he wrote in *My Literary Passions* (New York, 1895), p. 143: "each man's life among us is a romance of the Spanish model; it is the life of man who has risen, as we nearly all have, with many ups and downs."

graph from *Guzmán de Alfarache* (but there is no such recognition in Suárez Carreño's *Las últimas horas*, published in 1949, which is much the better novel); even as the protagonist of Alfred Kern's *Le Clown* (1957) encounters Felix Krull in Paris. To be sure, Pío Baroja's loafers had greeted the first years of the twentieth century; and the young Dos Passos made clear his admiration for them.[42] But the modern possibilities of the form would not be fully revealed in Spain. I can but recall here the many correspondences and affinities that supported it and prepared the way for its revival after World War II: Gide and Pirandello, Céline and Brecht, Steinbeck and Orwell, Henry Miller and Kerouac, Malaparte, Chaplin, and Fellini.

Together with irony, there was "dis-couragement"—the devaluation of courage. Most characteristic of recent years, in this connection, is a loss of gravity in the writer, who, no longer a prophet or a leader, "stops being a bird," says Roethke, "yet beats his wings." It is no longer fashionable to make declarations concerning the future of man. Threatened with events which no one controls, the novelist hesitates to show men truly risking, or even shaping, their own lives. In the midst of bankrupt revolutions and the orthodoxy of disbelief, Camus' *homme révolté* is no more a hero of our time than the powerless antihero. From *Lazarillo* to our day, it seems to me, the picaresque has been an outlet for the expression of human alienation. And today the *pícaro* remains what he has always been: the coward with a cause.

[1961]

[42] Cf. John Dos Passos, *Rosinante to the Road Again* (New York, 1922), pp. 87-88.

On the Uses of Literary Genre

The concept of genre occupies a central position in the study of literary history, very probably, because it has succeeded so well and for so long in bridging the gap between critical theory and the practice of literary criticism. As every student of the subject knows, the theory of genres is coextensive with the history of poetics. Since Aristotle and Plato, it has normally subsumed philosophical inquiries which were vaster and more ambitious than itself. On the other hand, it has traditionally served as a practical instrument for poets as well as critics. While on a certain level the age-old debate on the nature of literary genres was following its course, the criteria under discussion were proving their fruitfulness on the level of individual criticism. If it appears to be a fact that speculative thinking—"theory" in the broader sense—has been particularly relevant in a practical way to, curiously enough, the creation and the reading of poetry, the question that naturally arises is whether there is much that one can learn from this important conjunction. The theorist asks himself, in other words, whether the critical effectiveness of the concept of genre should nourish his understanding of the original issues. If what we can observe is the persistently beneficial effects of a continuing problem, do the effects, then, shed any real light on the problem? Can the relationship be reversed, and the workings of criticism be made to have some sort of repercussion on theory? Is it possible to avoid concentrating on either speculation alone or a pragmatic escape from the issues?

Doubtless there is no forgetting the aesthetic and logical difficulties with which the subject is fraught, and which Benedetto Croce expressed most forcefully for his time. It is not sufficient to dispose of them by merely admiring the actual uses and the long-lasting pertinence of artistic genres— by pointing out, for example, that Croce himself wielded generic categories quite profitably in a number of his books. The challenging question is whether theorists should have learned from the fact that the notion of genre is so much more successful than other approaches—than the study of rhetorical figures or, I think, the analysis of style—in eliciting not just the singular quality but the *form* of a literary work.

Modern criticism has repeatedly demonstrated that the vocabulary of genre theory, paradoxically enough, adapts itself most sensitively to the apprehension of individual works. The instances that I have in mind are from the Hispanic field: Américo Castro on Cervantes, Amado Alonso on the historical novel, Stephen Gilman on *La Celestina*. There are, of course, many others. In the area of fiction alone, one need only recall Albert Thibaudet, Ramon Fernandez, György Lukács, Northrop Frye; the misreading of Balzac and Stendhal by nineteenth-century academic criticism precisely for lack of a theory of the novel; the value, too, of contemporary speculations on the essay or the prose poem; the reappraisal of theatrical conventions after Brecht and Beckett. Generally, the nineteenth and twentieth centuries constitute a second great period of creative reassessment in the history of European genre theory. The first of these periods was the Renaissance (and its aftermath the Baroque). Bernard Weinberg's admirable *History of Literary Criticism in the Italian Renaissance* (1961) has taught us among other things that a crucial relationship existed during the second half of the sixteenth century in Italy between the flowering of the theory of genres, in the tradition of Aristotle, and the practical criticism prompted by the extended quarrels over the *Divina Commedia* as epic poem, Speroni's *Canace e Macareo* as tragedy, Ariosto and Tasso and the new *romanzo* form, Guarini's *Pastor Fido* and both tragicomedy and the pastoral. The appearance of masterpieces like *Orlando Furioso* had provided the impetus for a restatement of theory.[1] Con-versely, the field of poetics was regarded not as remotely ab-stract, but as directly relevant to the interpretation and the composition of single works. The controversies and the un-easiness concerning the new narrative procedures, with re-gard especially to Ariosto and the "romance," doubtless were a background condition for the invention of *Don Quixote*, even as the criticism of Guarini and the new tragicomedy would have an impact some years later on the quarrel over *Le Cid* and on neoclassical dramatic writing in France. Clearly, these junctures and events would prove to be highly influential. From Montaigne's trial of the essay to Cervantes' experimentations with the short story, the dramatic interlude, and the long narrative, it is difficult to underestimate the con-nection between the theoretical restlessness of the sixteenth century, in the area of poetics, and the ability to start anew, to confront boldly expanding circles of experience, on the part of the greater writers of the period.

The lesson that may be derived from the empirical rele-vance of artistic genres is perhaps the following: a genre is an invitation to form. Now, the concept of genre looks for-ward and backward at the same time. Backward, toward the literary works that already exist. Forward, in the direction of the apprentice, the future writer, the informed critic. A genre is a descriptive statement, but, rather often, a declara-tion of faith as well. Looking toward the future, then, the conception of a particular genre may not only incite or make possible the writing of a new work; it may provoke, later on, the critic's search for the total form of the same work. Clearly, what is at stake is the idea of form in the tradition of Aristotle's *Poetics*—the very context in which the Euro-pean history of genre theory appears to make sense. On this occasion, I can only recall briefly that in the Aristotelian sys-

[1] Cf. Bernard Weinberg, *A History of Literary Criticism in the Italian Renaissance* (Chicago, 1961), ii, 812.

tem form and matter are the two intrinsic "causes" that account for the mode of being of an object. As the object is analyzed after it has been made, an effort of abstraction is needed in order to distinguish between the two elements that have gone into its making: the matter of which the object was made; and the form, or principle of *informing* and structuring, which made it the actual object that it is. Craig LaDrière has made very clear that the student of literature ought to be able to distinguish between the form-matter issue and the form-content or form-expression dichotomies. If the matter of a work is confused with its "theme," "subject," or "content," then form becomes what remains after a work has been drained of its meaning.[2] Similarly, expression seems to imply that something was to be said before it was actually said. The impact and the expressiveness of a work of art are dependent on its form—in Mario Fubini's words, "quell'unica forma che in sé risolve gli infiniti contenuti."[3] What the "matter" of a literary work can be reasonably a part of, in LaDrière's sense, is language—language already shot through with formal elements, elaborated by the ages.[4] All previous forms, that is, become matter in the hands of the artist at work. If matter is what the poet informs, then prosody at that very instant is matter, meter is matter, and a motif or a plot is no more matter than is a design for composition or a principle of structure.

As I understand these issues (so elementary and yet so darkened with the patina of time), the crucial point for us is

[2] Cf. J. Craig LaDrière, "Form," in *Dictionary of World Literature*, ed. Joseph T. Shipley, 2nd edn. (New York, 1953), p. 168.

[3] "Genesi e storia dei generi letterari," in *Tecnica e teoria letterari*, vol. ıı of *Problemi ed orientamenti critici di lingua e di letteratura italiana*, ed. A. Momigliano et al. (Milan, 1951), p. 32; reprinted in Mario Fubini, *Critica e poesia* (Bari, 1966), p. 135. Further citations will be from *Critica e poesia*.

[4] Cf. LaDrière, "Form," p. 168.

this: *form is the presence in a created, man-made object of a "cause."* It is the revelation or the sign of a dynamic relationship between the "finished" artifact and its origins in previous life and previous history. The genuinely great work of art vibrates and "moves" still from the artist's ability to proceed from one order of life to another by virtue of his modeling, reshaping, informing skills. Form is the visible manifestation later of this victorious process of formation, making, *poiēsis.*

The important corollary, as far as genres are concerned, is the fact that a preexistent form can never be simply "taken over" by the writer or transferred to a new work. The task of form-making must be undertaken all over again. The writer must begin once more to match matter to form, and to that end he can only find a very special sort of assistance in the fact that the fitting of matter to form has *already* taken place. To offer this assistance is the function of genre.

The idea of a genre like tragedy or the elegy has been most useful as a generalization when it has suggested to the writer what holds the different parts of an elegy or of a tragedy together: when the genre theorist, that is, has stepped away from the single work in order to discern or to recommend not a certain matter or a certain form but a principle for matching one to the other. Looking backward, a genre is a descriptive statement concerning a number of related works. Looking forward, it becomes above all—to revise slightly my earlier words—an invitation to the matching (dynamically speaking) of matter and form. During the Renaissance, this effect was well grasped by those theorists who did not submit to the common dichotomy (particularly in the tradition of Horace's *Ars poetica*) of *res* and *verba*. (For example: the definition of the elegy in terms of either meter or subject matter alone.) Some critics, faced with this division into surface structure and voluntary content, would then recur to the services—i.e., to the unifying function—of genre. Such was the case with Giovanni Battista Pigna in his *Poetica Horatiana* (1561): "if materials, words, and verse are to be fitted together," Professor Weinberg explains, "some principle of fittingness must be established: this may be the vague notion of appropriateness . . . involved in appropriateness to genre. Pigna uses the latter principle."[5] A number of modern critics, it seems to me, do very much the same. Like Pigna, they have sought in genre a "principle of fittingness." They have observed that generic models, to a greater degree than rhetorical or stylistic norms, postulate and suggest that general informing drive which makes possible the emergence, beyond *res* and *verba*, of a unified artistic whole. The writer who in the process of writing a comedy, for example, discovers that neither a comic style nor a comic theme will be sufficient, can find in the structural model of the comic genre a much broader and more effective invitation to the matching of matter and form.

The validity of these criteria is confirmed by the fact that they allow us, in addition, to distinguish between the more characteristic or "central" genres and the classes or the statements that one usually regards as either peripheral or irrelevant. I am referring to three familiar kinds of definition. First, to briefly sketch the three, there is the examination of content alone (the "essence" of tragedy, or the "ideas" of the Russian novel) or of surface form (meter, for example). If the central thrust of generic definition is the association of matter with form, then statements such as these fall short of real genre. At best, they permit us to pose the question: What is the missing component?—the answer to which means a step in the direction of genre. Let us grant, for instance, that *terza rima* is not a genre. Why, then, is the poetic epistle a genre, with which this meter has often been linked? If the

---

[5] Weinberg, *A History of Literary Criticism*, I, 158.

sonnet is a generic category too, what are the traditional goals that one should associate with its stanzaic scheme? The Gothic novel, in Austin Warren's opinion,[6] or the historical novel gradually became genres during the nineteenth century insofar as it was recognized that they demanded and continued to demand a special sort of informing effort from the narrative imagination. So much, then, for this first type of definition: like the thematic distinction between, say, a still life and a nude, it is merely irrelevant to the problem of genre. But the distinction between an oil painting and a fresco is, instead, peripheral; or perhaps introductory. It is characteristic of a second class, dealing with technique and craftmanship. On this point it is difficult to disagree with Croce, whose idealism led him to deny any significance to material techniques. The Aristotelian response—basically, that we have "matter" as yet not formed—points to a similar conclusion. The differences that exist between the various artistic vehicles—between poetry read, recited, and staged, or between a gouache and a pastel—do not coincide with the overall structural models we call genres. The use of a technique or of a medium requires skill, know-how—but a "how" that does not as yet pertain to form. These are the premises of the informing effort, and the challenge that is implicit in them manifests full well that pure "matter" is to be found not only in personal experience or in society but in the conditions of a certain medium. Like the particular language a writer employs (for example, the arbitrary system of vocalic sounds that he must use), these conditions are conventional. Thus one notices that the technical premise, or set of premises, of a form is often called a convention, a term which underlines the radical need for passage from the order of experience to the order of artistic form: in Harry Levin's words, "a convention may be tentatively described as a necessary differ-

[6] Cf. René Wellek and Austin Warren, *Theory of Literature* (New York, 1949), p. 243.

ence between art and life."[7] One might say that conventions are an invitation, if not to a form, to a specific art.

The third class, even broader than the second, is composed of the essential modes often called "universals." The most widely accepted approach to these has been the tripartite division into "narrative" (or "epic"), "dramatic," and "lyrical." It is a paradox of literary study that despite the conspicuous growth of Orientalism since the early nineteenth century, and the persistent reliance of literary criticism on literary history, these Greco-Roman modes continue to be assigned some sort of "ultimate" value by numerous writers. Besides, the scholars who qualify these modes, or offer alternatives to them, are inclined to retain, nevertheless, a comparable vision of permanence—the same archetypal assumptions beyond history. Among critics writing in German, from Schiller to Emil Staiger, this has been particularly true; and in the case of Schiller, of course, highly fruitful. But there are three very elementary observations on this broad subject that one feels obliged to formulate. I do not doubt or deny, first, that the search ▪ for universals will be a central task for future literary studies, as it is for linguistics today. Second, this search will surely depend on the assimilation of a great deal of knowledge concerning the non-Western literatures, or to put it in academic terms, on the work of comparative literature scholars who have been trained as Orientalists. (I assume that we are not dealing with Kantian a priori assumptions but with the products of the critical observation of literary history. Even within the bounds of Western literature, the tripartite division into narrative, drama, and lyric has been insufficient for several centuries now. The rise of the essay as a genuine —certainly, since Montaigne, not spurious or marginal— literary genre has made the point quite clear.) Third, one must stress that these essential modes or universals do not co-

---

[7] *The Gates of Horn* (New York, 1963), p. 18.

incide with the historically determined, practically oriented, form-conscious categories that we have been calling genres. The latter distinction was firmly made by Goethe in one of the prose commentaries to the *West-östlicher Divan*, in which the older poet was anxious to draw from his recent experience of Oriental poetry some understanding of what is and what is not permanent in literature. (The same relation between being and becoming, in a sense, that his admired Arabic and Persian poets knew so well.) Allegory, the ballad, the drama, the elegy, the epistle, the fable, the idyll, the ode, the novel, parody, the romance, satire, and several others, Goethe thought, are merely *Dichtarten*—poetic kinds, species, or modes. They compose a miscellaneous group, as some of them seem to be named after their content, others after external aspects, and only a few according to their "essential form" ("so findet man, dass sie bald nach äusseren Kennzeichen, bald nach dem Inhalt, wenige aber einer wesentlichen Form nach benamst sind").[8] These kinds or modes should not be confused with the three basic "natural forms," *Naturformen der Dichtung*: the epic (or narrative), the lyric, and the drama. The three natural forms can be, and usually are, blended within an individual work: for example, in a French tragedy the exposition is narrative, the middle is dramatic, and the end may be called lyrical. Thus, it appears that in Goethe's thought the three ultimate archetypes were not only "natural" (as opposed to "conventional")—they were "inner forms" too, as opposed to externals. In fact, Goethe mentions in passing the mistaken taxonomy of the naturalist who collects only the external characteristics ("äussere Kennzeichen") of minerals and plants.[9] Moreover, his terms suggest that the evolution of poetry since the Greeks manifests the shifts and permutations of *Dichtarten* or

---

[8] "Noten und Abhandlungen zu besserem Verständnis des West-östlichen Divans," in *Goethes Werke* (Weimar, 1888), VII, 117.

[9] *Ibid.*, VII, 120.

genres and modes that are really "accidental." The genres, one might say, are contingent, because they are a function of historical change, and of the character and development of nations: only the archetypal inner forms are "necessary."[10]

The generic classifications of neoclassicism were, on the one hand, superficial and inconsistent; on the other, they showed no sense of history. Goethe's use, in the *Noten und Abhandlungen zum Divan*, of terms like "inner" or "essential" form[11] indicates that he had little patience with the first of these defects. As for the second, it seems at first glance that Goethe was applying a historical dimension or point of view to the synchrony of neoclassical genre theory. Stasis could not be accepted on any level by the author of "Die Metamorphose der Pflanzen." Nevertheless, history does not alter all forms—all "inner" forms—and there remains the distinction between the three universal archetypes and the different genres or modes. It is of course difficult to determine—not only in the case of Goethe—whether such a conclusion is the product of a general and unprejudiced review of historical data, or of a compromise between theory and history. But neither the literary critic nor the naturalist in Goethe could be expected to assume an all-out "evolutionist" position. Thus, the division into archetypes and genres appears to perpetuate the old Renaissance distinction between genus, species, and differentiae. The Renaissance theorist would normally call genus a fundamental form of "imitation," in Aristotle's sense, such as imitation by means of language, as distinct from a

[10] Cf. *loc.cit.*

[11] On Goethe's use of "inner form" (derived from Shaftesbury), cf. René Wellek, *A History of Modern Criticism: 1750-1950* (New Haven, 1955), I, 203. On Goethe's idea concerning the natural forms of poetry, Professor Wellek remarks (p. 213): "the principle implied is obviously that of Goethe's own metamorphosis of the plants: the view that there is an *Urpflanze*, of which all the other plants are merely variations. There was also an *Urpoesie*, out of which the three genres grew by separation."

child's imitation of his mother or a painter's reproduction of what he sees, or also, within this form, from dramatic or narrative imitation.[12] At any rate, the Renaissance theorist would usually regard as a species what is today considered a genre —a species resulting from the introduction of certain particulars or differentiae into the genus. Classical logic assumed that genus was a class more extensive (though perhaps less "comprehensive") than species. Aristotle (in *Topica* 1. 5. 102a) had defined genre, "genos," as the essential attribute that is applicable to a plurality of things which are specifically different from one another.[13] Man was a species of the genus animal, the rose a species of the genus flower, and both could be identified through specific differentiae. In other words, the confusion of modern genre theory is partly due to the fact that what we now call genre was once considered more specific than generic, and that we are left without an accepted term for genus. In sixteenth-century Spain the Aristotelian theorist Alonso López Pinciano, author of *Filosofía antigua poética* (1596), called "especie" what the modern Spanish critic considers a "género"; and this distinction persisted for at least two centuries.[14] In eighteenth-century England, Hugh Blair or Dr. Johnson still used "species" as the ordinary term for "literary kind."[15]

In an article published more than thirty years ago, Karl Viëtor argued persuasively for the distinction between universals and genres. Goethe's *Naturformen* he called *Grundhaltungen*—fundamental attitudes. The narrative, the lyrical, the dramatic (*Epik, Lyrik, Dramatik*) are not artistic patterns or shapes or figurations, nor are they attitudes toward the artistic object or the public. They spring from the poet's

---

[12] Cf., for example, Alonso López Pinciano, *Philosophía antigua poética*, ed. Alfredo Carballo Picazo (Madrid, 1953), 1, 242.

[13] Cf. José Ferrater Mora, "Género," in his *Diccionario de Filosofía*, 4th edn. (Buenos Aires, 1958), p. 581.

[14] Cf. Pinciano, *Philosophía antigua poética*, p. 240.

[15] Cf. Wellek and Warren, *Theory of Literature*, p. 338, note 8.

elementary modes of experience, of action and reaction in the world.[16] To call the difference between these attitudes "psychological" would be too simple, for they involve a passage from ordinary experience to creative resolution, from the human being to the poet. One might say, negatively, that their status is not entirely aesthetic. On the other hand, the ode, the elegy, the sonnet are true genres: *Gattungen*. Viëtor, in a few masterful pages, explains that the characteristic feature of a genre can be found neither in the "outer form" alone, nor in the "inner form," nor in the traditional content. All three concur, in the *shaping*, for example, of a sonnet: the tension between its two physically asymmetric parts, the psychic compression and release, the dialectics of feeling and reflection all fulfill an indispensable function. But as some of these traits may be encountered also in an elegy by Schiller or a Hölderlin ode, it becomes necessary to detect a generic structure (*gattungshafte Struktur*) implying a principle of construction or organization of the different parts of the ode, the elegy, the sonnet. These are the structural norms which the poet employs and may also modify, since the nature of genres, unlike that of universals, is historical.

My concern here is not with universals and the many problems that they raise.[17] Our theme is genre, and I have made clear already that I welcome the distinction between universals and genres. There remains the question of the relationship between the two. When I pointed out a moment ago

[16] Cf. Karl Viëtor, "Probleme der literarischen Gattungsgeschichte," *Deutsche Vierteljahrsschrift für Geistesgeschichte und Literaturwissenschaft*, IX (1931), 425-427; reprinted in Viëtor, *Geist und Form* (Bern, 1952), under the title "Die Geschichte literarischer Gattungen." Further citations will be from *Geist und Form*.

[17] If universals are experiential or psychological, is it not misleading, willfully so, to continue to use poetic-generic terms like "narrative," "dramatic," "lyrical"? A convenient concept and term is Northrop Frye's "radical of presentation," cf. *Anatomy of Criticism* (Princeton, 1957), pp. 246-247.

that what we call genre today was once considered more specific than generic, and that we are left without an accepted
term for genus, I might have added that the situation was
fortunate. For now the concept or the function of genre could
be properly isolated and understood. As the link was finally
broken between genus and species, it became possible to
speak of genus in different ways (i.e., of universals, "ulti-
mates," "types," *Naturformen, Grundhaltungen*) and of
species as well (i.e., genres, or modes, or styles) without retaining the traditional assumption that the two need be logically and genealogically related.

Viëtor did not go so far. He took for granted that a genre
like the ode, or the elegy, or the sonnet was a subgroup *of* the
universal *Lyrik*; and that every genre had to spring, indeed
could only spring, from one of the universal attitudes.[18]
Likewise, in the fourth chapter of the *Anatomy of Criticism,*
Northrop Frye assumes that the larger categories flow into
the classes of genre and subgenre. Frye subdivides his four
basic genres, which are "Epos," "Prose," "Drama," and
"Lyric," into a number of "specific forms" (thus reverting to
the older genus-species filiation). This is not the place to discuss the role these components play within Frye's system of
relations and correlations. As far as genres are concerned, we
need only extend Viëtor's own premises. Any "vertical" system (vertical as a genealogical tree is, with the branch of the
elegy growing from a thicker lyrical branch and sharing a
common trunk, etc.) fails to recognize the fact that universals and genres belong to different orders, and can only
be grasped by means of different criteria. Only the genre is
a structural model, an invitation to the actual construction of
the work of art. A lyrical attitude or assumption or style may
be perceived on a certain level of a literary work, while on
another level we may remark that it has been designed or

[18] Cf. Viëtor, *Geist und Form*, p. 294.

organized in accordance with a particular generic model, and though these two strata may of course run together or overlap in a number of places, there is little that the critic can gain by postulating that some kind of causal link exists between the two.

The same point can be made by recalling the observation with which this essay began: that one notices in the patterns of genre, as used by practical critics, a special proximity to overall form. A genre, in this sense, is a problem-solving model on the level of form. A "radical of presentation" like, say, the narrative, is a challenge—but the kind of challenge that sets up a confrontation between the poet and the "matter" of his task. More problems are raised than solved by the writer's determination, vis-à-vis the blank page, to "tell a story." But let us suppose that he is facing a particular genre like the picaresque novel. Let us say—hastily—that the picaresque model can be described in the following way: it is the fictional confession of a liar. This is already a provocative notion. Besides, the writer knows that the picaresque tale begins not *in medias res* but with the narrator's birth, that it recounts in chronological order the orphaned hero's peregrinations from city to city, and that it usually ends—that is, it can end—with either the defeat or the conversion of the "inner" man who both narrates and experiences the events. What is at stake now, it seems to me—what is being constructively suggested—is not the presentation but the informing drive (in Viëtor's words, *Gestaltungsdrang*)[19] that makes the whole work possible. Within the process of writing, the "radicals" and the "universals" fulfill their function at a very early stage; details of rhetoric and style play essential but partial and variegated roles; and only the generic model is likely to be effective at the crucial moment of total configuration, construction, *com-position*.

[19] Cf. *Geist und Form*, p. 294.

Now, genres change, unlike "radicals" or "universals." As they change, they affect one another and the poetics, the system to which they belong, as well. Although genres are chiefly persistent models, because they have been tested and found satisfactory, it has been generally known since the Enlightenment—since Vico, since Voltaire's *Essai sur la poésie épique*—that they evolve, or fade, or are replaced. As a matter of fact, a few superior writers of the sixteenth century (Montaigne, the anonymous author of *Lazarillo de Tormes,* Cervantes) had stimulated the invention of the essay and the novel, the two genres which, together with the lyric, would dominate much of modern literature. Though not always as successfully, this trend would be continued, and would accelerate after the Romantic period. Thus, it seems important to reconsider the terms of generic theory from the point of view of *new* genres. Let us recall some of the criteria that have been used in this discussion: empirical relevance, form-making, invitation to the matching of matter and form, informing drive, problem-solving model, principle of construction, process of writing, moment of composition. As I review them, it seems evident that they imply two things: process and instrumentality.

Insofar as they do, I find myself in agreement with the main ideas of Mario Fubini in his well-known essay on "Genesi e storia dei generi letterari." There is much that the historian can learn, Fubini observes, from the arguments and the speculations touched off in the past by the introduction of new (i.e., not amenable to accepted genre theory) works. The main lesson is that all genres are potentially useful—and expendable. Let us admit, with Croce, that a genre is an external class in aesthetic terms. Let us also remember that—*felix culpa!*—the sixteenth-century debate on whether *Orlando Furioso* was a "poema epico" or a "poema romanzesco" demonstrated that although no single generic norm could possibly do justice to a masterpiece like Ariosto's, the combined use of several genres would allow the critics to surround and seize, so to speak, their quarry. Taken together, the different genres are like coordinates through which the individual poem can be apprehended and understood. (Fubini's own metaphor is of web and woof, *trama*: "così, protagonista del discorso, l'individuo poetico traspare attraverso la trama delle definizioni generiche, che valgono a farcelo meglio conoscere.")[20] Now, this sort of effect is obvious in the case of a much-discussed innovation like *Orlando Furioso*. But the same applies to traditional works. Generic statements, Fubini stresses, are instrumental—i.e., essentially critical. The process of classification that genre theory implies is but one part of a broader process of definition and interpretation. If the nexus between a genre and a single work is rather puzzling, we need not be reminded of the virtues, and even the necessity, of studious puzzlement. Genres, in other words, condition and incite the questioning of literary works. The dynamics of the history of genres shows that this basically fruitful questioning never ceases.

At the same time, we must avoid lingering too much over the point of view of the *critic*. Literary works have to exist, of course, before they can be questioned, and it is a mistake to assume that poetics is intended primarily for scholars and aestheticians. The traditional target of poetic theory has been the writer. For many centuries there were schools, in the broader meaning of the word, for the poet to join, where not only practical but theoretical teachings were shared. The young poet went to "school" insofar as he admitted, one might say, that to write was not to remain alone—that there were important principles and techniques he could not possibly discover within the brief span of his own life: *ars longa, vita brevis*. No poet is likely to raise his voice in an environment devoid of poetic models; and even today the formal

[20] *Critica e poesia*, p. 129.

model called genre exerts some normative impact—not in the old knuckle-rapping sense, but insofar as it offers a challenge, a foil, a series of guidelines. I realize, of course, that the poet, the critic, and the theorist converge in a number of situations, or even coincide. Fubini's emphasis on the critic's angle of vision may well have been justified by the fact that since Dante and Tasso, Manzoni and Carducci, the superior poet in Italy has often been a theorist-critic too. Yet it seems necessary to distinguish between functions, if not persons. When I began by recalling the critic's success in applying generic standards to individual works, it was in the hope that this a posteriori detection of structure would reflect or confirm the poet's original ability to shape and recreate through the intermediary of genre. If one tends to concentrate, as Fubini did, on the *critic's* discovery of the instrumentality of genres, instead of the poet's, one is not in the best position to discern the chief merit of the generic model, which is, as I said earlier, its pertinence to total literary form-making.

The distinction between the functions of the poet, the critic, and the theorist, particularly with regard to new genres, becomes clearer in practice whenever we apply the three broad criteria—or angles of vision, or perspectives— which are most generally relevant to the subject. These criteria may be briefly described as follows. First, there is the temporal perspective. The idea of a genre must come into existence or be detected before it can be operative as a norm or as a practical model. It can be the result of an a posteriori contemplation of literary works—i.e., an afterthought, a product of the critic's attempt to classify and order his materials. Northrop Frye, to take a fairly recent example, has recommended that the name of "anatomy" be given to one of the basic forms of prose fiction, which offers, unlike the "novel" or the "romance," primarily intellectual patterns (as in Rabelais, or *Candide*, or the utopias). Historians of Spanish literature, who are familiar with the nineteenth-century genre called *costumbrismo* or sketch of manners (Mesonero Romanos, Estébanez Calderón, and others), have looked backwards and applied the term retroactively to the *Siglo de Oro* (Quevedo, Zabaleta, Francisco Santos). We may note in passing that the two terms overlap, to a certain extent, so that *costumbrismo* can be considered a version of the anatomy (and the dialogue in Hispanic prose between the novel and the anatomy perhaps comparable to the dialectics of the romance and the novel in American fiction). Now, the generic "process" involves not only the acceptance of new classifications and descriptions but possibly the passage, as a consequence, from criticism to poetry. The a posteriori class detected by the critic, and recognized by the theorist, may go on to have an impact on the writer's awareness of the potentialities of his medium, and thus become operative as a genre a priori. Where an academic term like "anatomy" is concerned, coming as it does centuries after Rabelais and even Robert Burton, this seems hardly likely, though not impossible. It is a matter, after all, of relative distance—between period and period, and between critic and poet. There are many situations in which this distance proves to be small: the rise of tragicomedy in the sixteenth and seventeenth centuries, for example, especially after the debate over Guarini's *Pastor Fido*; or, in our day, the influence on contemporary writers of terms and notions coined and used in quick succession by enterprising journalists, publishers, advertising men, and academic critics (such as the French *nouveau roman*). The process of generic description and classification is never quite closed, and the diachronic fluidity of genre theories is much more real than their apparent solidity at a single moment in history. Consequently, what our temporal perspective can most usefully discern is simply whether or not a generic model belongs to a particular synchronic system, that is to say, to the poetics of a particular literary period. Whether or how the term was integrated later into another synchronic system, is a different problem, requiring the use of different criteria.

We are thus led to ask, secondly, to what extent a class or a model is, so to speak, "official." The question is whether a new genre has entered the "inner circle" of the poetics of a period. After all, the very notion of a new genre is ambiguous: if it is a genre, then it is relatively authoritative, and therefore not "new" in the sense of "unknown," "unfamiliar," or "untried." The so-called new genre comes into being through a peculiar process of acceptance, which is substantially different from that of the new poem or of the individual masterpiece. The poem achieves instant existence, as it were, merely by being read and "published." The generic process, of course, is rather slow (Montaigne the writer was recognized much before the essay form was, for example). But what is more significant is that although both the new work and the new genre imply a reading public, the emergence of the latter demands a special sort of critical approval: the readers, acting as critics or even theorists, decide that a viable model exists. This is the start of a process whereby the form gradually becomes "official." I am assuming that a difference exists between the status of the model at an earlier and a later stage of the process; or, in synchronic terms, that one ought to distinguish between the larger repertory of norms that is available to a certain generation and the codified, accepted classes composing what is usually considered the "poetics" of that generation. As far as synchrony is concerned, Renato Poggioli has proposed an important distinction between the explicit norms of a literary period and what he calls its "unwritten poetics." Before Thomas Mann, Marcel Proust, and James Joyce could begin their more ambitious works, they had in mind a certain idea of the novel with which their practice could interact: "in other words, those writers worked within a vague, vast, and yet limited circle of literary possibilities: a circle constituting by itself a modern poetics of the novel."[21] Besides, Poggioli added, the need for such implicit standards is not a phenomenon limited to our time:

"Although this fact has escaped the conscious attention of most literary scholars, unwritten poetics have existed in every age, either alone, or alongside written ones, the last alternative being characteristic of neo-classical periods. In primitive ages, we have only unwritten poetics; in eclectic, composite, and decadent epochs, they predominate over the written ones; in classical or neo-classical periods they are less influential than the written ones, affecting preferably those special or minor currents which flow apart from the main stream."[22]

The sixteenth century, which I called earlier the first great period of creative reassessment in the history of European genre theory, cannot be regarded as a neoclassical period, in the context of Poggioli's terms. The new genres and the as-yet-uncodified examples of the Renaissance did not fail to affect the creative mainstream; neither was it an eclectic or a decadent epoch of the sort in which written poetics languish. It was a moment of dynamic contact between traditional artistic principle and practical innovation. The written and the unwritten poetics did not evolve on two separate, disconnected levels. Among the Italian theorists of the late sixteenth century, the main difference between an "Ancient" like Giason Denores and a "Modern" like Battista Guarini consisted in the fact that the former maintained the absolute validity of certain immutable principles, while the latter defended the multiplication of genres and the changes brought about by the demands of new audiences.[23] But both the

---

[21] Renato Poggioli, "Poetics and Metrics," in *Comparative Literature. Proceedings of the IInd Congress of the I.C.L.A.*, ed. Werner P. Friederich (Chapel Hill, N.C., 1959), I, 194; reprinted in Poggioli, *The Spirit of the Letter* (Cambridge, Mass., 1965), pp. 343-354.

[22] "Poetics and Metrics," p. 195.

[23] Cf. Weinberg, *A History of Literary Criticism*, II, 1074-1105.

ancients and the moderns were quite willing, under the cloak of either permanence or change, in theoretical terms, to make room practically in their systems for the new genres, that is to say, to take over and legitimate some of the fields covered by the unwritten poetics of the time. Cervantes, who was familiar with some of the Italian theorists, confronted most lucidly the generic dynamics of his day, and the fruitful interaction that existed between the written and the unwritten codes. Though this is an instance that would require extended study and information, I refer to it in passing with the theoretical aims of this discussion primarily in mind. I do not know whether the pastoral novel was actually an "official" or an "unofficial" genre when *La Galatea* (1585) was begun, but I suspect that to leave the question open might be the closest to the truth, that is, to the situation in which Cervantes lived and worked. At the time of the debate over the *Pastor Fido,* which took place soon afterwards, it was argued that the long pastoral was a legitimate expansion of the eclogue. And the extensive narratives by Sannazaro and Montemayor were already well known and recognized. We may assume that the pastoral novel still belonged to the circle of "unwritten poetics" when Cervantes started *La Galatea*; that although the official class of the epic poem was available to every sixteenth-century poet, Cervantes chose not to compose an epic in *octavas reales* on the victory of Lepanto; that as far as the stage was concerned, he wavered between the accepted tragic structure and the developing popular forms; and that he confronted simultaneously the written and the unwritten norms of the day—the whole expanding circle of contemporary poetics—when he wrote his most syncretic and original work, *Don Quixote*. The modern novel, of course, from Cervantes to our time, could be described as an "outsider" model that writers insist on regarding as essentially incompatible with the passage from an unwritten poetics to an "official" system of genres.

Cervantes' response offers a singularly suggestive comment on the situation and the challenge every writer is obliged to face, namely, the necessity of an active dialogue with the generic models of his time and culture. This dialogue is active in the sense that the poet does not merely choose among the standards that are accessible to him—he makes possible their survival; and he determines *which* are the preferable or the pertinent or the potentially "new" norms. I have just recalled, under our first two perspectives, some of the ways in which readers or writers take part in a continuing process of classification and description, involving both a priori and a posteriori classes, or in which they decide the viability of new genres, whether "official" or not. In other words, I have been stressing the dependence of genres, and of their diachronic fluidity, on the *choices* that are constantly being made by poets, critics, and theorists. Under our third perspective, what one wishes to clarify is the *nature* of the choices that occur. For I am referring to a very broad spectrum of phenomena. In the case of the theorist (or of the writer functioning as theorist), at one end of the spectrum, one finds that the choice is usually logical, or allegedly so. At the other end of the spectrum, the decision of the poet will tend to be "existential." These are, I think, the truly fundamental differences. As far as the logical posture is concerned, I am aware of the fact that it subsumes a variety of procedures. The theorist may wish to define a series of norms or abstractions derived from a *reductio ad unum* of the instances at hand, either with inductive methods (analytical or historical) or with deductive ones (based on philosophical or aesthetic principles). The norm may be an essential idea that the individual work can only reflect most imperfectly (in the Platonic tradition: "in a sense," writes Bernard Weinberg concerning such sixteenth-century "Ancients" as Giason Denores, "they see the forms as Forms, which are always the same, which make no concessions to times or audiences, which impose upon the poet a strict obedience to unalterable rules"),[24] or it may be a real entity which the work actually exemplifies (*universalia sunt realia*). The Horatian and Aristotelian theorists of the Renaissance did not limit themselves to any one of these alternatives. But what doubtless occurred in almost all cases was that genres were being *defined*.

The air of unreality one finds in the tradition of classical and neoclassical poetics has to be ascribed to this most widespread assumption, to wit, that genres are sharply delimited objects that are "out there," confronting the critic or the reader, requiring above all an effort of verbal definition. Nevertheless, aesthetic models were never "hard" data. As the readers, the poets, and some of the critics knew, and as the history of poetics manifests, generic norms have constantly demanded both a reaffirmation of their validity and a renewed perception of their nature (for a form can never be "taken over," as we observed earlier: it must be "achieved" all over again, from the start, with each single work). Logically speaking, it is a thankless task to define a being whose limits and character are largely dependent on the results of the definition. The modern novel highlights this circular quandary particularly well. But it is the problem of all genres, as theorists and historians have come to realize. Karl Viëtor, to recall an eminent example, stressed at the end of his well-known essay the crucial importance of this difficulty. How is it at all possible to write the history of a literary genre, he asked, when we do not possess firm generic norms in the first place, and must instead derive those norms from the survey of a multitude of single facts?[25] Viëtor went on to say that this is a problem all hermeneutics, all historical writing, have to face, as Schleiermacher well knew, and Dilthey, Simmel, or Huizinga (and, of course, Marxist dialecticians). In practice the historian does as well as he can, which some-

[24] *Ibid.*, II, 1104.
[25] Cf. *Geist und Form*, p. 305.

times is very well indeed. In order to write his *Geschichte der deutschen Ode* (1923), Viëtor himself relied on the ancient models, the progressive testing and retesting of initial standards, and the slow emergence of the history of the ode as a sequence and a species of growth (*Wachstumsvorgang*).[26] This is a problem, one might say, that no one resolves, that never disappears, but (in some cases) slowly, gradually dissolves.

So much for the theorist and the critic-as-theorist, who, under this particular perspective, find themselves a long distance away from the poet and the practical critic. (My concern, I repeat, is with functions, not personal idiosyncrasies.) The problem of definition is quite foreign to the preoccupations of the creative writer. The author of, say, a tragedy, is not necessarily concerned with the entire history of the genre or with the accuracy of his critical views. He looks forward to the interaction between a contemporary model—a "working hypothesis"—and his own poetic efforts and gifts. When a poet (or a reader, or a practical critic) observes the changing limits and elusive character of a group of works in which he is actively interested, he does not stop to define—he *decides*. This is the crucial distinction that Robert C. Elliott has made quite clear in an important article, "The Definition of Satire," with reference to Wittgenstein's strictures concerning "concepts with blurred edges" and the definition of games:

"How does then one know whether *x* (which perhaps seems a borderline case) is a satire or not? Following Wittgenstein, one looks at a number of satires about which there is no question—which are at the center of the concept, so to speak—and then decides whether work *x* has resemblances enough to the undoubted examples of the type to be included in it. The point is: this is not a *factual* question to be settled by examining the work for the necessary and sufficient prop-

---

[26] Cf. *Geist und Form*, p. 308.

erties which would automatically entitle it to the name *satire*; it is a *decision* question: are the resemblances of this work to various kinds of satire sufficient so that we are warranted in including it in the category—or in extending the category to take it in?"[27]

If a writer or a critic has decided that a group of works does exist, on the basis of certain significant resemblances, what matters then is the effectiveness of such a resolution, and the ways in which it helps him to understand and emulate those works. (There are a number of masterpieces one could regard as products of "incorrect" decisions.) This does not mean that the writer is obeying a sheer whim or a rootless impulse of the mind (as might perhaps be the case with the definition of games Wittgenstein discusses). We are speaking here of aesthetic responses (or, in a strict sense, of a position based on an aesthetic experience): for example, a response to satires as literary artifacts. These are decisions, then, *about* artistic form, and the writer who is making them is well on his way to his goal: the process of composition may have begun. The age-old interaction between poetics and poetry is not due merely to the opposition between model and creation, but to the conflict between the operations of two different approaches toward models, the logical and the existential-aesthetic. In the final analysis, these two approaches imply different kinds of subject-object relationships: the theorist naturally tends to move some steps away from, and to consider as an object, the form which for the poet is inseparable from the actual exercise of his skills.

Finally, I should like to stress that literary genres have always tended, in the European tradition, to constitute *systems*. I am speaking here, of course, as I have throughout this essay, of genres as formal models, as the core of the theoreti-

[27] Robert C. Elliott, "The Definition of Satire," *Yearbook of Comparative and General Literature*, XI (1962), 23.

cal endeavor called poetics. ("After all," writes Renato Poggioli, "like its ancient counterpart, modern poetics is but a system of literary *genres*.")[28] This is made particularly clear by the authors of poetics in the Aristotelian tradition (from Francesco Robortello to Northrop Frye), and in terms of periods by the second half of the sixteenth century in Italy, which marked a high point in the history of systematic speculation concerning poetry. One may wish to recall, in this connection, such lesser-known accomplishments as Giovanni Antonio Viperano's subtle symmetries (in his edition of Cicero's *De optimo genere oratorum*, 1581), based on Averroës' differentiation between poetry of praise and poetry of vituperation, or Francesco Patrizi's bold new poetics of the "marvelous" (*La deca istoriale*, 1586); or the celebrated efforts of Julius Caesar Scaliger in his *Poetices libri septem* (1561).[29] Scaliger, in the words of Bernard Weinberg, "is basically an orderly thinker, capable of seeing the necessary consequences of his distinctions and of creating a subordination of his ideas to guiding principles. One remarkable effect of this quality is that he recognizes, after developing his own system, that it is contradictory to that of Aristotle."[30] What matters most, as far as the structure of poetics is concerned, is not whether these writers accepted the precise terms of Aristotle or of Horace, but the fact that they all ordered their conclusions on the basis of certain guiding principles. In the manner of their humanist and medieval predecessors, the authors of Renaissance poetics seldom failed to indicate the place of their subject in the overall scheme of the arts and sciences. The order of poetics was expected to reflect, or be a part of, the great order of philosophy.[31]

Nevertheless, this is an order that was often forgotten or

---

[28] "Poetics and Metrics," p. 194.

[29] Cf. Weinberg, *A History of Literary Criticism*, I, 209; II, 743-750, 765-786.

[30] *Ibid.*, II, 744.

[31] Cf. *ibid.*, I, Chap. I.

denied. Since the Romantic period and the breakdown of the neoclassical code, that is to say, since the apparent disintegration of a widely accepted body of theoretical assumptions concerning literature, critics and historians have been inclined to concentrate on the individual work, the single author, the isolated genre. If by "atomicism" one sometimes means the attempt to isolate the single parts of a system, to pry the element apart from the field or the mass to which it belongs, then the modern study of literature, in keeping with its Romantic origins, has been generally atomistic. Even the scholar who attempts to cover an entire historical period is not likely to rely too heavily on poetics as a unifying factor. Actually, the synchronic meanings of order—order as arrangement, classification, coordination—have normally been subordinated to the linear or diachronic meanings—chronological order, sequence of styles, evolution of forms, etc. The fact that so many genres have served, so to speak, as countergenres, and so many styles as counterstyles (praise and vituperation, tragedy and comedy, pastoral and picaresque, and so forth), is interpreted most often from a temporal point of view: for example, as parody, refutation, polemics, reversal. But the confrontation of genres may be due to a kind of coexistence on the level of experience or of the imagination, rather than to mere substitution or dialectical succession. The plays of Goldoni cannot be understood, Mario Fubini explains, solely within the history of comedy. The festive forms of writing, like laughter itself, appear rather often in the midst of seriousness.[32] Whether poetry itself—whether the totality of the significant works that come together in the poetic experience and the imagination of an epoch—provides the historian with a genuine order or a system, is surely a most difficult question to answer. Yet the shape of poetics need not provoke such doubts. The code, if not the message, is a coherent whole. One cannot but agree with Professor

[32] Cf. *Critica e poesia*, p. 149.

Fubini when he suggests some of the ways in which the itinerary of genres can be regarded not as the evolution of independent norms, nor as the survival of timeless "structures," but as the history of changing theoretical systems.

[1965, 1968]

Genre and Countergenre:
The Discovery of the Picaresque

Bibliographical research, of which the works of Antonio Ro-dríguez-Moñino offer today an eminent example,[1] provides the student of literature with a very substantial problem: that of the relationship between a poem and its readers. As every-one suspects in the most generic way—*scripta manent*—art can and often does succeed in conquering time. But how does literature, in addition, traverse space? Is one of these dimen-sions a condition of the other? This is what a certain branch of the sociology of literature, of which Robert Escarpit is the persuasive advocate, attempts to clarify. These studies deal with the aftermath of poetic creation by examining the his-tory of *books*. As a poet's words are published, multiplied, and distributed among other men, the main instrument of publication, the book, develops into the vehicle not of mere one-to-one communication but of broad social diffusion. A book, in this sense, "is neither more nor less than its diffu-sion," as Professor Escarpit explains:

"Since, in a little space, it has a high density of intellectual and formal content, since it can easily be passed from hand to hand, since it can be copied and reproduced at will, the book is the simplest instrument which, from a given point, can liberate a multitude of sounds, images, feelings, ideas, facts, by opening the gates of time and space to them—and then, joined with other books, can reconcentrate those dif-fused data in countless other points scattered through the

[1] This chapter is a translation (and a development) of "Luis Sánchez, Ginés de Pasamonte y los inventores del género picaresco," in *Homenaje al Prof. Rodríguez-Moñino* (Madrid, 1966), I, 221-231.

centuries and the continents in an infinity of combinations, each different from any other."[2]

These changing combinations require the passage of historical time. Moreover, they imply a temporal process on an aesthetic level. The publication of a poem is comparable to the performance of a drama or of a symphony only to the extent that it makes *possible* a series of future readers. A theatrical performance can bring about an immediate contact between author, director, actor, text, and audience. Where written literature is concerned, an extensive process unfolds that is both temporal and spatial. The book requires certain intermediaries in order to make its appearance—the editor, the printer, the bookseller—but it can only presume or anticipate a reader. As the real readers multiply, a collective sort of communication begins to take place. A second printing, and a third, or a fifth, particularly if these spread out in space, tend to prove that the audience has ceased to be hypothetical. Thus, the publishing history of a book manifests a process of actualization that is both aesthetic and sociological. The "after-the-fact" sociology of literature does not show how poetry reflects or refracts social patterns (usually a circular issue). It highlights, rather, the power to affect those patterns, that is, the ways in which literature alters a society's awareness of itself.

Bibliographical data allow us to reconstruct decisive links in the process of actualization of single works. As an example, I will examine in the first part of this article the early career of *Lazarillo de Tormes*. The study of this career, which coincided with the birth of the picaresque narrative— a crucial step, in turn, in the rise of the modern novel—will draw us into the orbit of the theory of genres. In fact, it may very well be that of all the "combinations" and "reconcentra-

[2] Robert Escarpit, *The Book Revolution* (London and Paris, 1966), p. 19.

tions" that Robert Escarpit indicates, the most stable and the most significant *is* the formal model usually called genre.

I

In 1554 three little books entitled *La vida de Lazarillo de Tormes, y de sus fortunas y adversidades* appeared in Antwerp, Burgos, and Alcalá de Henares. None of the three is in all certainty the *first* edition. The hypothesis that an earlier edition, now lost, was published in 1553, has been advanced but never proved. Modern critics concur in rejecting the Alcalá version, which deviates most often from the other two and is marred by no less than six interpolations, obviously spurious. This leaves Antwerp and Burgos—two notoriously mercantile towns in the sixteenth century.[3] It should not be forgotten that printers were good businessmen from the start. Two centuries later Voltaire would point out that Dutch booksellers earned millions because certain Frenchmen had been blessed with wit and intelligence ("les libraires hollandais gagnent un million par an parce que les Français ont eu de l'esprit").[4] Toward the middle of the sixteenth century there were witty Spaniards too, as well as discriminating Flemish merchants.

Lazarillo de Tormes has had a genuine audience since the end of the sixteenth century and the start of the seventeenth. Why not since 1554, one might ask, that is, since the beginning of its existence as a book? A most competent student of

---

[3] Cf. J. Denucé, *Inventaire des Affaitadi, banquiers italiens à Anvers, 1568* (Antwerp, 1934); R. Doehaerd, *Etudes anversoises. Documents sur le commerce international à Anvers de 1488 à 1514*, 3 vols. (Paris, 1963); J. Finot, *Etudes historiques sur les relations commerciales entre la Flandre et l'Espagne au Moyen Age* (Paris, 1899); J. A. Goris, *Etude sur les colonies marchandes méridionales à Anvers* (Louvain, 1925); V. Vazquez de Prada, *Lettres marchandes d'Anvers*, 4 vols. (Paris, 1960); R. Carande, *Carlos V y sus banqueros* (Madrid, 1943), vol. 1.

[4] Quoted by Robert Escarpit, *Sociologie de la littérature* (Paris, 1966), p. 61.

the subject, A. Rumeau, has shown how limited the popularity of *Lazarillo* actually was during the reign of Philip II (1556-1598).[5] Four editions were offered to the public within the span of two years: in Antwerp (by the printer Martín Nucio), Burgos (Juan de Junta), and Alcalá de Henares (Salcedo), in 1554; and a second time in Antwerp (Guillermo Simón) in 1555. An early success is evident. Hence the odd contrast with what follows, or rather, fails to follow. The anonymous *Segunda parte* (published in Antwerp in 1555 by Martín Nucio and Guillermo Simón) is immediately forgotten. (It will only be reprinted, together with the first part, in Milan in 1587 and 1615; in Spain it will be published for the first time in 1844. This Flemish sequel clearly has played no part whatsoever in the history of the Spanish picaresque novel.) And even *Lazarillo* itself, after the flare-up of popularity in 1554-1555, will be reprinted rather seldom during the second half of the century—five times, to be exact, twice in Spain: Madrid, 1573; Tarragona, 1586; Milan, 1587; Antwerp, 1595; and Bergamo, 1597.[6] Furthermore, Rumeau explains that the Italian edition of 1597 (Bergamo) owed its existence to the fact that the editor, Antonio de Antoni, was anxious to sell the remaining copies of the 1587 Milanese printing, which had not been doing well, even though the Bergamo dedication tried to suggest the very opposite; and that one should also not take at face value the publicity-minded declarations found among the preliminaries of the 1573 censored edition (*edición castigada*), brought out in Madrid by the royal chronicler, secretary, and cosmographer Juan López de Velasco, according to whom *Lazarillo* had always been well received, particularly abroad ("fue siempre

[5] Cf. A. Rumeau, "Notes au 'Lazarillo.' Des éditions d'Anvers, 1554-1555, à celles de Milan, 1587-1615," *Bulletin Hispanique*, LXVI (1964), 272-293.
[6] These data are in E. Macaya Lahmann, *Bibliografía del Lazarillo de Tormes* (San José, Costa Rica, 1935). All bibliographical facts mentioned without a special footnote are to be found here.

a todos muy acepto, de cuya causa, aunque estaba prohibido en estos reinos, se leía y imprimía de ordinario fuera dellos)."[7]

The 1587 Milan edition opens with a dedication that is rather more honest. There the novel is presented as nearly forgotten, and worm-eaten with age: "la vida de Lazarillo de Tormes, ya casi olvidada, y de tiempo carcomida."[8] Thirty-three years, it is true, had passed. The censored edition was not being reprinted in Spain, actually, nor the uncensored text outside of the peninsula. Besides, I should like to call attention to yet another fact, which completes the picture without modifying it. The first French translation, published in Lyon in 1560, adds to the conclusion of the tale one more chapter—dealing with Lazaro's friendship with certain wine-loving Germans—which happened to be the first chapter of the *Segunda parte* or sequel published in Antwerp in 1555. The same addition can be found in the Antwerp editions of 1595 and 1602, by the heirs of the famous Plantinus, and in numerous later reprints (until Bordeaux, 1837). It would have been odd for the Flemish printers to decide to copy the innovation of a French translator (whose starting point had been the Antwerp original of 1554 or 1555). The opposite probably happened, as Gabriel Laplane suggests,[9] and one may postulate the appearance of an additional Flemish edition between 1555 and 1559, of which no copies are extant today, and to which the editor (perhaps Guillermo Simón) had added for the first time the opening chapter of the Antwerp sequel. We may also recall in passing that the Flemish original of *Lazarillo*—not the Burgos or the Alcalá text—was the basis for the 1573 *edición castigada*, the 1587 and 1597 reprints in Milan and Antwerp respectively, and the first

[7] Quoted by Rumeau, "Notes au 'Lazarillo,' " p. 274.

[8] *Ibid.*, p. 284.

[9] Cf. "Les anciennes traductions françaises du 'Lazarillo de Tormes' (1560-1700)," in *Hommage à Ernest Martinenche* (Paris, 1936), p. 148.

French and English translations (the latter by David Rowland, in London, 1586). The version of *Lazarillo* which attained real temporal and spatial diffusion during the *Siglo de Oro* in Spain and Europe—and thus became really a "book"—was the Antwerp text, whether complete or truncated, of 1554. Everything suggests that the first "discoverers" of the novel were living in Flanders.[10]

In Spain, the book was banned and condemned by the Grand Inquisitor's *Cathalogus librorum qui prohibentur* (Valladolid, 1559). The story was consistently irreverent, of course, and one may surmise that it was enjoyed as such by its first readers: the longest interpolation we encounter in the Alcalá text (1554) offers still another false miracle by the swindling pardoner. But these components were not enough to make *Lazarillo* steadily popular anywhere. The touches of anticlerical satire were not new—in this sense, they were the least original parts of the novel[11]—and their effect was likely to be short-lived. López de Velasco's cuts in 1573 did not affect the essential structure of the tale, that is to say, the sequence of situations and the narrative method on which the future picaresque novel, and its immense European success, would ultimately be based.

Today we know that *Lazarillo de Tormes* marked a crucial moment in the rise of the European novel. We know that this tale of a small boy's partial but enduring disaffection with a scandalous world has lent itself to numberless variations from the sixteenth century to our time. In the passages where we

[10] Cf. Rumeau, "Notes au 'Lazarillo,'" pp. 285-287; Laplane, "Les anciennes traductions," p. 149, note 10; *The Pleasant History of Lazarillo de Tormes*, ed. J.E.V. Crofts (Oxford, 1924), p. viii.

[11] Suffice it to mention the names of Juan de Lucena, Juan Maldonado, Gil Vicente, Torres Naharro, Diego Sánchez de Badajoz, Cristóbal de Castillejo as links within "una tradición ininterrumpida de sátira anticlerical y antimonástica cuyo más celebre representante en España es el Arcipreste de Hita," in the words of Marcel Bataillon, *Erasmo y España* (Mexico, 1950), I, 251.

see Lazarillo wandering from town to town, looking for a shelter and a master, we recognize easily enough an early figuration of the freedom and the quest that are the burden of modern novelistic heroes. There is no doubt but that *Lazarillo* inaugurated with singular skill, within the Spanish literary curve spanning *La Celestina* and *Don Quixote*, the presentation of the hopes and failures of men who, orphanlike but inquiring, far removed in practice from any abstract canon, test their knowledge as they grow older and confront or work out the compromises that will determine their lives.

Yet, as we return to the sequence of events in the sixteenth century, all such developments become virtual once more. The historical view forces us to conjecture that what did take place might not have happened at all. At best, we are justified in singling out the factors that were most favorable to a particular series of possibilities. During the decades of the *Siglo de Oro*, a Spanish novel, or any Spanish text, enjoyed exceptional conditions for influence and propagation. We have seen that the original Castilian text of *Lazarillo* was printed not only in Spain but in the Low Countries and in Italy—and shortly afterwards in France as well. This initial "space"—the dimensions of a publishing world—coincided with the mercantile support for the Hispanic conquest and colonization of America. Nevertheless, the rhythm of acceptance of *Lazarillo* was slow. A genuine audience, as Robert Escarpit will remind us, presupposes the convergence of the factors of space and time. To the spatial diffusion of our proto-picaresque novel, in other words, a certain temporal continuity was still to be added.

To decipher an absence is always hazardous. Why, one asks, was this rhythm of acceptance so slow? In its day, of course, the position of *Lazarillo* was truly singular. That is to say, in the middle of the sixteenth century, a novel, or a genuine pre-novel, was unusual and isolated indeed. The fact that an original work remains without immediate effect or consequences, surely is an ordinary occurrence in the history of the arts. (*Lazarillo*, as Marcel Bataillon has stated, was "un commencement absolu.")[12] Also, it often happens that a new work stimulates a great deal of interest at first, only to be forgotten just as quickly, for it has not been understood or assimilated. Thus, the first triumph of *Lazarillo* was followed by decades of relative indifference. Particularly in the career of the visual arts, there are a number of similar cases—for example, the delayed impact of Goya in the nineteenth century. The great Giotto, who died in 1337, remained without successors for almost a century in the midst of one of the most intense periods of creativity in the history of painting. "For a hundred years after Giotto," Berenson observed, "there appeared in Florence no painter equally endowed with dominion over the significant."[13]

The author of *Lazarillo* had no successor for nearly fifty years. In 1599 Mateo Alemán—the humanist, *cristiano nuevo,* and businessman from Seville—published his *Guzmán de Alfarache*, ending the isolation of the earlier novel. Today the thematic and formal differences between *Lazarillo* and its followers seem worthy of consideration. On a certain level, *Guzmán de Alfarache* (a didactic and dogmatic monolith) and *Lazarillo de Tormes* (compassionate and pluralistic) seem nearly antithetical. But the seventeenth-century reader very probably had his eye on another level, where the two works converged. The result of this convergence was a common *género picaresco*, which did not come into being until 1599, of course—just as the heroic couplet did not exist until Chaucer had enough admirers and imitators, as John Livingston Lowes once pointed out: "'The heroic couplet,' says Professor Manly, with the utmost truth, 'originated . . . suddenly. Chaucer wrote heroic couplets, and there they were.'

[12] *Le roman picaresque*, ed. Marcel Bataillon (Paris, 1931), p. 5.
[13] *The Florentine Painters of the Renaissance* (New York, 1909), p. 20.

But when Chaucer wrote heroic couplets, and there all at once they were, the heroic couplet did not thereby spring into existence as a convention. It became that later, when other poets, following Chaucer, looked upon it and saw that it was good, and wore it threadbare."[14] What matters to us here, likewise, is the reaction of Mateo Alemán's contemporaries. As we shall see in a moment, the acceptance of either *Lazarillo* or *Guzmán* was second to the main development: the surge of popularity of the model, the pattern, the genre, which they sustained not singly but conjointly.

Guzmán de Alfarache was one of the first authentic best sellers in the history of printing. Its huge success immediately transformed a narrative form—in Lowes's terms—into a convention. The evidence suggests that Luis de Valdés was not far from the truth when he affirmed, in the "Elogio" heading the *Segunda parte* of 1604, that twenty-six different editions and no less than fifty thousand copies had appeared in four or five years: "¿De cuáles obras en tan breve tiempo vieron hechas tantas impresiones, que pasan de cincuenta mil cuerpos de libros los estampados, y de veinte y seis impresiones las que han llegado a mi noticia?"[15] The success of *Guzmán de Alfarache* around 1600 is well known. But critics

---

[14] John Livingston Lowes, *Convention and Revolt in Poetry* (Boston and New York, 1919), p. 48.

[15] Mateo Alemán, *Guzmán de Alfarache*, ed. S. Gili Gaya (Madrid, 1953), III, 59. See R. Foulché-Delbosc, "Bibliographie de Mateo Alemán. 1598-1615," *Revue Hispanique*, XLII (1918), 481-556. Foulché-Delbosc did not see an edition in-4° of *Guzmán*, similar to the *princeps*, published by Várez de Castro in Madrid in 1600 (there is a copy in the Biblioteca Nacional in Madrid); nor a reprint by Sebastián de Cormellas in Barcelona, 1599, where one reads at the bottom of the title page not "A costa de Angelo Tabano," but "Véndense en la mesma Emprenta" (Biblioteca Menéndez y Pelayo, Santander); nor another by Juan Mommarté, Brussels, 1600, with a title page that is slightly different from the one in the Biblioteca Nacional or that in the British Museum. Counting these editions, then, in addition to those Foulché-Delbosc saw, I obtain a total of twenty-five editions (of the *Primera parte* alone) previous to 1605.

have not observed that it also resulted in the resurrection of *Lazarillo de Tormes*; and that it sparked a "combination" (to use Escarpit's word), a double acceptance, a convergence, from which there arose, during the years immediately following the publication of *Guzmán* (1599), the idea of a *género picaresco*—an idea which was formulated for the first time by Ginés de Pasamonte in a passage of *Don Quixote* (1605): "mal año," said Ginés in a defiant moment, "para *Lazarillo de Tormes*, y para todos cuantos de aquel género se han escrito o escribieren" (Part I, Chap. 22). We shall return later to these provocative words.

Four editions of *Lazarillo* had appeared in 1554 and 1555. Then, for as long as a second phase lasted, from 1573 to 1595, the book had five reprintings. Now a third, very different phase begins: within four years, from 1599 to 1603, at least nine editions of *Lazarillo* will be published. Basically, its public will be the same as *Guzmán*'s. I cannot venture a guess as to its composition. But we do know that it was large. And a large literate audience of Spaniards around 1600 could not possibly coincide with the lower class. It was probably most akin not to the heroes of picaresque novels but to their authors, particularly Mateo Alemán. Its core, in other words, would have been the discontented middle class. (Generally speaking, the rise of the novel in sixteenth-century Spain seems to have been rooted not in the triumph but in the frustration of the bourgeoisie.)

The king, Philip II, had died in 1598. The start of a new reign had brought either fresh hopes or a greater degree of boldness to writers and printers. The *Primera parte de Guzmán de Alfarache* was published for the first time in Madrid, "en casa del Licenciado Várez de Castro," a printer's shop where it began to be sold around the first week of March 1599. The *tasa* (or right to charge a certain price) was fixed by Gonzalo de la Vega on March 4. (Curiously enough, the *aprobación*—or ecclesiastical license—had been granted on

January 13 of the previous year.)[16] Now, exactly nine weeks later, the printing house of Luis Sánchez in Madrid offered to the public an edition of *Lazarillo de Tormes*. The *tasa* for it was authorized by Gonzalo de la Vega on May 11.[17] In the meantime, *Guzmán de Alfarache* had begun to appear in the other kingdoms of the peninsula, as several alert publishers outside of Madrid tried to capitalize on the success of the Castilian edition. Sebastián de Cormellas, "a costa de Angelo Tabano, mercader de libros," brought out Alemán's long novel in Barcelona, with a license delivered on April 27.[18] (By this time a certain specialization had taken place in the trade, with the printer and the bookseller becoming two separate persons with different functions.) A second business-man from Barcelona, Miguel Menescal, followed suit, working with the printers Gabriel Graells and Giraldo Dotil.[19] In Aragon we find that it was Juan Pérez de Valdivielso, "a costa de Juan Bonilla, mercader de libros," who issued *Guzmán de Alfarache*, in Zaragoza, the *aprobación* having been granted on June 21, 1599. Besides, it seems that Sebastián de Cormellas proceeded to sell still more copies of the novel in his own printing shop; and that the original edition by Várez de Castro was immediately pirated in Madrid.[20]

We can now observe that *Lazarillo de Tormes* followed precisely the *same* itinerary. Luis Sánchez, as we just noted, brought it before the public in Madrid a few days after the initial success of *Guzmán de Alfarache*. Sebastián de Cormel-

---

[16] This *editio princeps* can be found in a number of libraries: the Biblioteca Nacional both in Madrid and Lisbon, the British Museum, Widener Library (Harvard University), the Hispanic Society (New York), and elsewhere.

[17] Cf. Lahmann, *Bibliografía*, p. 64.

[18] I have seen the copy in the Biblioteca Nacional in Madrid.

[19] It has the same *aprobación* as the edition by Cormellas (copy in the Hispanic Society).

[20] The Zaragoza edition has *aprobaciones* by Licenciado Mateo de Canseco (June 21, 1599) and by the Asesor Galván (June 22) (Biblioteca Nacional, Madrid; Wiener Hofsbibliothek).

las and Juan Pérez de Valdivielso, Alemán's editors in Barcelona and Zaragoza respectively, published *Lazarillo* too, also in 1599. (There is no *tasa* or *aprobación* in either printing, obviously because the edition by Luis Sánchez was pirated.)[21] These were not the sole occasions on which *Lazarillo* appeared to follow closely in the steps of the illustrious *Guzmán*. In Paris Nicolas Bonfons would print the latter in 1600, and *Lazarillo* in 1601; in Milan, Juan Baptista Bidelo brought both novels out in 1615, and so on.[22]

Yet—the story is not finished—*Lazarillo* was not reprinted between 1603 and 1607. This surprising pause may be attributed to the sudden advent of three competitors: the two sequels to *Guzmán de Alfarache* (the spurious continuation by Mateo Luján de Sayavedra in 1602, and Alemán's own *Segunda parte* in 1604); and, above all, the publication of *Don Quixote* in 1605. The success of Miguel de Cervantes' entry in the publishing race was so irresistible that *Guzmán de Alfarache*, the best seller, would not reappear until 1615, in Milan. If what most of these bibliographical data seem to indicate is the rise of a new genre, then an important consequence of this rise was the emergence of a diametrically opposed masterpiece, which itself was able to serve as seed for a "countergenre." Surely the facts of the case are unequivocal. On the editorial and literary levels, Cervantes' seminal novel was an inspired response to the challenge of the newborn picaresque genre.

II

These "negative" impacts or *influences à rebours*, through which a norm is dialectically surpassed (and assimilated) by another, or a genre by a countergenre, constitute one of the

[21] Cf. Lahmann, *Bibliografía*, pp. 67-68. I owe the data concerning the edition by Cormellas (Hispanic Society) to the courtesy of Professor Homero Serís. Valdivielso's Zaragoza edition is in the Bibliothèque Nationale in Paris.

[22] Cf. Lahmann, *Bibliografía*, pp. 69, 74.

main ways in which a literary model acts upon a writer. Yet this is an aspect of genre theory we tend to overlook. Since the early nineteenth century and the breakdown of normative systems of poetics, the subject has become more and more a province of historical scholarship. Thus one neglects the equally historical fact that the life of poetic norms and models has involved above all the poets, the dramatists, and the storytellers themselves.

With this fact in mind, I have tried to discuss in another essay ("On the Uses of Literary Genre") three perspectives or distinctions of some relevance not only to theorists or critics but to writers and readers as well. Briefly, these distinctions can be reduced to three questions: Is the norm under consideration a model that could have affected the writer (exerted an influence upon the work in progress), or is it a critic's "afterthought" and an a posteriori category (though liable as time passes to become an a priori model)? Is it an explicit norm and an accepted part of the authoritative systems of the day, or does it belong to the "unwritten poetics" of the period? Has it come into being by means of a process of definition on the part of critics and theorists, or as a result of the *decisions* of writers, readers, and audiences?

Let us now return to our practical example. We have just seen that the parallel publication and success between 1599 and 1605 of two Spanish novels created the appropriate circumstances for the emergence of a new model and for its immediate impact on an incipient countergenre: *Don Quixote* (1605) and its successors. Curious though I am about those exact "circumstances," there is little I can add, unfortunately, to the bibliographical-historical data presented in the first section of this essay. I propose the following comments less as evidence for a real sequence of events than as illustrations of a theoretical approach toward the subject.

Our best clue, I think, is fictional—for we find it in *Don Quixote*. The problem at hand, after all, is literary; and it even has to do with fiction. It might be argued that no evidence could be truer than that of one of Cervantes' own characters (since he himself played the main role), or more likely to illuminate what actually took place in the minds of the "real" readers of *Lazarillo* and *Guzmán*. But it would complicate matters unduly to introduce here one of the main topics of *Don Quixote* itself.

In the chapter following the adventure of Mambrino's helmet, Don Quixote meets a chain of galley slaves on the road, engages them in conversation, and undertakes finally to liberate them (Part I, Chap. 22). Not the least articulate of the galley slaves is the famous Ginés de Pasamonte, otherwise known as Ginesillo de Parapilla:

"Señor comisario," dijo entonces el galeote, "váyase poco a poco, y no andemos ahora a deslindar nombres y sobrenombres: Ginés me llamo y no Ginesillo, y Pasamonte es mi alcurnia, y no Parapilla como voacé dice, y cada uno se dé una vuelta a la redonda, y no hará poco."

"Hable con menos tono," replicó el comisario, "señor ladrón de más de la marca, si no quiere que le haga callar, mal que le pese."

"Bien parece," respondió el galeote, "que va el hombre como Dios es servido; pero algún día sabrá alguno si me llamo Ginesillo de Parapilla o no."

"¿Pues no te llaman así, embustero?", dijo la guarda.

"Sí llaman," respondió Ginés; "mas yo haré que no me lo llamen, o me las pelaría donde yo digo entre mis dientes. Señor caballero, si tiene algo que darnos, dénoslo ya y vaya con Dios, que ya enfada con tanto querer saber vidas ajenas; y si la mía quiere saber, sepa que soy Ginés de Pasamonte, cuya vida está escrita por estos pulgares."

"Dice verdad," dijo el comisario, "que él mismo ha escrito su historia, que no hay más que desear, y deja empeñado el libro en la cárcel en doscientos reales."

"Y le pienso quitar," dijo Ginés, "si quedara en doscientos ducados."

"¿Tan bueno es?", dijo Don Quijote.

"Es tan bueno," respondió Ginés, "que mal año para *Lazarillo de Tormes*, y para todos cuantos de aquel género se han escrito o escribieren: lo que le sé decir a voacé, es que trata verdades, y que son verdades tan lindas y tan donosas, que no puede haber mentiras que se le igualen."

"¿Y cómo se intitula el libro?", preguntó Don Quijote.

"*La vida de Ginés de Pasamonte*," respondió el mismo.

"¿Y está acabado?", preguntó Don Quijote.

"¿Cómo puede estar acabado," respondió él, "si aun no está acabada mi vida? Lo que está escrito es desde mi nacimiento hasta el punto que esta última vez me han echado en galeras."

("Señor Commissary," spoke up the prisoner at this point, "go easy there and let us not be so free with names and surnames. My just name is Ginés and not Ginesillo; and Pasamonte, not Parapilla as you make it out to be, is my family name. Let each one mind his own affairs and he will have his hands full."

"Speak a little more respectfully, you big thief, you," said the commissary, "unless you want me to make you be quiet in a way you won't like."

"Man goes as God pleases, that is plain to be seen," replied the galley slave, "but someday someone will know whether my name is Ginesillo de Parapilla or not."

"But, you liar, isn't that what they call you?"

"Yes," said Ginés, "they do call me that; but I'll put a stop to it, or else I'll skin their you-know-what. And you, sir, if you have anything to give us, give it and may God go with you, for I am tired of all this prying into other people's lives. If you want to know anything about my life, know that I am Ginés de Pasamonte whose life story has been written down by these fingers that you see here."

"He speaks the truth," said the commissary, "for he has himself written his story, as big as you please, and has left the book in the prison, having pawned it for two hundred reales."

"And I mean to redeem it," said Ginés, "even if it costs me two hundred ducats."

"Is it as good as that?" inquired Don Quixote.

"It is so good," replied Ginés, "that it will cast into the shade *Lazarillo de Tormes* and all others of that sort that have been or will be written. What I would tell you is that it deals with facts, and facts are so interesting and amusing that no lies could equal them."

"And what is the title of the book?" asked Don Quixote.

"*The Life of Ginés de Pasamonte.*"

"Is it finished?"

"How could it be finished," said Ginés, "when my life is not finished as yet? What I have written thus far is an account of what happened to me from the time I was born up to the last time that they sent me to the galleys.")[23]

If is of course impossible to know exactly what Ginés de Pasamonte means when he boastfully talks of a "género" of which *Lazarillo* is the prototype. We may notice, however, that the existence of such a genre was a matter of experience for him. Where theorists are inclined to "define," writers are rather more likely to "decide": Ginés de Pasamonte the writer (and Cervantes with him) is strongly determined not only to equal but to surpass *Lazarillo* and its successors ("It is so good . . . that it will cast into the shade *Lazarillo de Tormes* and all others of that sort"). In fact, the nature of his decision—that a group of works exists with which he proposes to compete—seems immeasurably less vague and more pertinent than the nature of the group itself ("all others of

[23] I quote from the translation by Samuel Putnam (New York, 1949), I, 172-173.

that sort that have been or will be written"). In this context, a genre is above all a challenge to the writer's will, and in that sense an inspiration or an influence. Ginés does not refer to it by means of any technical or cultured term (such as "especie," since "género" was usually reserved for the genus of imitation),[24] but with ordinary words ("all others of that *sort*," Putnam correctly translates). One witnesses here the spontaneous discovery of a class by a reader-critic belonging to the most vast of audiences. This vastness is what Cervantes, in his perspectivistic, illusion-creating, and problem-producing fashion, is able to stress and even exaggerate through the fiction of Ginés de Pasamonte.

It is difficult to ascertain today whether it was feasible for a real thief or a real galley slave to identify, as Ginés does, with the fictional galley slave Guzmán de Alfarache and to begin writing a book comparable to the real Mateo Alemán's. As I noted earlier, a large literate audience in seventeenth-century Spain could not have coincided with the lower class, and those who identified with the *pícaro* must have been mostly members of the discontented middle classes. But on a fictional level, and especially in *Don Quixote,* where the hero imitates the romances of chivalry and where literature becomes not a separate art but the environment and condition of living, the fact that a certain character feels that the picaresque existence is very near his own appears credible and almost reasonable. In this case the "realistic" narrative genre based on *Lazarillo* is doubly worthy of imitation—by Ginés de Pasamonte in his fictional life as a thief and also by Ginés the writer, who is fictional too, but whose *Vida* is moreover a narrative within a narrative. Ginés de Pasamonte may be viewed as a Don Quixote who not only experiences (without losing his mind) but writes down his life (a life which, as Don Quixote finds out early in Part II, another wrote for

---

[24] Cf. above, p. 117.

him): hence the amusement Cervantes obviously derives from the dialogue between the two novel-imitators, which may justify his having cast here Don Quixote as the straight man. Between the man and the writer, besides, one finds the reader or the critic, who is called upon to determine the existence of the literary genre to be imitated. Ginés, as a reader neither cultured nor ignorant, as a layman (or *ingenio lego*), combines a bold ability to recognize novelty with the generic mentality of his time, that is, with an immoderate fondness for classification, be it within or without the pale of traditional poetics.

I might add that Cervantes presents here the operations of "unwritten" poetics. One can say that Ginés de Pasamonte, like many Spanish readers after 1599, of whom he could be considered a fictional symbol (both by ourselves and by Cervantes) establishes a category a posteriori (i.e., a category which did not exist when *Lazarillo* was written) when he speaks of a newly born genre ("todos cuantos de aquel género se han escrito"); while mentioning at the same time a class of books in the process of becoming an a priori model, to be imitated by others in the future ("todos cuantos . . . se . . . escribieren": "will be written"). From *Gil Blas* to *Felix Krull,* the evidence proves abundantly the correctness of Cervantes' guess, or rather of Ginés de Pasamonte's.

For the two are of course distinct, as the same dialogue makes clear. A dialogue in Cervantes is a joining of critical perspectives, and it would be impossible for him to embrace fully either the technical simplicity of Don Quixote, as far as the narrator's craft is concerned, or Ginés de Pasamonte's allegiance to the picaresque form. It is Ginés, not the real author, who imitates *Lazarillo* and *Guzmán de Alfarache.* For it must be realized that although this passage refers explicitly to the former, it tacitly alludes to the latter. Mateo Alemán's hero, at the end of the very long last part of *Guzmán de Alfarache* (1604), writes his autobiography while serving a sentence in the king's galleys, as Alemán had announced he would in one of the preliminaries to the first part (1599). "He himself writes his life in the galleys," Alemán had said, who went on to explain that this is quite proper, and not incompatible with the expression of moral doctrine:

"El mismo escribe su vida desde las galeras, donde queda forzado al remo, por delitos que cometió, habiendo sido ladrón famosísimo, como largamente lo verás en la segunda parte. Y no es impropiedad ni fuera de propósito, si en esta primera escribiere alguna dotrina; que antes parece muy llegado a razón darla un hombre de claro entendimiento, ayudado de letras y castigado del tiempo, aprovéchandose del ocioso de la galera. Pues aun vemos a muchos ignorantes justiciados, que habiendo de ocuparlo en sola su salvación, divertirse della por estudiar un sermoncito para en la escalera."[25]

(He himself writes his life in a galley, where he has been forced to row as a consequence of the delinquent acts he had committed, having been a very famous thief, as the Second Part will copiously show you. And it is not improper nor untimely that he should write down matters of moral doctrine in the First Part; it seems quite reasonable, rather, for a man to do so who has a clear intelligence, some education and many years' experience, while taking advantage of his idle hours in the galley. We even know of ignorant men brought to justice who, instead of devoting those last idle hours to the salvation of their soul, spend their time studying a little sermon for use on the staircase to the gallows.)

Thus the adventures of Ginés de Pasamonte resemble Guzmán's much more than they do Lazarillo's, at least in their literal dénouement. On another plane, however, the differ-

[25] *Guzmán de Alfarache*, ed. Gili Gaya, I, 36, "Declaración para el entendimiento deste libro."

ences are quite substantial. At the end of Part II Guzmán undergoes a sudden religious conversion, though not so profound a one as to prevent him from recounting his former existence with considerable sympathy for the rogue and the swindler he once was. Doubtless Cervantes does not miss an opportunity to remember ironically Mateo Alemán, that great and crucial opponent who is alluded to not only in *Don Quixote* but in several of the *Exemplary Novels*.[26] It may be that one of these ironies points to the questionable authenticity of Guzmán de Alfarache's religious conversion, since Ginés de Pasamonte appears to associate himself with Guzmán without the slightest intention of ceasing to be the genuine rogue and swindler that he is. A second allusion is quite explicit, and has to do with the narrative uses of the first- and third-person forms of the verb. Joaquín Casalduero is one of the few critics who has observed that Cervantes is stressing in this passage the pseudoautobiographical aspect of the picaresque genre,[27] while suggesting a basic polarity between this aspect and the techniques of the "countergenre" for which *Don Quixote* stands. With his well-known ambiguity, Cer-

[26] As far as *Don Quixote* and *La ilustre fregona* are concerned, this is a problem that demands detailed study. I will limit myself here to a critical conjecture and a biographical fact: it seems that many of the literary-structural ironies and censures formulated in *El coloquio de los perros* (regarding the abuse of sermons and moral discourse, the tendency to digress, the lack of form, the wordiness, the fact that if the dogs in the story turn out to be *pícaros*, the *pícaros* themselves, *mutatis mutandis*, should be regarded as dogs, or rather, as mere "cynics") have *Guzmán de Alfarache* as their object. Secondly, it is suggestive that when Mateo Alemán emigrated to America in 1608, never to return to his native country, he read during the crossing and brought to Mexico with him a copy of the recently published first part of *Don Quixote*—which was confiscated upon arrival by the Inquisition. Cf., on the latter, A. S. Bushee, "The 'Sucesos' of Mateo Alemán," *Revue Hispanique*, xxv (1911), 421-422, note 2.

[27] Cf. Joaquín Casalduero, "Notas sobre 'La ilustre fregona,'" *Anales Cervantinos*, iii (1953), 6; and *Sentido y forma del Quijote* (Madrid, 1949), p. 113.

vantes both praises and ridicules *Lazarillo, Guzmán,* "and all others of that sort that have been or will be written."

The dialectics of genre and countergenre are essential to the understanding of a particular axiological structure. In the context of the dialogue between Don Quixote and Ginés de Pasamonte, *género* means essentially "fictional autobiography"—as implicitly opposed to the third-person narrative or "fictional history." (This is a polarity, I need not stress, that will dominate the poetics of the novel, from Alemán-Cervantes to Defoe-Fielding, *Werther*-Scott or Balzac, etc.) As such, *La vida de Ginés de Pasamonte* is supposed to exhibit indubitable virtues as well as defects. On the one hand, its title, like those of *Lazarillo* and *Guzmán* (*La vida de Lazarillo de Tormes, y de sus fortunas y adversidades* and *Primera parte de la vida del pícaro Guzmán de Alfarache*), begins with the words "La vida de." The novelist's task, to paraphrase Ginés, does indeed consist in prying into other people's *lives.* His purpose cannot be grasped by means of any pre-Renaissance emphasis on "character." For the novel presents, recounts, unfolds not characters but lives—even as Ginés refuses to identify himself independently from the *vida* that he has written down. (Hence the wonderfully loose and apparently inconsequential exchange concerning his name and surname: Ginés merely wishes to be as responsible for his name as he is for his identity as presented in *La vida de Ginés de Pasamonte.*) To this end, i.e., the presentation of *a* life, the autobiography or pseudoautobiography is most effective: it reproduces the original chronology of events ("from the time I was born up to the last time that they sent me to the galleys") and gives the impression of being truthful or true to life—in Ginés' words, "que trata verdades" ("that it deals with facts"). The use of the first-person form of the verb adapts itself singularly well to the concealment of all thematic deceptions and lies ("mentiras"). Since *Lazarillo,* the most eminent example of this is the picaresque genre, whose roguish hero need not respect the truth of other people's lives as a storyteller, any more than he does their property in everyday practice.

Should Ginés (if this is his name) the writer be more honest than Ginés the thief? The reader is led to ask himself this question, and to interpret in his own way the facts: *La vida de Ginés de Pasamonte* is presented by its author, with the commissary's consent, as a truthful autobiography. Nevertheless, Cervantes stresses most explicitly the problem of narrative structure. A dramatic or epic character possesses, to be sure, some sort of identity; but how does one shape a "life"? The supposed proximity to "life" of the autobiographer is exacted at a very high cost: that of formlessness—and perhaps, as a consequence, of meaninglessness. Any life that is narrated by its own subject must remain incomplete and fail to achieve artistic unity or, very simply, the status of art.

Narrative form demands a "second" or "third" person expressing a consciousness that is extrinsic to the sequence of events. Only such a consciousness can make possible the writing, in Aristotelian terms, of either "poetry" or "history." The saturation of the picaresque with the narrator's individual and willfully limited point of view is most remote from history. And it is one of the ironies of Cervantes that *Don Quixote*, as told by the Arabic chronicler Cide Hamete Benengeli, apparently emulates the structural and presentational virtues of history. It seems to me, to a large extent, that it actually *does*; and that this is an irony one cannot afford to take too lightly. The novel as it emerges in the sixteenth century, after the great Florentine historians and the chroniclers of the conquest of America, owes much to this crucial *rapprochement* between literature and history—to the organization and detailed recreation and tolerant understanding of the concrete wealth of experience by a "third" person. Cervantes, at any rate, penetrated deeply into these polarities.

He quickly saw and judged that the most daring and characteristic feature of the picaresque story was its pseudoautobiographical nature, while his own work as a whole would prove that he had chosen to reject the techniques which Ginés de Pasamonte had so enthusiastically embraced.

The acceptance of a genre is normally an extended process, embracing several stages. The elevation of a single book or of a series of books to the rank of a formal model is secured above all by the readers (or by the writers and critics before they write, i.e., as readers). In our case, we may regard Ginés de Pasamonte as the representative or the fictional symbol of this reading public. Yet still another symbol would be needed for an earlier stage in the acceptance of the picaresque, that is to say, for the intermediaries who brought the novels to a particular audience: the printers. Toward the beginning of the sixteenth century, printers fulfilled all three of the functions that would subsequently be divided into a number of different specialties or professions: the selection, the printing, and the sale of books. In other words, they were editors and booksellers as well. Later in the sixteenth century, as I showed with regard to the editions of *Lazarillo* and *Guzmán*, printers would begin to delegate the actual sale of books to special dealers. But they did not relinquish as yet the crucial editorial or selective role. As Robert Escarpit stresses in his *Sociologie de la littérature*, "les premiers imprimeurs sont déjà des éditeurs-accoucheurs. Leurs choix ont un caractère créateur. Ainsi c'est à Caxton, qui les a imprimés parmi les premiers, que Chaucer, Gower, Lydgate, Malory, etc., auteurs déjà anciens, doivent une résurrection à la vie littéraire que leur maintien en manuscrit leur eût probablement interdite."[28]

In the Spanish context of my subject, the representative of this creative function could be Luis Sánchez, who was re-

[28] *Sociologie de la littérature*, p. 60.

sponsible not only for the resurrection of *Lazarillo* in 1599 but for its association in Madrid with *Guzmán*—a pairing that was imitated immediately in Barcelona, Zaragoza, Paris, and elsewhere[29]—thus grouping physically the two master-pieces and promoting the rise of a model. Unfortunately, we do not know enough about him. His father, Francisco Sán-chez, had run a modest printing shop in Madrid during the second half of the sixteenth century. Luis, who inherited the shop, distinguished himself by publishing a number of very fine works. According to Pérez Pastor, he was said to employ the best craftsmen available: "tuvo en su imprenta los mejores oficiales en aquella época."[30] Luis Sánchez, moreover, was an educated person. We know that he composed Latin poems as preliminaries for some of the books he printed.[31] We may suppose that he possessed a measure of humanistic learning and an effective interest—whether critical or commercial—in the newer trends in writing. It was, at any rate, men like Ginés de Pasamonte and Luis Sánchez who made possible the birth of a genre.

[1965, 1968]

[29] Cf. above, p. 145.
[30] Cristóbal Pérez Pastor, *Bibliografía madrileña* (Madrid, 1891), I, xxix.
[31] Cf. *ibid.*, I, nos. 465, 670.

Literature as Historical Contradiction:
El Abencerraje, the Moorish Novel,
and the Eclogue

Written between 1550 and 1560, *El Abencerraje*, like its contemporary *Lazarillo de Tormes*, marks a clear beginning in
the history of European literature. Each of these brief and
anonymous tales is deservedly regarded as a masterpiece.
Each gave rise ultimately to a new narrative genre: in the
case of *El Abencerraje*, to the Spanish *novela morisca* and its
European posterity, usually called the Hispano-Moorish
novel, or more simply, the Moorish novel. To be sure, the
itinerary of a genre, i.e., the continuing modification of a formal model, is a process of change. When the object of one's
study, moreover, is a genre with a clear beginning, one ex-
pects to discover considerable differences between the
seminal masterpiece—the innovator—and the later products
for which this prototype acted more as an incitement than as
an established canon to be respectfully imitated. These considerations are especially relevant, I think, to the Moorish
novel and the singular status of *El Abencerraje,* "the first of
the Abencerrajes," the generic model of which I will attempt
a reading in this essay.[1]

A certain dimension of *El Abencerraje* (a dimension only,
to which no one would dare reduce today the entire novel
and its complex, delicate texture) achieved considerable popularity in its time: the figure of the noble, chivalrous Moor

---

[1] Most of this essay has appeared in the Introduction to my edition
of *Lazarillo de Tormes and El Abencerraje* (New York, 1966), pp.
35-47. In addition, I have translated some of the material in a more
detailed article, "Individuo y ejemplaridad en el *Abencerraje*," in
Collected Studies in Honour of Américo Castro's 8oth Year (Oxford,
1965), pp. 175-197.

and the story of his deeds in love and war, set against the splendid but melancholy background of the last years of the Moslem kingdom of Granada. This literary type, and situation, for which there existed numerous precedents in the literature of the Spanish Middle Ages, especially in the ballads and chronicles of the fifteenth century, entered prose fiction for the first time in *El Abencerraje* and, a few years later, was developed by Ginés Pérez de Hita in his famous *Guerras civiles de Granada*. The first part of the latter, actually called *Historia de los bandos de los Zegríes y Abencerrajes,* appeared in 1595; the second, titled *Segunda parte de las guerras civiles de Granada,* in 1619. Both parts of the Spanish original were reprinted numerous times.

These two prose narratives, *El Abencerraje* and *Las guerras civiles de Granada,* made possible the European renown of the sentimental Moor of Granada, as the two coalesced in the imagination of their readers (in a manner somewhat comparable to the emergence of the picaresque model through the joint impact of *Lazarillo de Tormes* and *Guzmán de Alfarache*). The numerous translations of Jorge de Montemayor's *Diana,* to which *El Abencerraje* had been added by an enterprising printer for the 1561 Valladolid edition, were one of the conditions of this development. The various translations and adaptations of Perez de Hita's best seller constituted another. Montemayor's celebrated pastoral was translated into French by Nicole Colin in 1578, into English by Bartholomew Young in 1598, and reprinted in more than one language many times thereafter. In Italy, Francesco Balbi da Correggio wrote in Spanish the *Historia de los amores del valeroso moro Abindarráez y de la hermosa Jarifa* (Milan, 1593), a long epic based on *El Abencerraje* and on the combination of Christian and Moslem characters, as in Ariosto's poem; and during the seventeenth century similar materials were introduced by Celio Malespini into his *Ducento novelle*

(1609). In France, after Pierre Davity's collection *Travaux sans travail* (1599) and the success of Pérez de Hita, the gallant Moor became somewhat of a fad. When Voiture visited Spain in 1602, his fascination with these themes was such that he composed several Spanish ballads in the style of the *romances moriscos* included in Pérez de Hita's book. The title of a novel by Madame de Villedieu, *Galanteries grenadines* (1672), suggests most clearly the spirit in which the story of Abindarráez and Jarifa was probably appreciated by the authors of French seventeenth-century novels in the heroic-sentimental manner: by Mademoiselle de Scudéry in her eight-volume *Almahide* (1660-1663) and especially by Madame de Lafayette in *Zäide, histoire espagnole* (1670), an important step in the art of the author of *La Princesse de Clèves* (1678), which marks, of course, a crucial date in the history of the European novel.

In the eighteenth century the vogue of the Spanish Moor was associated with the beginnings of literary exoticism and its use in the *conte philosophique,* somewhat as the Incas and other extinct cultures were. Florian's *Gonzalve de Cordoue ou Grenade reconquise* (1791) was finished during the French Revolution, and its noble knights proved to be in love with not only the usual Oriental beauties but the notion of liberty. Finally, Chateaubriand's *Les aventures du dernier Abencérage* (1826) obtained considerable popularity and confirmed the credentials of our story, with its combination of gallantry and selflessness, passion and death, as a thoroughly Romantic legend. No other "death of a culture" seemed less painful or more glorious than that of Arabic Andalusia. American readers are most familiar with Washington Irving's tales of *The Alhambra* (1832) and other works in the same vein, which contributed to the general appeal during the nineteenth century of the image of "Moorish" Andalusia as the most seductive and colorful part of Spain.

The vicissitudes of the genre have been studied with care and need no further rehearsal here.[2] At every point, it seems, the framework of the story made possible a certain conjunction of imaginative elements (sentimental or idyllic ones) with allegedly historical developments (the wars of the *Reconquista* in Spain, the decline of the last Moslem kingdom in Andalusia). Thus the first problem the critic meets is the need to elucidate the uses of *history* in Hispano-Moorish fiction. Florian had prefaced his *Gonzalve de Cordoue* with a book-length "Précis historique sur les Maures d'Espagne," and a majority of readers assumed that the tales of love and civil war in Granada blended fiction with events that could be regarded as historical. The Moorish narrative had thus become an early form of the kind of "historical novel" in which legendary and factual materials, past occurrences and contemporary standards mingle comfortably. But this was not always recognized. The type of the Andalusian Moor had given rise to a myth in both the literary and the historical senses of the term, and it seems clear that his appeal was due largely to the enhancement of an attractive fiction by a dramatic historical background, and vice versa. Did this apply also, we may now ask, to the original *El Abencerraje*? How authentic, how relevant is its historicity?

Simple questions such as this barely conceal, I am afraid, an array of difficult problems. I ask my readers to exercise some patience as they consider with me the row of further questions and topics our theme will demand: What components of the Moorish novel were historical? In what ways does the historicity of a literary work manifest itself? Can it

[2] On the history of the Hispano-Moorish novel, cf. Barbara Matulka, "On the European Diffusion of the 'Last of the Abencerrajes' Story in the Sixteenth Century," *Hispania*, xvi (1933), 369-388; María de la Soledad Carrasco Urgoiti, *El moro de Granada en la literatura. Del siglo XV al XX* (Madrid, 1956); and the Introduction to Antonio de Villegas, *El Abencerraje*, ed. F. López Estrada and J. E. Keller (Chapel Hill, N.C., 1964).

be recognized in poems or in stories where the historical in-humanity of man has been exchanged for a vision of justice or an ideal of harmony? Can an effort of the imagination (rather than of "realism") such as the Moorish novel or the pastoral offers, succeed in contradicting (or "negating," in Hegel's and Marcuse's sense) the conditions of contemporary society? Does the eclogue, that most poetic retreat from civil-ization, depend on the city it abhors and would forsake? What are the precise literary means by which the author of *El Abencerraje* constructed his "exemplary" dream world?

I

There are a number of details and particularly of charac-ters in the first of the Moorish novels which, if viewed *sep-arately*, are historical. Rodrigo de Narváez was in fact a famous captain who had contributed decisively to the cap-ture of Antequera by Prince Don Fernando in 1410; as a re-ward he was appointed the governor of that city, which he defended until his death in 1424.[3] The Abencerrajes, of North African origin (the name may have derived from the Banū Al-Sarrādj, whose native town in Spain was Córdoba) were one of the most powerful clans in Arabic Andalusia during the fourteenth and fifteenth centuries, constituting a kind of praetorian guard in Granada.[4] Historians emphasize

[3] On the historical background of *El Abencerraje*, cf. the extensive Introduction by Francisco López Estrada to his edition of *El Aben-cerraje y la hermosa Jarifa* (Madrid, 1957). This is an invaluable study of all main aspects of the subject.

[4] Cf. *ibid.*; Luis Seco de Lucena, "La leyenda de los Abencerrajes," in *Archivos del Instituto de Estudios Africanos*, v (1951), 35-51; and the copious bibliographies on the Abencerraje theme that may be found in Carrasco Urgoiti, *El moro de Granada*; López Estrada's edition; and the edition by Estrada and J. E. Keller. The etymology of "Aben-cerraje" is, as far as I know, not undisputed. The etymon "son of the saddler" ("hijo del sillero") was mentioned early in the sixteenth century, cf. Hernando de Baeza, in *Relaciones de algunos sucesos de los últimos tiempos del Rey de Granada* (Madrid, 1868), p. 9; and

the significance of loyalty to lineage or "spirit of kinship" ("'aṣabiyya," which the fourteenth-century philosopher of history Ibn <u>Kh</u>aldūn regarded as the fundamental motive force in history)[5] among Andalusian Arabs, whose communities were frequently threatened by family clashes and blood feuds. The story of the massacre of the Abencerrajes in Granada, probably in 1472, as a result of palace intrigues, was told in Christian chronicles of the period, albeit briefly and in nearly fictionalized form.[6] These are the two most important historical components in the novel—Rodrigo de Narváez and the Abencerraje clan—although there are others.

On the other hand, Narváez, whom the novelist introduces as the governor of both Alora and Antequera, could not have been the governor of Alora, a city captured from the Arabs in 1484, sixty years after Narváez's death, during the final and successful war against Granada which Ferdinand and Isabella conducted from 1482 to 1492. In the opinion of certain critics, the unknown author of *El Abencerraje* might have confused the first Rodrigo de Narváez with one of his descendants who succeeded him in the governorship of Antequera, or with some other Christian knight who showed

---

maintained today, for example, by Emilio García Gómez in "Sobre los epitafios de dos caballeros Abencerrajes," *Al-Andalus*, vii (1942), 296-297. The second edition of *The Encyclopedia of Islam* (Leyden and London, 1960), i, 98, announces for a later volume "Al-Sarrādj, Banū."

[5] Cf. the article by Francesco Gabrieli in *The Encyclopedia of Islam*, 2nd edn., i, 681; and by the same author, "Il concetto della 'aṣabiyyah nel pensiero storico di Ibn <u>H</u>aldūn," *Atti della R. Accademia delle Scienze di Torino*, lxv (1929-1930), 473-512. On 'aṣabiyya in Andalusia, cf. Julio Caro Baroja, *Los moriscos del reino de Granada* (Madrid, 1957), pp. 47-49.

[6] Cf. Baeza, *Relaciones de algunos sucesos*, p. 9; and Fernando del Pulgar, *Crónica de los Reyes Católicos*, ed. J. de Mata Carriazo (Madrid, 1943), ii, 39.

clemency toward a captured Abencerraje, like the celebrated Don Alonso de Aguilar. Or, what is more likely and entirely characteristic of the author's attitude, it may be that he mingled different periods with considerable freedom, introducing into his story various elements that added a historical flavor and enabled him to use as a background the atmosphere of the "frontier wars" near Granada in the fifteenth century. The principal method adopted by the author was to place a fictional idyll celebrating values similar to those of the romances of chivalry not in a fabulous land and in a remote period, as was usually the case in such novels, but rather in a historical and geographical setting marked by conflict and, above all, very familiar to his readers.

Rodrigo de Narváez was already a renowned, legendary captain when the novel was written. His reputation, as we shall see, plays a role in the story itself. The calamitous end of the Abencerrajes was already a legend in the first half of the sixteenth century. Narváez and the Abencerrajes appeared in well-known *romances fronterizos* (ballads dealing with the frontier wars between Christian Spain and the Moslem kingdom of Granada). Thus, for example, in the ballad "De Granada partió el moro":

> Oído lo había *Narváez*
> que está sobre la barrera,
> y como era buen cristiano,
> el corazón le doliera. . . .[7]

> (This had been heard by *Narváez*,
> Standing right by the wall,
> And as he was a good Christian,
> He felt deep grief in his heart. . . .)

[7] *Romancero español*, ed. L. Santullano (Madrid, 1943), p. 597. The ballads not footnoted are well known and can be found in any collection of *romances*.

Or in the celebrated "Romance de Alhama":

> Mataste los *bencerrajes,*
> que eran la flor de Granada;
> cogiste los tornadizos
> de Córdoba la nombrada. . . .

In Byron's translation ("A Very Mournful Ballad on the Siege and Conquest of Alhama"):

> By thee were slain, in evil hour,
> The Abencerrage, Granada's flower;
> And strangers were received by thee
> Of Cordova the Chivalry. . . .

We also meet the words "la flor de Granada" in *El Abencerraje*: "Hubo en Granada un linaje de caballeros que llamaban los Abencerrajes, que eran la flor de todo aquel reino. . . ." ("In Granada there lived a line of nobles named the Abencerrajes, who were the flower of that entire kingdom. . . .");[8] while we know that the "Romance de Alhama" was published in the *Cancionero de romances* printed in Antwerp in 1550 or earlier. Moreover, not only Rodrigo de Narváez, Prince Don Fernando, and the Abencerrajes, but Alora and Antequera and other Andalusian cities appeared in *romances* and other popular poems of the fifteenth and sixteenth centuries. One need only recall the illustrious "Alora, la bien cercada," dealing with the siege of the city. A "Romance de la pérdida de Antequera" is also one of the older *romances fronterizos* ("La mañana de San Juan, / al tiempo que alboreaba. . . ."), comparable to "De Antequera partió el moro," dealing also with the Christian conquest of the city; while "Suspira por

---

[8] *Lazarillo de Tormes and El Abencerraje,* ed. C. Guillén (New York, 1966), p. 114. (This text will be quoted hereafter.) The English translation used throughout is John Esten Keller's, from the edition by F. López Estrada and Keller. I am grateful to Professor Keller for permission to quote his translation in this discussion.

Antequera / el Rey moro de Granada" offers a thoroughly fictional scene of individual sorrow.[9] In fact, the well-known ability of the Spanish ballad tradition to personalize cities, and to personalize, above all, the loss of a city and the intense nostalgia of the vanquished, is particularly visible in the Antequera poems.

The personification of cities is a trait of classical Arabic poetry, and it leads sometimes to the offer of an exchange between two cities, as if they were women, or of a ransom—for example, in a famous poem by Abū Tammām (805-845) celebrating the capture in 838 of the Byzantine fortress city of 'Ammūriya (Amorium):

> They [the polytheists] had a mother for whom, had they
>   hoped she might be ransomed, they would have
>   given as ransom every loving mother and father,
> Comely of face withal, so fit of physique that she re-
>   duced Chosroes to impotence, and utterly repelled
>   Abū Karib.
> From the age of Alexander or (even) before that—the
>   forelocks of the nights might have become white,
>   yet she has not become white;
> A virgin, deflowered not by the hand of any accident
>   (of fortune), neither has the ambition of time's
>   turns aspired to (possess) her. . . .[10]

---

[9] For the various ballads on the conquest of Antequera, cf. Francisco López Estrada, *La conquista de Antequera en el romancero y en la épica de los siglos de oro* (Seville, 1956), also published in *Anales de la Universidad Hispalense*, xvi (1955), 133-192.

[10] A. J. Arberry, *Arabic Poetry* (Cambridge, Eng., 1965), p. 52. The translation is Professor Arberry's. In the words of Ramón Menéndez Pidal, in *Flor nueva de romances viejos* (Buenos Aires, 1939), p. 244: "los poetas árabes llaman frecuentemente 'esposo' de una región al señor de ella, y de aquí el romance tomó su imagen de la ciudad vista como una novia a cuya mano aspira el sitiador. Esta imagen no se halla en ninguna literatura medieval sino en la castellana. Sólo después, cuando los soldados españoles llevan consigo el Romancero a Alemania y Países Bajos, vemos surgir la concepción de la ciudad sitiada como

In the Antequera ballad cycle, a moving example is "En Granada está el Rey moro" (published by Juan de Timoneda in his *Rosa de amores,* 1573), where the Moorish king goes so far as to offer Granada in exchange for Antequera:

> En Granada está el Rey moro,
> que no osa salir della.
> De las torres del Alhambra
> mirando estaba la vega.
> Miraba los sus moricos,
> cómo corrían la tierra.
> El semblante tiene triste,
> pensando está en Antequera.
> De los sus ojos llorando
> estas palabras dijera:
> —¡Antequera, villa mía,
> oh quién nunca te perdiera!
> Ganóte el rey don Fernando,
> de quien cobrar no se espera.
> ¡Si le pluguiese al buen Rey
> hacer conmigo una trueca,
> que le diese yo a Granada,
> y me volviese a Antequera! . . .[11]

(The Moorish king is in Granada, for he does not dare to leave her. From the towers of the Alhambra, he was looking on his lands. He saw how his own Moors were skirmishing all around. His countenance is afflicted, his thoughts are of Antequera. His eyes weeping all the while, these are the words that he said: "Antequera, my own city, oh who could have ever lost you! King Fer-

---

una novia, ya refiriéndose a Magdeburgo y a su sitiador Walenstein (1629), ora a otras muchas ciudades holandesas, danesas y suecas."

[11] I quote the version in F. López Estrada, *La leyenda de la morica garrida de Antequera en la poesía y la historia* (Seville, 1958), pp. 62-63. (Unless otherwise indicated, translations are my own.)

nando was your conqueror, but one can deal with him
no more. If only it pleased the good king to barter with
me just once! And I would give him Granada, if he returned Antequera! . . .")

And contemporary critics—most recently, Francisco López
Estrada—have justifiably stressed the poetic effectiveness of
the "Morica de Antequera" ballads, the opening of which
(first printed in the *Cancionero llamado flor de enamorados*,
1562) is the couplet:

> ¡Si ganada es Antequera,
> ojalá Granada fuera![12]

> (Ours now is Antequera,
> If only Granada were!)

The appeal of such poetry, evident and overwhelming
though it still is today, must not be forgotten if one is to understand the peculiar historicity of *El Abencerraje*. It seems
clear that the poetic transfiguration of these historical events
and characters—not as an end in itself but as the vehicle of
the poem—had begun much before *El Abencerraje* was composed. They had already been transferred, as it were, to the
popular imagination, and our author was not interpreting
these elements directly so much as he was capitalizing on
their legendary vitality and poetic power.

El Abencerraje did not spring essentially from a transformation of the past, or a longing for it, but from a poetic and

---

[12] Cf. the study by López Estrada, *La leyenda de la morica*. It should
also be recalled that, after *El Abencerraje* was printed, and after "new"
ballads were composed using its materials, the *romances* of Antequera
and the Abencerraje legend continued to be associated and to be
presented jointly to the readers. The Cracow Library preserves a rare
pliego suelto or chapbook called *Romance de la hermosa Xarifa y
Abindarráez que comiença La mañana de San Juan. Con las Coplas del
Vil muy sentidas, y otras: Si ganada es Antequera. Y Despierta, Juan,
por tu fe*, printed in Granada by Hugo de Mena in 1573. See also
López Estrada, *La leyenda de la morica*, p. 28.

fictional effort which succeeded in offering, above all, a forceful contrast with the historical present. This is a contrast based not only on the conventionality or the "unreality" of the novel as a fictional creation but on a polarity of values. (The former—a writer's freedom from the limits of social experience—is of course a condition of the latter—the liberation of an audience of readers from prevailing contemporary values.) The readers of *El Abencerraje* around 1560 must have been highly sensitive to the image of tolerance that the novel proposed, particularly the dissidents and *cristianos nuevos* (Christians of Semitic origin), who were painfully aware of the problem posed by the presence in their midst of thousands upon thousands of *moriscos* (Spanish descendants of the Moors, many of whom still lived as Moslems) and by the simultaneous suppression through *raison d'Etat* of all religious and ideological differences. In *El Abencerraje*, which was probably written between 1550 and 1560 (though the best version was published in 1565 as part of a miscellany by Antonio de Villegas entitled *Inventario*),[13] the

[13] Four different versions of *El Abencerraje* were printed in the sixteenth century, of which only the last three are dated. Though the first two are clearly older and related to each other, critics do not agree on their chronological order. The four texts are: (1) *Parte de la corónica del ínclito infante don Fernando*—the first words on the title page of a book written and printed probably between 1550 and 1561. This book includes a long dedication by an anonymous "corrector" to his master Don Jerónimo Ximénez de Embún, and may have been published in Zaragoza. It exists today in only one copy, of which the last third is missing. Artistically it is a clumsy adaptation, of inferior quality. (2) A very similar text printed in Toledo in 1661 by Miguel de Ferrer. The first page of the only extant copy is missing, but the rest is complete. It includes the dedication to Ximénez de Embún by his servant. It provides us with a slightly more satisfactory form of the *Corónica*. (3) A text that was added to an edition of the celebrated *Diana* of Jorge de Montemayor, in Valladolid, 1561, probably by the printer Francisco Fernández de Córdoba. Montemayor had died in Italy a few months earlier. This is the version which was most widely read, as it was reprinted many times together with the *Diana*. It elaborates a great deal on earlier texts, particularly when the subject

ethical energies released by friendship and love overcome all
collective divisions caused by religion, culture, national antagonisms, and war. The author's vision of personal understanding among enemies, of individual contact and sympathy
despite religious or racial differences, by means above all of

---

is love, in keeping with the rhetoric of Montemayor's pastoral. (4) The
text included in the *Inventario* by Antonio de Villegas, published in
1565 in Medina del Campo by Francisco del Canto. An enlarged edition of the book appeared in 1577, in the same city, with no substantial
changes in *El Abencerraje* (though its title later became the most widely
accepted one: *El Abencerraje y la hermosa Jarifa*).

As texts 1 and 2 are similar, we really have three types. Each of these
differs considerably from the other two. The editor of the *Diana*, for
example, added a love poem in seven stanzas; Antonio de Villegas, the
tale of the affair between Narváez and a married woman. The modern
critic must therefore make a choice. Fortunately it is not a difficult
one. In almost everyone's opinion one of the three versions is indubitably superior to the others. The elegance, the concision, the poetic
unity that we admire in *El Abencerraje* are to be found, above all, in
Villegas' *Inventario*.

The question of authorship is very far from being solved. Villegas
doubtless retouched the version we find in his book, this being sufficient
proof of his stylistic competence. In recent years F. López Estrada and
Marcel Bataillon have been inclined to think that Villegas, furthermore,
was the original author. This is an attractive hypothesis, as Villegas
was a fine poet in his own right, though a gloomy one. But the
Inventario is a miscellany of poetry and prose, as the title suggests,
and there is not enough internal evidence to prove beyond doubt that
a single hand was responsible for the entire collection. In fact, certain
passages in the Villegas *El Abencerraje* can be clarified or improved
by comparison with the other texts. The same applies to the other two.
Thus a second possibility has been mentioned, that of a lost text, or
series of texts, on which our three extant types would have been based.
This idea is badly in need of proof but does not contradict any of the
facts we know. Thirdly, it has been suggested that Villegas himself
was the author of the lost original manuscript; when the *Corónica*
and the *Diana* appeared in 1561, he would have decided to recast and
improve his own text for publication—an ingenious idea, but the most
hypothetical of all. Besides, it does not account for the few cases in
which the *Inventario* version is not as clear as the others (see note 101
to my edition of *El Abencerraje*). For further details and bibliography
(M. Bataillon, A. Rumeau, K. Whinnom, F. López Estrada), cf. my
article "Individuo y ejemplaridad en el *Abencerraje*," p. 18, note 42.

individual self-mastery, is expressed most simply in the concessive clause that appears twice in the text: "aunque las leyes sean diferentes" ("though our religions may be different").

In 1559 two sumptuous autos-da-fé were celebrated in Valladolid—the second, on October 8, attended by the young monarch Philip II—and a comparable one took place in Seville, where a large number of persons, *because* their "leyes" were different, were disgraced, whipped, garroted, burned alive. *El Abencerraje,* in other words, exemplifies the capacity of the literary imagination for historical contradiction, or for contradiction through historical allusiveness.

It could be retorted that *El Abencerraje* embodies the memory of, or a nostalgia for, the more humane forms of existence belonging to earlier times in Spain, as preserved in poetic folklore or the prose chronicles of the fifteenth century, and that it is basically a carry-over from the past. This apparently sensible position calls, in turn, for a fourfold reply. First, it should be quite clear that these relics from the past, which *El Abencerraje* supposedly gathers, are not historical documents or the genuine material of history. They have been transfigured, as we have just seen, into poetry. The values inherited by *El Abencerraje* could only be of the sort that literature and folklore are able or likely to convey. Secondly, it seems just as evident that only those values are "carried over" to the present which a continuing effort of the will preserves as pertinent to its own aspirations and contemporaneous surroundings. (Even a conservative attitude tends, as we know, to echo and expand a primary response to the present.) This applies especially to folklore, since the status of a folkloric piece coincides necessarily with its renewed acceptance by a certain community: as Petr Bogatyrev and Roman Jakobson once pointed out, not only the deviant or the startlingly new—say, a Sade or Lautréamont—but the merely individual ceases immediately to exist in the area of folklore unless it proves to be socially functional and sanctionable.[14]

We have, thirdly, some historical evidence at our disposal. Although the question of *El Abencerraje*'s origins—its authorship and earliest appearance in print—remains obscure, the precious few facts we have establish a link between the novel and its contemporary audience. The anonymous *El Abencerraje* has come down to us in four different printed versions, of which one of the oldest is entitled *Parte de la corónica del ínclito infante don Fernando*—the first words of the title page of a little book set in Gothic type, written and published, as far as we know, between 1550 and 1561, and printed probably in Zaragoza, the capital of Aragon. This book includes a long dedication by an anonymous "corrector" to his master Don Jerónimo Ximénez de Embún, a "caballero mesnadero" or minor nobleman from Aragon. Ximénez de Embún was the lord of the small towns of Bárboles, Oitura, and Cascallo (southwest of Zaragoza), and of other lands in Figueruelas and Alagón.[15] Now, Bárboles and Oitura are located in a district called La Almunia de Doña Godina, which was inhabited almost exclusively by *moriscos* during the sixteenth century—that is, until their final banishment in 1610. According to the census that was taken at the time of their expulsion, the little village of Bárboles (which still boasts today a church tower of unmistakable Islamic flavor) had forty-two Moorish households.[16] The prosperity of these

[14] Cf. Jakobson and Bogatyrev, "Die Folklore als eine besondere Form des Schaffens" (1929), reprinted in R. Jakobson, *Selected Writings* (The Hague and Paris, 1966), IV, 1-15.

[15] Cf. F. López Estrada, "El 'Abencerraje' de Toledo, 1561," *Anales de la Universidad Hispalense*, XIX (1959), 47ff.

[16] Cf. Henri Lapeyre, *Géographie de l'Espagne morisque* (Paris, 1959), p. 109. According to J. M. Lacarra, approximately a fifth of the population of Aragon—some 64,000 *moriscos*—were expelled in 1610. And a large part of the *morisco* literature that has remained from the sixteenth century is Aragonese. Cf. J. M. Lacarra, "La repoblación del valle del Ebro," in *La reconquista española y la repoblación del país,*

fertile, well-irrigated lands depended on the expertness and capacity for toil of the Moorish inhabitants. Thus there was an economic foundation for the sympathy which a landowner like Ximénez de Embún showed for the *moriscos* who tilled his fields. The nobles' attempts to defend the descendants of the Moors and prevent their expulsion are recounted in such documents as the trial of Don Sancho de Cardona, admiral of Aragon, who was prosecuted by the Inquisition on account of his advocacy of the *morisco* cause.[17] Especially in Aragon, financial self-interest and cultural protection were closely related.[18] Thus it does not seem surprising that an early version of *El Abencerraje* should have been prepared for, and dedicated to, just such an Aragonese nobleman. Don Jerónimo Ximénez de Embún was, besides, a man bold and courageous enough to address an official protest to the Inquisition concerning the treatment of the descendants of the Arabs, despite the fact that he was himself—as Francisco López Estrada has discovered—a *cristiano nuevo* of partly Jewish origins.[19]

We should not allow ourselves to forget, fourth, when

---

ed. J. M. Lacarra et al. (Zaragoza, 1951), p. 68: "todavía en el siglo XVI había pueblos enteros en que, salvo el cura, el notario y el tabernero, todos sus habitantes eran moriscos y alardeaban de su condición y de su fe, y cuando se decretó su expulsión in 1610, varios pueblos y aldeas quedaron totalmente despoblados." I wish to thank the parish priest of Bárboles, Mosén Luis Andués Romero, for his information and assistance. He has pointed out to me the interesting fact that his parishioners, though generally devout, have to this day remained singularly indifferent to the adoration of images and saints.

[17] Cf. Pascual Boronat, *Los moriscos españoles y su expulsión* (Valencia, 1901), i, 443ff.

[18] Cf. "Los moriscos aragoneses, según un autor del siglo XVII," in Caro Baroja, *Razas, pueblos y linajes* (Madrid, 1957), p. 84.

[19] Cf. López Estrada, "El 'Abencerraje' de Toledo, 1561," 51; Antonio Paz y Melia, *Papeles de Inquisición*, 2nd edn. (Madrid, 1947), no. 1434, p. 459; and Julio Caro Baroja, *Los judíos en la España moderna y contemporánea* (Madrid, 1961), ii, 262.

speaking of the Moorish novel, that the historicity of a work of literature is not necessarily a function of its uses of the *past*. (We mean by historicity, in this context, the role of the social, political, economic processes of a society not as the humus or the origin but as a basic dimension of a finished literary work.) The historical imagination cannot be defined by the degree to which it is retrospective, past-oriented, memory-bound. It issues just as genuinely from a human being's commitment to his own time, from his involvement in the "life" around him—the lives, the processes, and the durations that envelop his own. Several instances of this—to broaden our frame of reference for a moment—come readily to mind. In the twentieth century, a number of intellectual disciplines demonstrate the looseness of the relationship that exists between the historical imagination and chronological distance. These are disciplines that make it possible to investigate a period in the past without a substantial interest in history. An event or a document of the Renaissance may be interpreted nonhistorically by an anthropologist, a structural linguist, a formalist in literary criticism. On the other hand, the opposite occurs in epochs that are permeated with a historical sensibility. The nineteenth century provides the most splendid instances of the ability to view contemporary matters through the keenest of historical intelligences. The novels of Balzac, Stendhal, Turgenev, Dostoevsky, Galdós—nearly all the great nineteenth-century novelists, in fact—illustrate this point. It has long seemed to me that the distinction between Galdós' *novelas contemporáneas* (dealing with contemporary settings) and his *episodios nacionales* (depicting chronologically the history of Spain since the Battle of Trafalgar) was not profound. I am aware of the special tasks the historical novelist, properly speaking, chose to confront; but the admirers of Manzoni and Scott will admit without difficulty that the genre of the historical novel shared an important dimension of historicity with other genres whose materials, décors, or formal strategies were not *expressly* dependent on political, social, or economic events.

These literary phenomena cover, to be sure, a wide range. As a preliminary approach to this variety of works and forms, it may be helpful to apply the following categories: on the one hand, the distinction between *present* and *past*, as referential objects for a literary work; and, on the other, the distinction between *implicit* and *explicit* techniques, as modes of reference to these objects. In this manner, we may observe that a poem denotes the present while connoting the past as a historical object; that a novel narrates social or political events from the past while alluding much more significantly to the readers' and the author's own time, and so on. *El Abencerraje,* in this sense, appears to exemplify a certain sort of literary paradox: its explicit uses of the past (filtered essentially through folklore) offer a link with history and an experience of history less authentic and less meaningful than its implicit responses to the present.

This paradox is not incidental or fortuitous. It manifests for us on this occasion one of the most important and original features of the *literary* work of art in general. This is the power of suggestiveness with which every student of literature is familiar, because it spans the history of poetic forms from Sappho to Mallarmé and the modern Symbolist tradition, from the medieval mystical treatise to the Romantic fragment, the plays of Chekhov, the contemporary short story or prose parable. As I have tried to show in another essay,[20] the verbal artifact is fundamentally *allusive* because it possesses the potential (which may or may not be fulfilled) for conveying meanings or achieving effects that are never quite stated or made explicit. The verbal work of art is able to communicate infinitely more than what it audibly "says" in so many words. This broader, expanding range of effects is at-

---

[20] Cf. "Stylistics of Silence," pp. 221-279 of this volume.

tained not in spite of the fact that the writer failed to develop his meaning, but because he chose to be concise or indirect. Some of the techniques of allusiveness are very plain indeed: dramatic or narrative irony; abrupt or truncated endings; dialogue, not only on the stage but in the short story, ballad, poetic epistle, or epistolary novel; the use of a sequence of events to create a situation which can then be made to "overflow" beyond the characters' visible actions and articulated words; clashing themes or clusters of themes, unresolved paradoxes, dynamic metaphors, and so on. What is more arduous is to perceive and study the general ways in which the meanings of a verbal work of art are conveyed *not by its explicit components* but by the interrelationships existing among them. The explicit components are linguistic utterances or discourses of varying length but of necessarily concentrated character, since articulated speech must function, of course, in temporal progression and within necessary limits or constraints. They are, in brief, both partial and verbal. And they derive from linguistic strategies that constitute, generally speaking, what we usually call *style*. The interrelationships among these components, on the other hand, based though they are on language, are essentially tacit, implicit, "silent." They make possible the structures that reverberate in the reader's mind between and above the sounds. These unifying, ultralinguistic relations constitute the especially "literary" or artistic constructions we usually call "*form*." They are, as such, expressive and aesthetically functional, even though they may not coincide at any moment with a single linguistic utterance, a single image, a single event or dramatic situation. Thus the literary work of art uses language in order to transcend it; and it develops a style in order to surpass it. The allusive techniques I have just described are but one aspect of the tendency of the literary artifact to assemble forms that are highly expressive and, beyond a certain point, silent and *metaverbal*.

II

The Moorish novel, then, does not occupy a peculiar position in the history of literature. *El Abencerraje* alludes to contemporary history by means of silent contradictions. It offers a vision of peace and unity against the background of past wars between Christians and Moslems, while connoting contemporary struggles and religious conflicts. It has this dimension and this effect in common with other literary genres and modes, of which the oldest and probably the most central and enduring is the pastoral. The idyllic dream of *concordia* emerging from *discordia* is an exercise in dialectics which often is much more than implicit. In his *Philosophy of History* Hegel affirms that one of the conditions of historical progress is the fact that imperfection involves the very opposite of itself—perfection—as a seed, impulse, or potentiality, and that this contradiction goes on to be annulled or resolved in time.[21] It seems evident, conversely, that a fictional picture of perfection is experienced by the reader or the spectator as the antithesis of the imperfections among which he lives. As far as the pastoral is concerned, it has traditionally held forth the most stylized of alternatives to ordinary experience—the singing shepherd's Arcadia—while giving voice to the most ordinary and profound longing for peace, innocence, and happiness. It is the honesty of the longing, the urgency of the dream, and the ways in which they imply their origins in sorrow and frustration, that make the best pastoral poems more than artificial attempts to emulate the structural beauties of Virgil.

In a brilliant essay on the pastoral, "The Oaten Flute," Renato Poggioli comments at length on an episode in Tasso's *Gerusalemme Liberata* (Bk. vii), "Erminia's stay among the shepherds," as an example of what he calls the "pastoral

[21] Cf. *Vorlesungen über die Philosophie der Geschichte*, ed. Theodor Litt (Stuttgart, 1961), p. 109.

oasis": Erminia, a maiden disguised in armor in order to save Tancredi, a wounded knight whom she loves, flees a group of pursuing Crusaders and takes refuge in an isolated community in the woods. These oases or interludes, in which happiness and peace are inserted in a framework of injustice and war, appear in the *Aeneid*, the *Divina Commedia* ("Qui sarai tu *poco tempo* silvano . . ." [*Purg.*, Canto xxxii]), *Orlando Furioso, Os Lusiadas, Don Quixote, As You Like It*: "pastoral poetry," Poggioli explains, "makes more poignant and real the dream it wishes to convey when the retreat is not a lasting but a passing experience, acting as a pause in the process of living, as a breathing spell from the fever and anguish of being."[22] In other words, the pastoral as interlude within a broader literary work makes most explicit its antithetical role. But this is evidence for the dynamics of the bucolic aspiration in general, which is an "invitation," as Poggioli stresses, to seek truth and peace of mind by forsaking the strife of civil war and social living.[23] Within the *Gerusalemme* or *Don Quixote*, the genre acts as countergenre. But this is a function of its ability to counter history.

The third and fourth lines of Virgil's First Eclogue (of which Ernst Robert Curtius writes, with characteristic enthusiasm, that it is an essential key to the literary history of Europe: "from the first century of the Empire to the time of Goethe, all study of Latin literature began with the first eclogue")[24] express, as the poem begins, *historical* flight and loss: "nos patriae fines et dulcia linquimus arva,/ nos patriam fugimus." Meliboeus addresses Tityrus, contrasting the latter's fate with his own. Tityrus, an old slave, lies at ease in the shade—"lentus in umbra"—playing his music, for he has been

---

[22] "The Oaten Flute," *Harvard Library Bulletin*, xi (1957), 154.

[23] Cf. *ibid.*, pp. 147-150.

[24] Cf. *Europäische Literatur und lateinisches Mittelalter* (Bern, 1948), p. 195. I quote from the translation by Willard R. Trask (New York, 1953), p. 190.

to Rome and gained his freedom. Meliboeus has been banished from his house and fields, and while the first image offered by the poem is that of Tityrus' peaceful repose, this image is intensified by the emotional involvement of the speaker, the exiled Meliboeus, a victim of strife and *war*:

> Tityre, tu patulae recubans sub tegmine fagi,
> silvestrem tenui musam meditaris avena:
> nos patriae fines et dulcia linquimus arva,
> nos patriam fugimus: tu, Tityre, lentus in umbra
> formosam resonare doces Amaryllida silvas.

(Tityrus, thou where thou liest under the covert of spreading beech, broodest on thy slim pipe over the Muse of the woodland: we leave our native borders and pleasant fields; we fly our native land, while thou, Tityrus, at ease in the shade teachest the woods to echo fair Amaryllis.)

The same polarities—repose and movement, song and exodus, peace and war—reappear in the Ninth Eclogue: "but our songs, Lycidas," regrets Moeris, "have no more power among warring arms than Chaonian doves, as they say, when the eagle comes":[25]

> . . . sed carmina tantum
> nostra valent, Lycida, tela inter Martia, quantum
> Chaonias dicunt aquila veniente columbas.

At this point the bucolic song, which is both the framework and the climax of the pastoral, is not considered capable of dispelling the disasters of war. It is well known that the idyllic picture of happiness and innocence is but one moment in a long process of conflict and purgation that Virgil bequeathed to European literature as the overall framework of

---

[25] I quote here and above from J. W. Mackail's translation, *Virgil's Works* (New York, 1934), pp. 265, 291.

the pastoral. As the reader progresses through the *Eclogues* (as arranged for publication by Virgil in 38 or 37 B.C.),[26] he traverses a sequence of different stages or levels of poetic fiction. I have just noted that the first of these phases, introduced by the First Eclogue, is historical, evoking the ways in which civil disorders reach and threaten man in his well-being. In a recent summary, Jacques Perret calls this phase "les épreuves de la terre" (following Paul Maury).[27] The Second Eclogue, he adds, concentrates on "les épreuves de l'amour," and the great sorrows they bring. The Third Eclogue displays the liberating effects and beauties of song (that is, art as theme, experience and power within art): "dans un cadre que rien ne saurait venir troubler, c'est le divin loisir. Nous sommes ici au niveau de la pastorale, dans cet univers qui s'ébauche chez Théocrite, qui s'épanouira dans l'Europe du XVIe siècle."[28] In the Fourth Eclogue the shepherds' music goes on to encompass prophecy and myth, "révélations surnaturelles." The Fifth Eclogue presents the apotheosis and spiritual ascent of Daphnis, the ideal shepherd, of whom Gallus, the unworthy, the exile from Arcadia, is the inversion and "antitype" in the Tenth Eclogue. Between the Fifth and the Tenth Eclogues, it appears that the process we have just seen, from the disorders of history to the triumphant harmony of the spirit, is reversed.

Contemporary scholars, from Paul Maury to Jacques Perret and Brooks Otis,[29] have made much of these extraordinary

[26] Cf. Brooks Otis, *Virgil* (Oxford, 1963), p. 97. The manner in which the growing distance from the reality of country life in Virgil's Arcadia goes hand in hand with a certain approximation to history and "truth" is expressed sensitively by Friedrich Klingner in his *Virgil* (Zurich and Stuttgart, 1967), p. 14.

[27] Cf. Jacques Perret, *Virgile* (Paris, 1965), Chap. II.

[28] *Ibid.*, p. 16.

[29] Cf. Paul Maury, "Le secret de Virgile et l'architecture des Bucoliques," *Lettres d'Humanité*, III (1944), 71-147; Perret, *Virgile*, pp. 15-24; Otis, *Virgil*, pp. 128-143.

structural symmetries (the Ninth Eclogue being an echo of the First, the Eighth of the Second; the Seventh of the Third; the Sixth of the Fourth; with the Fifth, the apotheosis of Daphnis, in the center, and the Tenth as a reversal of the Fifth), and it is not for the layman to comment upon such intricacies. It is enough, for the purposes of this essay, simply to stress two basic dimensions of the *Eclogues*: their historicity; and the dynamics of their total form. The threshold (the First Eclogue) and the final stage (the Ninth and the Tenth) dramatize the conflict between contemporaneous history and song. The outer covering of the poetic structure is historical, and the reader must journey through it. Nothing is more erroneous than a static view of bucolic fiction. The pastoral dream, as Virgil reshaped it and transmitted it to his successors, falls far short of offering a picture of happiness, innocence, and perfection only. The poets of the Renaissance were able to bring considerable power to their longings for peace and harmony by inserting them within the traditional dynamics of the pastoral.

Garcilaso de la Vega's *Egloga primera*, the most celebrated and influential poem of the Spanish Renaissance, was published not long before *El Abencerraje* (in 1543, in the posthumous *Las obras de Boscán y algunas de Garcilaso de la Vega*), and I should recall briefly its uses of the dynamics of the pastoral. It follows very closely the structure of Virgil's Eighth Eclogue, which, as we have just seen, echoes the Second Eclogue and its emphasis on the "trials of love." But this phase in Virgil was preceded by the image of contemporary history and the "trials of the earth" (the First and Ninth Eclogues). Garcilaso, within a single eclogue, maintains the same movement, as the reader proceeds from historical fact to the sorrows of fictional love. The extensive dedication to the Viceroy of Naples, at the start of the *Egloga primera,* evokes war and Spanish imperial history as the polar opposite of *otium*, poetic leisure, music. It also anticipates the poet's own death within the same introductory framework, which is not only historical, collective, or remote, then, but individual and profoundly temporal as well. Historical events and individual experience are not merely balanced by means of an ordinary polarity between *negotium* and *otium*, war and peace—they touch and mingle in the common dimension of time:

> . . . espera, que *en tornando*
> a ser restitüido
> al ocio *ya* perdido,
> luego verás ejercitar mi pluma
> por la infinita innumerable suma
> de tus virtudes y famosas obras,
> > *antes que me consuma,*
> faltando a ti, que a todo el mundo sobras.
>
> *En tanto que este tiempo que adivino*
> viene a sacarme de la deuda, un día,
> que se debe a tu fama y a tu gloria . . . ,
> > y *en cuanto* esto se canta,
> escucha tú el cantar de mis pastores.

(. . . *wait*, for *when again* I have been restored to my lost leisure, you will see my pen devoted at once to the infinite sum of your virtues and famous deeds, *before* I die, neglecting you, who exceed everyone. *While this time which I foresee is approaching*, to discharge me *some day* of the debt which is owed to your fame and glory . . . , and *until* this is sung, listen to the song of my shepherds.)[30]

It is only from this history-framed presentiment of the poet's death that the fictional time of the eclogue, covering a single day, from sunrise to sunset, is allowed to emerge.

[30] I quote Elias Rivers' translation in his *Renaissance and Baroque Poetry of Spain* (New York, 1966), pp. 53-58.

The cycle of the day is, traditionally, a support for poetic conceptions of harmony and cosmic order. It spans in the *Egloga primera*, as in Virgil's Eighth Eclogue, the songs of two shepherds. The lament of Garcilaso's first shepherd, Salicio, whose passion is unrequited, remains essentially within the limits of the "trials of love," though it also brings into question the liberating effects of music and art (the level, in Maury's view, of Virgil's Third and Seventh Eclogues). Salicio's feelings are earthbound, horizontal in their career, doomed to wandering and roaming, like the endlessly flowing river which is the prevailing symbol of his song. Generally, Salicio's words are attuned to the flow of the neighboring water. At one point, especially, he recalls that he once dreamed of a river that had lost its course:

> sin saber de cuál arte,
>   por desusada parte
> y por nuevo camino el agua se iba;
> ardiendo yo con la calor estiva,
> el curso enajenado iba siguiendo
>   del agua fugitiva.

(Not knowing how it happened, the water would change its course and flow another way; burning with the summer heat, I would try to follow the diverted course of the fleeing water.)

Here the commonplace of the "topsy-turvy world"—the "impossibles" or *adynata* of Theocritus (as in the Idyll 1, line 132, followed by Virgil in line 26 of the Eighth Eclogue)[31]—is placed in a dream, personalized and adapted to a song in which rivers and tears flow constantly but with no visible end in sight. But Salicio complains in vain. Unlike Alphesiboeus, the *last* shepherd in Virgil's Eighth Eclogue,

[31] Cf. Otis, *Virgil*, pp. 116-118; and Curtius, *European Literature and the Latin Middle Ages*, Chap. v, p. 7.

he fails to charm back and recover his lost love through the orphic power of song (although he awakens the compassion of nature). The effects of singing, which are all joy in the "third stage" of Virgil's eclogues, are presented but also restricted by Garcilaso.

In contrast, the following stages are introduced as the spiritual progression of Nemoroso, whose song closes the *Egloga primera*. Though the natural dimensions of the bucolic poem persist in the lament of Nemoroso, they portray the mutability not of the heart but of all reality, and speak not of psychological but of metaphysical error. Instead of a "horizontal" river, the sun is now the prevailing symbol—of vertical ascent and truth. It implies, in the simple words of Lorenzo de' Medici, "il sole della donna mia."[32] For those forms of spiritual Renaissance humanism of which Neoplatonism is the best representative, light is the bearer of truth,[33] and a ladder permitting the soul's ascent toward absolute Beauty through love. Nemoroso sings:

> como al partir del sol la sombra crece,
> y en cayendo su rayo se levanta
> la negra escuridad que el mundo cubre,
> de do viene el temor que nos espanta
> y la medrosa forma en que se ofrece
> aquella que la noche nos encubre,
>   hasta que el sol descubre
>   su luz pura y hermosa:
>   tal es la tenebrosa

---

[32] Cf. Lorenzo de' Medici, *Opere*, ed. A. Simioni (Bari, 1939), p. 45. This is the prose commentary on the sonnet "Quel, che'l proprio valore e forza eccede. . . ."

[33] Cf. C. C. Gillispie, *The Edge of Objectivity* (Princeton, 1960), p. 88; and on light metaphysics in general, "Luz," in José Ferrater Mora, *Diccionario de filosofía*, 5th edn. (Buenos Aires, 1965), II, 99ff.; and Joseph A. Mazzeo, "Light Metaphysics, Dante's 'Convivio' and the Letter to Can Grande della Scala," *Traditio*, XIV (1958), 191-229.

> noche de tu partir, en que he quedado
> de sombra y de temor atormentado,
> hasta que muerte el tiempo determine
> que a ver el deseado
> sol de tu clara vista me encamine.

(As upon the sun's departure shadows lengthen and when its rays go down there rises the black darkness that covers the world, whence comes the fear that strikes us and the terrible shapes assumed by those which the night conceals from us, until the sun reveals its pure and lovely light: so is the shadowy night of your departure, in which I am left tormented by shadow and fear, until death shall set the time which will take me to see the longed-for sun of your fair sight.)

Here the natural course of the sun, as described in the first part of the stanza, has become but the vehicle of the poet's symbolic meaning. The cycle of the day, no longer a support for natural harmony, yields to the metaphysics of light and the dark night of *this* world, of earthly reality alone. The outer sun yields to the inner light of understanding precisely as night is about to fall.

I know of no better presentation of the cycle of the day as spiritual process—and hence, of the *Egloga primera*—than the following passage from Hegel's lectures on the *Philosophy of History*:

"Imagination has often pictured to itself the emotions of a blind man suddenly becoming possessed of sight, beholding the bright glimmering of the dawn, the growing light, and the flaming glory of the ascending Sun. The boundless forgetfulness of his individuality in this pure splendor, is his first feeling—utter astonishment. But when the Sun is risen, this astonishment is diminished; objects around are perceived, and from them the individual proceeds to the contemplation of his own inner being, and thereby the advance is made to the perception of the relation between the two. Then inactive contemplation is quitted for activity; by the close of day man has erected a building constructed from his own inner Sun; and when in the evening he contemplates this, he esteems it more highly than the original external Sun. For now he stands in a conscious relation to this Spirit, and therefore a free relation."[34]

The acute experience of time and the forebodings of death ("En tanto que este tiempo que adivino") with which the poem began, now rejoin the setting of the sun ("el tramontar del sol") as the poem quietly ends. Garcilaso has integrated into the basic setting, form, and images of his great eclogue the dynamics of the pastoral. And he has thereby traversed within a single poem the stages represented in Virgil by the first four Eclogues and perhaps the Fifth.

In the case of the eclogue as in that of the Moorish novel, the dynamics of form allow a prevailing theme to allude to its opposite in historical reality. Peace, harmony in love, or the light of understanding and truth, imply, within a dynamic form, their origin in war, discord, and darkness. Moreover, a successful poem like the *Egloga primera* shows that these

[34] *The Philosophy of History*, tr. J. Sibree (London and New York, 1900), p. 103; Hegel's words (cf. *Vorlesungen über die Philosophie der Geschichte*, ed. Litt, p. 168) are: "Man hat oft die Szene geschildert, wenn ein Blinder plötzlich sehend würde, die Morgendämmerung schaute, das werdende Licht und die aufflammende Sonne. Das unendliche Vergessen seiner selbst in dieser reinen Klarheit ist das Erste, die vollendete Bewunderung. Doch ist die Sonne heraufgestiegen, dann wird diese Bewunderung geringer; die Gegenstände umher werden erschaut, und von ihnen wird ins eigne Innere gestiegen und dadurch der Fortschritt zum Verhältnis beider gemacht. Da geht der Mensch dann aus tatlosem Beschauen zur Tätigkeit heraus und hat am Abend ein Gebäude erbaut, das er aus seiner inneren Sonne bildete; und wenn er dieses am Abend nun anschaut, so achtet er es höher als die erste äusserliche Sonne. Denn jetzt steht er im Verhältnis zu seinem Geiste und deshalb in freiem Verhältnis."

polarities can be more than rhetorical. As far as Garcilaso is concerned, it has often been said that his poetry implies a kind of balance between "arms" and "studies," *armas y letras, sapientia et fortitudo*—in brief, between the warlike and the intellectual faculties that so-called Renaissance courtiers or gentlemen were expected to reconciliate. It has also been maintained that the joint encomium of *armas* and *letras* was a distinctive feature of the *Siglo de Oro*. In the words of Ernst Robert Curtius: "Nowhere else has the combination of the life of the Muses and the life of the warrior ever been so brilliantly realized as in Spain's period of florescence in the sixteenth and seventeenth centuries—it suffices to call to mind Garcilaso, Cervantes, Lope, and Calderón. All of them were poets who also served in wars. Neither France (excepting Agrippa d'Aubigné, who, however, wrote poetry *invita Minerva*) nor Italy can show anything of the sort. . . . It is the glory of the Spanish empire that there the ideal of *armas y letras* is most highly esteemed.[35] Suddenly one breathes the atmosphere (redolent with mythomania) in which the idea of national literature thrives. The model of literary history implicit in such a context (the legacy of Greece and Rome subdivided into national continuities) is sharply distinct, of course, from the comparatist's: literary history, I would say, as the coexistence and confrontation of international processes and "durations." Whether one considers the Spanish Golden Age as a confrontation of movements and collective styles or not, a minimal requirement is that our concept of the *Siglo de Oro* should admit of historical change. The monistic notion of period as homogeneous synchrony is a special and misleading fallacy of literary history.

The attitude of the poet toward *armas* varied considerably in Spain from the reign of Charles V, the apogee of imperial expansion and crusading fervor, to the last decades of the six-

---

[35] *European Literature and the Latin Middle Ages*, p. 178.

teenth century, as the reign of Philip II drew to a close; and the awareness of exhaustion and decline increased during the seventeenth century. The voices of doubt and disaffection surely grew louder and more numerous as the years went by. But it should be stressed that the tensions and suspicions played from the start a central role in what Américo Castro has portrayed as an "age of conflict" (*edad conflictiva*). Especially in *La realidad histórica de España*, Américo Castro has thrown new light on the inner insecurity, or rather the blending of "inseguridades" and "firmezas," which underlay Spain's moment of international power and the values that made it possible.[36] The voices of criticism, prophecy, and irony are most often, to be sure, those of the *cristianos nuevos*. They led ultimately to such well-known formulations during the seventeenth century as Quevedo's famous sonnets on national decline; or the exhortations in the *Epístola moral a Fabio* (ca. 1613)—long regarded as anonymous—to forsake conquest and economic ambition:

> ¿Piensas acaso tú que fue criado
> el varón para el rayo de la guerra,
> para surcar el piélago salado,
>
> para medir el orbe de la tierra
> o el cerco por do el sol siempre camina?

(Do you perchance think that man was created for war's thunderbolt, to plow the salty sea, to measure the earth's globe or the orbit ever followed by the sun?)[37]

But similar questions were raised much earlier by novelists and poets. At the end of *Lazarillo de Tormes* (1554), the roguish hero ironically tarnishes the military triumphs of

[36] Cf. Américo Castro, *La realidad histórica de España*, 2nd edn. (Mexico, 1962), Chap. III; and *De la edad conflictiva*, 2nd edn. (Madrid, 1961).

[37] *Renaissance and Baroque Poetry of Spain*, ed. and tr. Elias Rivers, p. 255.

Charles V by associating them with his own dishonorable social climbing. Américo Castro quotes a meaningful stanza by the poet Francisco de Medrano (1570-1607) in which the consciousness of greatness and power does not exclude feelings of melancholy concerning *both* war and peace:

> Ya lo muelle nos daña
> de la paz, de la guerra ya la saña.
> España triste gime,
> de la fortuna en la más alta cumbre;
> que la sobra y oprime
> de su gran majestad la pesadumbre;
> y máquinas que el cielo
> no apoya, vienen con su peso al suelo.[38]

(Now the softness of peace harms us, now the fury of war. Spain moans sadly, on the highest pinnacle of Fortune; for it considers superfluous and oppressive the heaviness of its great majesty; and the constructions which heaven does not support, tumble down to earth with their weight.)

The particular tensions I am discussing here, with regard to the Moorish novel and the pastoral, were but a small component, then, of a broader confrontation.

Already in Garcilaso, as we have just seen, the *topos* of "arms" and "studies" is no more than superficial. The balancing of warlike action and poetic leisure at the beginning of the *Egloga primera* is merely a frame, an ordering device; what is actually expressed or conveyed, within the symmetry of the rhetoric, is different from not only the form but the *content* of the commonplace. It has to do with time and the inner presentiment of death. This is the initial emotion and the personal-historical experience from which, on this occasion, the pastoral fantasy will spring. Can the same be ob-

---

[38] As quoted by Castro, *La realidad histórica de España*, p. 100.

served in the later career of the pastoral in Spain? I shall limit myself to suggesting the following "model" for this particular confrontation (as part of a larger confrontation of processes or durations).

As the pastoral grows and comes to full bloom, not long after the death of Garcilaso, it favors especially the form of the extended narrative in prose (interspersed, as in Sannazaro's *Arcadia*, with poetry). The development of the pastoral doubtless coincides with the growth of disaffection and disillusionment in the *edad conflictiva*. It also takes its place within a system of contemporary poetics (more or less "official" or codified) in the area of the prose narrative. The main polarity in this area is that between the romances of chivalry, on one side, and the pastoral, the Moorish novel, and the picaresque, on the other. The romances of chivalry dramatize the warlike virtues in man. As a genre, they reach their peak during the first half of the sixteenth century. *Palmerín de Inglaterra*, published in 1547, is probably the last chivalric romance of real value. The masterpieces of the genre, the Catalan *Tirant lo Blanch* (1490) and *Amadís de Gaula,* were written before the end of the fifteenth century. The career of the romance of chivalry as a literary "duration" goes back, essentially, to the Middle Ages, though it "endures" through the sixteenth century. After *Palmerín de Inglaterra*, toward the middle of the century, its decadence becomes quite clear. The antithesis to the romance of chivalry appears with the publication of three exceptional shorter works between 1550 and 1560: Bernardim Ribeiro's *Menina e moça* (1554), *Lazarillo de Tormes* (1554), and *El Abencerraje* (ca. 1660). Three evolving narrative genres will follow these masterpieces: the pastoral, from Jorge de Montemayor's *Diana* (first published shortly before 1560), Alonso Pérez' *Diana* (1564), and Gil Polo's *Diana enamorada* (1564) to Cervantes' *La Galatea* (1585) and Lope de Vega's *Arcadia* (1598); the picaresque, with Mateo Alemán's *Guzmán de Alfarache*

(1599); and the Moorish novel, with Pérez de Hita's *Historia de los bandos de los Zegríes y Abencerrajes* (1595). All three genres express, though in sharply different ways, a basic dis-affection with contemporary history. When we consider these genres as temporal durations, it seems evident, from a cursory glance at the dates, that the florescence of the pastoral precedes that of the Moorish novel and the picaresque, even as all three concur with, or contribute to, the decline of the romance of chivalry. The final stage in the process is the triumph of the picaresque (whose hero is a born outsider, and a neocynical comedian on the stage of history), which does not begin until 1599, but will last through a large part of the seventeenth century (until Francisco Santos' *Periquillo el de las gallineras*, 1663). Our "model," in short, shows a passage from implicit to explicit techniques as modes of reference to contemporary history.[39]

[39] Did the Moorish novel have any historical impact? When one studies the interaction between historical processes and literary ones, it is important to clarify the effects produced *by* literature on social realities. Bruno Snell went so far once as to say, in *The Discovery of the Mind* (tr. T. G. Rosenmeyer [Cambridge, Mass., 1953], p. 292), that Virgil had strengthened his contemporaries' desire for peace and exerted an influence on the political ideology of the Augustan age. It would require another essay to consider the impact of the Moorish novel as a whole, and I shall indicate very briefly what the working hypothesis for such an essay might be. I would underline the differences existing between *El Abencerraje* and Pérez de Hita's *Guerras civiles de Granada* (1595). The former did not merely portray an idyllic Moor in an idyllic setting, in such a way as to inspire only what Renato Poggioli calls the "pastoral catharsis" (cf. "The Oaten Flute," p. 174): a wish fulfillment purging the reader of the wish to act, or compensating for the renunciations imposed on him by the social order. *El Abencerraje* offered an image—of moral fiber and social communication—of the kind that can touch and "modify" the reader. This positive ethical-historical vision, based on a "double portrait" (not of the Moor alone but of the exemplary Christian hero, Rodrigo de Narváez) no longer plays a central role in the works of Pérez de Hita and his followers. In the meantime, the fashion for the gallant, sentimental Moor had arisen, particularly in the *romancero nuevo* (artistic ballads composed and signed by known writers). In these ballads the Moor

I I I

Only in *El Abencerraje*, then, was Rodrigo de Narváez the governor of *both* Alora and Antequera. Let us begin our reading of the novel by asking why this is so. I have just recalled that cities enjoyed a kind of poetic life in the *romancero*. They played in these ballads an affective, nearly personalized role, as in the exchange between Granada and

---

was isolated and torn out of context. A powerful poetic image—powerful and significant enough not only to contradict but to affect social fact—had yielded to the colorful literary "type" of the gallant Moor.

It is an error to continue speaking, as a number of Hispanists have since Georges Cirot, of *maurophilie littéraire* with regard to these ballads, or Pérez de Hita, or Lope de Vega's *El remedio en la desdicha*. These works could not give voice to any genuine "maurophilia" for the simple reason that they did not postulate the existence of the Moor as such, that is, they did not recognize his identity. It is true that a sense of cultural "otherness" developed during the Renaissance, but only after the Moor had been replaced by the *morisco*, and the Spanish writer had become fixed in medieval attitudes toward the former. The object of the new "anthropological" curiosity would be the Turk in the East (Andrés Laguna's *Viaje de Turquía*), the non-Spanish Moslems of North Africa, the Indians of epic poetry and the chronicles of the conquest of America. But no poet wrote an epic on the subject of the conquest of Granada, which lasted the same number of years as the Trojan War. No *Granada conquistada* or *liberada*, in the manner of Tasso, was written by a Spaniard. When "otherness" appeared in this area, its object was of course the rebellious *morisco* and the immense ghettos in which he lived in Spain, and we know the severity which Cervantes and Lope de Vega, despite their praise of the gallant Moor, showed toward the real *moriscos* at home.

Had *El Abencerraje* been understood better and imitated more fruitfully, racial and religious tolerance might have been strengthened in Spain. But the necessary conditions were lacking for both developments. Basically, the exaltation of the Moorish knight, always a nobleman, was far from being incompatible with a profound scorn for the *morisco*, who was always plebeian. The enthusiastic praise of the gallant Moorish knight—who, in the final analysis, was not different from a Christian nobleman—could only intensify everyone's impatience with the stubborn *moriscos*, who persisted in their faith, their ways, their otherness. As a matter of fact, these contrasts may have facilitated the decision to banish all *moriscos* from Spain in 1610.

Antequera which the king of Granada himself proposes in "En Granada está el Rey moro."[40] Now, Rodrigo de Narváez faces a double responsibility. It is one of the features of the text to multiply such dualisms, not only through the constant rhythmic balancing and fondness for symmetries which are characteristic of the author's hand,[41] but by means of actual situations. When Narváez leaves Alora in search of warlike feats, the road he takes suddenly forks: "y yendo por su camino adelante, hallaron otro que se dividía en dos" ("as they made their way along the road, they found it divided into two ways"). Thus he is obliged to split his forces into two groups, even as he is used to defending both Alora and Antequera—"que tenía a cargo ambas fuerzas, repartiendo el tiempo en ambas partes y acudiendo siempre a la mayor necesidad" ("and therefore he had two fortresses under his command; he divided his time between them and would hasten to the defense of the one in the greater danger")—almost as if they were two persons whom he was pledged to protect. Later, Abindarráez the Moor will find himself divided between the beautiful Jarifa and Narváez himself, an emotional and moral dilemma on which the plot is based. This correspondence between places and persons, between geographical space and the dimensions of love, friendship, or desire, underlies the brief ballad Abindarráez sings:

[40] Cf. Ramón Menéndez Pidal, *Romancero hispánico* (Madrid, 1953), I, 70.

[41] The Abencerraje, for example, carried in his hand a heavy and beautiful lance with *two* points ("una gruesa y hermosa lanza de dos hierros"), the number of the points being the same as the number of adjectives qualifying the lance; the Abencerrajes were killed by the king of Granada because "hizo a dos de estos caballeros un notable e injusto agravio" ("committed against *two* of these gentlemen a notable and serious offense"), i.e., a double offense doubly qualified. But of course the most different situations can be equally symmetrical, and what matters in *El Abencerraje* is the growing process of reconciliation and ethical improvement finding its way through the so-called Renaissance symmetries.

Nacido en Granada,
criado en Cártama,
enamorado en Coín,
frontero de Alora.

(Born in Granada,
Reared in Cártama,
Love-struck in Coín,
On the frontier of Alora.)[42]

The division of the kingdom of Granada into Moslem and Christian cities frames and surrounds the wandering, restless life of the Abencerraje. And the hero's later separation from his beloved Jarifa will reflect the banishment of his entire lineage from the loveliest "woman-city," Granada.

Images of severance, disjunction, disunion are basic and wide-ranging in the story. Human beings, it seems, are in constant peril of separation, spatially and emotionally. This danger threatens not only individuals but entire political or religious communities. One of the aspects of *El Abencerraje* that might have been historically allusive is precisely this experience of history *by* its characters—as conflict and division, which will be superseded ultimately by ethical values of universal, unifying import.

Abindarráez himself is, of course, no mere orphan, individually uprooted. As the last of the Abencerrajes, he is the victim of a kind of total orphanhood, a conclusive break with his entire ancestry (which was destroyed or expelled by the king of Granada). It is surely impossible not to think of other collective disasters, like the expulsion of the Jews in 1492, of

---

[42] The author will underline throughout the work movement in space, on the one hand, and, on the other, haste, delay, temporal urgency. As far as time is concerned, most of the work occupies, like a neoclassical play, less than twenty-four hours; and these hours are filled with a sense of urgency, of the need to engage in valuable actions. Narváez himself will not allow time to pass by in vain ("pasar el tiempo en balde").

which certain Spanish readers must have been reminded by the fate of the Abencerrajes. His ancestors, Abindarráez recalls, were banished by the same king who had favored them earlier (as the Spanish Jews were banished by the class and the king, Fernando the Catholic, who had been their protectors): "vees aquí ... cuántos podrían escarmentar en las cabezas destos desdichados, pues tan sin culpa padecieron con público pregón; siendo *tantos y tales y estando en la favor del mismo Rey,* sus casas fueron derribadas, sus heredades enajenadas, y su nombre dado en el reino por traidor" ("behold here ... how many men could learn through the experience of these unfortunate ones, who blameless suffered public disgrace; *though numerous and powerful as they had been in the king's favor,* their houses were torn down, their estates given into the hands of others, and their name proclaimed traitorous throughout the kingdom"). Abindarráez, at any rate, feels bound to perpetuate and uphold the values of his noble ancestors: "por parescer a aquellos donde vengo, y no degenerar de la alta sangre de los Abencerrajes, antes coger y meter en mis venas toda la que dellos se vertió" ("so as to be worthy of my forbears and so as not to degenerate from the noble blood of the Abencerrajes, but rather to gather and pour into my veins all of theirs that was shed"). Abindarráez remembers and wishes to restore. But he does not, as yet, consciously heal. The images of separation that have just been mentioned are countered, on another level, by a number of moments expressing a basic yearning for unification, for understanding and reconciliation, by means of sentimental and moral impulses; first of all, by the presentation, both intense and delicate, of the hero's love for Jarifa.

The Abencerraje's exile as a boy in Coín was compensated for by the company of motherless Jarifa, in whom he found a sister. The ambiguous theme of brotherhood turned into love, or of the vacillation between the two (a classical theme —Pyramus and Thisbe in Ovid, for example—developed in

Greek romances and in related medieval forms, like the medieval cycle of Floire and Blancheflor, leading to Boccaccio's *Filocolo*),[43] assumes a crucial function in our story. The *amours enfantines* of Abindarráez and Jarifa call to mind the medieval tale of Floire and Blancheflor, who were inseparable:

> Ensemble vont, ensemble vienent
> Et la joie d'amours maintienent
>
> . . . .
> Ensemble lisent et aprennent. . . .[44]

In their childhood Abindarráez and Jarifa were inseparable companions: "nunca me acuerdo haber pasado hora que no estuviésemos juntos. Juntos nos criaron, juntos andábamos, juntos comíamos y bebíamos" ("I can hardly recall an hour that we were not together. Together they reared us, together we walked, together we ate and drank"). Only childhood could permit such extreme closeness. Adult life, by contrast, will mean necessarily the imminence of separation or the need to struggle against it. Childish love represents not only an unconscious Platonic love but a union too perfect to survive in the later years of life. (In Boccaccio's *Filocolo* the

---

[43] Concerning the ambiguous confusion between love and the feeling of brother and sister, one should distinguish between what Cervantes calls in the *Persiles* "hermanazgo fingido," "feigned brotherhood," that is to say, lovers pretending to be brother and sister in order to protect themselves in a dangerous situation or to test their chastity; and the story of two children who are reared as if they were brother and sister. The former can be found in Heliodorus' *Theagenes and Chariclea* and in some of the Spanish sixteenth-century imitations of the Greek romance, like Alonso Núñez de Reinoso's *Clareo y Florisea* (1552), as well as in Scarron's *Roman comique*, Voltaire's *Candide*, and, of course, Genesis 20:2. The latter may be encountered in Longus' *Daphnis and Chloë* and in the cycle of Floire and Blancheflor, as well as in certain classical myths, approaching incest, like the tales of Byblis and Caunus, Yphis and Ianthe in Book IX of Ovid's *Metamorphoses*.

[44] *Floire et Blancheflor*, ed. M. M. Pelan (Paris, 1956), pp. 213-214.

young hero is perfectly happy so soon, so very soon, that he can think of no further goals or reasons for which to live.)[45] Abindarráez and Jarifa will pass from innocence—as brother and sister—to love in the most natural manner, without intermediaries or stratagems for seduction, that is to say, without the trappings of sixteenth-century sentimental novels or of the Spanish imitations of *La Celestina*. Yet a day comes when the most painful of all breaks takes place: the transformation of brotherly love into a "rabiosa enfermedad," a "raging illness," implying both distance and the possibility of sexual desire. This fall from innocence takes place in a garden—an Andalusian earthly paradise fragrant with jasmine—and culminates in the admirably evocative and concise scene of the fountain.

The scene has Platonic and mystical overtones but is neither of the two. Abindarráez dares to express to Jarifa his mixed brotherly feelings, while he averts his eyes and sees her reflection in the waters of the fountain, as well as, he adds, an even truer image in his soul:

"—Hermano, ¿cómo me dejastes tanto tiempo sola?
Yo la respondí:
"—Señora mía, porque ha gran rato que os busco y nunca hallé quien me dijese dó estábades, hasta que mi corazón me lo dijo. Mas decidme ahora, ¿qué certinidad tenéis vos de que seamos hermanos?
"—Yo—dijo ella—no otra más del grande amor que te tengo, y ver que todos nos llaman hermanos.
"—Y si no lo fuéramos—dije yo—¿quisiérasme tanto?
"—¿No ves—dijo ella—que a no serlo, no nos dejara mi padre andar siempre juntos y solos?
"—Pues si ese bien me habían de quitar,—dije yo—más quiero el mal que tengo.

---

[45] Cf. *Il Filocolo*, ed. S. Battaglia (Bari, 1938), p. 74.

Entonces ella, encendiendo su hermoso rostro en color, me dijo:

"—¿Y qué pierdes tú en que seamos hermanos?

"—Pierdo a mí y a vos—dije yo.

"—Yo no te entiendo,—dijo ella—mas a mí me paresce que sólo serlo nos obliga a amarnos naturalmente.

"—A mí sola vuestra hermosura me obliga, que antes esa hermandad paresce que me resfría algunas veces.

Y con esto bajando mis ojos de empacho de lo que le dije, vila en las aguas de la fuente al proprio como ella era, de suerte que dondequiera que volvía la cabeza, hallaba su imagen, y en mis entrañas la más verdadera."

("—Brother, why have you stayed away from me so long?

"—My lady,—I replied—because I have looked for you a long time and could find no one who would tell me where you were, until my own heart told me. But now tell me: how certain are you that we are brother and sister?

"—Only through the great love and affection I have for you,—she said—and seeing that everyone calls us brother and sister.

"—And if we were not—I said—,would you love me as much?

"—Don't you realize—she said—that if we were not, my father would never allow us to be alone together?

"—Then I said:—If they were to take this joy away from me, I would prefer the pain that I suffer.

Then her beautiful face was suffused with color and she said:

"—And what are you losing from the fact that we are brother and sister?

"—Losing you and myself—I replied.

"—I do not understand—she said.—Rather it seems to me that being of the same blood, we are naturally obliged to love one another.

"—Your beauty alone obliges me, for on the contrary that kinship seems to chill me sometimes.
Then I lowered my eyes quickly in embarrassment at what I said, and I saw her in the waters of the fountain just as she was, so that no matter where I turned my head, I found her likeness, and most of all I found it in my heart.")

The passage from one image of Jarifa to another, each less material than the one which preceded it, has been compared by Francisco López Estrada to an "escala platónica." This affinity is as certain, for the Spanish reader, as the memory of a stanza in the *Cántico espiritual* by Saint John of the Cross:

> ¡Oh cristalina fuente,
> si en esos tus semblantes plateados
> formases de repente
> los ojos deseados
> que tengo en mis entrañas dibujados!

(Oh crystal spring, if only in your silvery face you would suddenly let take shape the eyes I long for, which I have engraved in my heart!)[46]

Yet on a literal level, the growth and the climax of the love between Abindarráez and Jarifa will be neither Platonic nor mystical. The union of two persons, the abolition of space as the condition of the severance and the distance existing between not only two communities or two cities but two human beings, is what the characters' desire initially signifies; and this significance need not be extended into any dimension be-

---

[46] *Renaissance and Baroque Poetry of Spain*, p. 132. I thank Professor Raimundo Lida for suggesting this parallel to me. (One may note in passing that Saint John of the Cross took holy orders in Medina del Campo, where Villegas lived and worked, in 1563.) The inevitable and ubiquitous presence of the image of the beloved is also reminiscent, of course, of Petrarch's obsession with Laura *in vita* and *in morte*, cf. *Rime*, cxxvii, 12-14; cxxix, 27-29, 40-48, and *Epistolae metricae*, i, 7, 148: "et liquido visa est emergere fonte. . . ."

yond the earthly one. The multiplication of Jarifa, from a direct visual impression to the reflection in the water of the fountain, to the image in Abindarráez's inner being ("entrañas"), unfolds an obsession: not only the effects of desire but the wish to avoid any separation on the part of the lovers, who are so completely united spiritually. The primacy of the image preserved in the Moor's "entrañas" (a term rather more physical than "alma" or "corazón") indicates both the strength of his emotions and the fact that their object is a complete human being. In their youthful innocence, Abindarráez and Jarifa have perhaps not discovered as yet the "dualism" of body and soul. That the Abencerraje's feelings are neither unphysical nor solely physical, but above all integrative, is powerfully shown by a classical reminiscence.

For the entire scene rests on a discreet allusion to the metamorphosis of Salmacis and Hermaphrodite in Book IV of Ovid's *Metamorphoses* (ll. 285-388):

"Acuérdome que, entrando una siesta en la huerta que dicen de los jazmines, la hallé sentada junto a la fuente, componiendo su hermosa cabeza. Miréla, vencido de su hermosura, y parescióme a Salmacis, y dije entre mí:

—¡Oh, quién fuera Troco para parescer ante esta hermosa diosa!"

("I recall that one day during siesta I entered a garden which was called the Garden of the Jasmines. She was seated at a fountain arranging her beautiful hair. I gazed at her overcome by her loveliness, and she seemed to me like Salmacis. I said to her under my breath:

—Oh, that I might be Trocus to appear before this beautiful goddess!")

And a few moments later:

"Diciendo esto, levantéme, y volviendo las manos a unos jazmines de que la fuente estaba rodeada, mezclándolos con arrayán hice una hermosa guirnalda y, poniéndola sobre mi cabeza, me volví a ella coronado y vencido. Ella puso los ojos en mí, a mi parescer, más dulcemente que solía, y, quitándomela, la puso sobre su cabeza."

("So saying, I arose and setting hand to some jasmines by which the fountain was surrounded, and mingling the blossoms with myrtles, I made a lovely garland and I put it on my head, going to her crowned in defeat. Letting her eyes rest upon me in a way sweeter than usual, she removed the wreath from my head and placed it on her own.")

Abindarráez calls Jarifa a goddess, first of all, because she is so beautiful. But why does he compare her with Salmacis? In Ovid, Salmacis is a rather idle nymph, with hardly any other occupations than combing her hair, bathing, watching herself in the water, picking flowers. The scene of the fountain in *El Abencerraje* preserves some of these details, while it also transforms them. (One need only reread, for example, the translation of Ovid's *Metamorphoses* by Jorge de Bustamante [ca. 1540], where Salmacis is portrayed arranging her hair, bathing, and making garlands to crown herself as in victory.)[47]

The situation is ancient and well known, in literature and folklore. "Innombrables sont les légendes," writes Gaston Bachelard in *L'Eau et les rêves*, "où les Dames des fontaines peignent sans fin leurs longs cheveux blonds."[48] The gift of

[47] Cf. *Las Metamorphoses, o Transformaciones del muy excelente poeta Ovidio* . . . (Antwerp, 1551), fol. 59v. Cf. R. Schevill, *Ovid and the Renaissance in Spain* (Berkeley, Cal., 1913), p. 148. A number of years ago Marcel Bataillon indicated the connection between the text by Bustamante and the scene of the fountain; cf. "Salmacis et Trocho dans 'L'Abencérage,'" in *Hommage à Ernest Martinenche* (Paris, 1936), pp. 361ff., reprinted in *Varia lección de clásicos españoles* (Madrid, 1964).

[48] *L'Eau et les rêves* (Paris, 1947), p. 114. Cf. Paul Sébillot, *Le Folklore en France* (Paris, 1905), II, Chap. 2, "La puissance des fontaines," and p. 200. Sébillot recalls that the primitive Christian churches were

garlands, to celebrate a victory in the arena of love, was frequent in classical literature; but it could also be encountered in the amorous symbolism of Saint John of the Cross:

> De flores y esmeraldas
> en las frescas mañanas escogidas,
> haremos las guirnaldas,
> en tu amor florecidas,
> y en un cabello mío entretejidas.

(Of blossoms and emeralds, gathered on cool mornings, we shall make garlands, flowery with your love and woven together with one of my hairs.)[49]

These unifying symbols—the interweaving of garlands and hair, the association of the water of a fountain with love—support and deepen the allusion to the metamorphosis of the two lovers in Ovid.

The story of Salmacis was familiar in Spain, and had been translated or adapted long before Juan de Mena and Jorge de Bustamante by Alfonso X, El Sabio, in the *General estoria* (thirteenth century). The name of Salmacis' lover, the son of Hermes and Aphrodite, had become since the *General estoria*, mysteriously enough, "Troco."[50] Now, when Abindarráez

---

often built on the site of fountains associated with pagan cults and myths.

[49] *Renaissance and Baroque Poetry of Spain*, p. 134.

[50] Cf. note 20 to my article "Individuo y ejemplaridad en el Abencerraje," as well as M. R. Lida de Malkiel, "*La General estoria*: notas literarias y filológicas," *Romance Philology*, XIII (1959), 7, 25; and Marcel Bataillon in his review of F. López Estrada, *Bulletin Hispanique*, LXII (1960), 202. Trocus evoked the notion of change (Sp. *trocar*, change or exchange), first applied perhaps to Smilax's lover in Ovid, Crocus, who was transformed into a flower; then to Hermaphrodite (the tale of Crocus and Smilax appearing in both Ovid and the *General estoria* just before Salmacis and Hermaphrodite); and then also to the animal *trocus*, which fertilized itself, as in Gr. *trochos*, "wheel," and Sp. *rueda*, "sunfish."

longs to be like Troco, or Trocus, this does not simply mean that he wishes to appear before the goddesslike Jarifa-Salmacis. "Oh, ¡quién fuera Troco para parescer ante esta hermosa Diosa!" ("Oh, that I might be Trocus to appear before this beautiful goddess!")—we read in our text, which is based on Antonio de Villegas' *Inventario*. But the implication is clearer in the *Corónica* version, where the words of the Moor are: "Oh, ¡quién fuese Troco para poder *siempre estar junto* con esta hermosa ninfa!" ("Oh, that I might be Trocus to be *always together* with this beautiful nymph!").[51] For the core of the story in Ovid is this: a young man, the son of Hermes and Aphrodite, has refused the advances of Salmacis, the nymph of a pool. She has asked him, at first, to kiss her like a sister: "*sororia . . . oscula*" in Ovid (Bk. IV, ll. 334-335), or in the *General estoria*, "algunos besos cuemo los leuarie de ti una tu *hermana*."[52] But the nymph of the fable, exactly like the hero of *El Abencerraje*, is not satisfied with mere brotherliness. At her wish her body becomes one with the young man's, in the water of the pool, and a single being, Hermaphrodite, results from their union.

Similarly, young Abindarráez wishes so much to preserve and intensify the closeness he and Jarifa had enjoyed as children, under the guise of being brother and sister, that he associates himself with Trocus. And the author of *El Abencerraje*, in his delicate but bold manner, pursues the theme even further. A few lines later another classical myth, the story of Narcissus, echoes the allusion to Hermaphrodite, just as the latter had been prepared for by the theme of ambiguous brotherly love. We have already read that Jarifa's face

[51] Cf. Keith Whinnom, "The Relationship of the Three Texts of 'El Abencerraje,'" *Modern Language Review*, LIV (1959), 508.

[52] *General estoria*, ed. A. García Solalinde, L. A. Kasten, and V.R.B. Oelschläger (Madrid, 1957-1961), II, 214b. This particular detail in Ovid is missing in the translation by Bustamante and in the prose *glosa* in the *Copilación de todos las obras del famossísimo poeta Juan de Mena . . .* (Toledo, 1548), fol. xvii.

was reflected in the waters of the fountain. Now Abindarráez asks himself what would happen if, unlike Narcissus, who fell in love with his own appearance, he could become one with Jarifa's image on the water—as an alternative, one might say, to the full union experienced by Trocus:

"—Si yo me anegase ahora en esta fuente, donde veo a mi señora, ¡cuánto más desculpado moriría yo que Narciso! Y si ella me amase como yo la amo, ¡qué dichoso sería yo! Y si la Fortuna nos permitiese vivir *siempre juntos*, ¡qué sabrosa vida sería la mía!"

("—If I should now drown myself in this fountain, where I see my lady, how less would I be blamed than was Narcissus! And if she loves me as I love her, how happy I would be! And if Fortune should permit us to live *together forever*, what a delightful life mine would be!")

Again, the ties with Renaissance Neoplatonism are strong. It was common for the Neoplatonic poet to bemoan the incompleteness of the fusion of the lover with his beloved. A powerful instance in Spanish is a sonnet by Francisco de Aldana (1537-1578):

> ¿Cuál es la causa, mi Damón, que estando
> en la lucha de amor *juntos* trabados
> con lenguas, brazos, pies y encadenados
> cual vid que entre el jazmín se va enredando,
>
> y que el vital aliento ambos tomando
> en nuestros labios, de chupar cansados,
> en medio a tanto bien somos forzados
> llorar y suspirar de cuando en cuando? . . .[53]

(What is the reason, my Damon, that while being joined *together* in the struggle of love, with tongues, arms and

---

[53] Francisco de Aldana, *Poesías*, ed. Elias L. Rivers (Madrid, 1957), p. 9. On the Neoplatonic theme (Leone Ebreo), cf. Rivers, *Francisco de Aldana* (Badajoz, 1955), p. 157.

feet, and chained together like the grapevine that entangles itself with the jasmine, and that while panting for breath with our lips, weary of sucking, we are forced, in the midst of so much good, to weep and sigh from time to time? . . .)

These words elevate to a Platonic level, as Elias Rivers indicates, the more direct description of physical love in the *De rerum natura* of Lucretius (Bk. IV, ll. 1105-1111):

Denique cum membris conlatis flore fruuntur
aetatis, iam cum praesagit gaudia corpus
atque in eost Venus ut muliebria conserat arva,
adfigunt avide corpus, iunguntque salivas
oris, et inspirant pressantes dentibus ora;
nequiquam, quoniam nil inde abradere possunt
nec penetrare et abire in corpus corpore toto.

(Then when their limbs are intertwined and they are at the point of enjoying the flower of youth, when the body has a foretaste of its joys and Venus is about to sow the woman's fields, each greedily clasps the other's body, joining the moisture of their mouths and panting as teeth press on lips; but all in vain, for neither can take anything away, nor can one whole body penetrate and enter the other.)[54]

But our text is both syncretic and original. The Moor's complaints and hopes in *El Abencerraje* are closer to the spirit of the pastoral lament. Traditionally, the shepherd was separated from the person he loved; and he struggled to remedy this condition through the orphic power of song. The polarity of separation and union (where the key terms, in Spanish, were *juntar* and *apartamiento*) was essential in both the divine eclogue of Saint John of the Cross and the human

[54] I quote the Russel M. Geer translation of *On Nature* (Indianapolis, New York, and Kansas City, 1965), p. 149.

eclogue of Garcilaso. As far as the latter is concerned, the bitterest lament may be found in the *Egloga primera*, and in the radical isolation from which Salicio suffers:

> Por ti el silencio de la selva umbrosa,
> por ti la esquividad y *apartamiento*
> del solitario monte me agradaba;
> por ti la verde hierba, el fresco viento,
> el blanco lirio y colorada rosa
> y dulce primavera deseaba
>
> . . . .
>
> Materia diste al mundo de esperanza
> de alcanzar lo *imposible* y no pensado,
> y de hacer *juntar lo diferente*,
> dando a quien diste el corazón malvado,
> quitándolo de mí con tal mudanza
> que siempre sonará de gente en gente.

(Because of you the silence of the shady forest, because of you the *unsociable remoteness* of the lonely woods used to please me; because of you I longed for the green grass, the cool breeze, the white lily, the red rose and sweet springtime. . . . You gave the world cause to have hope of achieving the *impossible* and unthinkable, and of making *different things join*, by giving your perverse heart to whom you did, taking it away from me with such an abrupt change that the news of it will always resound from nation to nation.)[55]

The scene of the fountain in *El Abencerraje* brings together, in short, a number of traditional motifs, and reaches its peak in the wish of Abindarráez-Trocus to avoid any "apartamiento" by means of the fusion of his body with that of Jarifa-Salmacis. This is the most powerful image of unification in the novel, transcending all internal and external dual-

[55] *Renaissance and Baroque Poetry of Spain*, pp. 56, 58.

isms. The *union of the two lovers*, in other words, implies the *unity of each*. And it becomes gradually associated in the reader's mind with the *other* forms of division—geographical, social, religious—which the novel as a whole proposes to heal.

I V

A little later in the story, circumstances—or rather, the will of Fortune—will separate the lovers. Their reunion, in the midst of war, will not be the result of love alone. The generous assistance of Rodrigo de Narváez, the famous captain, will make possible both their happiness and the parallel growth of a lasting friendship. In the process, certain moral values will emerge, enriching the texture of the story. The unifying power of friendship, loyalty, disinterestedness will appear singularly important. Some observations on the origins and generic features of the novel will help to clarify this point.

In *El Abencerraje* the most varied traditions and literary conventions of the Renaissance meet. I have already singled out mythological allusions, a typical theme of the Greek romance, echoes from the *romancero* and poetic folklore; one can recognize also certain verbal devices from the rhetoric of contemporary love poetry ("the prison of love," etc.), a brief tale from the Italian *novella* (the loves of Narváez, reminiscent of Masuccio Salernitano and Ser Giovanni Fiorentino), and other conventions.[56] I have also mentioned that

---

[56] There are more echoes from the *romancero* than I have been able to mention (the general weeping in Granada after the massacre of the Abencerrajes, like "toda Córdoba lloraba" in the ballad "Pártese el moro Alicante"; the poetic use of numbers, Alora's "cincuenta escuderos hijosdalgo," as in the ballad "Cabalga Diego Laínez"; the description of the Moor's sumptuous and colorful dress, which was traditional, in the "Romance de Alatar," cf. López Estrada's edition of *El Abencerraje*, p. 105). The tale of the love of Narváez, and especially the hunting image in it, is related either to a story in Ser Giovanni Fiorentino's *Il Pecorone*, published in 1548, or to a tale in

the so-called Moorish novel continues to express the values of the romances of chivalry—courage, beauty, loyalty, honor, generosity, justice—at a time when the popularity of these improbable and interminable narratives was beginning to wane.[57]

There is still another factor which becomes evident at the very start of Antonio de Villegas' version of *El Abencerraje*:

"Este es un vivo retrato de virtud, liberalidad, esfuerzo, gentileza y lealtad, compuesto de Rodrigo de Narváez y el Abencerraje, y Jarifa, su padre y el Rey de Granada; del cual, aunque los dos formaron y dibujaron todo el cuerpo, los demás no dejaron de ilustrar la tabla y dar algunos rasguños en ella."

(This is a living portrait of virtue, liberality, prowess, gallantry and loyalty set down about Rodrigo de Narváez and the Abencerraje and Jarifa, and about her father and the King of Granada. In it, although the two made up and laid the background for the entire story, the others did not fail to decorate the canvas and to add some outlines to it.)

We are told that the author is about to offer us a double portrait, not of Narváez and the Abencerraje separately but of

---

Masuccio Salernitano's *Novellino*, cf. J.P.W. Crawford, "Un episodio de 'El Abencerraje' y una 'Novella' de Ser Giovanni," *Revista de Filología Española*, x (1923), 281-287.

[57] Concerning *El Abencerraje* and the romances of chivalry, one fact should be mentioned: *El Abencerraje* presents one of the last secret marriages in Spanish literature previous to the Council of Trent, which prohibited them. Marriage by oath, not *in facie Ecclesiae* but in the presence of witnesses, was illicit but valid, and it took place frequently in the romances of chivalry: the marriages of Elisena and King Perión, Amadís and Oriana in *Amadís de Gaula*; of Palmerín with Polinarda in *Palmerín de Inglaterra*, etc. Jarifa's father in *El Abencerraje* must approve her marriage after the fact, as King Lisuarte had Oriana's— cf. Justina Ruiz de Conde, *El amor y el matrimonio secreto en los libros de caballerías* (Madrid, 1948).

the two together, drawn simultaneously—a collective sketch to which Jarifa, her father, and the king of Granada will add a few "touches" of their own. This brings to mind, above all, the "collective biographies" of the fifteenth century, anthologies of heroism intended to celebrate the deeds of great men. Their authors—Gutierre Díez de Games, Diego de Valera, Fernán Pérez de Guzmán, Fernando del Pulgar—emulated Plutarch, Suetonius, and Valerius Maximus insofar as they stressed the *ethos* of admirable men and adapted their selection of historical facts to this purpose. As for the classical appreciation of fame, it was a fundamental motive in the lives of these exemplary heroes.[58]

The fame-seeking heroism of the medieval knight, however, was directed toward the future. A certain length of time separated the exemplary hero, the ethical model, the superior man, precisely because they were all these things, from their possible rivals or imitators. The glorious person could become through the intermediary of the written word an example for later men, even as the hero himself was expected to have learned from the great models of antiquity. Mosén Diego de Valera (1412-1488), for example, in the *Memorial de diversas hazañas*, recounted great deeds "porque los hacedores de aquéllas y los descendientes suyos sean acatados con la reverencia y honor que les pertenece, y por ejemplo suyo otros se esfuercen a tales obras hacer"[59] (so that their doers and their descendants may be respected

[58] Cf. María Rosa Lida de Malkiel, *La idea de la fama en la Edad Media castellana* (Mexico and Buenos Aires, 1952). The idea, expressed at the beginning of *El Abencerraje*, that Spain produces heroes worthy of great fame but not the chroniclers capable of perpetuating the memory of their exploits, is a commonplace of Spanish fifteenth-century historical writing and biography (as in the Introduction to Fernán Pérez de Guzmán's *Loores de los claros varones de España*). On the origins of the commonplace, cf. Lida de Malkiel, pp. 146-147.

[59] *Memorial de diversas hazañas*, ed. J. de Mata Carriazo (Madrid, 1941), p. 4.

with the reverence and honor which they deserve, and that through their example others may strive to accomplish such works). It was exactly in this spirit that Fernando del Pulgar had written a brief sketch of Rodrigo de Narváez, in the collective biography called *Claros varones de Castilla* (1486).[60]

The biographical portrayal of famous men found its justification, then, in their *exemplary function*. This function had been characteristic of the Middle Ages, and of the development of the *exemplum* from a mere anecdote or *sententia* to a fuller portrait or an extended narrative presentation: "*exemplum (paradeigma)* is a technical term of antique rhetoric from Aristotle onwards and means 'an interpolated anecdote serving as an example.' A different form of rhetorical *exemplum* was added later (*ca.* 100 B.C.), one which was of great importance for after times: the 'exemplary figure' (*eikon, imago*), i.e., 'the incarnation of a quality': 'Cato ille virtutum viva imago.' "[61] The rhetorical origin of the *exemplum*—as part of an orator's repertory of persuasive devices—is important, for it clarifies the status of famous men in a fifteenth-century biography like Fernando del Pulgar's. The word *exemplum* applied both to the act and to the written account of it.[62] In fact the two were indivisible, and a great life demanded the written word in order to fulfill its exemplary role. Regarded as an *exemplum*, the individual hero would assume an ultraindividual significance and exert a special ethical effect: that of perpetuating an ethical norm through its historical connection with human behavior. It should be understood that the exemplary hero did not merely uphold certain moral qualities, or certain values, as norms. He *proved* as persuasively as possible, by the force of his own

[60] Cf. *Claros varones de Castilla*, ed. J. Domínguez Bordona (Madrid, 1923), pp. 113-117.

[61] Curtius, *European Literature and the Latin Middle Ages*, p. 59.

[62] As indicated by Hildegard Kornhardt in her study of the subject, "*Exemplum*" (Göttingen diss., 1936); cf. Curtius, p. 60, note 71.

example, the relevance of the norm to individual conduct, or vice versa, man's ability to put it to actual practice. In this sense, the *exemplum* is repetitive and looks backward to a persistent norm.

For this reason, it does not always coincide with the *figura,* the meaning of which for the Middle Ages has been masterfully illuminated by Erich Auerbach. Based as it was on the original relationship between Judaism and Christianity, between the Old and the New Testaments, the significance of a figure such as Joshua—Joshua as *figura Christi*—was both historical and prophetic. If A was a *figura* of B, then B would represent its fulfillment and its truth. In Canto 1 of Dante's *Purgatorio* the truth and the fulfillment of the historical figure of Cato of Utica would be shown as having taken place after his death, through the realization of God's knowledge in history.[63] Thus the *figura* was prophetic, forward-looking, and historical, while the *exemplum* was moral, rhetorical, directed toward individual praxis rather than general truth.

Now, in *El Abencerraje,* as in other sixteenth-century Spanish narratives which we tend to regard today as forerunners of *Don Quixote,* something markedly different occurs: the goals of exemplary behavior are no longer to be found *outside* the work—for example, in the future reader, or the hero's descendants—but in the *story itself.* The written word is no longer the necessary mediation between the exemplary individual and his successor, or between the *figura futurorum* and its subsequent historical fulfillment. Instead, the word dramatizes, in "novelistic" fashion, the direct impact of one life upon another, and the processes whereby men attempt to come to terms, within the span of their earthly existence, with the demands of the superior ideal or the abstract norm.

---

[63] Cf. Erich Auerbach, "Figura," and "Typological Symbolism in Medieval Literature," in his *Gesammelte Aufsätze zur romanischen Philologie* (Bern and Munich, 1967), pp. 55-92, 109-114.

This is the promise that was held out in the introductory paragraph by Antonio de Villegas, quoted earlier, concerning the "twin portrait" of Rodrigo de Narváez and the Abencerraje, and the further decorative touches added by the other persons in the story. Those in the novel who learn from the exemplary hero, from the perfect knight, or are his rivals, are such characters as Abindarráez, Jarifa, her father, and the king of Granada. The perfect knight is, of course, Rodrigo de Narváez.

The prestige of Narváez follows him everywhere and lifts up the spirits of all those who fight with him or against him. A friendship grows and develops between Narváez and Abindarráez, based on mutual admiration and *caballerosidad*. Consequently, the Moor (who to all extents and purposes behaves like a Christian dressed as a Moor) feels obliged not only to deserve Jarifa's love, but, as a true Abencerraje, to be worthy of his friendship with Narváez. Hence a series of conflicts, as well as of self-perfecting and ennobling actions: Abindarráez, more youthful and impulsive than the mature Narváez, learns to control his own wishes and to teach Jarifa, by word and example, to master her own. Thus a kind of chain reaction takes place, leading to the final competition, in the ability for self-sacrifice and knightly generosity, between the various characters in the story, including Jarifa's father and the king of Granada (who, as the introductory paragraph promised, add a few "rasguños" to the picture). But in the final analysis, none succeeds in outdoing Rodrigo de Narváez (who had learned earlier, when he was a younger man, to curb his own will and conciliate loyalty with love, as the final tale of his frustrated affair with a married woman makes clear), though they all have been guided and lifted up by his example.

At each step, each phase of this ethical process, the impact of one person on another has been essential. The efficient cause of improved conduct has been not a moral concept but the individual who has embodied it and thus become a living *exemplum* for the other or others. This attachment of a moral concept to a concrete thing or person is what modern philosophy, especially since Nietzsche, often approaches by means of the term "value." Within a single work of narrative fiction, the impact of one character upon another, in such a way as to convey a value, is what René Girard in his important book *Mensonge romantique et vérité romanesque* (1961) calls "médiation intérieure." In *El Abencerraje*, as in other sixteenth- and seventeenth-century works marking the emergence of the novel as a new literary genre, the reader witnesses and coexperiences a sequence of internal mediations, in Girard's sense. Yet this is not the core, I think, of *El Abencerraje*, nor is the hero of most modern novels a mere mediator. The notion of internal mediation underlines the fact that a certain fictional character "imitates" another who serves as a model, as a guide, or even as an idol to be worshiped. The series of personal impacts that I have brought out in *El Abencerraje* have a great deal to do, rather, with what I might call "incitement" or "inspiration."

There are significant differences between these two kinds of phenomena. Aimless or "godless" people are generally expected or obliged to imitate. Through a substitute *imitatio Christi*, they thus make possible the transmission of a moral concept or an article of faith. In such cases the center of gravity tends to remain the belief, as the very notion of imitation often assumes some weakness or mediocrity on the part of the imitator who puts the concept or the belief into practice. On the other hand, the "inspired" or "incited" character needs the example of another character, of a superior human being, in order to really act as he would wish to act—in order to improve not his ideals but his behavior. By incitement I mean the human impact that makes possible the actualization of what had remained latent until then. The modern novelistic version of the traditional *exemplum* stresses not the type and the *figura* but their temporal actualization in the present.

The emphasis, then, is not on the moral goal or the faith but on the moral qualities needed to actually embody them—courage, generosity, etc.—and to manifest them as *values*. In the broadest terms, one might say that it is not Christ but his incarnation that is being emulated or mediated. What the novelist shows is the process of incarnation by which ideals become the blood and flesh of individual lives.

In this manner the "inspired" person goes on to occupy his rightful place in an exemplary process: in what Honoré d'Urfé (an admirer of Spanish pastoral romances and, like the author of *El Abencerraje*, of the Neoplatonic and Neostoic writing of his time) calls in his *Epîtres morales* (1603) a "continuous chain of grandeur":

"Juge par là, Agathon, si cette souveraine bonté ne nous fait pas hausser à elle par les degrés de la science; et si cette grandeur n'est pas une chaîne continuée, qui des hommes va jusques à Dieu. Quant à la grandeur des vertus morales, c'est sans doute que de nous elles vont continuant jusques à lui. Et enfin que tu l'entendes mieux, reçois pour fondement ce paradoxe que te vais dire. Nulle vertu n'est vraiment vertu qui ne soit extrêmement vertu. . . . Tout homme donc qui désire être vertueux, faut qu'il recherche de l'être extrêmement, autrement il ne méritera point ce nom. . . . J'ai nommé cette proposition un paradoxe, d'autant que la commune opinion est, de même qu'Aristote, que les vertus morales sont médiocres, et qu'elles ont deux extrémités vicieuses. . . ."[64]

[64] *Les Epistres morales de Messire Honoré d'Urfé* . . . (Lyon, 1620), pp. 326-327 (I have modernized the spelling). The first edition of the *Epistres* appeared in 1598; the epistle quoted here (II, 9) was added to a second edition, in 1603. D'Urfé, like Corneille, a more famous interpreter of moral self-perfectioning and "grandeur," knew his Spanish writers well. In the *Epistres morales* he mentions such pastorals as the two *Dianas*, by Montemayor (which included *El Abencerraje*) and Gil Polo, and Cervantes' *La Galatea*. Cf. Soeur Marie Lucien Goudard, *Etude sur les Epistres Morales d'Honoré d'Urfé* (Washington, D.C., 1937).

Such exemplary behavior, supported during the Renaissance by Neoplatonic and Neostoic thought, implies two basic corollaries: that all men embody the same higher values and are *united* by them; and that they thereby achieve a great deal more than the fulfillment of their personal goals— they participate, by surpassing themselves, in universal ethical attitudes. The love of Abindarráez for Jarifa in this sense has a different scope than the knightly virtues he shares with Narváez: human beings are united by love as individuals only, by superior conduct with values greater than themselves. It is true that just as virtuous men may lead others closer to the supreme good, in Neoplatonic terms the love of a beautiful person leads to infinite beauty. But the exemplary process dominated by Narváez in *El Abencerraje* appears to stress the former course rather than the latter.

The highest norms of behavior are to be found in man himself, in his conscience and capacity for self-perfectioning. Without doubting the teachings of the church, the humanist observes and admires their approximation to individual experience: no moral force is more persuasive than the example of a single, extraordinary human being. In *El Abencerraje*, no qualifications or equivocations are tolerated regarding moral norms (stylistically, the small number of adjectives is striking). But the author dramatizes their actualization, thereby making heroism more accessible to men. It is not difficult to imagine the profound effect *El Abencerraje* could have had on Cervantes, who probably discovered in it the qualities but not the flaws of the romances of chivalry: an instance of knightly superiority that did not call for parody, as the story itself showed that Narváez could guide the sanest of men. Let us not forget that at the end of his first sally (Part i, Bk. 5), of his first imitation of Amadís, Don Quixote, badly beaten and defeated, found solace in the tale of the Moor Abindarráez and the governor of Alora and Antequera.

The art of the pastoral, says Friedrich Klingner in his book on Virgil, allows the reader to desire and foresee a world that is sound and whole again.[65] *El Abencerraje* offers a comparable kind of healing. The governor of Alora and Antequera inspires an exemplary, gradual, dynamic process of unification that may lead us, in our minds, to surpass dualisms and efface divisions. Nevertheless, the pastoral and the Moorish novel belong to different classes of literary creation. The eclogue, like all retreats from civilization—"Beatus ille qui procul negotiis"—turns away from the pain and the frustration on which its protests and its dreams are built. The novel's imaginative effort never ceases to involve its origins in reality through contradiction. Its expanding forms embrace and dispute the structures of contemporary social life. Its principal images and processes suggest and construct a world from which history could not possibly be excluded, and in which civilization itself could become sound and whole again. To contradict is not to conquer or to liberate. The ultimate object of the healing is the reader's own historical experience.

[1965]

[65] Cf. Klingner, *Virgil*, p. 15.

III

Stylistics of Silence

I

It has become common for the critic of poems to assume the attitude of an uncertain Oedipus before the sphinx. We hear frequently about the riddles, the enigmas, and even the mysteries of poetic creation. These perplexities are, most probably, a function of the very advances that have taken place in the formal analysis of poems. The repertory of methods and instruments available for the detailed interpretation of literary texts has doubtless been refined and expanded to a considerable degree during the last thirty years. Yet the more penetrating the critical intuition, the more vigorously there emerges the riddle of artistic "form." This is an area where knowledge leads—if not to tragic expiation —to an increased awareness of irrevocable limits. A peculiar insight into the problematic nature of their craft appears to await the formalist and the critic of style as the ultimate reward for their efforts. In the following essay, I would like to discuss some of the things that we mean when we still speak, after all is said and done, of the "mystery of poetry" (*el misterio de la poesía*).

I have in mind especially two groups: the Anglo-American writers who have been named "New Critics"; and the Hispanic researchers into poetic style whose principal teachers have been Amado Alonso and Dámaso Alonso. One could gather many contemporary testimonies to a growing refusal to manipulate, sift, or disunite the materials of which poems are made. In one of his last books, for example, Richard P. Blackmur raises the alarm. I shall mention but one brief passage from *The Lion and the Honeycomb* (1955). Blackmur revives an old suspicion: the feeling that a poem manifests an

intuition that is at once everywhere and nowhere at all, so
that words may be able to intertwine, multiply one another,
release their expressiveness, and thus give rise to something
of indefinite contour—something to which we cannot point
and say "there it is." On this occasion Blackmur uses the
term "symbol": "What writing creates—what goes on after
the writing has stopped—may sometimes be called symbol.
It is a symbol when it stands, not for what has been said or
stated, but for what has not been said and could not be said,
for what has been delivered by the writing into what seems
an autonomous world of its own. Symbol is the most exact
possible meaning, almost tautologically exact, for what
stirred the words to move *and* what the moving words
made."[1] Let us notice how Blackmur seems to identify, in
passing, the ineffable with the unexpressed: "what has not
been said" with "what could not be said." From other angles,
not always as interesting, other American writers have envisaged the obstacles which obstruct the road of the formalist
critic.[2] In France, Paul de Man, in a strong article, has suggested that it is a dead-end street.[3]

Let us now observe, in order to clarify the terms of the
problem, the ways in which two Spanish critics interpret *el
misterio de la poesía*. I should like, first, to comment on a
genuine monument of modern critical analysis: Dámaso
Alonso's *Poesía española* (Madrid, 1950). This is a systematic
book, based on a rigorous methodology. It is also personal,
ebullient, intense, nearly autobiographical, and never marred

[1] *The Lion and the Honeycomb* (New York, 1955), p. 224. See also
p. 191. The present essay is a translation, with some modifications
and additions, of "Estilística del silencio (en torno a un poema de
Antonio Machado)," *Revista Hispánica Moderna*, XXIII (1957), 260-
291.

[2] Cf. Karl Shapiro, *Beyond Criticism* (Lincoln, Nebr., 1953), and
Philip Wheelwright, *The Burning Fountain* (Bloomington, Ind., 1954).

[3] Cf. Paul de Man, "Impasse de la critique formaliste," *Critique*, no.
109 (June 1956), 483-500.

by the "dissociation of sensibility." The author, as he writes, seems to proceed from one surprising discovery to another. His double inquiry—practical (the elucidation of some poems from the *Siglo de Oro*) and theoretical (the establishment of a methodology)—assumes at times narrative forms. The critic recalls those moments in his life that best exemplify the "ways" (*vías*) of his approximation to poetry— namely, the three essential kinds of literary knowledge: the reader's, the critic's, and the scientist's. His task is presented as an ascent (destined to stop short of "the peak" [p. 12]), a critical ladder, a "path of analysis" ("camino de análisis" [p. 306]), the itinerary of a new Don Quixote; and, finally, as the siege of an impregnable fortress: "the castle has not been taken. We have circled it; we have explored its walls, its sentry-paths, its outskirts. Only intuition, only the whistling arrow clears the walls and reaches the inner mansion. There light reigns" ("el castillo no ha sido ganado. Hemos girado en torno a él, hemos reconocido sus muros, sus rondas, sus arrabales. Sólo la intuición, sólo las saetas silbadoras salvan los muros y llegan hasta la interior morada. Allí reina la luz" [p. 634]). Thus one recognizes gradually the nature of what the author, toward the end of the book, calls a "struggle" ("lucha") both with the reality of literature and with himself (p. 633). On the one hand, as we have just seen, the vocabulary of the believer or the mystic is frequently employed. On the other, the scientist ("hombre de ciencia") recurs to such terms and images as "célula fotoeléctrica" ("photoelectric cell"), "simbiosis" ("symbiosis"), "matemática fidelidad," "hiperestesia sinestética," "relaciones eléctricas," "inducciones a distancia," and so on. This dual frame of reference is operative, more or less explicitly, throughout the book; and it allows one to comprehend words like these: "we are exactly at the edge of the mystery. The mystery is called love, and is called poetry . . . My God, my God, why do we touch poetry with our incompetent hands, when we know nothing of its mystery, which is Your own?" ("estamos exactamente en la orilla del misterio. El misterio se llama amor, y se llama poesía . . . Dios mío, Dios mío, ¿por qué tocamos con nuestras ineptas manos a la poesía, si no sabemos nada de su misterio, que es el tuyo mismo?" [concerning Garcilaso's "Eclogue III," p. 105]). What is really the mystery that underlies such questions and exclamations? Let us remember the distinction (formulated, if I am not mistaken, by French Catholic writers) between "problem" or "secret" or "riddle," on the one hand, and, on the other, "mystery." "Secret," to be very brief, designates what is hidden, unknown, not yet known; "mystery," the unknowable—postulating perhaps a God. As far as the meaning and structure of a Spanish poem are concerned, they are not, for the formidable and extraordinarily gifted critic who is Dámaso Alonso, inscrutable or unattainable. However, it is only the reader's or the critic's intuition that is able to seize them. The man of *science* cannot possibly work out laws that are applicable to a single, unique object. The professional student of poetry encounters a mystery—i.e., an object beyond the reach of scientific method—as soon as he attains the limits of his discipline. (The book's subtitle is: *Ensayo de métodos y límites estilísticos.*)

What may remain a secret for certain literary critics becomes a mystery for those who experience with some intensity the frustration of their scientific ambitions. There is a dividing line here which Dámaso Alonso has traced with energy and clarity. The scientific study of poems is surrounded by two "intuitive" acts: at one end, there is a "previous" intuition (which is twofold: the critical intuition, vis-à-vis the poem, and the choice of the method to follow [p. 121]), and at the other, "before the peak," a perception of ultimate unicity: "foreseeable progress in the techniques of stylistics makes me think that a total knowledge of the unicity of the artistic object is the limit of such advance.

Limit, in the mathematical sense: stylistics may approximate indefinitely its goal, but without ever touching it" ("el progreso previsible para las técnicas estilísticas me hace pensar que el conocimiento total de la unicidad del objeto artístico es el límite de ese avance. Límite, en sentido matemático: la Estilística puede acercarse indefinidamente a esa meta, pero sin tocarla nunca" [p. 13]). For our critic, in other words, *the poem itself is not a mystery*—it is not, for example, essentially obscure or ambiguous. On the contrary: it is a "criatura nítida, exacta" (a "terse, exact creature"). These adjectives are central in the work of Dámaso Alonso: *nítido, exacto*. The critic, above all, sheds a bright light on the sharp-cut, perfect poem. The great poem is a "prodigy of mathematical rigor" ("prodigio de matemático rigor" [p. 351]). The problem is to seize it fully, to discover the secret of the perfect criticism of style.

A comparable sense of wonderment before the precision and the power of poetic creation is to be found in the analyses of individual poems which Francisco García Lorca has published in recent years. These analyses are exceptionally detailed. I do not know of any other readings—any "new criticism" of poems—that offer as sensitive and fine a response to every aspect of verbal texture. (Let no one decry "formalism" who has not risked this, who has not returned from the critic's Hades and palpably experienced the difficulties of stylistic analysis.) I recall particularly the long and thorough study of a ballad by Góngora, "Hermana Marica." García Lorca brings out the vocalic effects and rhythmic arrangements whose interaction gives life to the words and the clauses. His exegesis seeks to attain the last, most minute components of the ballad's sound. The critic's initial target is the acoustic image—Saussure's *signifiant*. García Lorca's ability to search out and illuminate the innumerable, near-infinite parts of *poetic* sound (as distinct, one might say, from the limited number of phonemes operative in ordinary language) matches his awareness of the amazing, enigmatic richness of poetic creation: "a study that starts from the mere *significans* is an available approach—perhaps the surest, if not the best —to the mystery of poetic creation, which the reader relives in the act of aesthetic enjoyment" ("el estudio desde el mero significante es una vía abierta, si no la mejor, quizá la más segura, para acercarse al misterio de la creación poética, en cuya reviviscencia por el lector radica el acto de la fruición estética").[4] Now, it appears that the riddle does not reside in the poem itself. The radical mystery is that of poetic *creation*. The critic is impressed above all with the marvel, the miracle, of the moment when an "absolutely" perfect poem was born. What made it possible? The instinctive mastery of the writer? His conscious purpose? It does not matter: we cannot, we need not, know. Our starting point must be the perfect correspondence between the order of the sounds and the level of the meanings; and we must therefore strive to awaken in the reader's sensibility those distant strata in which the subtlest aspects of language become effective.

Criticism should energize *in us* that particular relationship with language, that intimate love and possession of its power, which was and still is the premise not only of Góngora's genius but of that of every poet-in-the-making. The mystery is in the etymon: poetry as making. Only a thorough analysis of what was made can lead us back to the mystery of the making. There are two possible reasons, Francisco García Lorca adds, for objecting to such a method: "the first is partially legitimate only: the destruction, be it provisional and preliminary, of the irreducible unity of the artistic object. The other is wholly spurious: to declare solely relevant to unattainable zones of sensibility, to attribute to the world of the unknowable and the ineffable, a series of poetic facts which are largely amenable to ordered analysis" ("una, sólo

[4] Francisco García Lorca, "Hermana Marica (Análisis de un romancillo de Góngora)," *Le Torre*, III (1955), 146.

en parte legítima; la destrucción, aunque sea provisional y previa, de la unidad irreductible del objeto artístico. Otra, en todo bastarda; diputar como propio de zonas inexplorables de la sensibilidad, atribuir al mundo de lo incognoscible y lo inefable, una serie de hechos poéticos que en gran medida se entregan al análisis ordenado").[5]

I would not wish to echo these objections. Yet there are questions that linger and remain curiously troublesome. Some of the terms, I think, that are current in the formal study of poems, some of the assumptions on which it rests, deserve further discussion and clarification: not only "style" or "form," but what we mean when we mention a "series of poetic facts," or the "elements" that constitute a poem. How numerous are the facts or the elements? How do they begin, and where do they end? What is the precise goal of the formalist's analysis? We are speaking of a discipline which pretends to grow into a body of knowledge, to lend itself to theory, and—in that sense—to become a "science." Is there such a thing as a branch of knowledge that does not circumscribe its object of study? Before the "limits of stylistics" can be ascertained, it would be useful to determine the limits of the verbal "object," of the artifact made of language. The problem resides, of course, in the combination of artifact *and* language, i.e., in knowing whether the limits of the linguist's "object" are the same as the critic's, and the extent to which they overlap.

With regard to this problem, an interesting contrast exists between the two groups of textual critics to whom I have just referred: the Anglo-American and the Hispanic. Ezra Pound has said that language is "the most powerful instrument of perfidy."[6] The New Critics, in the midst of their commitment to the intrinsic reading of poems, or as a result of it, have stressed such factors as irony, ambiguity, and paradox; so

---

[5] *Ibid.*, p. 157.
[6] *Literary Essays* (London, n.d.), p. 77.

much so that no one is shocked to hear R. P. Blackmur, late in his career, proclaim that symbols stand for what the poets have not said. Now, these are factors that do not coincide as completely with the verbal texture of a literary work as the notion of "style" usually does. The New Critics, to tell the truth, did not rely unduly on the tools and terms of modern linguistics. They did not come to literary criticism *from* the technical study of language. The Hispanic critics did, generally speaking: their *Estilística*, like the German *Stilistik* whose most illustrious practitioner is Leo Spitzer, prides itself on the constant and timely use of the vocabulary not only of ancient rhetoric but of contemporary linguistics. In this sense, they have made the age-old tradition of philology relevant to the sensitive comprehension of poems. A concomitant of this seems to be their extraordinary confidence in the poem as a mathematically perfect *verbal* construction that is essentially amenable to *linguistic* analysis.

The boundaries of the poem, according to this view, concur nicely with those of its language. This does not mean, naturally, that the character, or the uses, of verbal signs are the same in poetry as in common speech. In fact, there are a number of elementary premises that students of poetry generally accept, all tending to draw a line between ordinary language and poetic language. As I understand them, they are, very briefly, the following.

1. Nonliterary language tends to be linear: vocal actualization requires succession in time. Further, it tends to be self-oblivious: new clauses dislodge earlier ones; and even the repetition of an idea or a feeling assumes the character of a new start, a fresh attempt to make words relevant to a practical situation in real life. Poetic language tends to be both linear (otherwise no rhythm could arise) and simultaneous—or better, *incremental*. Like a house in the making, a poem is a process in which new components are placed around previously existing ones. (Literature as a whole ex-

hibits a comparable continuity. A poem is incremental like a building; a literary system, like a city.) By such constant self-reliance, the poem *can* become a self-enclosed sign.

2. On this basic sequence of sounds and meanings, ordinary language superimposes above all the form (or structure) of syntax. In poetry the form of syntax comes into unceasing contact (or collision) with other forms and reiterative orders that are equally functional: the rhythm within a line of verse, the pattern—above it—of the lines themselves, the recurrence of sounds and meanings, the arrangement of rhymes and stanzas. The process of poetic language is *manifoldly* incremental—on a number of simultaneous levels. It offers not a single form but a dynamic coexistence of *several* levels of form.

3. Each natural language employs a restricted quantity of phonemes. In Castilian Spanish, in which only twenty-four phonemes are at work, the ear distinguishes between the vocalized *d* sound in *nada* ("nothing")—somewhat similar to the *th* in the English *father*—and the more explosive *d* in *mando* ("command"). However, if one puts this distinction to what Louis Hjelmslev has called the "commutation test" (based on whether a phonic change brings about a change in meaning), one notices that it does not normally affect the signified (*signifié*, or *significatum*) aspect of any verbal sign. The two sounds are variants of the same phoneme /d/.[7] In poetry, on the contrary, the difference is operative. One need only recall three lines on the subject of mystical love, rich with the vocalized or soft *d*, from Saint John of the Cross's *Dark Night of the Soul*:

> ¡Oh noche, que juntaste
> Amado con amada,
> amada en el Amado transformada!

[7] Cf. André Martinet, *Eléments de linguistique générale* (Paris, 1960), pp. 24-25, 67-69.

(Oh night, that joined
The Lover to the beloved,
The beloved in the Lover transformed!)

4. The preceding three lines show that a "commutation test" in the context of poetry involves much more than an individual portion of the linear sequence. It is not the part but the whole that is instantly changeable. What matters is the pertinence of the soft *d* sound not to *Amado* or to any single word, as might be the case with a phoneme, but to the entire sequence *Amado-amada-amada-Amado-transformada*. There is no simple one-to-one relationship between the *significans* and the *significatum* of the verbal sign. The entire poem is the predominant sign: this is what one means when one says that in poetry not only the overall forms but the smallest detail or "event" is, rather than contingent, necessary.

5. Thus one is in a position to understand why the connection between the two aspects of the verbal sign (*significans* and *significatum*) is not merely arbitrary in poetry. Ferdinand de Saussure, in a famous passage of the *Cours de linguistique générale*, proclaimed that the connection between the acoustic image *cheval* and the concept that it conveys was arbitrary and conventional. Emile Benveniste, in a well-known essay, challenged this notion.[8] I shall not enter into a technical dispute among linguists, with regard to ordinary language. As far as poetry is concerned, Dámaso Alonso has explained (in *Poesía española*, p. 28) that the link between *significans* and *significatum* is "motivated" in poetry, and I emphatically agree. (Dámaso Alonso calls this nexus "form.") He also stresses that the poetic *significans* is not merely a word or part of a word, but that it can be any complex of sounds belonging to any of the several strata that I earlier

[8] Cf. "Nature du signe linguistique," *Acta Linguistica*, I (1939), 23-29.

called "levels of form": a syllable, a rhythm, a vocalic intonation, a tonal variation, a pattern of rhymes, etc.; and of course the whole poem is an enormously complex *significans* (p. 27). Thus, it seems clear, to return to my own argument, that the question of the indivisibility of the two aspects of the poetic sign should not and cannot be taken up apart from that of the indivisibility of the different signs appearing successively in a poem: the sound *amada* and the psychic effect or psychic image *amada* are united by a necessary link because, or insofar as, *amada* is inseparable from *Amado-amada-amada-Amado-transformada.*

In both directions (from one aspect of a sign to another, and from sign to sign), the poem is a unified whole. It cannot be approached or grasped "atomistically." As Ernst Cassirer has shown, language makes it possible to transcend the ancient dichotomies of "spirit" and "nature," "body and soul."[9] To add a further example, one might wonder whether the Spanish word for "cat" can be made to function as a necessary sign. In "Gatos de Roma" ("The Cats of Rome"), Jorge Guillén accomplishes this, not instantaneously, but as a precipitate of the process of the *entire* poem:

Gatos de Roma

Los gatos,
No vagabundos pero sin un dueño,
Al sol adormecidos
En calles sin aceras,
O esperando una mano dadivosa
Tal vez por entre ruinas,
Los gatos,
Inmortales de modo tan humilde,
Retan al tiempo, duran
Atravesando las vicisitudes,
Sin saber de la Historia

---

[9] Cf. "Structuralism in Modern Linguistics," *Word*, 1 (1945), 114.

Que levanta edificios
O los deja abismarse entre pedazos
Bellos aún, ahora apoyos nobles
De esas figuras: libres.
Mirada fija de unos ojos verdes
En soledad, en ocio y luz remota.
Entrecerrados ojos,
Rubia la piel y calma iluminada.
Erguido junto a un mármol,
Superviviente resto de columna,
Alguien feliz y pulcro
Se atusa con la pata relamida.
Gatos. Frente a la Historia,
Sensibles, serios, solos, inocentes.

(The cats,
Not vagabonds but ownerless,
Sleeping in the sun
In streets without sidewalks,
Or waiting for a generous hand,
Perhaps, among the ruins,
The cats,
So humbly immortal,
Challenge time, persist
Through vicissitudes,
Know nothing of history
Which raises edifices
Or lets them crumble to pieces
That are still beautiful, now the noble supports
Of these figures: free.
The fixed stare of green eyes
In solitude, in leisure and distant light.
Half-open eyelids,
Blond fur and illumined calm.
Erect beside marble,

Surviving remains of a column,
A comely and happy someone
Spruces himself with wet paw.
Cats. Before History,
Sensitive, serious, alone, innocent.)[10]

Literature heals the dualisms, unifies the scattered fragments—pieces and broken columns, like those among which
Roman cats live—of language and its latent perceptions.
Saussure showed that language as a code and a potential
mental order was a structural whole and a system. He did not
maintain, of course, that the individual message or *parole*
was a structured unit. Yet a *poem*—with regard to both the
link between signifying and signified, and the connection between one sign and another—is. A poem exemplifies that particular use of language in which the single communication
becomes a complex of structures. Or to put it differently: *the
poem* transfers the qualities of system from the code to the
message.

So much for the poem as system, and for some of the
peculiarities of its uses of language. The formalist critic is in
a good position to describe these uses. But this is only a start.
We have not dealt with the further question: What are the
boundaries of the poem? To be sure, the poem is conveyed
by words. Yet we also know for a fact that language is capable, among other things, of transcending its own limits.
Whether it becomes in the process a kind of nonlanguage is
perhaps a terminological issue, on which it might not be fruitful to dwell. It should be more important to grasp the substantial problem to which formal analysis leads: that of the
limits, i.e., the outer dimensions and effects, of the verbal-
artistic "object." I have just recalled that literature tends to
strengthen the coherence of the linguistic message, by tight-

[10] From *Affirmation. A Bilingual Anthology, 1919-1966*, tr. Julian
Palley (Norman, Okla., 1968), p. 147.

ening its internal joints and articulations. It offers, in this sense, self-enclosed signs—signifying themselves. Does this also mean that it weakens or dissolves its links with an external *designatum*, a referential object or situation? "Gatos de Roma" is doubtless a little system, in which all connections cease to appear arbitrary. Does it, by the same token, fail to establish a necessary relationship with other realities than its own—to involve the readers more closely in a *designatum*? Obviously, it does not. The verbal work of art adds dimension to dimension in a manner no critic of style can afford to neglect—and which implies a sort of ultimate return, paradoxically enough, to the referential energy of ordinary speech.

In this context, there is much to be learned from the writings of Amado Alonso. Amado Alonso's frame of reference was not merely the structural approach to linguistic systems (meaning the verbal code or *langue*) but the study of the expressive strategies and emotional or affective means of *parole*, as in Charles Bally's idea of *évocation*.[11] He stressed the "contagious" and suggestive power of words ("contagio sugestivo"), and their ability not only to mean but to hint and imply.[12] In his long essay on Valle-Inclán's *Sonatas*, he discusses the expressive aura of the great stylist's language, and names it also *evocación*. "This emotional expressiveness," he explains, "results not only from the choice of words, but from their position in the sentence, the notions that neighboring words represent, and, most important, associations between the words used and others that are absent" ("esta expresividad emocional estará conseguida no sólo por la selección de los vocablos, sino por su colocación en la frase, por las nociones representadas en las palabras vecinas y, de modo

---

[11] In Bally's *Traité de stylistique française* (Heidelberg, 1919), Part v. On this point, cf. Giacomo Devoto, *Studi di stilistica* (Florence, 1950), p. 23.

[12] Cf. Amado Alonso, *Materia y forma en poesía* (Madrid, 1955), pp. 18, 44, 97-98, 101, 264-270.

muy importante, por las asociaciones que las palabras empleadas guardan con otras ausentes").[13] In the following pages, I shall attempt to show the importance of these "absent words." I shall analyze the various "absences" in a poem by Antonio Machado with the principal intent not of discerning the general features of Machado's art, but of underlining the *silent* aspect of poetic forms.

II

The Absent Poet

Let us read a poem from Antonio Machado's *Campos de Castilla*:[14]

A José María Palacio

Palacio, buen amigo,	1
¿está la primavera	
vistiendo ya las ramas de los chopos	
del río y los caminos? En la estepa	
del alto Duero, Primavera tarda,	5
¡pero es tan bella y dulce cuando llega! ...	
¿Tienen los viejos olmos	
algunas hojas nuevas?	
Aún las acacias estarán desnudas	
y nevados los montes de las sierras.	10
¡Oh mole del Moncayo blanca y rosa,	
allá, en el cielo de Aragón, tan bella!	
¿Hay zarzas florecidas	
entre las grises peñas,	
y blancas margaritas	15

---

[13] *Ibid.*, p. 264.

[14] The poem is well known and has already been commented upon. Cf. Luis Felipe Vivanco, "Comentario a unos poemas de Antonio Machado," *Cuadernos Hispanoamericanos* (Sept.-Dec. 1949), 541-565. I quote from Antonio Machado's *Obra poética*, ed. R. Alberti (Buenos Aires, 1944), pp. 165-166. The fairly literal English translation is my own.

entre la fina hierba?
Por esos campanarios
ya habrán ido llegando las cigüeñas.
Habrá trigales verdes,
y mulas pardas en las sementeras,   20
y labriegos que siembran los tardíos
con las lluvias de abril. Ya las abejas
libarán del tomillo y el romero.
¿Hay ciruelos en flor? ¿Quedan violetas?
Furtivos cazadores, los reclamos   25
de la perdiz bajo las capas luengas,
no faltarán. Palacio, buen amigo,
¿tienen ya ruiseñores las riberas?
Con los primeros lirios
y las primeras rosas de las huertas,   30
en una tarde azul, sube al Espino,
al alto Espino donde está su tierra . . .
                              Baeza, 29 abril, 1913

To José María Palacio

Palacio, my good friend,   1
Has spring begun
To clothe the branches of the poplar trees
Along the river and the roads? On the steppe
Of the upper Duero, Spring is slow,   5
But so fair and mild when it arrives!
Are there a few new leaves
On the old elms?
Still now the acacias will be bare
And snow remain on the mountain ranges.   10
Oh mass of the Moncayo, white and pink
Afar, so beautiful, in the Aragon sky!
Are there brambles in flower
Among gray rocks,
And white daisies   15

In the fine grass?
Over the belfries,
Storks will have started to arrive.
There will be green wheat fields,
And gray-brown mules on seedlands,   20
And farmhands sowing late crops
Under the April rains. Now the bees
Will be tasting rosemary and thyme.
Are there plum trees in bloom? Violets, still?
Furtive hunters, with decoys   25
For partridge under their long capes,
Will not be missing. Palacio, my good friend,
Do riverbanks have nightingales already?
With the earliest lilies
And the earliest roses of the orchards,   30
On a blue afternoon, go up the Espino,
The high Espino where her plot of earth lies . . .

                              Baeza, April 29, 1913

This epistle or poetic letter ends, like many letters, with a
practical request addressed to a friend: that he bring flowers
to the grave of the poet's wife. The flowers should be—this
is one of the links between the practical request and the rest
of the poem, cast as it is in an interrogative mode—the first
flowers of *spring*. I shall discuss shortly some of the aspects
and functions of the poetic letter. For the moment, I should
like to indicate a basic absence, to which the poem owes
much of its elemental, self-restrained, evocative power: the
absence of the poet himself.

Not once does the writer's "I" appear, in a composition
that is obviously emotional in tone and message. In a poetic
letter addressed to a friend, the first-person form of the verb
is never used. Constructions in the third person predominate, especially the impersonal forms: "*¿Hay* ciruelos en
flor?" ("Are there plum trees in bloom?"). The second person

is employed for the first and last time in the final request to Palacio: "*sube* al Espino" ("go up the Espino"). The seventeen verbs included by Machado (of which sixteen are in the third person) seem common, simple, colorless, with two or three exceptions: "siembran" ("sowing"), "libarán" ("will be tasting," "will drink"). We encounter twice "tienen" ("have"), "hay" ("there is"). Sometimes the variation consists in a mere shift of tense, from the present to the future: from "hay" to "habrá" ("there will be"). And therein may reside the clue. Machado focuses his attention on being, becoming, nonbeing. His verbs designate primarily not an action but the absence or presence of something. Above all, this mere existence or nonexistence is associated with time, situated within an all-embracing temporal flow: "llega," "habrán ido llegando," "quedan," "está vistiendo" ("arrives," "will have started to arrive," "remain," "has begun to clothe"), etc. When the verb "to be" serves to determine attributes or properties, these are referred to a temporal process too: "pero *es* tan bella y dulce *cuando llega*," "*Aún* las acacias *estarán* desnudas" ("But so fair and mild when it arrives," "Still now the acacias will be bare"). I shall go on shortly to consider the function of the more active verbs (the farmhands sowing, the bees savoring rosemary and thyme). I now wish to stress that the other verbs denote certain modes of existence in time: advent, duration, rebirth, decadence. Things are visible or are missing, "have . . . already," arrive, linger, disappear, and are reborn again.

Is this choice of verbs a sign of detachment, or of the sort of "objective" lyrical (or narrative) style in which a writer pretends to banish himself from his own work? Manfred Kridl once attempted to distinguish between a "poésie lyrique descriptive ou indirecte" and a "poésie lyrique pure ou directe." Kridl showed how the former kind of lyrical impulse may direct itself toward external description, dramatic dialogue, or narrative events, without any interference from the author's point of view.[15] The lyrical posture in our poem, however, is descriptive and indirect while harboring a direct intent as well. It *alludes* to the personal participation of a single "I" in a particular situation. It is the allusive power of the words that makes possible here a reconciliation between Manfred Kridl's two categories.

The poet first appears as the "I" implicit in the dialogue with the "you" of the poem: as the friend of José María Palacio. The second and third words, "buen amigo," manifest both the loyal affection felt by Machado, as he begins his letter, and the objective status of the correspondent. As we hear the first line:

Palacio, buen amigo,

we sense the sudden impact of the poet's own—quiet, humble —voice. I use the terms "hear" and "voice" consciously. We know that a poem can offer a greater or lesser degree of "reification" and spatialization; it can become, to be sure, a thing of beauty. The art of Machado, instead, restores us to the original source—oral, vocal, temporal—of the poetic utterance. The initial vocative—"Palacio, buen amigo"—establishes, much before the reader journeys in his imagination to the plains and mountains of Castile, the poet's voice firmly in the foreground of the lyric. The reader, located in the same place, will contemplate those "northern" lands as if standing by Machado's side, in Baeza, in Andalusia, where spring is early and exuberant. It is as if a brief but irresistible impulse at the start were enough to set off the entire lyrical movement. The nuance of an emotion, the convention of the epistle, the function of friendship, linking an "I" with a "you," are all concisely sketched in the first line. The name of Pa-

[15] Cf. Manfred Kridl, "Observations sur les genres de la poésie lyrique," *Helicon*, II (1939), 147-155.

lacio will not be repeated until line 27, where it rejoins and heightens once more the sentiments which the first line set in motion and which had remained thereafter mute but operative among all the other words.

The semipresence of the poet in the poem is perfectly appropriate, as we shall soon see, to the thematic texture of the work. But it also responds to a radical attitude, previous to any event or writing, on the part of the man and the poet. The anti-Romantic withdrawal of the writer as a singular man, of the self as mere subjectivity, limitation, and anecdote, the obstinate avoidance of the *Moi haïssable,* the disillusionment with sincerity, were significant features not only of the Symbolist tradition, from Mallarmé to Valéry, but of other literary trends toward the end of the nineteenth century. I can but touch upon this topic here. I will only quote from a letter in which Mallarmé makes his point concisely (Besançon, May 14, 1867): "c'est t'apprendre que je suis maintenant impersonnel, et non plus Stéphane que tu as connu—, mais une aptitude qu'a l'Univers Spirituel à se voir et à se développer, à travers ce que fut moi."[16] How is a poet, one might wonder, to convey any sensibility other than his own? How is he to avoid becoming a dramatist, narrator, or philosopher in verse? Through what "voices" can he speak? Now, if we are to grasp the nineteenth-century reversal culminating in the work and example of Mallarmé—after Hölderlin, of course, and Leopardi, and Baudelaire—we must not assume that modern poetry is a privileged expressive vehicle for the individual, for the singular sensibility or hypersensibility. Neither must we suppose that the alternative is inevitably dramatic or narrative. There is another way, a third mode, neither confessional nor dramatic, to which the Symbolist or post-Symbolist poet will often return. The poet, according to this mode, speaks in *his own voice*—he need not

---

[16] *Propos sur la poésie*, ed. H. Mondor (Monaco, 1946), p. 78.

be detached, dramatic, descriptive—but *not in the first person*. Machado in "A José María Palacio," as we have noticed, does not even use the first-person verb; but Mallarmé's observation, of course, is not essentially grammatical: the poet is "impersonal" insofar as he speaks *for others* (and is, in the original sense, a "prophet"), or even more, for the revelation or the discovery of an order or of a quality of being that rises above the traditional dualism between self and world.

To a certain extent the terms I am using go back to the oldest generic differentiation in the history of European poetics: the Platonic-Aristotelian distinction (*Republic* 392d-394d, *Poetics* 1448a) between literary forms in which the writer "imitates" others or "takes another personality," and those forms in which he speaks "in his own person" or in his own voice. (Homer, for example, spoke in his own person whenever he did not introduce dialogue.) At the same time, Aristotle thought, of course, that the writer imitated primarily "men in action." A firm notion of the lyric did not emerge from Greco-Roman theory, and the authors of the *artes poeticae* did not fully recognize until Petrarch and the Italian Renaissance that it was legitimate for a poet, speaking in his own voice, to impersonate no one, to "imitate" his own experience and formulate "concepts" produced by his own mind. This is the discovery which the nineteenth-century post-Romantic writer, in turn, according to an apparently dialectical historical process, would seek to transcend. For in the meantime, the uses of the poet's own "voice" and "person" had become identified with the most self-indulgent individualism, subjectivity, and so-called sincerity. And I should venture to add: when one rereads today—speaking as a layman—those pages of the *Republic* in which Plato denounces poetry, one is in a position to understand the Greek philosopher's disapprobation of the "dramatic mode," i.e., of the "imitation" (in the restricted sense of *mimeisthai*) of others: for the young citizen of the ideal state, could not poetry become an invitation to mutability, dispersion of character, irresponsibility? We have now proceeded, so to speak, from the "hateful He" to the "Moi haïssable." During the nineteenth century it was the facile use of the confessional mode, of the "sincere I," that was regarded more and more as illusory, erroneous, or morally reprehensible. That the task facing the modern writer was highly difficult and complex is made most clear today by the career of the great Portuguese poet Fernando Pessoa, who, in the most rigorous and self-punishing manner, consciously chose to identify himself with a series of fictional poets—Alvaro de Campos, Alberto Caeiro, Ricardo Reis—and thus to write under a number not of pseudonyms (superficial disguises for one's real voice) but of "heteronyms" (*other* lyrical voices). Pessoa was not able to overcome dialectically the ancient dualism of self and world, or to speak in his own person for an order of the real. He could only forswear, with desperate inventiveness, the existing conditions for a personal mode of poetry. "Falar," he wrote, "é o modo mais simples de nos tornarmos desconhecidos. E esse modo imoral e hipócrita de falar a que se chama escrever, mais completamente nos vela aos outros e àquela especie de outros a que a nossa inconsciência chama nós-próprios"[17] (Speaking is the simplest way of making ourselves unknown. And that immoral and hypocritical way of speaking which is called writing, conceals us most completely from others and from that class of "others" which our ignorance calls ourselves).

On the general subject of modern poetry, Martin Heidegger, whom Antonio Machado went on to read many years after the composition of "A José María Palacio" (as he had earlier studied, and reflected upon, Bergson), has proposed an apt metaphor. He has said that the function of the modern

---

[17] Fernando Pessoa, *Páginas de estética e de teoria e crítica literárias,* ed. Georg Rudolf Lind and Jacinto do Prado Coelho (Lisbon, n.d.), p. 42.

poet consists in serving as the "shepherd of Being" (*Hirt des Seins*). The concrete existence of men in the world and among things and other men makes possible the illumination of "Being" as underlying value and discovery. Antonio Machado himself, in the midst of either grief or faith, retains his "openness" to the world, his sense of participation in it, his ability to ask. The suppression of egocentric gesturing is closely related to the modern poet's special breadth of perspective: the perspective of the poet who may be the "shepherd of Being," or to put it in terms more appropriate to Machado, of becoming and time.[18]

The first silence that we have encountered, then, concerns the poet's own person. But this emptiness is counterbalanced by the allusive force of the basic structure of the poem: by its spoken character.

The Absent Friend

That is to say: the distant friend whom Machado remembers and imagines. I have in mind, actually, two things: the absence from which the poet suffers, and which encloses in its nostalgia the "you" of the poem, the friend who remained behind in Soria; and the allusive techniques by which both the first- and the second-person forms of the verb are concealed. As far as the latter point is concerned, it becomes necessary to glance at two principal features of the poem: the use of interrogation; and the epistolary form.

Every question postulates a dialogue (if only the self-questioning with which many poets, particularly since Mallarmé, have dramatized their lyrical monologues). As we read any of the questions in "A José María Palacio," all formulated in the third person, we cannot but be conscious of their destination.

[18] Cf. Egon Vietta, *Die Seinsfrage bei Martin Heidegger* (Stuttgart, 1950), p. 36.

¿Tienen los viejos olmos
algunas hojas nuevas?

(Are there a few new leaves
On the old elms?)

(ll. 7-8)

—writes Machado; and immediately, though allusively, the interrogated "you" seems to rise before us. I am referring to the dimension of dialogue that Stephen Gilman has elucidated in his study of *La Celestina*. A great many questions are asked in *La Celestina*: "just as the frequent exclamations express the sentiments of the 'yo,' so these questions enfold the 'tú' in what is being said."[19] A dialogue, Gilman adds, is the language resulting from the encounter between two lives. In our case, such an encounter must be limited to the mental processes of an epistle, even though most of the lines only allude to the identities of the questioner and the questioned. Machado has found the perfect device for his sleight of hand. With the help of a series of questions implying the beginning of a dialogue, the third-person of the verb fulfills also the functions of a second person.

One discovers the emotional force of an attitude that is, in fact, no more than semi-interrogative. The origin of the questions on which the poem is based is to be found somewhere between certainty and doubt, or between knowledge and ignorance. A number of constructions center on the future of probability:

ya habrán ido llegando las cigüeñas . . .

(Storks will have started to arrive . . .)

while others refer to events neither known to have taken place nor improbable:

---

[19] *The Art of the Celestina* (Madison, Wis., 1956), p. 22.

¿Hay ciruelos en flor? ¿Quedan violetas?

(Are there plum trees in bloom? Violets, still?)

These are not academic—feigned—questions, or idle conjectures. They are made possible both by a degree of certainty founded on the materials of memory and a degree of doubt with regard to the cyclical course of time. The poet remembers full well the spring months he experienced in Soria as a young man. Doubtless the blackberry bushes, the daisies, the plum trees will bloom sooner or later. But when, exactly, and in what combinations, and with what total effect? How is one to know whether the acacias are *still* bare, while at the *same* moment there are violets—those very early, humble flowers—*remaining*? Not only the poet's physical absence from Soria—from a particular spring in Soria—but the astonishing "multiplicity" of time is involved. The poet attempts, without mentioning the past, to rejoice in a similar but imperfectly imagined present. The questions addressed to Palacio allude silently to the full spectrum of emotions—remembrance and hope, nostalgia and melancholy—that can be derived from the silent passage of time.

The poem expands and comes into being gradually, step by step, as it proceeds from one question to another. It is precisely this repetition, this persistence of the interrogative mode that gives life to the desire from which the poem grows. The reader experiences a slow process of resurrection, as a distant natural scene becomes mentally real. He participates in the poet's wish to cancel distances and absences by means of words. The poet and the reader together attempt to ask Palacio what he knows and to imagine what he knows and sees. Palacio, of course, is *there*. But he is also the poet's "buen amigo" and, as such, the cornerstone of the poem in more ways than one. "Distance," Pedro Salinas has written, "is something more than a spatial and geographical reality that comes between two persons: it is a new psychological situation for both, which requires new treatment" ("Distancia es algo más que una realidad espacial y geográfica que se interpone entre dos personas: es una situación psicológica nueva entre ellas dos, y que demanda nuevo tratamiento").[20]

José María Palacio, I must emphasize, not only is but, above all, *was* the friend of the poet—when the poet's wife, Leonor (concerning whose death Machado writes elsewhere in *Campos de Castilla*), was living. Palacio knew and shared a good part of their life in Soria. Machado, now living in Baeza, does not limit himself to the solitary remembrance of things past—*only* past, and unrelated to the present. He grants no easy, no total victory to absence, separation, and the apparent discontinuity of time. He writes and questions, instead, the friend who knows and remembers a great many things—both public and private—of interest to both. There is no need, however, to mention explicitly the past. To have a friend, and to talk with him, is in itself an exercise in continuity, or perhaps a demonstration of permanence. Time, in this sense, does not corrode all. If love no longer exists, friendship may last. Palacio is a fixed point within the flow of time. He is an invaluable link not simply between two cities or two regions (Baeza and Soria, Andalusia and Castile) but between the present and the past, the living and the dead. This is, to be very brief, the situation to which the poem alludes.

The role of Palacio in the poem provides an indispensable link, too, between this situation and the reader. Let us suppose for a second that it did not exist (that the poem were not an epistle). It could be argued then that the author's meaning was not "allusive" but simply obscure or overly dependent on biographical information extraneous to the

---

[20] *El defensor* (Bogotá, 1948), p. 36.

words. There is no denying, however, as the poem stands, that Palacio establishes an effective connection between two cities and two moments in time, that he is a convincing proof of Machado's earlier relationship with Soria. On the other hand, the poet's posture could not tolerate too much clarity. Let us suppose also that he had chosen to speak in so many words of his dead wife's grave, at the poem's close: he might have written, for example, "my wife's grave" ("la tumba de mi mujer," "la sepultura de mi mujer," etc.) What would there remain, then, of the poet's indirect method, of his manifest desire to emphasize not a personal loss but the public renewal of spring and all living things? Machado wrote merely *su tierra,* "her earth," "her plot of earth"; and it should be noted in passing that the possessive pronoun in Spanish is ambiguous: *su* can signify "his" or "her." In this fashion, the poem rises in an intermediate area between concealment and explicitness—private obscurity and public clarity. I shall presently recall that this is characteristic of the letter, whether ordinary or poetic.

I have already indicated that the epistolary genre and the interrogative style are but two limited versions of a larger mode: they are forms of dialogue, in Gilman's sense—brief "encounters of two lives." In the history of literature these two forms have often met. Horace, the model for epistolary verse since the Renaissance, is exceptionally and masterfully fond of the question mark. He introduces two kinds of question most often: speculative ones, deriving from the Roman poet's moral or philosophical themes (for example, "Vir bonus est quis?" in the epistle [1, xvi, 40] on the false virtues the common people admire); and questions of a personal or familiar nature, as when Horace, separated from his friends, inquires about their activities ("Quid studiosa cohors operum struit?" in a letter [1, iii, 6] sent to a group of young noblemen studying abroad). Critics have subdivided the entire *Epistulae* in this manner: into, first, pieces of "philosophical" import; and second, friendly communications *ad familiares.* But, of course, as every reader of one of the great seventeenth-century Spanish poems, the "Epístola moral a Fabio," well knows, an *epístola moral* should also be an *epístola familiar.* The "moral" aspect of the poem prevents the letter writer from indulging too much in personal details of no general interest, on the one hand; while on the other, its "familiar" style forces the poet to bring moral philosophy down to earth, to make it comprehensible and vivid. To be sure, it is the blending of these two dimensions which best characterizes the achievement of Horace and the epistolary genre in general. The genre develops from a bold and poetically fruitful contrast between an ordinary or even colloquial style and a sweeping or even lofty intent. It makes possible, so to speak, a clash between style and theme. On a certain level, this clash echoes the basic tension and effort of the poetic letter: the attempt to make abstract thought seem relevant to a particular human being. The success of the attempt is based on the poet's ability to achieve an effective balance between the personal and the abstract—or, to return to my earlier terms, to speak in his *own* voice for *others.*

In our poem, neither the writer nor his correspondent is in the limelight. But their friendship permeates the whole, even as Garcilaso's affection for Boscán runs through this "familiar epistle" in the Horatian manner—the first, according to Elias Rivers, composed in Spanish. The moral theme in Garcilaso "is so gradually brought in," Rivers explains, "and so closely tied to the poet's friendship that it is never really impersonal at all; it is completely reshaped by the context, by the tone of the whole epistle."[21] There are a number of epistles in which

[21] Elias L. Rivers, "The Horatian Epistle and Its Introduction into Spanish Literature," *Hispanic Review,* xxii (1954), 176. Cf. also E. P. Morris, "The Form of the Epistle in Horace," *Yale Classical Studies,* ii (1931), 81-114; and Carlos Clavería, "Sobre las epístolas de Guiraut Riquier," in *Homenatge a Antoni Rubió i Lluch* (Barcelona, 1936), iii, 125-136.

the existence of the addressee is no more than a pretext, or a verbal stratagem. In our case, as in that of Garcilaso, the poetic utterance is indivisible from the friend who "knows" and is capable of reading between the lines.

There are other reasons for not underestimating the sort of association, of mental and emotional "encounter," which is central to a genuine letter as understood by Pedro Salinas in his masterly essay on the subject. Salinas' conception of the letter is not that of speech "across space," or a long-distance conversation. For writing is in this area too—despite all that may be intimate, colloquial, or informal in a letter—distinct from speaking. "More than kisses, letters mingle souls," wrote John Donne. And one might add: they do so on a surprisingly "objective" level. Letter writing, that is, can always prompt a process of alienation, objectify a man's image of himself, present his "I" as an "other." Confessional though it often is, and close to the order of experience, it implies also, like all writing, the possibility of a "moment of truth": detachment, clarity, devotion, or the recognition of subterfuge by the author—by the "I" confronted with its own "other." "El escribir," Salinas states, "es cobrar conciencia de nosotros"[22] ("Writing is the achievement of self-awareness"). A possible effect of the self-awareness induced by writing is paradoxical enough: unlike the speaker, the writer may not pretend for very long that his identity coincides with his exact words.

Machado's poem manifests in a most exemplary fashion the vital situation on which a "familiar epistle" necessarily rests. A poetic letter does not belong to the large body of literature in which an author addresses himself primarily to an *unknown* public by means of a presumably self-sufficient language. Neither is it, on the other hand, a mere exercise in conversation with a friend. The epistle seeks, rather, the form

---

[22] *El defensor*, p. 26; cf. Donne, "To Sir Henry Wotton," l. 1.

of a unilateral "versation" in which language strives to re-create the conditions of a con-versation, that is to say, of a situation based on shared and unspoken assumptions.[23]

Absence and Time

Our poem issues from the confluence of two emotions or experiences: absence and time. I have discussed mostly up to now the various kinds of absence, as well as the method through which a difficult problem is solved: the need to give voice to what does *not* exist, to articulate emptiness, depriva-tion, nonbeing. The entire poem leads to the request that Palacio visit the grave of the poet's wife. It ends with the memory of Leonor. Her death, the poet's youth, the distant past are all alluded to. Yet, in the context of "A José María Palacio," the term "memory" is not enough. The poem does not look essentially toward the past. Leonor's past death and present absence are related to a much broader and not

[23] I have in mind the concept of "situation" proposed by Charles Bally in *Le Langage et la vie*. It rests on an initial distinction between written and spoken language. In conversation, speech is supported by extralinguistic elements, such as—in the case of a man and his wife, for example—the realities which the speakers have experienced together, or share at the moment of speech, and therefore take for granted. Thus speech is often elliptical, and *does not have to be allusive*. But literary works are often allusive insofar as they need to refer to previous or undeveloped situations, or to historical experiences, as Jean-Paul Sartre makes clear in "Pour qui écrit-on?" (*Situations* [Paris, 1948], vol. II). It is obvious that in a number of literary genres the written words are linked with internal situations; for example, in Hemingway, or for that matter, the *Divina Commedia*, dialogue may constantly al-lude to an implicit situation; or in the plays of Chekhov, a dramatic situation may allow the playwright to drastically reduce dialogue. Cf. Bally, *Le Langage et la vie* (Geneva and Lille, 1952), p. 76. The notion is picked up by Francisco Romero, "Comunicación y situación," *Revista de Filología Hispánica*, V (1943), 244-250; and Alfonso Reyes, *El deslinde* (Mexico, 1944), p. 175. For a more recent view, see Lein Geschiere, "Fonctions des structures de la phrase française," in Geschi-ere, Bernard Bray, and Sem Dresden, *La Notion de structure* (The Hague, 1961), p. 20.

merely intimate picture of presences and absences, departures and growths, renewals and various other temporal processes. Obviously, there is much that Machado could not and would not *say*. Had he developed fully all the possibilities of his theme, the product might have been another poetic exercise in remembrance, nostalgia, or grief. If, conversely, none of the writer's more private sentiments had come into play, we might fail to sense emptiness or nonexistence at all. Somewhere between the twin poles of indifference (to both life and death) and nostalgia (of existence in the past), one may discover a feeling for *absence*: i.e., not for the things that once were, but for those that *are not*. Absence manifests the blending of existence and nonexistence in the world around us. As distinct from nostalgia and disillusionment, which were characteristic of Romantic poetry, the metaphysical concern with nonbeing is clearly predominant in several of the greater poets of the West from Baudelaire and Mallarmé to Wallace Stevens.

Machado's allusions fulfill a function comparable to that of certain symbols in Mallarmé. Both techniques may be regarded as responses to the challenge formulated in "Le nénuphar blanc": "résumer d'un regard la vierge absence." To recall briefly Mallarmé's prose poem: the writer has an appointment with an unknown woman; she fails to appear; the writer picks up a blossom in which emptiness is enclosed, a "nénuphar blanc," "qui ne se gonfle d'autre chose sinon de la vacance exquise de soi . . ."[24] Here a flower symbolically joins being to nonbeing. A still more famous flower, "l'absente de tous bouquets," serves to express elsewhere the effort of the mind to transcend the given boundaries of the real. To be sure, this not merely the task of poets, and in *Reason and Revolution* Herbert Marcuse quotes "l'absente de tous bouquets" while suggesting a parallel between the

[24] Stéphane Mallarmé, *Oeuvres*, ed. H. Mondor and G. Jean-Aubry (Paris, 1951), p. 286.

power of negation in Hegel (the dialectical recognition of the absent, of that-which-is-not, as part of a historical process dependent on the ability of men to denounce the limits of the factual) and the search for an authentic language in Mallarmé, Villiers de l'Isle-Adam, Breton, Brecht. "The absent," states Marcuse in this context, "must be made present because the greater part of the truth is in that which is absent."[25]

Hence the relevance for Machado of a profound feeling for time. In the Hegelian tradition it is the passage of historical time which makes nonbeing tangible. Machado's poetry is pervaded with an awareness of temporal processes in the life of man and in nature. This overwhelming concern with time runs through some of the more significant literary works produced immediately before and after World War I. In 1913 (the date of "A José María Palacio"), *Du côté de chez Swann* and *L'Evolution créatrice* are first published; and Thomas Mann begins to plan his *Zauberberg*, which the war would postpone. For the purposes of this analysis, I shall use the thought of Bergson as our principal framework.

The questions concerning temporal occurrences in "A José María Palacio"—"Has spring begun / To clothe the branches. . . ?" and the others that follow—are all asked and felt *from a distance*. The spatial dimension that is implicit in them is directly responsible for a part of their emotional force. Evidently the difference between the rhythms of the seasons in Castile and in Andalusia is relative to space. We should first notice the ways in which spatial distance accentuates one's consciousness of the passing of time.

Man's experience of space, in the philosophy of Bergson as in the intuition underlying Machado's poem, subsumes distance, division, *separation*. The different objects occupying space are impenetrable to one another and, ordinarily, het-

[25] *Reason and Revolution*, 3rd edn. (Boston, 1960), p. x.

erogeneous. What direct experience can I possibly have of a distant landscape or a natural event which my senses cannot perceive? Here time must come to my rescue, through the exercise of memory. Yet it is not the same to remember an object in order to assume its existence in the present, or its pertinence to my present actions and life, as to recapture its pastness. In the latter case, the full use of memory may represent a "désintéressement de la vie," an "inattention à la vie."[26] In the final analysis, physical separation has a negative impact. If "A José María Palacio" did not include a number of questions and statements dealing with time, if the poet had only felt the distance separating him from the streets of Soria and the plains of Castile, the tone of the poem would be negative as well. And to use his own words, Machado would find himself sadly "al borde del sendero," "on the edge of the footpath" of life.

Other sources must account for the "interest" and the "attention" urging on the questions and the statements in the poem. The author's combined experience of space and time is richer and more ambiguous than the mere acceptance of solitude. This ambiguity was scarcely insinuated in the brief poem I have just quoted from:

> Al borde del sendero un día nos sentamos.
> Ya nuestra vida es tiempo, y nuestra sola cuita
> son las desesperantes posturas que tomamos
> para aguardar . . . Mas Ella no faltará a la cita.

> (On the edge of the footpath we sit down one day.
> Now our life is time, and our only concern
> are the desperate postures that we choose to take
> so as to wait and wait . . . But It won't miss the date.)
>
> (*Del camino,* xxxv)

---

[26] Cf. Henri Bergson, *L'Energie spirituelle* (Paris, 1920), ch. v, and *Matière et mémoire* (Paris, 1946), ch. ii.

The melancholy of this early poem enfolded, actually, a seed of hope, as one realizes after reading "A José María Palacio." Hope seemed to be discarded by the spatial image at the start ("Al borde del sendero"); but it was restored by the following line: "Ya nuestra vida es tiempo. . . ." Insofar as the footpath is emblematic of the course of life, which immediately becomes identified with time, which in turn becomes all one's life, it is no longer feasible to withdraw from it—to sit on the edge of a reality that embraces *all*. The self-contradiction at the heart of the poem is most instructive: it consists in the passage from a disjunctive spatial image to the idea of all-enclosing, all-conquering time.

If space divides, time unites. I know of no formulation in Bergson which suggests this more simply and admirably than the following words: "nous ne durons pas seuls. . . ."[27]

Nous ne durons pas seuls: that time is both multiple (it subsumes several "tracks") and unitary (it is shared by all beings and things) is a large part of what "A José María Palacio" conveys to the reader. The ways of time branch off, precisely because they cover all beings and things, into an infinite number of footpaths. Our poem suggests a very complex experience of duration (in the traditional sense of *duratio*: time lasting—what remains, lives still, has *not yet* ceased to exist) as a sum or a combination of numberless durations that are "parallel" but, chronologically or rhythmically speaking, different. This is the temporal *structura structurarum* Machado's poem unfolds. First of all, there is the basic lag between the tardy spring of Castile and the earlier flowering of vegetation in Andalusia. The place and date in Andalusia are: Baeza, April 29. From the vantage point of a spring that is well advanced, that has left behind the transitional period between one season and another, Machado looks back in the direction of a slower and also more modest spring. Beneath

---

[27] *Essai sur les données immédiates de la conscience* (Paris, 1911), p. 81.

this principal contrast between Baeza and Soria—this basically dual structure—a number of additional subdivisions and detailed variations are drawn in. Luis Felipe Vivanco, with all the sensibility and knowledge needed to enter into the "Virgilian" atmosphere of the poem, has clarified in a useful article some of the features of the Castilian spring. At one end of the process are the sierras, still covered with snow, and the acacias, which grow green rather late but then quickly when they finally do.

> Aún las acacias estarán desnudas
> y nevados los montes de las sierras.
>
> (ll. 9-10)

At the other end, at the time when fruit trees have begun to bloom, the violets of February and March have faded.

> . . . ¿Quedan violetas?   (l. 24)

The other elements of the poem find their places between these two poles. Some are indicated with relative certainty, that is, without a question mark: storks, wheat fields, bees. The fruits and flowers the poet asks about are less advanced: poplars, elms, brambles, daisies, plum trees.[28] Also:

> ¿tienen ya ruiseñores las riberas?
>
> (Do riverbanks have nightingales already?)
>
> (l. 28)

A row of late-starting or slow temporal processes, then, distinct from one another but characteristic of spring in Soria, are opposed to a second cluster of processes (imagined, again, by the reader) which make up the quick reawakening of nature in Andalusia. Envisaged as a whole, all these processes compose a variegated picture of the rebirth of things.

[28] Cf. L. F. Vivanco, "Comentario a unos poemas de Antonio Machado," p. 559.

Machado knows that time is an unifying factor. (Bergson had compared the inner experience of time—his *durée*—to a melody whose notes occur in succession but are indivisible: a kind of interaction would take place, without interruption of continuity, between the various stages in a flow of qualitative change. Similar claims have been made, of course, with regard to public, natural, or geological time.) Machado also alludes at the end of the poem, rather more briefly, to what no one feels obliged to stress: that there is "a time for dying." These are some of the essential components of a poetic intuition of time that is not merely ambivalent but subtly intricate and suggestive. By "poetic intuition" I mean to suggest the general distinction between a narrator's and a poet's approach to temporal experiences. A novelist such as Stendhal or Tolstoy may develop "horizontal" dimensions by letting the reader share the actual flow, the tick-tock of time. A poet like Machado informs as succinctly and as allusively as possible a temporal emotion that is "vertically" profound, finite, nearly instantaneous, and yet open to the breadth and width of human becoming.[29]

I have been insisting upon the positive aspects of a temporal experience that is neither simple nor conventional. It is not simple, in that it offers not only an image of time as a "cluster of durations" but a confrontation with the rebirth and new youth of nature, on the one hand, and with absence, separation, mortality on the other. We are not dealing, of course, with a mere contrast between the career of nature and the life of human beings. A radical ambivalence (bridging, perhaps, as I said earlier apropos of modern poetry, the Romantic distance between "self" and "world") affects any existence or thing *sub specie temporis*—including, in the final analysis, time itself: the ultimate polarity between linear and

[29] Cf. Martin Heidegger, *Sein und Zeit* (Halle, 1927), p. 331: "Die Zeitlichkeit ist wesenhaft ekstatisch."

cyclical time. As an example of this, let us recall the closing of the poem:

> Con los primeros lirios
> y las primeras rosas de las huertas,
> en una tarde azul, sube al Espino,
> al alto Espino donde está su tierra . . .
>
> (With the earliest lilies
> And the earliest roses of the orchards,
> On a blue afternoon, go up the Espino,
> The high Espino where her plot of earth lies . . .)

The reader visualizes a spacious spring scene, and in the midst of it a grave. The beauty of a clear, sunny afternoon—a high hill, the Espino, silhouetted against a blue sky—surrounds and invades the cemetery. In other words: "her plot of earth" is an integral part of the spring scene. This integration is what the poem has gradually accomplished. From a temporal point of view, the point is crucial: the all-embracing flow of time comprehends the death (regarded as a past event) of a woman once loved, one's memory of her person (in the present), her absence, and finally, the tangible presence of her grave. (By calling the latter *tierra*, Machado accentuates its natural, physical status.) Such a combination of meanings involves a number of reciprocal effects: doubtless the life and death of a single human being are now incorporated into a universal temporal order; but youth, on the other hand, and rebirth, and beauty, coexist visibly with mortality and nonexistence. These meanings converge most clearly in the image of the flower. Machado's roses and lilies celebrate simultaneously the *vert paradis* of a past irrevocably lost and the radiance of a new season. Funeral flowers and yet (unlike the violets mentioned earlier) rich, splendid emblems of spring; innocent bearers of happy tidings (should one remember the lilies of the Annunciation, pictured in innumerable works of art?) and yet so vulnerable to the laws of time, the lilies and the roses compose together a symbol as ambivalent as the *nénuphar blanc*. It should be added, however, that one must not isolate the symbol unduly from the collective scene to which it belongs: "Con los *primeros* lirios / y las *primeras* rosas de las huertas." The adjective *primero*, employed twice, underlines the fact that these are not simply individual flowers: they are "durations" within a greater and more comprehensive "cluster of durations."

I have also said that the temporal experience suggested by Machado—heavily "literary" or old-fashioned though the theme of spring can be—is not conventional. His roses, it seems to me, have little to do with those flowers in Ausonius (or Ronsard, or Malherbe, or Herrick) that are doomed in advance to decay, and thus serve as incentives to live merrily while you may. This particular *topos* assumes that time follows a descending curve. Machado's flower *in its moment of greatest beauty* is associated with the death of others. Time is also the dimension of growth, hope, vigor, genesis. It is not a mere process of "slow dying." Every human being, confronted with mortality, "lasts" as long as he lives, and lives as long as he lasts—in unison with all the other beings of whose total "duration" he is an integral part.

The one-sided levity of the *carpe diem* tradition is foreign to our poem. Stylistic affinities exist with certain odes of Horace (1,2; IV,7, among others) where verbs and adverbs converge on a picture of natural change. For example, in the "Ode to Torquatus" (IV,7):

> Diffugere nives, redeunt iam gramina campis
>   arboribusque comae;
> mutat terra vices et decrescentia ripas
>   flumina praetereunt....[30]

---

[30] Horace, *The Odes and Epodes*, tr. C. E. Bennett, Loeb Classical Library (Cambridge, Mass. and London, 1927), pp. 310-311.

(The snow has fled; already the grass is returning to the fields and the foliage to the trees. Earth is going through her changes, and with lessening flood the rivers flow past their banks . . .)

But spring, Horace adds, will be "trampled underfoot by summer, destined likewise to pass away." In poetry such as this the passing of the seasons supports and confirms the fugacity of all things. The course of time is unequivocal. When seen from the perspective of a *single* human life, it discloses no other horizon than death. For many centuries the commonplaces of classical rhetoric and the thematics of Christianity have maintained and broadcast the language of *contemptus temporis.*

Spring itself has often served as a pretext rather than a text in European literature. I refer not to the sensual portrayal of spring as a collective, natural process in the folkloric "May songs" of the Middle Ages, but to the conception of the Provençal troubadours: there it acts as a foil or background for the self-enclosed feelings of the poet. Spring is a public, predictable event. But the poet is "different" and alone. Above all the reader observes the harmony or—most generally—the disharmony between the setting and the hero, the world and the self, the externals of spring and the inwardness of the individual soul. Obviously this is the egocentric attitude which Machado (like the great Catalan poet Verdaguer in his "La plana de Vich," as Vivanco notes) chooses to reverse. In "A José María Palacio" it is not the coming of spring that fails to occupy the foreground; it is the poet himself. The processes of spring are here the mold in which the writer's principal intuition—regarding the nature of time—has been cast.

Machado's readers sense full well his resignation, his philosophical stance, his melancholy, or rather, his slow return from melancholy. But the poem manifests also a feeling of plenitude. Time is not just illusory or destructive. Maybe the gods, thought Hölderlin, are in need of man, who lives in temporality, who knows desire, expectation, memory, creation. The consciousness of time as the dimension of plenitude finds its climax perhaps in the wonder caused by the dawning, the beginning, the awakening or reawakening of things: "the experience of genesis," "the sense of an origin" ("la emoción del origen"), as it has sometimes been called.[31] "O bonheur!" writes Flaubert in the *Tentation* of 1874, "bonheur! J'ai vu naître la vie, j'ai vu le mouvement commencer."

> ¿Tienen los viejos olmos
> algunas hojas nuevas?   (ll. 7-8)

Machado's wonder at the renewal of life and the rebirth of things, clad as it is in questioning, poised on the edge between being and nonbeing, could scarcely render more purely "the sense of an origin"—or to recall Hofmannsthal's definition of the superior poem, "a presentiment of blooming" ("eine Ahnung des Blühens").[32] The solidarity of time, of duration shared by all, does not contradict one's consciousness of a "not yet"—of not having *yet* died. Genesis and death meet and fuse in a single line of verse:

> ¿Hay ciruelos en flor? ¿Quedan violetas?
>
>   (l. 24)

From Absence to Presence: Poetry as Process

Earlier in this essay I discussed the peculiar continuity of literary communication. Poetic language, I suggested, tends

[31] Cf. Walter F. Otto, "Die Zeit und das Sein," in *Anteile. Martin Heidegger zum 60. Geburtstag* (Frankfurt am Main, 1950).

[32] In such poems "zugleich ein Hauch von Tod und Leben zu uns herschwebt, eine Ahnung des Blühens, ein Schauder des Verwesens. . . . Jedes vollkommene Gedicht ist Ahnung und Gegenwart, Sehnsucht und Erfüllung zugleich" ("Das Gespräch über Gedichte," in *Gesammelte Werke. Prosa II*, ed. H. Steiner [Frankfurt am Main, 1951], p. 110).

to be incremental. Like a house in the making, a poem is a process in which new components are deliberately added to ones already in place. *Verba manent*: the words do not vanish or cease to be operative after they have fulfilled their original function. On the other hand, one should notice how a poet makes use of the successive or *temporal* dimension of speech; the special mode of permanence of poetic language— the way words "remain"—is a kind of mental accretion.

Of this our poem is a clear instance. Thematically, "A José María Palacio" presents the birth of a landscape: spring as gradual resurrection. Formally, it comes into being through a parallel process of expansion. We can now see that the experience of genesis, "the sense of an origin," grants the poem its dynamic structural principle. It *grows*—as the flowers of spring grow; it is a matter of *croissance,* to use Valéry's term: "cent instants divins ne construisent pas un poème, lequel est une durée de croissance et comme une figure dans le temps."[33]

As the poem begins we first receive an impression of volume and distance. There is a vast panoramic view, wide and far-reaching like so much of Castile. The eye follows the valley of the river Duero, until it meets the mountains on the frontier of Aragon. Poplars are silhouetted against the plain. If only they were green, they would stand out and underline the curve of the river. Details are subordinated to the whole. We are provided with a landscape and a view; above all, we are beholders.

Spring remains uncertain; no more than a few new leaves can be expected from the ancient elms. And the next element is negative: the acacias are still bare; after which the disappointed eye returns to the snowcapped mountains of winter, to the airiness and the space that a visual perspective requires:

[33] *Variété III* (Paris, 1936), p. 15.

> Aún las acacias estarán desnudas
> y nevados los montes de las sierras.

(ll. 9-10)

But now the particulars become less bulky, more precise, more intimate. Suddenly bramble bushes (on a rocky hillside still) make their appearance, as well as the first, lowly flowers: white daisies among the grass. The unity of the visual field is being broken while the poet busies his imagination with smaller and smaller things: bushes, bees, violets. On this occasion, too, the introduction of detail and the reduction of distance reveal the observer's increasing concern.[34] In fact, the poet ceases to be an observer or a spectator. To be sure, the reader keeps the Castilian countryside well in mind. But it is no longer a landscape.[35] It has become a setting: beings and things are not there primarily to be contemplated, but to be lived with.

The renewal of spring appears to affect all participants, to populate the poem and quicken its rhythm. It involves human beings as well as "nature." The plains, the mountains, and the trees of Soria are now succeeded by some of the things men do or build in order to make a physical environment their own—churches, ploughed fields—and finally by the men themselves: the farmhands, the hunters. This process is made most visible by the acceleration occurring in the second half of the poem. But it had begun earlier, though with a more limited palette and cast of characters—soon after the last reference to the snowcovered mountains and the naked poplars and acacias. The double coloration of the Moncayo, white and pink—with or without snow—had brought us to the frontier of spring. At that point we encountered the first signs of a change of seasons, the first flowering: the "brambles in

---

[34] Cf. José Ortega y Gasset, *La deshumanización del arte*, in *Obras completas* (Madrid, 1955), iii, 360-363.

[35] Cf. Romano Guardini, *Form und Sinn der Landschaft in den Dichtungen Hölderlins* (Stuttgart and Tübingen, 1946).

bloom"; and then the flowers themselves, the daisies growing in a grass of which we may only imagine the color. But of course, our springtime setting must grow green again. Soon we discover "green wheat fields." In the meantime, space has been filled with movement: storks have flown across the vertical lines of the church towers. There follow the seedlands, the greenness and the rain, the fertility, the peasants working with the animals—much of this in a single, accelerating sentence marked by the reiteration of the conjunction *y*:

> Habrá trigales verdes,
> y mulas pardas en las sementeras,
> y labriegos que siembran los tardíos
> con las lluvias de abril. . . .
>
> (ll. 19-22)

We find only two verbs designating an action: *siembran, libarán*. I have stressed already the visual values of the poem's opening. Now the other senses come into play—smell and taste:

> . . . Ya las abejas
> libarán del tomillo y el romero.
>
> (ll. 22-23)

One hears, further on, based on alliteration of rolled *r*'s, the voice of the nightingale:

> ¿tienen ya ruiseñores las riberas?   (l. 28)

And then the social, nearly aristocratic, pleasures of the hunt. Our setting has become a little world. Yet precisely at this moment, just when the experience of time becomes most intense, through a growing identification of the poet's inwardness with the entire springtime scene, Palacio is addressed again. All that is absent and alluded to reenters our consciousness, rejoins the overall process of spring. The humble, dying violets are associated with the plum trees in bloom, in a final transition to the ambiguity of the last four lines.

The process of growth has not stopped: logically enough, the Castilian spring, with whose modesty Machado had sympathized earlier, bursts forth in splendor as the poem closes. Its last components are the most pleasurable: nightingales, lilies, roses. Machado is saying to Palacio: do not visit the grave until spring has fully come into its own. By the same token, the poet appears to become a spectator once more. I have been emphasizing the linear development of "A José María Palacio." On another level, its form is cyclical. As the poem closes, broad vistas are being opened again. The reader looks into the distance, as he did earlier toward the "montes de las sierras" and the "cielo de Aragón." But the view is no longer the same. The circle of the poem is rather like a spiral. Spring will reach its peak before long. On the day that Palacio will accomplish his mission, the orchards of Soria will be filled with flowers under a radiant blue sky.

The Stylistics of Allusion: Methodology

The stylistic analysis of literature is based normally on the following assumption: that a perfect junction exists between the "signifying" and the "signified" elements of a work. Whether the formalist begins with the minute examination of phonetic and grammatical materials and then goes on to explicate their sense (what Dámaso Alonso calls "forma exterior"), or proceeds from the sense to the words (his "forma interior"), the fact remains that he hopes to discover the principles governing the necessary adequacy of the meaning of a literary work to its verbal designs.

The poem that we are studying requires a different set of assumptions and methods. I have just shown that "A José María Palacio" overflows with allusive meanings. Our problem, then, is this: we have observed that the total *significatum* of the poem—the complex of notions and emotions it conveys —is a product not only of the words and the sentences that are *there*, that are visible (or audible), that are demonstrably articulated, but of the *absent* words suggested by those that are present. A verbal construct is not like a visual sign: a mere examination of the visible leads to an overestimation of what is only superficial or partial. If the *significatum* encloses a series of essential "silences," is it reasonable to look in the written structures of the poem—grammatical, rhythmical, etc.—for a perfect adjustment to what is really said? Is this a legitimate method? If we were to follow it without demur, we would be forced to admit that the suggestive aspects of the work are not expressive; we would confess that the "silences" are not objective components of the poem but figments of the reader's imagination; and assume that they are not among the causes of the poetic experience we have been commenting upon.

But this is not what we have seen and understood. Let anyone who is in doubt read and reread the poem as honestly and sensitively as he can; and let him ask himself what the source is of the lyrical emotion which undeniably, irresistibly descends upon the reader with the very first lines of the poem:

> Palacio, my good friend,
> Has spring begun
> To clothe the branches of the poplar trees
> Along the river and the roads? ...

This emotion, I think, derives essentially from the evocation and the self-restraint working between the lines and the words: from the interrogative mode, the serenity of the poet, the psychological situation implied. One could also speak of a tone of voice, an attitude, as necessary conditions for the poetic effect that is achieved. At any rate, the foundations of the poem, from whatever angle we may wish to approach them, clearly subsume the various choices we have already singled out: the self-effacement of the "I," the function of the person to whom the questions are addressed, the relevance of friendship (tolerant of so many silences), the framework of the past, of memory, death, and the area of meaning where a forward-looking concept of time and a consciousness of nonexistence meet.

I am not denying, of course, that the "present" verbal structures and devices are responsible for the overall effect of the poem. But I am concerned with the nature of this responsibility. My point is that we are not confronted with the kind of causal relationship to which the study of *style* is usually restricted. This kind could be described as a one-to-one relationship: the structure or the device produces *directly* the effect. It could be set down symbolically as: A = B. The *significans* A is joined to the *significatum* B. It is assumed that A has been articulated fully by the poet; and that B and A are "joined" as the two aspects of a visible *sign*—what is seen and what is meant—are fused: a sort of coincidence, rather than a causal linkage, is to be recognized.

The alternate assumption, which I venture to support, is that successful poetic form presupposes *also* a basic connection between the latent or tacit parts of the *significans* and the words actually uttered or written. The first task of stylistic research should consist in observing the adequacy of the written words to the absent words. The theoretical model would be: A + X = B. That is to say: a series of written components (A) plus a series of unwritten ones (X) make possible the total impact of the poem. The efficiency of A is proved by its ability to move in the direction of X, and *then*, together with X, to disclose B. The phonetic and grammatical components considered in isolation can only lead us to perceive a meaning from which the aftermath of all the unwritten premises has been subtracted (A = B − X).

Further, the added quantity X belongs, I think, to the very base of the poetic pyramid: it is closely tied to the sounds and the grammatical resources of the poem; it is like an invisible supplement to these sounds and resources. The "silences" should be regarded as a part of the *significans*. If our subject were a visual sign, they would embrace colors and spatial proportions. As far as the verbal work of art is concerned, this particular cohesiveness should be understood very probably as one of the aesthetic functions of language. The bond between A and X on the level of the *significans* is an extension of the systematic properties of a poem. Earlier in this essay I recalled that there is no restricted one-to-one nexus between signifying and signified in a poem: between, for example, the sound *amigo* and the meaning of *amigo*. The poem as a whole is a single sign. A brief utterance such as *amigo* is pertinent to extensive strata or series in the poem—for example, to the *entire* first line ("Palacio, buen amigo") to the assonance in *í-o* found in the fourth line ("del río y los cam*í*nos"), and so on. Literary language transfers the qualities of system from the linguistic code to the poetic message by creating a network of reciprocal relationships between all the parts of a single sign. Now, if "A José María Palacio" were not a successful poem, not a single sign, not a finished complex of forms, the numerous allusions it offers would make up a vague halo on the periphery of the poetic utterance. Insofar as it is a little system, however, the silences (including such larger or generic structures as the function of the epistolary form, which cannot be circumscribed by any element of "style") become part and parcel of the poem itself. A work of literature is a compound of explicit statement and allusive form. It refers constantly to what lies apparently beyond itself: to an underlying "situation" in "A José María Palacio"; in other poems, to contemporary history, etc. A basic virtue of a writer's "style"—and by style we usually mean the visible portion of the iceberg—resides in the adequacy of the explicit statements to the allusive forms.

I will attempt to show this adequacy in "A José María Palacio" by means of a few examples. Generally speaking, the poem manifests the allusive power of a "low" style—a *sermo humilis*—in modern Spanish. This style at once conceals and reveals a great deal of inner tension. To be sure, we are far from the uninspired parsimony of much ordinary prose. One admires Machado's serenity and self-control. How does a man whose verbal reserve hides a wealth of feeling express himself? In two ways, perhaps: on the one hand, in a leisurely yet concentrated manner, with numerous pauses and unusual clarity of syntax; on the other, with sudden contrasts or reversals, repetitions or exhortations, and a lack of transitions, seeming somewhat harsh at times. Essentially, this style betrays a difference or distance between the "inner" and the "outer" man, between our visible or audible appearance and our "invisible" selves. Thus the qualities I am pointing out all derive from a combination of inner intensity and external simplicity of means.

Pauses. Nothing is more characteristic of reserve in the exercise of speech. The beginning of the poem, for example, includes a number of enjambments. After the initial vocative, a silence of the kind that follows the beginning of a letter or of a speech ("Palacio, buen amigo") prepares the unhurried start of the first question, the object of which does not become clear until the third line; meanwhile, a slight delay separates not only the verb from its predicate but the two parts of the compound verb "está vistiendo" ("is clothing"):

> ¿está la primavera
> vistiendo ya las ramas ... ?

The delay coincides with the reader's expectation. Not so in the next enjambment, where the repetition of *de* soothes our impatience:

> ... las ramas *de* los chopos
> *de*l río y los caminos? ...

And the words surface slowly, also through the pause between the next two lines:

> ... En la estepa
> del alto Duero. ...

This technique recalls to a certain extent the "soft enjambment" ("encabalgamiento suave") in Garcilaso, studied by Dámaso Alonso.[36] And it represents a heightening by syntactical means of the constant passage from speech to silence which takes place, of course, after every line of verse—as Mallarmé acknowledged in "Mimique": "le silence, seul luxe après les rimes."

CONTRASTS. Within the overall gentleness and moderation of the poem, there are moments that disclose a change of emotional attitude. Usually they respond to the appearance on the surface or "outside" of the poem of sentiments previously maintained "inside." On two occasions this change is rendered by a shift from the prevailing interrogative mode to an exclamation. At the end of the second sentence, the poet exclaims briefly:

> ¡pero es tan bella y dulce cuando llega! ...

Less restrained now, the understated emotion will flow out more freely a little later (and allow itself the repetition of *bella*):

> ¡Oh mole del Moncayo blanca y rosa,
> allá, en el cielo de Aragón, tan bella!
>
> (ll. 11-12)

The sense of release is denoted by the extension of the same vocalic sound at the beginning of each of these lines: *o-ó*, first (*Oh mole*), and then *a-á* (*allá*). The reader views and shares the gradual liberation of a repressed aggregate of emotions.

---

[36] Cf. *Poesía española*, p. 69.

RECURRENCES. There are fourteen sentences. If we discard the exclamations and the ending, we find but two syntactical modes: the question (six sentences) and the future of probability (five). There are three kinds of questions, all very simple. Verb, subject, and predicate—i.e., the order most likely to accentuate the interrogatory purpose:

> ¿*Tienen* los viejos olmos
> algunas hojas nuevas?　　　　(ll. 7-8)

Just once we have verb, predicate, and subject:

> ¿*tienen* ya ruiseñores las riberas?
> 　　　　　　　　　　　　(l. 28)

The third kind is extraordinarily bare and unadorned:

> ¿*Hay* zarzas florecidas ... ?
> .　　.　　.　　.　　.　　.　　.　　.
> ¿*Hay* ciruelos en flor? ¿*Quedan* violetas?
> 　　　　　　　　　　　　(ll. 13, 24)

Every question begins with a verb. The uses of the future of probability, on the other hand, are rather more varied. The alternation between these two constructions prevents monotony. But the intertwining of the two fulfills a more significant function as well.

I have already discussed the poet's vacillation between half-certainty and half-doubt. The method I propose to follow here does not consist, however, in moving directly from syntax to *significatum*. My concern is with the strategies of implication and allusiveness. I am trying to show how certain forms of verbal sobriety are linked with different manifestations of psychic tension in order to create for a restrained complex of emotions its most appropriate mold. Now, there are certain aspects of style that permit us to distinguish between these two forces: for example, the self-restraint indicated by the numerous pauses; or the intensity suggested by the exclamations and other sudden changes in emotional direction. What is the main effect, then, of these grammatical recurrences?

In his study of the poetry of Vicente Aleixandre, Carlos Bousoño points out that repetition can cause what he calls "negative dynamism" ("dinamismo negativo"). Thus, in our poem the recurrence of questioning supports the generally slow gait of the language, not only because all the questions converge on a single goal (in Bousoño's terms, they are "imágenes que encubren una misma realidad"),[37] but insofar as they obey the same pendular, cyclical rhythm. On the other hand, the constant return of the same modes, the same oscillation between one construction and another seems to give voice to a near-obsession or at least a persistent need: a continuity of inner effort. The reader perceives the slow tick-tock of an *emotion*.

Actually, no recurrence is complete, and there is no duplication. For example, let us observe with care the repetition of *primeros* and of the request to climb the Espino—"sube al Espino"—as the poem closes:

> Con los *primeros* lirios
> y las *primeras* rosas de las huertas,
> en una tarde azul, *sube al Espino*,
> *al alto Espino* donde está su tierra . . .

There is a noticeable blending of recurrence and change. Machado opposes two pairs, the second term of which is like an extension, a stretching, a gentle "pull" of the first:

> los primeros lirios
> las primeras rosas de las huertas
>
> sube al Espino
> al alto Espino donde está su tierra

[37] Cf. Carlos Bousoño, *La poesía de Vicente Aleixandre* (Madrid, 1950), pp. 145-150.

Machado's apparent symmetries make possible, then, an immeasurably more profound effect of style: the alternation between tension and distension. Let us now analyze some of these crucial delays or lengthenings of *tempo*.

PROTRACTED RHYTHMS. No rhythm can be modified or broken, obviously, before it has been established. This is one of the most elementary devices of literary expression: writers set up patterns in order to have an opportunity to upset them. (The upsetting, to recall another truism, is normally more significant than the pattern: hence the uselessness in this area of statistics, computers, and other quantitative tools.) In "A José María Palacio" there are a great many symmetries, parallelisms, internal assonances, and other harmonious relations. For example, the bisyllabic words enclosing an assonance: "chopos," "olmos," "ramas," "zarzas," "blancas," "capas," "pardas," "allá," "habrá"; and also "acacias," "faltarán"; even though the rhyme demands an assonance in *é-a*. Let us reread the brief quartet:

> ¿Hay zarzas florecidas
> entre las grises peñas,
> y blancas margaritas
> entre la fina hierba?   (ll. 13-16)

The pendular movement is due to a neat parallelism based on the number two. The first and third lines obey the same rhythm. The prosodic accents fall, besides, on the same sequence of vowels—*á, a, í, a*:

> Hay zárzas florecídas
>
> .   .   .   .   .   .
>
> y blán cas margarítas

The third line, in fact, is restricted completely to the stressed vocalic sounds *i* and *a*. Moreover, these constitute an additional assonant rhyme. As for the second and fourth lines, they offer nearly perfect symmetries on the vocalic, syntactical, and rhythmical levels:

> éntre las gríses péñas,
>
> .   .   .   .
>
> éntre la fína hiérba?

There the placing of an accent on the fourth syllable creates a contrast with the neighboring lines, bringing out sharply the *i* sound. For the following heptasyllabic—still another seven-syllable line—"Por esos campanarios," returns to what had been the predominant rhythm since "Palacio, buen amigo,"

> y bláncas margarítas
>
> .   .   .   .
>
> Por ésos campanários,

and to a row of three *a*'s in succession: *campanarios*; which in turn set up a contrast with the prosodic third-syllable stress on *i* in the next *endecasílabo* (less frequent than the accent on an even syllable):

> ya habrán ído llegándo las cigüéñas. . . .
>
> (l. 18)

echoing an earlier line, just as leisurely:

> y nevádos los móntes de las siérras.
>
> (l. 11)

This rhythm is repeated further on, in lines 22, 23, and, above all, 28, where it brings to a halt the acceleration of the central section of the poem and restores the earlier *tempo lento*:

> ¿tiénen yá ruiseñóres las ribéras?

Another example will clarify this fundamental opposition between symmetry (syntactical, vocalic, accentual) and protraction or prolongation (rhythmical). Let us notice the remarkable parallelism already present in the first four lines. In order to underline it, I shall cut off the two hendecasyllabics and reduce them to the status of heptasyllabics:

> Palacio, buen amigo,
> ¿está la primavera
> vistiendo ya las ramas ...
> del río y los caminos? ...

Four seven-syllable lines of identical rhythm. But the third and fourth lines are, so to speak, stretched, expanded, in agreement with the syntax:

> vistiendo ya las ramas *de los chopos*
> del río y los caminos? *En la estepa*

There the temporal delay is flagrant. As the poem opens, however, this particular rhythmical form is operative in a far subtler and softer manner. Yet it must be sought out, for, as we have seen earlier, the entire intonation of the poem is rooted in the first line.

The initial heptasyllabic, by virtue of its sense and of the pause corresponding to the comma, is composed of two counterbalanced parts:

> Palácio / buen amígo.

Likewise, the first word appears to divide into two sections—*Pala-cio*—of which the second functions just as *-migo* does with respect to *buen a-*: as a brief, delaying addition.

This first line offers something like a paradigm, which the rest of the poem "unfolds" on a number of levels (*Palacio, buen amigo* includes the five vowels of the Spanish phonological system, while its two prosodic accents single out the two extremes of the latter, *a* and *i*, which will become predominant in the poem), and it would require a great deal of space to do it justice. I will only indicate here its crucial rhythmical role: the *tempo* of prolongation or delay it imparts to the poem from the start, thus helping to set its unhurried, serene, reflective tone. There is an undeniable pause after the second syllable of *Palacio*, and a more marked one, of course, after the whole word: rather than an iambic, we have an amphibrachic (‿ ′ ‿) rhythm. The pause may be due to the repetition of the broad vowel *a*, followed by a mute fricative (the Castilian *c*) lending itself to prolongation: *PalaC-io*. For an essential fraction of a second, at any rate, one notices the first delay or suspension. It is precisely this suspension that the second hemistich echoes and extends: *buen ami-go*. And what is more important, above it a larger protraction takes place, involving the entire second hemistich with respect to the first:

> Palacio . . .
> buen amigo.

The main effect of the line, and its principal function as paradigm, resides in this extension from the first to the second hemistich. The passage from the triad to the tetrad produces a muted but unquestionable phenomenon of distension and release.

In deference to my readers, I will not analyze in any further detail the ways in which the rest of the poem elaborates this rhythm. I will only add that a numerical law should not be inferred from the initial three to four relationship. To be sure, this proportion, with some variations, is repeated immediately (inasmuch as the second syllable of *está* is heavily stressed):

> Palacio / buen amigo
> está / la primavera
> vistiendo / ya las ramas. . . .

But other numerical combinations are also at work in the poem. We have in lines 27 and 28:

...Palacio, buen amigo, / ¿tienen ya ruiseñores las riberas?

where the earlier extension is itself extended. There emerges from all these combinations a "formal" relationship which they have in common. We need only recall, for example, the contrast between the symmetrical rhyme scheme of the Spanish *romance*—the punctual return of the assonance after every second line—and the frequent shifts from a seven- to an eleven-syllable line. The stylistic "law" of the poem resides, then, in the general interaction between two factors: *symmetrical regularity* and *temporal extension*. The poem offers, within a harmonious framework, a sequence of "extensions" corresponding to the gradual release of an inner complex of "silent" emotions.

Motion and Emotion

It should not be necessary, in closing, to return to the *significatum* of our poem, which I have discussed at length as an exercise in the exegesis of allusion, nor to attempt an unavoidably superficial survey of the poetry of "silence" from Wordsworth to Lorca, with passing references to Flaubert's *chaudron fêlé*. This tradition is well known to the students of Rodenbach and Maeterlinck, Pascoli and Gide, Norwid and Ungaretti, and of course Stendhal and Hemingway; of the theater of Stanislawski and Chekhov; and of Charlie Chaplin and Marcel Marceau as well.[38] "Les paroles que nous pro-

[38] I have discussed this tradition and some of these writers in the Spanish version of this essay, "Estilística del silencio," pp. 27-31. In the text above I allude to *Madame Bovary*, Rodenbach's *Le Règne du silence*, and, *inter alia*, this notation of July 31, 1905 in Gide's *Journal 1889-1939* (Paris, 1948), p. 170: "mais j'admire à présent tout ce que je suis arrivé à n'y pas dire, à *réserver*. Je songe longuement à cette vertu que peut devenir chez un écrivain 'la réserve'. . . ." Cf. Natalia Benedetti, *La formazione della poesia pascoliana* (Florence, 1939), p.

nonçons n'ont de sens," said Maeterlinck, "que grâce au silence où elles baignent."[39] Let us assume that a "poetry of silence" exists and, in a last homage to Antonio Machado, ask a final question with regard to its nature and status as a species of art.

My hypothesis is this: the contrast between symmetry and temporal delay in "A José María Palacio" is but an individual instance of a more general aesthetic condition: the interaction in a literary work of art between a principle of unity and a principle of expansion.

For our analysis has confronted us with a paradox. We have isolated and identified a surprising fact, to wit, that the "silences" of a poem—the allusive structures built into it— which seem to enjoy no phonetic body, i.e., which do not seem to be perceived by the senses, are among the first causes of the poetic effect. Now, most aestheticians recognize that the roots of an aesthetic experience are sensorial.[40] The behold-er, the listener, the reader *perceive* a "created" object. The color or the sound in a work of art is so "opaque" as to act upon us, first and last, as a color or a sound: it does not "transparently" permit us to indulge in daydreaming, cen-trifugal associations, conjectures as to likenesses, and so on. We are riveted, through our senses, to an immediate, pres-ent object. We perceive a poem aesthetically, writes Eliseo Vivas, "when we read it with rapt, intransitive attention on

---

55; and on the Polish poet Norwid, Czeslaw Milosz, "La poésie polonaise," *Preuves*, no. 166 (Dec. 1964), p. 14: "c'est ce don de bal-butiement qui est pour moi le fruit le plus précieux de la culture du sol linguistique par les symbolistes."

[39] *Le Trésor des humbles* (Paris, 1917), p. 23.

[40] *Aisthètèrion* meant "organ of sense" in Greek, and *aisthètikos* "capable of sense perception," "sensitive." In this sense, too, A. G. Baumgarten, who coined the term "aesthetic," gave this definition of a poem in his *Meditationes philosophicae* (1735): "oratio sensitiva perfecta."

its full presentational immediacy."[41] Works of art *captivate* us: absorbed, fascinated, nearly hypnotized in some cases, we annul and revoke whatever lies beyond these artistic objects: our minds and bodies surrender willingly to such captors.

It should be added and emphasized, however, that the appreciation of art, precisely because it is "captivating," knows no simple material limits. The sensuality of the experience accounts, to be sure, for its concentration on a finite object. But it makes possible also an intensity or depth of involvement, on the part of the observer's whole being, that one cannot readily visualize in terms of physical boundaries. I venture to think, in fact, that this experience should not be visualized at all. The perception of language, whether ordinary or poetic, engages essentially the ear, not the eye. The enjoyment of literature (as Wilhelm Meister and the Romantics well knew) can be more aptly compared to the enveloping effects of music (or of architecture) than to the distant observation of easel painting. It is a prerequisite of literary criticism to discard all *visual* conceptions of *form*. For they have led too often to an overestimation of contour, distance, and contemplation. They turn participants into spectators and apply to aesthetic events a strict dualism of self and world. It seems to me that poetry, instead, is experienced dynamically, intimately, and "in the round." Considered as an object, a work of literature is a small semiotic system. From the point of view of the reader, who brings it to life, it should be regarded as an environment.

Literary form (actually a complex of forms, in the plural) is not static. It *moves*. This is one of the lessons of the "poetry of silence." A process of expansion occurs within the order of the poem and as a product of that order. But it does not tend necessarily toward vagueness or open-endedness. It leads

[41] *Creation and Discovery* (New York, 1955), p. 76. See also Arthur Szathmary, "Symbolic and Aesthetic Expression in Painting," *Journal of Aesthetics and Art Criticism*, XIII (1954), 86-96.

from a network of recurrences to a complementary structure of silences or allusions, from the inner to the outer circles of a singular environment. The phonetic substance of the poem evokes imaginary "spheres" at the same time that it controls them, for the suggestiveness of words is a function of their inexhaustible ability to captivate. Américo Castro has shown, with reference to Cervantes, what "contagious vitality" the written word can have.[42] This vitality is not easy to measure or to circumscribe; but it should not be detached from its formal origins. It may very well be that every genuine poem relates a principle of unity to a principle of expansion. Is this dynamic and dialectical relationship one of the distinctive features of the verbal work of art? Does it parallel an endless movement back and forth between language and silence? Does it make absence aesthetically perceptible? Does it bring to the imagination, to the farthest circles of a poetic sphere, the qualities of a sensual experience? Is it a continuing process of motion and emotion, expansion and contraction, breathing in and breathing out, like the pulsations of a little world? Is this one of the conditions, perhaps, of *el misterio de la poesía*?

[1957]

[42] Cf. "La palabra escrita y el 'Quijote,'" in *Hacia Cervantes*, 3rd edn. (Madrid, 1967), p. 374. In the context of Professor Castro's idea, there would be much to be learned from the study of Herder's conception of the literary art (as distinct from the other arts) as energy (*Energie*) based on the force (*Kraft*) of words as mental images: see I. *Kritisches Wäldchen* (1769).

IV

On The Concept and Metaphor
of Perspective

In the fourth chapter of their *Theory of Literature*, René
Wellek and Austin Warren discussed the fallacies of "relativism" and "absolutism" as critical approaches to literature.
Relativism, by referring the literary work exclusively to the
values of its own time, ignores its continuing identity and for-
feits any effective instrument of valuation. Absolutism dis-
dains all relations between literature and history, or submits
them to doctrinaire preconceptions. The answer to both, the
authors proposed, was "perspectivism," an intermediate attitude signifying "that we recognize that there is one poetry,
one literature, comparable in all ages, developing, changing,
full of possibilities."[1] Poetic works should be referred to the
values of their own time *and* of subsequent periods. Their
meaning results from a process of temporal accretion which
is like an accumulation of critical perspectives. Perspectives,
then, are both critical (they are illuminations of the work of
art) and historical (they belong to the process of literary history). They combine the procedures of literary criticism with
those of literary history understood as a dynamic and temporal process, while avoiding the extremes implicit in both:
individualistic chaos (criticism) and dogmatism (historicism). All these ideas, I should note, particularly for the
benefit of those few comparatists who have no Spanish, are
related to a general attitude in twentieth-century thought for
which José Ortega y Gasset was the most eloquent spokes-

[1] (New York, 1949), p. 35. "On the Concept and Metaphor of
Perspective" was first printed in *Comparatists at Work. Studies in
Comparative Literature*, ed. Stephen G. Nichols, Jr., and Richard
B. Vowles (Waltham, Mass., 1968), pp. 28-90.

man. Actually, in an earlier version of the same chapter, René Wellek made clear his acquaintance with Ortega's uses of the term perspectivism.[2]

My own concern with perspectivism was awakened many years ago by my reading of Ortega y Gasset and René Wellek. The training of a Hispanist-comparatist indeed owed, in my not untypical case, a great deal to both. It made possible the following survey of the metaphor of perspective, which I know full well cannot do justice to either the great range of the subject or the technical requirements of every individual part. I propose it as a preliminary essay and an effort to bring several approaches—several perspectives—to bear on a single metaphorical area which doubtless is still "developing, changing, full of possibilities."

I

Perspectiva, or *ars perspectiva,* derives from the Latin verb *perspicere,* meaning "to see clearly," "to examine," "to see through," and also "to regard mentally," "to ascertain." *Perspectiva* was a medieval Latin noun used to designate optics, the science of sight, which, since it rested on the application of Euclidian laws to vision, was considered a branch of geometry—"ancella," Dante calls it in the *Convivio* (Treatise II, Chap. 13)—and a part of the academic *quadrivium.* But Landino, in an early commentary on one of the passages in the *Divina Commedia* dealing with such optical phenomena as reflection and refraction, wrote that perspective "é parte di filosofia e parte di geometria"[3]—a significantly broader definition. The high esteem in which scholastic writers held optics is made particularly clear by Roger Bacon in his *Opus majus* (1267), where it plays a central role. Bacon

[2] Cf. "Six Types of Literary History," in *English Institute Essays* (New York, 1946), p. 121.

[3] As quoted by A. Parronchi, *Studi sulla dolce prospettiva* (Milan, 1964), p. 10.

relies on the medieval tradition represented most originally by the Arabic scientist Alhazen (Ibn al-Haitham, ca. 965-1039), whose writings on optics were translated into Latin by Gerard of Cremona in the twelfth century, and his follower, the thirteenth-century Polish writer Witelo. Bacon followed tradition, then, in affirming not only that sight was the noblest of the five senses, but that no other science could offer the beauty, sweetness, and usefulness of optics: "sed nulla tantam suavitatem et pulchritudinem utilitis habet."[4] These words remind us of the prestige which optics enjoyed during the Middle Ages and which certain Florentine artists of the Quattrocento had in mind as they confronted the problem of projecting the three dimensions of space on the flat surfaces of painting.[5]

I have noted that the verb *perspicere* meant both "to see clearly" and, metaphorically, "to regard mentally," "to ascertain." It should be remembered at this point that the identification of light and the perception of light with divine or higher truths had been a continuing symbol in Mediterranean cultures since earliest historical times. Broad though the topic is, it must be kept in mind as a frame of reference for later uses of perspective as a cognitive metaphor. The Middle Ages had derived the conception of God as light from three main sources: Greek and Roman philosophy, the Bible (Psalms 36, John 1:1-9 and 8:12, James 1:17, for example), and Judeo-Arabic thinkers like Ibn-Gabirol. Metaphysical speculations concerning the nature of light—an important feature of thirteenth-century scholasticism—revolved to a large extent around one question: that of the relationship between corporeal and spiritual light.[6] Two principal traditions

[4] *The 'Opus Majus' of Roger Bacon*, ed. J. H. Bridges (Frankfurt am Main, 1964), II, 3.

[5] Cf. Parronchi, *Studi sulla dolce prospettiva*. On the contribution of Alhazen, see H. Bauer, *Die Psychologie Alhazens* (Münster, 1911).

[6] On this topic, see J. A. Mazzeo, "Light Metaphysics, Dante's 'Convivio' and the Letter to Can Grande della Scala," *Traditio*, XIV

were influential, the first of which affirmed that physical light was indivisible from spiritual light, as Augustine had stated;[7] while the other held that these were basically distinct entities, in agreement with Thomas Aquinas, who thought that to designate both by means of the same word was a verbal rather than a conceptual coincidence: "nihil enim prohibet unum nomen imponi rebus quantumcumque diversis."[8] Scholastic philosophers took a number of different positions. Yet these appear to share a common view of the universe as a ladder or a hierarchy of light, and of light itself as a link—whatever its ontological status—between the spiritual and the physical orders. The *Divina Commedia* progresses, of course, from the visual aberrations occurring in the darkness of hell to the illumination of paradise, where the well-known optical phenomenon of *abbaglio* (a glare so dazzling that, like the brilliance of the sun, it cannot be stared at) requires in Canto xxx the acquisition of "novella vista" by Dante the pilgrim.

Most relevant to our topic is the consistent use in this context—as the very notion of spiritual light implies—of visual events as vehicles of knowledge. In the sixth book of the *Republic* (508-509), Plato had stated analogically that the supreme Good makes the world intelligible even as the sun makes it visible. Among the Romans, the Stoics were the first to utilize consistently the word *lumen* with regard to various forms of understanding.[9] And during the Middle Ages "it was

---

(1958), 191-229; and J. Ferrater Mora, "Luz," *Diccionario de filosofía*, 5th edn. (Buenos Aires, 1965), II, 99ff.

[7] Cf. *De genesi ad litteram*, IV, xxviii, 45 and XII, iv, 15, 18; and *Soliloquiorum libri duo*, 1,3; also Mazzeo, "Light Metaphysics," p. 199.

[8] *In Aristotelis librum de anima commentarium*, ed. A. M. Pirotta (Turin, 1959), II, XIV, 416, p. 105.

[9] Cf. F. H. Sardemann, *Ursprung und Entwicklung der Lehre von lumen rationis aeternae, lumen divinum, lumen naturale, rationes seminales, veritates aeternae bis Descartes* (Kassel, 1902), p. 20.

common scholastic doctrine that sight shares knowing with the intellect and that thought had, when dealing with first principles, something of the immediacy of light."[10] Since the light of the sun appears to stream downward in the direction of the earth, the finite world was regarded as the will of God "above," and light as a universal bond inviting man to raise his thoughts to Him. Sight remained the dimension of cognitive ascent for Renaissance Neoplatonism, and Lorenzo the Magnificent experienced *abbaglio* most intensely when he dared to gaze on the sunlike beauty of his beloved.[11] During the seventeenth century, reason would be called a "lumière naturelle" by Descartes and Leibniz,[12] while the traditional fusion of God with light would find what is perhaps its most eloquent expression in the famous incantation in Book III of *Paradise Lost* ("Hail, holy light, offspring of Heaven first-born!"). As Marjorie Nicolson has shown, it would remain for Newton to incorporate optics fully into the laws of nature, as far as both scientists and poets were concerned.[13]

The secularization of vision, and of its association with knowledge as well, in other words, is a process which spans the history of European culture. It cannot be understood without taking into account the crucial contribution of painting since the Renaissance. The fusion of vision with knowledge in general, in a secularized form, persists until the present day, as the itinerary of the metaphor of perspective in its progress from optics to philosophy, from Alhazen and Roger Bacon to Ortega and Bertrand Russell, will, I hope, demonstrate.

[10] Mazzeo, "Light Metaphysics," p. 212.

[11] Cf. Lorenzo de' Medici, *Opere*, ed. A. Simioni (Bari, 1939), pp. 45, 96-97, and *passim*.

[12] Cf. Descartes, *Principes Philosophiques*, I, 30; and Leibniz, *Die philosophischen Schriften* . . . , ed. C. I. Gerhardt (Hildesheim, 1960-1961), VI, 494, 496.

[13] Cf. M. H. Nicolson, *Newton Demands the Muse* (Hamden, Conn., 1963), Chap. 2.

II

Art historians have devoted much study in recent years to the career of visual perspective since the Renaissance, often on a highly technical level, and I shall limit myself here to a commentary on, and to adapting for my purpose, some of the ideas developed by Panofsky, Krautheimer, Parronchi, Francastel, and others. The origins of artistic perspective are, for a layman, obscure. Illusionistic shapes can be found in Giotto, as Roberto Longhi has shown, but these are only fragments;[14] and, in general, the use of isolated motifs like canopied buildings and square-tiled floors by Trecento painters did not produce unified or centralized spaces. Between the 1430's and the 1450's, certain Florentine artists discovered the applicability of the *perspectiva communis* (optics) to a *perspectiva artificialis* (in the visual arts), or, in Italian, *prospettiva*, by virtue of their exceptional gift for both artistic creation and the kind of scientific experimentation which would culminate later in the work of Leonardo. Filippo Brunelleschi, fundamentally an architect, was familiar with the mathematics of construction, i.e., with the pertinence of geometry to art. For the purpose of architectual surveys, he devised experimental paintings on wood, one of which, for example, represented the Piazza della Signoria; its top was cut out, so that an observer standing in the right spot could look through the opening and find that the skyline of the buildings in the painting coincided with that of the real buildings. This was hardly practical, as two preliminary drawings were needed, a ground plan and a vertical elevation.[15] A few years later Leon Battista Alberti, in his *Della pittura* (1435-1436), succeeded

[14] Cf. R. Longhi, "Giotto spazioso," *Paragone* (Arte), III (1952), 18-24.

[15] Cf. E. Panofsky, *The Life and Art of Albrecht Dürer*, 4th edn. (Princeton, 1955), pp. 247ff.; R. Krautheimer, *Lorenzo Ghiberti* (Princeton, 1956), Chap. 16; and Parronchi, *Studi sulla dolce prospettiva*, pp. 226ff.

in simplifying the discoveries of Brunelleschi and his followers, as well as in raising them to the level of an artistic theory.

"Chi mira una pittura, vede certa intersegazione d'una piramide": Alberti imagined that Euclid's visual pyramid, the apex of which is the observer's eye, was intersected by a flat plane, transparent as if made of glass ("non altrimenti, che se essa fosse di vetro tralucente"). This flat section became the surface of the painting, which no longer acted as such, but rather as an opening, an open window ("una finestra aperta") on the contents of the visual pyramid.[16] Thus the purpose of painting could be defined as the representation of things seen ("rappresentare cose vedute"),[17] a definition which Alberti the humanist associated with the myth of Narcissus: "che dirai tu essere dipingere altra cosa che simile abbracciare con arte, quella ivi superficie del fonte?"[18] (This curious analogy supports Alberti's insistence on the idea that the artist finds individual self-achievement in his work, as it also suggests that realism in art amounts to a sort of Narcissism on the part of all beings and things represented.)[19] In three-dimensional terms—made possible by the laws of perspective—the canvas is an open window on the contents of a truncated pyramid, and in two-dimensional terms it is comparable to the reflection in a mirror. Finally, for practical purposes Alberti devised an abbreviated perspective scheme based on a checkerboard system: the orthogonals composing the checkerboard floor or ground level were to converge on a vanishing point on the horizon, "and the problem of determining the gradual diminution of equidistant transversals

---

[16] L. B. Alberti, *Della pittura*, in *Kleinere kunsttheoretische Schriften*, ed. H. Janitschek (Vienna, 1877), pp. 69, 79.

[17] *Ibid.*, p. 99.   [18] *Ibid.*, p. 93.

[19] Though with a particular degree of beauty and truth. The notion that reflected images (images in a mirror or in a fountain) are more truthful than the objects they represent is Neoplatonic. Cf. my discussion of the "scene of the fountain" in *El Abencerraje*, p. 200 of this book.

was solved by the simple device of running an oblique line"—
from an elevated point on the side, representing the eye
level of a person in the painting—"across the convergent
orthogonals."[20]

Florentine perspective remained a fruitful artistic convention for four hundred years. It is generally recognized today,
however, that "convention" also means in this case a limited
and creatively limiting premise—a fruitful differentiation between art and non-art. That the perspective scheme was a
conventional interpretation is made clear by the fact that it
fell so far short of being either faithful to the visual perception of men or "true to life" in a broader sense. This and other
aspects of the subject were completely renovated in 1924 by
Erwin Panofsky in a memorable article called (after Ernst
Cassirer) "Die Perspektive als 'symbolische Form.'" Panofsky showed that perspective is a significant and illusionistic
form that does not coincide with the nature of perception. It
is an abstraction of what we see. It does not distinguish between "visual images," where other sensory and psychological data operate, and "retinal images," projected on the
concave surface of the eye. The fact that images are projected not on a concave but on a flat surface causes the well-
known effect of marginal aberration (also present in photography). Perspectives ignore both the real curvature of our
field of vision and the three-dimensional effect created by
two eyes. Kepler, for example, noticed that the straight flight
of a comet is perceived as curved by the observer, and assumed that men were influenced by the new art of perspective in not realizing their error.[21]

For clarity, I shall reduce the principal assumptions of perspective to the following:

[20] Panofsky, *Dürer*, p. 247.
[21] Cf. E. Panofsky, "Die Perspektive als 'symbolische Form,'" in
Vorträge der Bibliothek Warburg (*1924-1925*), pp. 258-330.

1. Painting is a mimetic fiction concerned with visual appearances—with Alberti's *cose vedute*. (A positive delight in *trompe l'œil* will be especially noticeable in the seventeenth century. As an example one may cite an entry in John Evelyn's *Diary* for February 27, 1644; Evelyn, while visiting Richelieu's villa in Rueil, admired a perspective painting of the Arch of Constantine, of which he wrote later: "The sky and hills which seem to be between the arches, are so natural, that swallows and other birds, thinking to fly through, have dashed themselves against the wall. I was infinitely taken with this agreeable cheat.")[22]

2. The central projection and unified space of the painting are absolutely dependent on the fiction of the single beholder, i.e., on a unifying "point of view." It is not the thought of God, critics have said, or the cohesion of things as they really are on which the *system of the painting* rests, but the perception and understanding of the observing human being. Various beholders, various points of view, however, can serve as different but valid supports for several reproductions of a single scene.

3. The point of view is attached both to a single and an immobile eye. One of the perspective apparatuses proposed by Albrecht Dürer in his *Underweysung der Messung* (1525; revised edition, 1538) called for a glass plate between the painter and the subject, as well as a device or chin rest to keep the painter's head from moving (see Figure 1).[23] This

---

[22] *The Diary of John Evelyn*, ed. W. Bray (Washington and London, 1901), I, 53.

[23] Ruskin, in his Introduction to the *Elements of Perspective* (1859), *The Works of John Ruskin*, ed. E. T. Cook and A. Wedderburn (London, 1901), xv, 241, asks the student to sit near a window and consider every pane as a "glass picture," and he adds, "but, to do this, you must hold your head very still. You must not only not move it sideways, nor up and down, but it must not even move backwards or forwards; for if you move your head forwards, you will see more. . . ."

fixed, monocular convention represents the most extreme contradiction of ordinary experience.

4. Objects are represented as having the same sizes and positions *in relation to one another* as they actually do when viewed by the single eye. Perspectives are relational.

5. These structures, or the connection between them as they are seen and their representation on the surface of the canvas, can be measured and are amenable to geometrical thinking. It was of course an aesthetic principle of the Italian Renaissance that beauty is a harmony of the parts with respect to the whole, and a mathematically correct system of relationships. This would make possible the rationalist theory which was developed during the seventeenth century and was called by Dilthey, with special reference to Leibniz, the natural system of aesthetic norms: "since . . . all harmonious relationships participated in the absolute order and harmony of the universe, there had to be, as the rationalist theorists believed, one and the same principle for beauty in the arts and in nature."[24] In this sense the geometrical connotations of perspective succeeded in bringing painting nearer to the status of music and the *artes liberales,* in turning it into a Pythagorean art.

6. The most important relational structure is distance, and things are seen in depth *with regard to the point of view,* that is to say, as more or less remote from the spectator. As Pierre Francastel suggests, it would be instructive to connect this view with the notion of "psychic distance" as wielded by anthropologists, who find it does not exist among those primitive peoples who regard the world as an unbroken continuum.[25] The idea of perspective can readily be associated with a growing epistemological dualism, with a rigorous split be-

24 K. Müller-Vollmer, *Towards a Phenomenological Theory of Literature. A Study of Wilhelm Dilthey's Poetik* (The Hague, 1963), p. 60.
25 Cf. P. Francastel, *Peinture et société* (Lyon, 1951), p. 87.

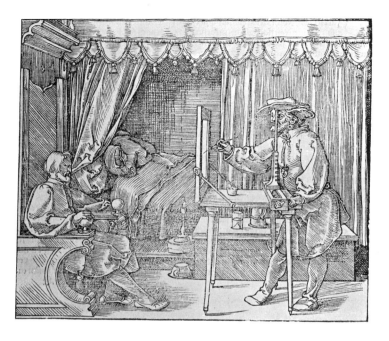

1. A Man Drawing a Portrait of a Sitting Man through
a Sight on a Glass pane. Albrecht Dürer
(From *Underweysung der Messung*)

2. The Miracle of the Healing of the Irascible Son. Donatello
(Padua, Sant'Antonio)

3. The Viaticum of Saint Bonaventura. Francisco de Zurbarán or
School of Zurbarán

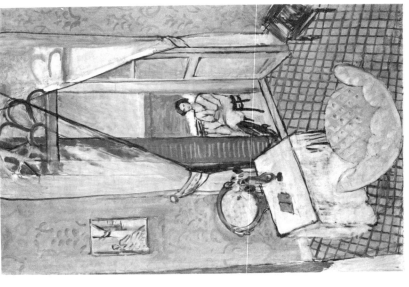

5. Large Interior at Nice. Henri Matisse
(Courtesy of the Art Institute, Chicago)

4. Anamorphic Portrait of Edward VI. Unknown Artist
1543, after Holbein
(The National Portrait Gallery, London)

tween subject and object as in the Cartesian distinction between mind and *res extensa*.[26]

I have discussed the concept of perspective by isolating it —as most metaphors based on it will—from any individual use in any particular context. This should nearly suffice for the purposes of this essay. The historical view, nevertheless, cannot be lost sight of. The actual practice of perspective, as art historians show, varies a great deal not only from painter to painter or from period to period, but with regard to the very stress that the perspective scheme can be given. It can become a significant structure or stay in the background of the painting. It can be a "symbolical" and functional form or a mere preliminary, technical device. It can be a basic mimetic method, a formula for representing "things seen," or an aesthetic pattern within a set of patterns, an invitation (as in Paolo Uccello's famous *Battle of San Romano*) to the formal beauties of geometry. I will now consider briefly, as illustrations, two individual works: a well-known one from the Quattrocento—a Donatello—and a seventeenth-century Spanish picture, not as widely known, from Zurbarán's *Seville*.

[26] Historians have drawn parallels between the rise of perspective during the Renaissance and the seventeenth century, and certain cultural assumptions of the period: the opening of empirical reality to the notion of infinity and the growing primacy of the theory of knowledge, from Nicholas of Cusa to Kant. Cf. Panofsky's suggestion in "Die Perspektive als 'symbolische Form,' " p. 287: "man könnte die Funktion der Renaissanceperspektive geradezu mit der Kritizismus, die der hellenistisch-römischen Perspektive mit der des Skeptizismus vergleichen." In his later *Dürer* (4th edn., pp. 261ff.) Panofsky mentions these parallels: the Renaissance inserted "historical distance" between itself and the past, as the picture does between the image and the point of vision (is this historical distance not a later idea, in our sense of the term?); the mind of man was placed in the center of the universe (i.e., the earlier reference to "Kritizismus"); and Renaissance aesthetic canons were based on correct mathematical relationships (a point mentioned in my fifth assumption). I shall discuss in a later section of this essay the problems raised by such parallels.

Donatello's bas-relief *The Miracle of the Healing of the Irascible Son* (for the Basilica of Sant' Antonio in Padua; see Figure 2) provides us with an early example of the enthusiastic application of linear perspective. The entire work depends on the convention of the truncated pyramid and on the controlling function of the point of view. The boxlike pyramid, in the first place, stresses distance and depth. It makes clear the priority of space. Into the "container" of the area limited by the surrounding buildings, human figures have been inserted, like landmarks or spatial indicators—and with all the difficulties implicit in the effort to fit life into mathematical coordinates. Space is a continuum previous to life. It separates one person from another and can only be covered in its entirety by the human eye. For the function of the point of view is such, in the second place, that objects and persons have been arranged in agreement with it. They have been located so as to be conveniently visible. Seeing actually "happens" in the work itself, and the observer feels invited to join the spectators *in* it, to lean on his own balustrade and watch the stagelike scene, to participate in the benefits of vision.

El Viático de San Buenaventura (Genoa, Galleria di Palazzo Bianco; see Figure 3), not always attributed to Zurbarán himself,[27] employs the perspective scheme as an occasion and a setting for symbolical form. The visual pyramid is extended into the distance, as the crowded foreground (occupied by no fewer than ten human figures) is followed by the strangely empty spaces in the back. It is as if the lines of the

[27] Paul Guinard adduces persuasive reasons against the attribution of this painting to Zurbarán, in his *Zurbarán et les peintres espagnols de la vie monastique* (Paris, 1960), pp. 80-81. In his opinion the canvas is not only physically too large to have been a part of the Saint Bonaventura cycle in Seville (four of which were by Zurbarán, four by Francisco Herrera); stylistically, he finds it "à mi chemin de Zurbarán et de Herrera." I am thankful to Professors Edith Helman and José López-Rey for this information. I might add that I, as a layman, have no difficulty in seeing this magnificent picture as a Zurbarán.

perspective scheme had been continued, through sheer technical routine, beyond the area where the action occurs. (Saint Bonaventura, gravely ill, is unable to swallow; as he prays, the Host imbeds itself miraculously in his chest.) Yet the artist's use of perspective is not an afterthought or a fortuitous matter. The foreground prepares carefully for the presence of the empty room behind it, by means of the lines of the canopy over the bed, the carpet on the floor, the very position of the bed and the pyramidal arrangement of the figures beside it. Thus we are led to observe the empty room, of which two features stand out: the book-lined walls; and the soft light filling the void, falling from a high window, its path paralleling that of the rays of sun directed toward the saint's chest. The distant emptiness makes possible this silent encounter of light, airiness, and learning. Saint Bonaventura was of course an illustrious theologian and writer. Light, the most incorporeal of material phenomena, adds to his last communion a transition between one world and another. The metaphysics of light, which I discussed earlier, coincide here with the consolations of theology. Saint Bonaventura had believed, in Joseph A. Mazzeo's words, that "God is the true light, and that light is more properly to be predicated of spiritual than corporeal things. . . . For Bonaventura, light was not only the hierarchical principle and the principle of continuity in the corporeal universe, but he also accepted the Augustinian view that light is that by which the body is united to the soul and by which the soul rules the body. Its status as the corporeal substance most like spirit made it a kind of connecting link between the spiritual and corporeal orders."[28] The rays of light here not only signify but actually represent a ladder awaiting the ascent of the dying saint's soul. And the miraculous events in the foreground of the painting are indivisible from the mysteriously empty spaces

[28] Mazzeo, "Light Metaphysics," pp. 205-206, 207.

in the back, nearly supernatural, radiant with the light which "is more properly predicated of spiritual than corporeal things."

When Dürer traveled from Venice to Bologna in 1506 in order to study *die Kunst der Messung*, the art of measurement, which he, like other Northern painters, had approached in an empirical fashion, he was seeking a proficiency which only an elite of artists and theorists had attained. A set of practical rules had been collected by Johannes Viator (Jean Pélerin) in his *De artificiali perspectiva* (1505; second edition, 1509). But the true theory or "art" of perspective was developed later, by a series of sixteenth-century publications, such as Dürer's own *Underweysung der Messung* (1525, 1538) and the works of Hyeronimus Rodler (1531), Augustin Hirschvogel (1543), Sebastiano Serlio (1547), Wenzel Jamnitzer (1548), Federigo Commandino (1558), Daniello Barbaro (1559), Jean Cousin the Younger (1565), Jacques Androuet (1576), Giacomo Barozzio da Vignola (1583), Lorenzo Sirigatti (1596), Guido Ubaldo del Monte (1600), and several others.[29] Many of these writers were geometricians, architects, or engineers. Venice, Nuremberg, and Holland, particularly, would see the publication of treatises on perspective during the sixteenth and seventeenth centuries which would make it possible for a specialized science to become common knowledge and a crucial influence on general visual habits.

Daniello Barbaro, in *La prattica della prospettiva* (1559), was one of the first to write of "anamorphoses," i.e., enigmatic pictures so contrived as to make sense only when seen obliquely or from a certain angle: for example, Erhard Schön's *Vexierbilder*, the signature in Holbein's *The Ambassadors* (1533), or the anamorphic picture, after Holbein, of Edward

[29] On these and other facts concerning the history of perspective theory, see A. Flocon and R. Taton, *La Perspective* (Paris, 1963), pp. 49ff.

VI (1543). (See Figure 4.) This vexing sort of visual trickery was but an extension of the illusionistic power implicit in perspective, and of the notion that the characteristics of vision could control the visible contents of the painting. An important affinity would develop between the possibilities of perspective and the so-called Baroque styles in the arts—a subject too complex and too familiar to be more than alluded to here. I need only recall the fondness for fiction and *trompe l'œil* in the seventeenth-century Baroque theater, its perspective backcloths and curtains (like the curtain described by Calderón in the Prologue to *Fieras afemina amor*: "era su perspectiva de color de cielo, hermoseado de nubes y celajes"),[30] the crowding of illusions into the truncated pyramid of the stage—now seen from the front only, as through a larger version of Alberti's "finestra aperta," by the immobile spectator. The Baroque builders of palaces and gardens and their followers—the architects of Versailles, the Tuileries, Saint Petersburg—converted into stone, tree-lined alleys, or panoramic avenues the structural requirements of the point of view.[31] In an excellent essay Richard Alewyn has explained that the "impatient culture" of the age did not easily tolerate emptiness in either time or space. Of this he finds a symbol in the elaborate fêtes and courtly celebrations of the later seventeenth century, and in the love of decorative makebelieve: human bodies seemed in need of splendid costumes, human crowds of dances and masquerades, sentences of conceits and metaphors, and blank walls of perspective frescos capable, like mirrors, of enlarging or transcending the limited spaces at hand.[32]

During the same period the geometrical premises of perspective theory were being extended considerably by such

[30] *Comedias* (Madrid, 1762), VIII, 414.
[31] Cf. Flocon and Taton, *La Perspective*, p. 61.
[32] Cf. R. Alewyn, "Feste des Barock," in *Aus der Welt des Barock*, ed. R. Alewyn et al. (Stuttgart, 1957), pp. 101-111.

scientists as Girard Desargues, whose interest in the subject led him to formulate the general theory of conic projections (*Pratique de la perspective*, 1636). While the notion of perspective became common knowledge, its mathematical support was also being elaborated, and ultimately grew so complex as increasingly to confuse both the ordinary reader and the ordinary artist. It seems clear from the bric-a-brac of a book like Burton's *Anatomy of Melancholy* that many a layman was puzzled and had trouble distinguishing between the miracles of magic and those of optics.[33] Indeed, in 1635 Father Jean-François Niceron, O. M., published a treatise called *La Perspective curieuse, ou Magie artificielle des effets merveilleux de l'optique.* In their useful survey of the topic, Albert Flocon and René Taton have commented upon the divorce between painters and perspectivists toward the end of the seventeenth century. One might add that the alienated parties actually were mathematics and art, whose earlier collaboration had sustained the discoveries of the Quattrocento. It was a memorable day when the engraver Abraham Bosse (1611-1678), who had tried to teach his students the geometrical views of Desargues, quarreled with the fashionable Lebrun and was expelled from the Académie de Peinture.[34] Approximately at this time, as we shall see later, the concept of perspective was turned into a philosophical metaphor by the mathematically trained Leibniz.

[33] Burton speaks of "perspective pieces" (paintings) and of "perspectives," meaning magnifying glasses, with the same sense of wonder; cf. *The Anatomy of Melancholy* (London, 1827), 1, 420: "to do strange miracles by glasses, of which Proclus and Bacon writ of old, burning glasses, multiplying glasses, perspectives, *ut unus homo appareat exercitus*, to see afar off, to represent bodies, by cylinders and concaves, to walk in the air. . . ."

[34] Cf. Flocon and Taton, *La Perspective*, p. 59. There were also the simplifiers, of course; in 1661 P. Bourgoing published in Paris a *Perspective affranchie de l'embarras du point de vue.*

III

Turning to the uses of the term in literature, it is not surprising to notice that the analogy or the metaphor of perspective arises first in Tuscany. A persuasive evidence of this is its appearance not only in cultured writing (as in the works of Giovan Maria Cecchi, 1518-1587)[35] but in the markedly popular and lusty songs that were sung in Florence during carnival celebrations. One of these *canti carnacialeschi* is the "Canto de' Simulatori," a stanza of which reads: "If wealth, wisdom and faith are falsely rendered from the outside by color, then he who believes in the clothing of those [deceivers] errs more than the others; for their language, intellect, and heart are full of unpleasant traits, and their being so pure and neat is but a sign of this; and it all derives solely from the fact that the whole world is done in perspective":

> Se la ricchezza, sapïenza e fede
> di fuor falsa il colore,
> dunque, chi al vestir di costor crede,
> fa più degli altri errore;
> perchè la lingua, l'intelletto e'l cuore
> hanno pien di dispetti,
> e l'esser puri e netti
> vi danno indizio; e questo sol deriva
> ché'l mondo é tutto fatto in prospettiva.[36]

The Dissemblers are familiar with perspective as a sign of deceit. Though the entire world may be "fatto in prospettiva," this truth becomes an error for those who unmask

[35] Cf. *Il donzello*, Act I, in *Comedie di M. Gianmaria Cecchi Fiorentino* (Venice, 1585), p. 7: "Il caso loro é prospettiva vera."

[36] *Nuovi canti carnacialeschi del Rinascimento*, ed. C. S. Singleton (Modena, 1940), p. 18. The poem is attributed to Guglielmo, "detto il Giuggiola." Cf. also *Tutti i trionfi, carri, mascherate, o canti carnacialeschi* (Lucca, 1750), II, 321.

it and look beyond externals, like the humble author of this popular song, who expresses an instinctive distrust of the visual as the conveyor of true knowledge. This derogatory meaning appears to have been central among early applications of the idea of perspective, either figurative or literal.

Metaphors based on perspective in painting—*perspectiva artificialis*—do not take hold, outside of Italy, until the early seventeenth century. Previous usage proceeds from the medieval *perspectiva* or optical science and designates instruments that improve or modify vision, like magnifying lenses or spyglasses. This meaning persists until the nineteenth century, and we still encounter it in Goethe, Gottfried Keller, or Browning, who exclaims in *Asolando* (1889):

> What would I give for the perspective glass
> At home, to make out if 'tis really so![37]

Browning speaks of the instrument with confidence, almost as a scientist might. Similarly, students of optics during the Middle Ages and the Renaissance often referred to their subject with admiration and respect: for example, Rabelais, who in connection with the phenomenon of *abbaglio*, which I discussed earlier, mentions the tradition of the "perspectifz"[38] (Alhazen, Witelo, Roger Bacon).

[37] "Inapprehensiveness," *The Complete Poetic and Dramatic Works of Robert Browning* (Boston and New York, 1895), p. 991. Cf. also G. Keller, "Der Schmied seines Glückes," *Die Leute von Seldwyla*, 4th edn. (Stuttgart, 1883), II, 64; and Letter of February 3, 1818, *Goethes Briefe* (Weimar, 1904), XXIX, 38. The German *Perspektive* appears to have been borrowed from the French *perspective*; cf. J. C. Adelung, *Grammatisch-Kritisches Wörterbuch der Hochdeutschen Mundart . . .* (Vienna, 1808), III, 694: "Gryphius suchte dieses Wort durch Schaukunst zu ersetzen, welches aber keinen Beifall erhalten hat."

[38] *Gargantua*, Chap. 10 in *Oeuvres complètes*, ed. P. Jourda (Paris, 1962), I, 46: "Car—comme le blanc exteriorement disgrege et espart la veue, dissolvent manifestement les espritz visifz, selon l'opinion de Aristoteles en ses *Problemes* et des perspectifz (et le voyez par experience quand vous passez les montz couverts de neige, en sorte que vous plaignez de ne pouvoir bien reguarder). . . ."

But a number of texts from the Renaissance and the Middle Ages throw a different light on the topic. They tend to stress that the image seen through the perspective glass is distorted or ambiguous, as if optical contrivances produced a kind of magic. The hero of Chaucer's "The Squire's Tale" receives from the King of Arabia a magical mirror where omens of future disasters may be read, and some of the curious bystanders advance the opinion that it consists

> Of anglis and sly reflexiouns

such as those that "Alocen and Vutulon" (Alhazen and Witelo) or other writers on optics had described when they wrote

> Of queynte mirours and of perspectyues.[39]

For mirrors were associated for a long time with witchcraft, or the aberrations of the senses. A Christian distrust of optics, besides, as a vain devotion to appearances, would be formulated in numerous sermons and in connection with comparisons or metaphors based on perspective—as, for example, in the characteristic words found in William Drummond of Hawthornden's *Cypress Grove* (1623): "All we can set our eyes upon in these intricate mazes of Life is but Alchimie, vain Perspective, and deceiving Shadows, appearing far other ways afar off, than when enjoyed and looked upon at a near Distance."[40]

The notion of distance, or of a distant view brought closer to the beholder, was a common denominator of the image seen through the perspective glass and the illusion of the *perspectiva artificialis* in painting, so that it is difficult to tell

[39] *The Text of the Canterbury Tales*, ed. J. M. Manly and E. Rickert (Chicago, 1940), p. 235. The *Roman de la Rose*, ed. E. Langlois (Paris, 1914-1924), ll. 18234-18387, also refers to these writers on optics.

[40] *The Poetical Works of William Drummond of Hawthornden* (Edinburgh, 1913), II, 80.

from a text like William Drummond's whether one kind of image or the other is being indicated.[41] Toward the end of the sixteenth century and the beginning of the seventeenth, outside of Italy, we encounter an important turning point in the history of our metaphor. The original meanings of the word, referring to optical effects, appear to have been grafted onto the newer frame of reference with which it was becoming associated. A certain significance or metaphorical purpose could be carried over from word to word even though the thing designated might have been different: to put it in other terms, connotation persisted even though denotation changed.

Three early seventeenth-century texts—from Jonson, Cervantes, and Bacon—will illustrate my point. At one end of the spectrum, Ben Jonson—Drummond's good friend—alludes clearly to optics, magic, and pseudoscience in *The Alchemist* (1610). His hero, a rogue and *simulatore*, owns a glass for swindling:

> He'll show a perspective, where on one side
> You shall behold the faces and the persons
> Of all sufficient young heirs in town,
> Whose bonds are current for commodity....[42]

But in Cervantes the association is less clear, and might allude to painting too. In the fourteenth chapter of the second

[41] Particularly in certain poems by the English metaphysicals. Cf. "Obsequies to the Lord Harrington," in *The Poems of John Donne*, ed. H.J.C. Grierson (Oxford, 1912), I, 272 (where "by perspective" is the equivalent of "diminished in proportion," which could apply to either an optical instrument or a picture, probably the former); and "Sinne II," *The Complete Works of George Herbert*, ed. A. B. Grosart (London, 1874), p. 48: "so devils are our sinnes in perspective" (i.e., devils are our sins represented, symbolized); an earlier line reads "as in sleep we see foul death": this *could* allude to painting, since the second line of the poem refers to it: "we paint the devil foul."

[42] *The Works of Ben Jonson*, ed. W. Gifford (New York, 1879), p. 359; cf. also *Every Man out of His Humour*, in *Works*, p. 151.

part of *Don Quixote*, the Knight of the Mournful Countenance, having just vanquished the Knight of the Mirrors, raises the visor of his helmet to discover his victim's identity: "Vio, dice la historia, el rostro mismo, la misma figura, el mismo aspecto, la misma fisonomía, la misma efigie, la perspectiva misma del bachiller Sansón Carrasco." With each repetition of the word *misma*, the tension between identity and appearance grows. The accumulation of nouns signifying appearance suggests the reader's, and Don Quixote's, comic surprise, but it also builds a kind of visual crescendo, with an increasing reference to the "engaño a los ojos" and the process of value-formation which surrounds, throughout the novel, the visual interpretation of single objects. The immediate context is visual—the verb *vio* is repeated four times within four sentences, and the stupendous nose of Sancho's counterpart, the squire Tomé Cecial, proves to be as illusory as the mirrors in his master's *nom de guerre*. The term *perspectiva* signifies here "aspect" in its most external and least reliable sense and could connote either painting (Cervantes might have read the theorists of perspective while in Italy) or the persistent attacks of the enchanter's magic against Don Quixote's less superficial truth. At the other end of the spectrum, Francis Bacon undoubtedly refers to painting when he states in one of his *Essays* (1625), concerning the wrong use of judgment by false scholars: "It hath been an opinion that the French are wiser than they seem, and the Spaniards seem wiser than they are. . . . It is a ridiculous thing, and fit for a satire to persons of judgment, to see what shifts these formalists have, and what prospectives to make superficies to seem body that hath depth and bulk."[43]

[43] "Of Seeming Wise," *The Complete Essays of Francis Bacon*, ed. H. L. Finch (New York, 1963), p. 68. The term "prospective" is probably an Italianism, as well as a plausible encounter of the forms deriving from *perspicere* (like "perspicacity," "perspicuous," and "perspective") with those deriving from the classical Latin *prospectus*, "a

IV

This fusion of, and confusion between, the real and the representational aspects of optical phenomena may be found also in the plays of Shakespeare, where the term is used a number of times—usually, commentators tend to think, with regard to the perspective glass.[44] Not so in *Richard II*, where it seems clear in one passage that Shakespeare has in mind the anamorphoses (single-angle, deceitful pictures) of the kind Daniello Barbaro had described in *La prattica della prospettiva* (1559). The passage where the simile occurs is not an isolated one thematically. It seems indivisible, in fact, from the salient theme I would like to examine: the visualization of grief.

Griefs and grievances, longlasting and unresolved, haunt the whole of *Richard II*. Grief is universally present, not as a product but as an underlying condition of the action:

> Comfort's in heaven; and we are on the earth,
> Where nothing lives but crosses, cares, and grief.
>
> (II, ii, 78-79)

Looking toward the future, the exiled Bolingbroke knows himself doomed to be "a journeyman to grief" (I, iii, 274), even as the deposed king can only remain the ruler of his sorrow:

---

view," *prospicere*, and the late Latin *prospectivus* (said of windows which permit a view, a prospect; Italian *prospettiva*, English "prospect"). The English "prospect" was an old medieval word, and the cultural derivative *perspectiva* could have been blocked in some cases by the living "prospect." Spanish *prospectiva* appears, as we shall see, in a fifteenth-century work by Alfonso de la Torre. John Ruskin (*Works*, XXIV, 478) thought it was a flaw of the English language that "prospect" and "prospection" should exist, but not "perspect" or "perspection."

[44] Cf., for example, *Henry V*, v, ii; *Twelfth Night*, v, i; *Sonnets*, XXIV, 4 (where the real and the painterly are fused).

> You may my glories and my state depose,
> But not my griefs; still am I king of those.
>
> (IV, i, 192-193)

Similarly, the king is aware of the special status of the griev-
ing soul:

> O that I were as great
> As is my grief, or lesser than my name!
>
> (III, iii, 136-137)

But the *perception* of grief is the crucial problem that concerns us in *Richard II*. It becomes necessary to show, however briefly, the relevance of images presenting hollowness,
emptiness, or the relationship between a contained substance
and its container. One may remember, for example, the comparison between the empty crown, the bucket, and the suffer-
ing soul:

> Now is this golden crown like a deep well
> That owes two buckets, filling one another,
> The emptier ever dancing in the air,
> The other down, unseen, and full of water.
> That bucket down, and full of tears, am I,
> Drinking my griefs, whilst you mount up on high.
>
> (IV, i, 184-189)

In the Duchess of Gloucester's house at Plashy, which is tem-
porarily empty, there is nothing to be seen

> But empty lodgings and unfurnish'd walls,
> Unpeopled offices, untrodden stones....
>
> (I, ii, 68-69)

As he approaches death, old John of Gaunt imagines his
future grave:

> Gaunt am I for the grave, gaunt as a grave,
> Whose hollow womb inherits nought but bones.
>
> (II, i, 82-83)

Thus the spectator is prepared to visualize the soul enclosed, enveloped, sealed off by the body—the "outer man" containing the "inner man":

> As if this flesh which walls about our life
> Were brass impregnable . . .
>
> (III, ii, 167-168)

—while the whole nation—"our sea-walled garden"—is like a fortress or a little world:

> England, bound in with the triumphant sea. . . .
>
> (II, i, 61)

Hollow objects can contain hidden substances, and a puzzling, ever-changing relationship can exist between container and contained, as well as between the traditionally divided soul and body. An important development of sixteenth-century literature is the increasing liberation of "inner man" from "outer man." Leo Spitzer has shown that in the medieval epic gestures revealed emotions: they were psychophysical.[45] Lionel Friedman has explained further that the radical Christian division in the Middle Ages of "dual man" (*homo duplex*) into the physical and the spiritual (*homo exterior* and *homo interior*) was balanced by certain correspondences existing between the two. Though the soul's life was regarded as invisible and the heart as hidden (*occulta cordis*), a symbolical connection remained between body and soul, and facial expressions or other externals were a *sign* of this connection. Thus writers did not pretend, or feel the need, to portray inwardness independently from outer appearances.[46] This situation is modified during the Renais-

---

[45] Cf. L. Spitzer, "Le vers 834 du Roland," *Romania*, LXVIII (1944-1945), 471-477.

[46] Cf. L. J. Friedman, "Occulta Cordis," *Romance Philology*, XI (1957-1958), 103-119.

sance—one may point to three examples: the prose of Machiavelli; the Spanish ancestors of the novel, like *Lazarillo de
Tormes* (whose hero is shaped by the uncanny ability of his
first master, a blind man, to dispense with vision); and Montaigne's attempt to seize the variable, fluctuating, elusive
homo interior: "ce n'est pas tour d'entendement rassis, de
nous juger simplement par nos actions du dehors; il fault
sonder jusques au dedans, et veoir par quels ressorts se
donne le bransle" (*Essais*, Bk. II, Chap. I). The Renaissance
and the Reformation were crucial stages in the process of
"interiorization" of European culture. The challenge that
Shakespeare faced, in this sense, was one of portraying the
homo interior by means of perceptible action on the stage—
or to put it most simply: of portraying the invisible through
the visible.

Lies, confessions, accusations of untruth, the formulation
of thoughts with regard to different strata of the inner or the
public personality as different situations arise—these occupy
many scenes of *Richard II* and emphasize its constant concern with treason: How does one unmask a traitor or discover a liar? Exile represents the banishment of the outer
man, while the inner person and its latent treachery remain
obscure or undisclosed:

> By this time, had the King permitted us,
> One of our souls had wand'red in the air,
> Banish'd this frail sepulchre of our flesh,
> As now our flesh is banish'd from this land.
>
> (I, iii, 194-197)

A man's reputation or honor is in part the unseeing confidence of others in his inner integrity:

> . . . that away,
> Men are but gilded loam or painted clay.
>
> (I, i, 178-179)

And the political matter of the play involves the realization that righteous behavior can be controlled too closely by externals, i.e., by the letter rather than by the substance of the law.

Sorrow, of course, can be externally caused or feigned, as in the parting of Aumerle from Bolingbroke upon the latter's banishment. The wind makes Bolingbroke shed a tear, while Aumerle prefers not to counterfeit feeling:

King Richard What said our cousin when you parted
with him?
Aumerle "Farewell!"
And, for my heart disdained that my tongue
Should so profane the word, that taught me craft
To counterfeit oppression of such grief
That words seem'd buried in my sorrow's grave.

(I, iv, 10-15)

Yet there are moments when inner grief can be *seen*, as when the king says to John of Gaunt:

Uncle, even in the glasses of thine eyes
I see thy grieved heart.

(I, iii, 208-209)

A closer reading of the play would show, in our terms, the varying conditions under which King Richard is reduced to acting as a mere *homo exterior* or surrenders to the outer glitter of language, while royalty is no more than an empty role. On those occasions the hero loses sight of his own grief, his inwardness, so that he is led, like a blind Narcissus, to question his face as if it could answer for the disappearing inner being. The famous scene of the breaking of the mirror implies such a level of self-reflection:

Bolingbroke   The shadow of your sorrow hath destroy'd
               The shadow of your face.
King Richard   Say that again.
               The shadow of my sorrow? Ha! Let's see.
               'Tis very true, my grief lies all within;
               And these external manners of laments
               Are merely shadows to the unseen grief
               That swells with silence in the tortur'd
                  soul.
               There lies the substance.

                                (IV, i, 292-299)

Thus we can recognize the relevance, earlier in the play, of Bushy's anamorphic simile (see Figure 4) and its complex presentation of the visualization of grief:

   Each substance of a grief hath twenty shadows,
   Which shows like grief itself, but is not so;
   For sorrow's eye, glazed with blinding tears,
   Divides one thing entire to many objects,
   Like *perspectives*, which rightly gaz'd upon
   Show nothing but confusion—ey'd awry
   Distinguish form; so your sweet Majesty,
   Looking awry upon your lord's departure,
   Find shapes of grief, more than himself, to wail;
   Which, look'd on as it is, is nought but shadows
   Of what it is not.

                          (II, ii, 14-24)

True perception requires what the dramatist Middleton calls "intellectual eyesight"[47]—or *insight*—through the "brass im-

---

[47] Cf. E. Engelberg, "Tragic Blindness in *The Changeling* and *Women Beware Women*," *Modern Language Quarterly*, XXIII (1962), 23. The original meaning of "insight" seems to have been "internal sight," "with the eyes of the mind"; cf. *The Oxford English Dictionary* (Oxford, 1961), V, 337.

pregnable" of the flesh, or, in the words of the Earl of Salisbury in *Richard II,* "the eyes of heavy mind" (ii, iv, 18).

I have dwelt at length on Shakespeare's splendid perspective simile in order to show not that it is the most central in the play, but, conversely, how readily it fits into a larger and more significant intellectual framework. Optical error is also a fallacy of understanding in this and other works where the metaphor of perspective appears. There is ultimately an important concentration not on the content of a given theme but on how it can be *known.* I have mentioned earlier that in a Donatello bas-relief the mechanics of vision control the nature of the visible. In Cervantes' narrative writing, the relationship between reality and the imagination becomes so basic as to bring sharply into focus the methods used for the presentation of fictional events. The artist in such cases is fundamentally concerned with how human experience can be perceived or known, and this in turn affects or enters the structure of the work of art. In *Richard II,* similarly, the career of grief seems no more problematic than its manifestation to the eyes of the characters and the spectators. This cognitive dimension based on vision surrounds and conditions the entire content of the tragic action on Shakespeare's stage.

We can begin to observe, at this point, how two separate historical processes belonging to the Renaissance gradually came into conflict: the first being a growing concern with the procedures of correct knowledge; the second, a confident delight in vision, as supported since the Quattrocento by the application of geometrical advances to painting. The metaphor of perspective became available to both these processes: it could give life to either knowledge or illusion. Within the overall process of "interiorization" in European culture, it seems to me that the distinction between the material and the spiritual in man would be replaced with increasing frequency by a simpler contrast between *l'homme visible* and *l'homme invisible* (to use Taine's terms in the Preface to his *History of English Literature*): the human spirit being, one might say, what we have trouble *seeing*. But I am anticipating, to be sure, and our next topic should be the career of the metaphor of perspective after the Renaissance.

V

During the later seventeenth century the term perspective will be applied with increasing frequency to the paintings themselves—sometimes called "perspective pieces"[48]—as well as to landscapes or vistas perceived in the same fashion. Thus the context of the poem, for example, is needed in order to clarify the fact that Dryden is describing a *picture* when he writes in the "Elegy of Mrs. Anne Killigrew"

> Of lofty trees, with sacred shades,
> And perspectives of pleasant glades. . . .[49]

Dryden's line could also have designated a *real* landscape, since the laws of perspective were generally regarded as being true to life. A perspective began to signify "a view," the contents of which are seen according to the Florentine pattern (using distance, vanishing point, etc.). As the painter's device had become a generalized visual habit, the term could alternate with ease between art and life. I should add that I have in mind in this essay primarily the linear perspective of Quattrocento origin, from which metaphorical usage mainly has derived. The later development of aerial perspective (rendered by means of fading or contrasting colors, light effects, etc.) provided the painter with *additional* procedures. These could achieve precedence over the linear pattern in the works of some artists, but they did not contradict

[48] Cf. R. Burton, *The Anatomy of Melancholy*, II, 2 and 4: "many pretty landskips and perspective pieces. . . ."
[49] *The Poetical Works of John Dryden*, ed. R. Hooper (London, 1891), II, 279.

or nullify it. A full study of the term perspective as signifying "a view," however, would probably have to stress the Romantic period. I am referring to the fondness in certain writers for misty, dewy vistas, infinite distances, sunset hours—
comparable to the softened hues of a landscape painted in
aerial perspective—as when Wordsworth gazes, in "Descriptive Sketches," on a stormy twilight:

> Eastward, in long perspective glittering, shine
> The wood-crowned cliffs, that o'er the lake recline. . . .[50]

Or when Chateaubriand uses the term metaphorically: "Il ne
faut pas toujours laisser tomber la sonde dans les abîmes du
cœur: les vérités qu'il contient sont du nombre de celles qui
demandent le demi-jour et la perspective."[51]

The growth of the metaphor during the seventeenth century appears to have been founded principally on the notion
of distance. The adverbial expression "in perspective" would
come to signify "afar," "in the distance" (as the even more
common "seeing things in perspective," "placing things in
perspective" would allude not only to context but to the relation between what is near and what is far). We meet this
meaning, for example, already in Lope de Vega's *Dorotea*
(ca. 1632). Fernando, Lope's hero, is ever the poet and lover
of words, beyond the mere activity of composing poems, and
his changing identity is inseparable from the constantly inventive use of language. As Celia observes: "Ves ahí lo que
te ha dejado don Fernando, versos, acotaciones y vocablos
nuevos . . ." (Act ii, Sc. ii). One of these "vocablos nuevos"
is *perspectiva*,[52] applied to land as seen from a distant boat

---

[50] *The Poetical Works of Wordsworth*, ed. H. Reed (Philadelphia,
1851), p. 32; see also "The Excursion," p. 629.

[51] *Le Génie du Christianisme*, Part ii, Bk. iii, Chap. i.

[52] Before *perspectiva*, the word *prospectiva* appears (Stephen Gilman
kindly tells me) in the *Visión delectable* (ca. 1440) by Alfonso de la
Torre, cf. *Biblioteca de autores españoles* (Madrid, 1855), xxxvi, 348.
It has there the medieval meaning of "optics."

"from what topsail do you discover the high crown of a tree,
land in perspective, the untidy fringes of the sea?":

> ¿En qué gavia descubres
> del árbol alta copa,
> la tierra en perspectiva,
> del mar incultas orlas?
>
> (Act iii, Sc. vii)

Nearly as promptly the identical notion of distance was
transferred metaphorically to *time*, usually with reference to
the future. The most expressive instances I know of this—
perspective as "mental view of the future," "outlook," "expectation"—are found in the letters of Madame de Sévigné,
whose imagination was capable of visualizing not only the
past, as critics have remarked, but the future too. "Vous me
donnez des perspectives charmantes pour m'ôter l'horreur
des séparations"[53]—she writes to her daughter, who, needless
to say, was the goal of her heart despite and in defiance of
every form of distance: "Du reste, je ne vous dis point que
vous êtes mon but, ma perspective, vous le savez bien."[54]
(Later on, with the growth of a sense of history, this metaphorical usage—"seeing in perspective," "needing perspective"—will refer not only to psychological but to historical
time.)[55]

[53] Letter of August 26, 1676 to Madame de Grignan.
[54] Letter of January 15, 1690 to Madame de Grignan. The term is
often used optimistically, as in *The Works of Oliver Goldsmith*, ed.
P. Cunningham (New York, 1900), iii, 197: "I saw a long perspective
of felicity before me." The adverbial expression "to have in perspective,"
"avoir en perspective," etc., has often a spatial application; cf. *Oeuvres
de Voltaire*, ed. Beuchot (Paris, 1834), lxx, 168: "Je suis, comme j'ai
toujours été, entre le lac de Genève et le mont Jura, ayant en perspective
les neiges éternelles des grands Alpes. . . ." But it soon comes to refer
to the future—to having a plan, a prospect, etc. Cf. Mme. de Sévigné,
Letter of November 1, 1688: "J'ai en perspective de vous allez voir, et
cette pensée me fait subsister."
[55] See Bertrand Russell's definition of "Perspective, historical" in the
Dictionary of Mind, Matter, and Morals (New York, 1952), p. 178: "The

Most useful for our purposes would be an investigation of the early adaptation of the metaphor to the processes of knowledge. There is evidence during the seventeenth century of the exact use by precise minds of the perspective figure and all its scientific trappings (the point of view, the visual pyramid, the vanishing point) with respect to judgment. To be sure, the passage from a metaphor for illusion to a metaphor for cognition had occurred earlier in individual cases, even with reference to the perspective glass.[56] At that time, however, mathematically educated minds brought their training to bear increasingly on the problems of human behavior. As there existed an exact method for correct visual interpretation, why should not analogous procedures be sought for the evaluation of moral situations? This tempting parallel was likely to arise, especially in France, during a period of growing rationalism. Even Pascal would mention with admiration the virtues of the pictorial point of view: "Si on est trop jeune, on ne juge pas bien; trop vieil, de même. . . . Ainsi les tableaux vus de trop loin—et de trop près; et il n'y a qu'un point indivisible qui soit le véritable lieu; les autres sont trop près, trop loin, trop haut ou trop bas. La perspective l'assigne dans l'art de la peinture; mais dans la vérité et dans la morale, qui l'assignera?"[57]

---

military superiority of Europe to Asia is not an eternal law of nature, as we are tempted to think; and our own superiority in civilization is a mere delusion. Our histories, which treat the Mediterranean as the center of the universe, give quite a wrong perspective." Also in this historical sense "perspective," which often means "view of the future," as we saw in the last note, refers to the ability to have "vision" (of the future). The University of California, which prides itself on having it, stresses in its "Academic Plan" for 1965-1975, *Unity and Diversity* (Office of the President, 1965), five overriding imperatives: "Growth," "Diversity," "Balance," "Freedom," "Responsibility," "Perspective."

[56] Cf. *Letters of Queen Elizabeth and King James VI of Scotland* (London, 1849), xciii, 173: "for I have not so small a perspective in my neighbors' actions. . . ."

[57] "Pensée 381," *Oeuvres de Blaise Pascal*, ed. L. Brunschvicg (Paris, 1921), xiii, 291. Cf. also "Pensée 383," xiii, 292.

In this thought La Rochefoucauld, half a century later, will substantially follow Pascal, though with the important omission of the question mark: "Les hommes et leurs affaires ont leur point de perspective: il y en a qu'il faut voir de près, pour en bien juger; et d'autres dont on ne juge jamais si bien que quand on en est éloigné."[58] The lucidity called for by La Rochefoucauld implies that a man cannot see himself, blinded as he is by self-love,[59] but can try to observe such other men as have the advantage of being more or less remote, if only the appropriate distance can be previously selected: "Comme on doit garder des distances pour voir les objets, il en faut garder aussi pour la société: chacun a son point de vue, d'où il veut être regardé; on a raison, le plus souvent, de ne vouloir pas être éclairé de trop près, et il n'y a presque point d'homme qui veuille, en toutes choses, se laisser voir tel qu'il est."[60] What La Rochefoucauld regards as right judgment, in other words, provides us with an early psychological example of what is often called "seeing things in perspective."

The first condition of this attitude is distance. Men can thus be judged correctly and objectively, just as natural bodies are measured by the surveying eye. In La Rochefoucauld's thought, man no longer towers aristocratically over nature, but is the far-off object of perspective vision, as Paul Bénichou has explained: "Il était un *moi* au dessus des choses, et il devient une *chose* comme les autres."[61] Yet this cognitive posture requires a degree of mental sympathy, of "insight," that would not be necessary if human beings, unlike objects, did not offer more than external surfaces to the beholder's eye. Judgment, La Rochefoucauld writes, is like a penetrating, all-pervasive light: "Le jugement n'est que la grandeur

[58] "Réflexions Morales," no. 104, *Oeuvres complètes*, ed. L. Martin-Chauffier (Paris, 1950), p. 258.
[59] Cf. "Maximes Supprimées," no. 563, *ibid.*, p. 335.
[60] "Réflexions Diverses," no. 2, *ibid.*, p. 361.
[61] *Morales du Grand Siècle* (Paris, 1948), p. 98.

de la lumière de l'esprit; cette lumière pénètre le fond des choses, elle y remarque tout ce qu'il faut remarquer, et aperçoit celles qui semblent imperceptibles."[62] The adequate choice of distance must be combined with the compensating effects of insight.

In his reflections concerning the *point de perspective* and the *point de vue,* La Rochefoucauld's conclusions bear a direct relation, as in Pascal, to the differences between youth and old age. Youth is too impetuous to be able to judge wisely. Old men retire too far from the society of other men. This withdrawal results not only in excessive distance but in a rejection of the perils and difficulties of understanding. Old men specialize in things which they can submit to their wishes and which are not likely to disappoint them. In fact, they deal with externals, with objects as mere objects: "Leur goût, détrompé des désirs inutiles, se tourne alors vers des objets muets et insensibles; les bâtiments, l'agriculture, l'économie, l'étude, toutes ces choses sont soumises à leur volonté."[63] The superior mind—*le grand esprit*—on the contrary, controls a wide range of insights: "Il discerne les objets éloignés, comme s'ils étaient présents; il comprend, il imagine les plus grandes choses; il voit et connaît les plus petites."[64] The ability to see things and people in perspective demands a constant coordination of the various levels on which the observer's intellectual vision must function, and a selfless objectivity. A case in point is La Rochefoucauld's final evaluation in his *Mémoires* of Cardinal Richelieu, where he recognizes the resentments caused by the cardinal's actions in particular areas but attempts to judge correctly, after all the evidence is in, the whole of his achievement. Thus the moralist's eye moves from external appearances to the intuition of inwardness, from the individual heart to the general manifesta-

---

[62] "Réflexions Morales," no. 97, *Oeuvres complètes,* p. 257.
[63] "Réflexions Diverses," no. 19 ("De la retraite"), *ibid.,* p. 400.
[64] "Réflexions Diverses," no. 16, *ibid.,* p. 384.

tions of human passions and humors, from the detail to the totality of a man's life. Perspective vision, in this case too, is that of "the eyes of heavy mind." Beyond its earthly range, there is little to be seen, for in La Rochefoucauld the glare of *abbaglio*, the field where vision fails, applies no longer to God or to the loved woman, as in Dante or Lorenzo the Magnificent, but (in violent recoil from the *ars moriendi* of a Montaigne) to death and its aftermath: "Le soleil ni la mort ne se peuvent regarder fixement."[65]

As we reach cognitive perspectives, we should take passing notice of the fact that the attendant metaphor of the "point of view" had also taken hold by La Rochefoucauld's time.[66] Actually, it seems that whereas the idea of perspective would remain a relatively cultured one, the notion of point of view, perhaps because it appears simpler, would obtain greater acceptance in everyday speech. I will not attempt to deal here with this extension of our subject. But in this respect an important distinction needs to be made, which will be of use to us later. A point of view is not always individual, or subjective in an individual sense. It can also be ultrapersonal. Dürer's perspective apparatus (Figure 1) did not necessarily set up a personal field of vision: a number of people could occupy the same position. This distinction becomes operative in the area of opinions or experiences collectively shared, such as politics, class prejudices, religion. Thus Mon-

---

[65] "Réflexions Morales," no. 26, *ibid.*, p. 247.

[66] Littré's *Dictionnaire de la langue française* (Paris, 1962) gives examples from Madame de Sévigné, Bourdaloue, Fontenelle, etc.; the *OED*, vii, 1051, quotes Coleridge and nineteenth-century writers; the *Diccionario de la lengua castellana* . . . , called "de Autoridades" (Madrid, 1726-1739), v, 435, gives Tomás Vicente Tosca's *Compendio matemático* (1670). The term obviously came into use as the result of a growing familiarity with perspective theory. "Viewpoint" seems to be a later abbreviation (*OED*, xii, 196: first example from the year 1856). "Standpoint," as I shall mention later, is a loan from the German *Standpunkt* (*OED*, x, 821: examples from the nineteenth century). *Gesichtspunkt* has been in frequent use since the eighteenth century.

tesquieu's fictional Persian writes as an outsider about a *Christian* point of view: "Le mariage, chez toutes les nations du Monde, est un contrat susceptible de toutes les conventions, et on n'en a dû bannir que celles qui auraient pu en affaiblir l'objet. Mais les Chrétiens ne le regardent pas dans ce point de vue."[67] The ultraindividual point of view, as we shall see later, will play a role in the discussions of modern perspectivistic philosophers.[68]

VI

With Leibniz (1646-1716) the language of philosophy seizes upon the mathematical premises of perspective theory. Early in his career Leibniz occupied himself with optics and the methods of perspective measurement. These topics are mentioned in his correspondence, and we know that he found J. Michaël's *De visu* stimulating reading.[69] Like Spinoza, who ground lenses, and Huygens, who was concerned with the construction of telescopes, Leibniz combined a mathematical turn of mind with a practical interest in optical instruments. It has been said that the development of the microscope supported some of his principal philosophical concepts.[70] Given all this, the fact that he recurred to the perspective figure is not too startling.

The figure of perspective appears in a number of his writ-

[67] "Lettre 116," in *Lettres Persanes.*

[68] It also enters everyday speech. The individual may regard as indispensable *his* "point of view," which is alone capable of revealing his particular experience of a thing. But there are moments in the workings of social or political institutions when the individual is expected to represent a *group.* If a prime minister, for example, appoints a commission to investigate a certain issue, and assigns to it a banker, a general, and an ambassador, we may surmise that he does not wish them to submit merely their personal opinions, but the "points of view" of the economist, the military man, and the diplomat, respectively.

[69] Cf. Y. Belaval, *Leibniz: Initiation à sa philosophie* (Paris, 1962), p. 60.

[70] Cf. H. W. Carr, *Leibniz*, 2nd edn. (New York, 1960), p. 96.

ings, from the early *Letter to Thomasius* (April 20-30, 1669) to the *Letter to the Electress Sophia of Hanover* (February 6, 1706), the *Théodicée* (no. 357), and such important late works as the *Monadologie* (no. 57) and the *Principes de la nature et de la grâce, fondés en raison* (no. 3). There are good reasons for thinking that this figure is nearly as relevant to the core of Leibniz's imagination as that of the sphere, which he "had continually in mind," H. W. Carr states, "and which served as the scheme of his system. . . . The center of the sphere is a point, but if you regard the center as belonging to the sphere and, so to speak, owning the waves which spread outwards, it is then a physical point, and it represents the unity of the whole sphere."[71] When asked by the Electress Sophia of Hanover to explain the relation between simple substances and other beings or things, Leibniz replied by comparing it to the manner in which numberless rays meet and form angles in the center of a sphere, though the center remains simple and indivisible. One may notice that the figure of perspective is an integral part of the figure of the sphere, for any portion of the latter can be considered as belonging to a perspective seen from the point of view of the center of the sphere, i.e., to one of the angles or the visual cones spreading out from a central eye. Thus the image appears to be intimately associated with Leibniz's world view, and it would be impossible to present the former without doing full justice to the latter. Suffice it to indicate here the existence of such an association, as well as the originality and elegance of Leibniz's passage, in this context, from metaphor to metaphysics.

In Leibniz's writings between 1668 and 1671 the idea arises

[71] *Ibid.*, pp. 81-82. I should also cite, among minor pieces in which the perspective figure appears, the *Conséquences métaphysiques du principe de raison* (as titled by Louis Couturat), written in 1676, and the *Système nouveau pour expliquer la nature des substances et leur communication entre elles* (1695).

that the soul is like a mathematical point—i.e., nonextensive
—on which all perceptions converge as perspective lines do
on a point of view.[72] This joins his rejection of Descartes' notion of substance as *res extensa*. Leibniz seeks a unit of substance which is at once real and, unlike atoms, has no parts,
is indivisible. This unit—the soul, later the monad—is, then,
nonspatial, like a point. The question which this concept
raises is that of the relationship between the soul and the rest
of the world, between the one and the many. The nature of
simple substances, Leibniz adds, is to have perceptions, and
in these perceptions the universe is represented. In Carr's
words:

"Perception is not an external relation, but an internal activity. To perceive is to *represent* composites. To represent the
simple would be meaningless. We do not, in fact, perceive the
simple substances which compose the universe, we perceive
the world which is composed of them. Our perception is not
the universe, it is the representation of the universe. In modern phrase we should say that knowledge, of which perception is a mode, is ideal or pictorial; it gives us not the real itself, but a representation of the real. To Leibniz, this is the
very meaning of individuality, because every representation
of the world must be individual."[73]

This is no mere idealism. The soul perceives composites of
which every simple part is real. The representation which the
soul obtains is partial and insufficient—but also provisional
and dynamic, since the soul is a growing activity moving from
simple perception (*percevoir*) to developed "apperception"
or consciousness (*s'apercevoir*). Each soul is a world in
miniature that represents the larger world outside with
greater or lesser distinctness, according to its individual nature, whereas God includes and knows all perfectly (*Letter*

[72] Cf. Belaval, *Leibniz*, pp. 60-61.
[73] Carr, *Leibniz*, p. 69.

to Sophia of Hanover). Here the image we are examining becomes useful to Leibniz, who will identify the individual
character of the soul, from which perception proceeds, with
the "point of view," and the order imposed by the soul on
representation, with "perspective." These figures imply a partial view of the whole by the single part, but they also show
that the relations between perceiving units and perceived objects are at once different and "truthful," as the *Théodicée*
states:

"Les projections de perspective, qui reviennent dans le cercle
aux sections coniques, font voir qu'un même cercle peut être
représenté par une ellipse, par une parabole, et par une hyper-
bole, et même par un autre cercle et par une ligne droite, et
par un point. Rien ne paraît si différent, ni si dissemblable,
que ces figures; et cependant il y a un rapport exact de
chaque point à chaque point. Aussi faut-il avouer que chaque
âme se représente l'univers suivant son point de vue, et par
un rapport qui lui est propre; mais une parfaite harmonie y
subsiste toujours."[74]

The indivisible unit of being will become the monad, which
is also connected with the rest of the world by means of perspectives, as Leibniz says in the classic example of the city in
the *Monadologie*:

"Et comme une même ville regardée de différents côtés paraît
tout autre et est comme multipliée perspectivement, il arrive
de même que, par la multitude infinie des substances simples,
il y a comme autant de différents univers, qui ne sont pourtant que les perspectives d'un seul selon les différents points
de vue de chaque monade."[75]

[74] *Essais de Théodicée*, no. 357, in *Die philosophischen Schriften*,
VI, 327.
[75] *Monadologie*, no. 57, in *Oeuvres philosophiques de Leibniz*, ed.
P. Janet (Paris, 1900), I, 716. The comparison with a city appears al-

It seems curious that a visual, external figure like the perspective scheme should be applied to metaphysical relations between nonspatial monads. In his early book on Leibniz, Bertrand Russell thought that he had detected a contradiction between the German philosopher's "subjective" view of space and the idea of the point of view, which calls for a degree of objectivity: "thus Leibniz had two theories of space, the first subjective and Kantian, the second giving an objective counterpart, i.e., the various points of view of the monad."[76] In other words, if spatial connections between monads are not real, how can perspectives, which occupy space, be objective? How is Leibniz able to avail himself of perspectives for a transition from nonextension to space?

Souls are qualitatively different from one another, and one such difference is the fact that each has a special point of view, from which its particular relation to other substances derives. Now, a bare scheme of the perspective figure is a simple cone or pyramid, and its apex can symbolize perfectly not only the nonextensive monad but its point of view, i.e., the actual place where the cone begins. Two points, as it were, coincide: that of the monad and that of its point of view, which results from its internal activity and nature. The comparison holds so far, and it is consistent with Leibniz's argument to affirm in this context that the point of view is metaphysically real, not just a cognitive event. Can we say the same of the rest of the perspective cone?

The monad-composed universe has no extension, no shape, no succession. Space and time enter only the monad's *representation* of the rest of the world. The qualities that are apprehended, such as the physical shapes of bodies, are only

---

ready in the *Letter to Thomasius* of April 20-30, 1669, *Die philosophischen Schriften*, I, 19; cf. also III, 622, and IV, 554.

[76] *A Critical Exposition of the Philosophy of Leibniz* (Cambridge, Eng., 1900), p. 122.

appearances, phenomena, like colors and sounds. These appearances are brought together in the process of representation by space and time. Extension is the condition of the monad's perception of multitudes of things.[77]

We do not have a subjective, Kantian space, dependent on a subject's mental structure as it perceives so-called objects. Space in Leibniz, though limited to the activity of representation, depends instead on the response of one substance to other substances, i.e., on the relation between one part and another part of the real. This response is called metaphorically a perspective. It rests on the actual organization of the monads in the nonextensive world they constitute. "Space and time in Leibniz's system belong to the world of appearance and not to the world of noumenal reality. Yet space and time are not themselves appearances, nor are they objects of perception, they belong to the *order* of perceptions. Space is the order of coexistence, time is the order of succession, in the monad's perceptions."[78]

The point of view, then, is metaphysically real. The perspective is a representational order which ontologically does not exist, but also is neither objective (since it structures appearances) nor subjective (since it rests on real relations between monads). The combination of the two is a mixed metaphor which may be qualified, in conclusion, by the following observations.

First, perspectives should not be regarded as illusory or erroneous—"as nought but shadows," in Shakespeare's words, "of what is not." They are not only "shadows" of what is, they are also exact, as the quoted passage from the *Théodicée* makes clear ("Rien ne paraît si différent, ni si dissemblable, que ces figures; et cependant il y a un rapport exact de chaque point à chaque point"). There is a mathematically correct and truthful relation between the various parts of a

---

[77] Cf. Carr, *Leibniz*, p. 91.
[78] *Ibid.*, p. 154.

given percept and its point of view. Just as space and time are not appearances, but orders of perceptions, perspectives are *exact orders of perception*. Monads can only know the real on the basis of phenomena, since only these are organized with precision and in agreement with a point of view.

The total figure, secondly, *combines* the ontologically existent point of view with the mirrorlike perspective. This articulation is crucial. The total figure at hand is a representational relation between different real entities. Thus Leibniz occupies a middle ground (and I wish to stress this in view of what later thinkers will sustain) between the ontological and the epistemological notions of perspective. Leibniz stresses that monads are subject to change, but that these changes proceed from a *principe interne,* not from external influences (*Monadologie,* nos. 10-11). The internal principle, with which the point of view is associated, is ultimately responsible for the development of the monad, for the order imposed on its perceptions. Thus, the point of view controls the perspective and the manner in which each soul experiences the universe.[79] Perspectives are cognitive, but not in any passive sense of the word.

In Leibniz's world view perspectives are, thirdly, legitimate and praiseworthy. I have already given some reasons for this. Furthermore, the universe (which God knows as a unity), as far as *created* substances are concerned, becomes infinitely mirrored and multiplied. There is a harmonious network of relations, which is not illusory but orderly, arranged in accordance with geometrically exact and understandable relations. How splendid that the universe should be both one and multiple, both like a single sphere and like a multitude of perspectives! The simile of the city in the *Monadologie,* which I quoted earlier, was followed by this

[79] The lines of the perspective figure, spreading from the apex outward, may also be regarded as forces, rays, tendencies, or efforts (*Letter to Sophia of Hanover,* ed. Gerhardt, vii, 566).

observation: "Et c'est le moyen d'obtenir autant de variété qu'il est possible, mais avec le plus grand ordre qui se puisse, c'est à dire c'est le moyen d'obtenir autant de perfection qu'il se peut."[80] And in the *Théodicée* the philosopher's rational delight is even clearer: "C'est comme dans ces inventions de perspective, où certains beaux dessins ne paraissent que confusion, jusqu'à ce qu'on rapporte à leur vrai point de vue, ou qu'on les regarde par le moyen d'un certain verre ou miroir. C'est en les plaçant et s'en servant comme il faut, qu'on les fait devenir l'ornement d'un cabinet. Ainsi les déformités apparentes de nos petits mondes se réunissent en beautés dans le grand, et n'ont rien qui s'oppose à l'unité d'un principe universel infiniment parfait."[81] Perspectives are a sign of God's preestablished harmony.

I should like to mention, finally, that Leibniz, unlike others, does not utilize the figure of perspective in order to underline distance or a strict dualism of subject and object. One is not confronted simply with a thinking mind that contemplates things. Perspectives are relations between equally real and active subjects. In this connection, too, the position of Leibniz is unique in the history of the metaphor.

We do not encounter it again, in a philosophical text, until much later, and it is only during the last eighty years that it has become frequent. The term "perspectivism"—according to José Ferrater Mora in an invaluable article to which the present essay is very much indebted[82]—was first used philosophically by Gustav Teichmüller in *Die wirkliche und die scheinbare Welt* (1882). The conception also reappears in Nietzsche. Before turning to Nietzsche, however, let us note the date of Teichmüller's book: 1882. The first group exhibi-

[80] *Monadologie*, no. 58, in *Oeuvres philosophiques*, I, 716.

[81] *Essais de Théodicée*, no. 147, in *Die philosophischen Schriften*, VI, 197. As in Shakespeare, anamorphoses are alluded to.

[82] Cf. "Perspectivismo," in *Diccionario de filosofía*, II, 405-408. On Teichmüller, cf. Julián Marías, *Ortega* (Madrid, 1960), I, 395-397.

tion of Impressionist painters had taken place in Paris in 1874. In 1877 Cézanne had painted his *Still Life: Jar, Cup, and Fruit* (Metropolitan Museum, New York); in 1881 Manet had completed his *Bar at the Folies-Bergère* (Courtauld Institute of Art, London). The Impressionist style had reached maturity, and some of its principal exponents were seeking new paths. By the same token, they were expressing a growing dissatisfaction with the conventions of Renaissance perspective; or they were experimenting with alternate procedures. From then on the prosperity of the metaphor of perspective will coincide with the decline of its literal uses in the visual arts (though not in commercial art).

These were the final stages of a convention which had been reduced much earlier, for many artists, to the status of a preliminary technique, a mere support for the painting, or even a *poncif*. In one of his "Antiquarian Letters" Lessing had described it as a mere device: "Denn die Perspektive ist keine Sache des Genies: sie beruht auf Regeln und Handgriffen. . . ."[83] For some of Lessing's contemporaries it was like a neoclassical rule, though perhaps a less substantial one than the three unities on the stage. A bad picture, in fact, could be painted with excellent perspective, as Diderot observed more than once.[84] The value of perspective was often considered pedagogical. It belonged to an apprentice's schooling in the

---

[83] *Briefe antiquarischen Inhalts*, IX, in *Gesammelte Werke*, ed. Paul Rilla (Berlin, 1955), V, 411. A characteristic example of the neoclassical view may be found in Dryden, who thought perspective was a Greek discovery forgotten in the barbaric Middle Ages and revived in the time of Raphael; cf. the epistle "To Sir Godfrey Kneller," in *The Poetical Works of John Dryden*, II, 274. On the other hand, Perrault, in order to praise the *Modernes*, had reproached the *Anciens* with not having had perspective. For a recent opinion on this—still today—unresolved issue, cf. J. White, *Perspective in Ancient Drawing and Painting* (London, 1956).

[84] For example, he describes in this fashion a painting by Hallé; cf. "Salon de 1767," in *Oeuvres Complètes de Denis Diderot* (Paris, 1821), IX, 42.

tradition of his craft, like drawing from natural models. In his *Gutachten über die Ausbildung eines jungen Malers,* Goethe writes that in his opinion a *young* painter cannot do without the study of anatomy and perspective.[85] The fact that perspective was often assigned a secondary role may partly explain why Romantic painters did not reject it at the time when medieval art in general was being rediscovered.[86] Another reason for this persistence is the eclecticism of much of nineteenth-century art and the role of a modern eclectic tradition, from Ingres (as Robert Rosenblum has recently interpreted him) to Picasso. The Beaux Arts school never envisaged the possibility of a real change, of course; and the question of perspective belonged to a broader tension between traditionalism and avant-garde.

Pierre Francastel compares to a "grille" the function of the perspective scheme in the works of the main Impressionist period: if placed, as it were, over the canvas, it does not conflict with it; but in the picture itself it serves as a mere framework, lightly alluded to.[87] This is especially clear in urban pictures like Monet's *Boulevard des Capucines* (1873), or later ones by Pissarro, like the *Place du Théâtre Français* (1898), where the vanishing distances of Parisian streets, or of the Seine River, are an occasion above all for the sensory and luminous effects with which the artist is concerned. During the 1880's, however, certain painters begin to produce pictures which dispense with, or even contradict, the "grille." Degas' interrupted rooms, figures cut off by the picture frame, diagonals plunging into shallow air; Gauguin's volun-

---

[85] Cf. *Gedankenausgabe* . . . , ed. E. Beutler (Zurich, 1949), XIII, 130. See also the conversations with Eckermann for December 13, 1826, and December 21, 1831, *ibid.*, XXIV, 186, 506.

[86] Cf. Ruskin, *Works*, XV, 17: "Turner, though he was a professor of perspective at the Royal Academy, did not know what he professed, and never, as far as I remember, drew a single building in true perspective in his life."

[87] Cf. *Peinture et société*, p. 153.

tary exile from familiar images, for the sake of fictional spaces and surfaces;[88] Cézanne's unwillingness to "seduce" (Malraux's word) with appearances, to subordinate the surface of the painting to the content of the pictorial illusion[89]—all these constitute important steps in a new inquiry. I have mentioned earlier Cézanne's *Still Life* in the Metropolitan Museum, which was painted in 1877, and about which Sam Hunter writes: "He stresses flatness here by juggling perspective . . . Cézanne's great innovations shattered with one blow all painting formulas based on traditional Renaissance perspective."[90]

"Das *Perspektivische*, die Grundbedingung alles Lebens. . . ."[91] These plain words startle the reader of the Preface to *Jenseits von Gut und Böse* like a road sign barely warning of what follows. Teichmüller's *Perspektivismus*[92] is wielded by Nietzsche in his most mobile and provocative manner and strikes off a number of original sparks, particularly in the book just quoted and *Die fröhliche Wissenschaft*. Yet the different texts converge on a single trend of thought. The starting point is the old notion of perspective as visual *illusion*, as an infinite series of arbitrary appearances perceived by countless individuals. "But, why not appearances?" Nietzsche asks characteristically. Are they not the product of man's imagination, of his creative interpretation of mute nature ("die Natur ist immer wertlos")?[93] "Wir, die Denkend-Empfindenden, sind es, die wirklich und immerfort etwas *machen*, das noch nicht da ist: die ganze ewig wachsende Welt von Schätzungen, Farben, Akzenten, Perspektiven,

---

[88] Cf. *ibid.*, pp. 166, 193, and *passim*.

[89] Cf. C. Greenberg, *Art and Culture* (Boston, 1961), pp. 52-54.

[90] *Modern French Painting, 1855-1956* (New York, 1956), p. 118.

[91] F. Nietzsche, *Werke*, ed. K. Schlechta (Munich, 1955), II, 56.

[92] I have not been able to see Teichmüller's book, but it appears from the text that Nietzsche had it in mind on more than one occasion: cf. *Werke*, II, 221, 599.

[93] *Ibid.*, II, 177.

Stufenleitern, Bejahungen und Verneinungen." ("It is we, who think and feel, that actually and unceasingly *make* something which did not before exist: the whole eternally increasing world of valuations, colours, weights, perspectives, gradations, affirmations and negations."[94]) It is only moral prejudice to believe that truth is superior to appearances and evaluations: "Man gestehe sich doch so viel ein: es bestünde gar kein Leben, wenn nicht auf dem Grunde perspektivischer Schätzungen und Scheinbarkeiten." ("One must admit so much: there could be no life at all except on the basis of perspectival estimations and appearances."[95]) The new concept of *value* is clearly the relevant one in this context, and for Nietzsche *Perspektiven* belong most often to the area of *Wertungen*, to the formation and creation of values.

The term seems appropriate to Nietzsche's later thinking in at least two ways. First, the notion of perspective as visual appearance supports readily his insistence on error and fallibility as the condition of our lives and of the necessity for the philosopher to comprehend the deep-seated impulses that lead the greatest of men to entertain particular opinions and sustain particular fallacies: "Wir finden Gründe über Gründe dafür, die uns zu Mutmassungen über ein betrügerisches Prinzip im 'Wesen der Dinge' verlocken möchten."[96] Perspectives, secondly, underline the endless multiplicity of interpretations any single phenomenon may suggest to an original thinker. All men are more or less interpretative, all being is in need of meaning, and this very fact can only be grasped through the individual mind's peculiar perspectives:

"Wie weit der perspektivische Charakter des Daseins reicht oder gar ob es irgendeinen andren Charakter noch hat, ob

---

[94] *Loc. cit.*; "The Joyful Wisdom," tr. Thomas Common, in *The Complete Works of Friedrich Nietzsche*, ed. Oscar Levy (repr. New York, 1964), x, p. 235.

[95] *Ibid.*, ii, 599.   [96] *Ibid.*, ii, 598; cf. also p. 860.

nicht ein Dasein ohne Auslegung, ohne 'Sinn' eben zum 'Unsinn' wird, ob, andrerseits, nicht alles Dasein essentiell ein *auslegendes* Dasein ist—das kann, wie billig, auch durch die fleissigste und peinlich-gewissenhafteste Analysis und Selbstprüfung des Intellekts nicht ausgemacht werden: da der menschliche Intellekt bei dieser Analysis nicht umhin kann, sich selbst unter seinen perspektivischen Formen zu sehn und *nur* in ihnen zu sehn."

("How far the perspective character of existence extends, or whether it has any other character at all, whether an existence without explanation, without 'sense' does not just become 'nonsense,' whether, on the other hand, all existence is not essentially an *explaining* existence—these questions, as is right and proper, cannot be determined even by the most diligent and severely conscientious analysis and self-examination of the intellect, because in this analysis the human intellect cannot avoid seeing itself in its perspective forms, and *only* in them.")[97]

Nietzsche is perfectly aware of the visual origin of the metaphor and even refers to it in order to stress the subjective nature of values. The perspective figure is subordinated here—in our terms—to the "point of view," to the apex of the visual angle; and the very act of seeing is considered an essentially personal and inventive effort:

"Hüten wir uns nämlich, meine Herren Philosophen, von nun an besser vor der gefährlichen alten Begriffs-Fabelei, welche ein 'reines, willenloses, schmerzloses, zeitloses Subjekt der Erkenntnis' angesetzt hat, hüten wir uns vor den Fangarmen solcher kontradiktorischer Begriffe wie 'reine Vernunft,' 'absolute Geistigkeit,' 'Erkenntnis an sich';—hier wird immer ein Auge zu denken verlangt, das gar nicht gedacht werden kann, ein Auge, das durchaus keine Richtung haben soll, bei

---

[97] *Ibid.*, II, 249-250; "The Joyful Wisdom," tr. Common, p. 340.

dem die aktiven und interpretierenden Kräfte unterbunden sein sollen, fehlen sollen, durch die doch Sehen erst ein Etwas-Sehen wird, hier wird also immer ein Widersinn und Unbegriff vom Auge verlangt. Es gibt *nur* ein perspektivisches Sehen, *nur* ein perspektivisches 'Erkennen'; und *je mehr* Affekte wir über eine Sache zu Worte kommen lassen, *je mehr* Augen, verschiedne Augen wir uns für dieselbe Sache einzusetzen wissen, um so vollständiger wird unser 'Begriff' dieser Sache, unsre 'Objektivität' sein."

("But let us, forsooth, my philosophic colleagues, henceforward guard ourselves more carefully against this mythology of dangerous ancient ideas, which has set up a 'pure, will-less, painless, timeless subject of knowledge'; let us guard ourselves from the tentacles of such contradictory ideas as 'pure reason,' 'absolute spirituality,' 'knowledge-in-itself':— in these theories an eye that cannot be thought of is required to think, an eye which *ex hypothesi* has no direction at all, an eye in which the acting and interpreting functions are cramped, are absent; those functions, I say, by means of which 'abstract' seeing first became seeing something; in these theories consequently the absurd and the nonsensical is always demanded of the eye. There is only a seeing from a perspective, only a 'knowing' from a perspective, and the *more* emotions we express over a thing, the *more* eyes, different eyes, we train on the same thing, the more complete will be our 'idea' of that thing, our 'objectivity.' ")[98]

These perspectives—one might add in modern terms—are not simply "figurative." Nietzsche raises the concept of perspective (in other passages also, where the stress is more pragmatic and biological), and that of vision in general, to the level of a process of *evaluation* and creation which is closer to the achievement of twentieth-century artists than to

[98] *Ibid.*, II, 860-861; "The Genealogy of Morals," tr. Horace B. Samuel, in *The Complete Works of Friedrich Nietzsche*, XIII, p. 153.

the geometrical objectivity of the old Florentine convention. In this sense he destroys the older idea, reliant as it was on the conception of a mimetic sensibility, and on a dualism of subject and object.[99] Nietzsche's seer is not only an active inventor but a lover of multiplicity and contradiction. The latter is what "perspectives" make clear. The active subject is able to control and exploit a variety of points of view on a single object as well as the contrasts they imply. By having "several eyes," by combining various points of view—almost like a Cubist painter—he contributes to the endless richness of being.[100]

VII

In the twentieth century "perspectivity" makes numerous and varied appearances, especially after World War I. It responds to an attitude well attuned, and not only in philosophy proper, to a period when no single truth seemed likely to suffice, and some form of eclecticism, of cosmopolitan doubt, of intellectual pluralism, or of inexhaustible historical curiosity tempted numerous minds. Are we con-

[99] On this point, cf. K. Löwith, *Nietzsches Philosophie der ewigen Wiederkehr des Gleichen* (Stuttgart, 1956), Chap. 6.

[100] I have discussed only one direction of Nietzsche's perspectivism. In another direction it tends toward pragmatism, the idea that intelligence is an instrument that life creates with a view to action, and life an interplay of forces constantly striving to surpass one another and themselves. Perspectives are vehicles of *Triebe*—biological and vital impulses: cf. *Werke*, III, 903. These forces work within the limits, and according to the needs, of each being; they act on others through limited channels: "Der Perspektivismus ist nur eine komplexe Form der Spezifität. Meine Vorstellung ist, dass jeder spezifische Körper danach strebt, über den ganzen Raum Herr zu werden und seine Kraft auszudehnen (sein Wille zur Macht)" (*ibid.*, III, 705). On this level perspectives are not necessarily personal or conscious, but rejoin collective needs (and what I call elsewhere the ultrapersonal point of view). On this aspect of Nietzsche's perspectivism, cf. R. Berthelot, *Un Romantisme utilitaire. Etude sur le mouvement pragmatiste* (Paris, 1911-1913), I, Chap. I.

fronted here with a species of relativism? With a blank check to all firmly held "points of view," all intellectual idiosyncrasies? With a crude confusion between the "one man, one vote" principle in political democracy and the ways of knowledge? Normally the notion of perspective seems most appropriate not to an all-out relativism, but to the idea that a "point of view" has to yield a "right perspective" on the real, that a diversity of approaches must necessarily be circumscribed, or supported in each case by an adequate methodology. Indeed the main stress is often negative, as the perspectivist is conscious above all of his limits as a perceiver of the truth, of his inability to grasp totalities and construct systems. On some occasions perspectivism has been regarded as a sort of historicism—the realization that every activity in the history of culture is relative to the historical and social conditions of the period in which it took place.[101] And it has been attributed to the thinkers whose ancestors, broadly speaking, one may consider to have been Dilthey and Herder. Certain abuses of the German-style *Geistesgeschichte* and history of ideas, such as the failure to evaluate properly individual achievement, or the intoxication with period by period generalizations, obviously fall into this category. But perspectivism describes rather more accurately the work of those historians who, like Dilthey himself, regard *Weltanschauungen* as basic existential attitudes.[102] To the perspectivist, historicism does not produce valueless chaos. It suggests that every world view provides us with an ultraindividual aspect of truth, with a partial but loyal perception of man, his history, and the values he has created. These are the distinctions, I think, that ought to determine the relevance of "perspectivism" to such writers and fields as Spengler's biolog-

[101] Cf. the article "Prospettivismo," *Enciclopedia filosofica* (Venice and Rome, 1957), III, 1671.

[102] Cf. Müller-Vollmer, *Towards a Phenomenological Theory of Literature*, p. 40 and elsewhere.

ically determined relativism, Georg Simmel, the *Umweltlehre* of the biologist Jakob von Uexküll, Max Scheler, Karl Jaspers, Karl Mannheim's *Soziologie des Wissens*, Erich Rothacker, Kenneth Burke, the historicists in literary criticism or art history, and José Ortega y Gasset.

I shall discuss here a few philosophical instances from Spain, England, and America. José Ortega y Gasset gave currency to the metaphor of perspective among Spanish readers during and after World War I. That the idea was central to his thought has been shown by Antonio Rodríguez Huéscar in a valuable book, *Perspectiva y verdad: El problema de la verdad en Ortega* (Madrid, 1966). I can only refer my readers to Huéscar's exhaustive account of the numerous meanings—at least thirteen—that the term assumes in Ortega's writings. But I must also direct their attention to a question of method which is pertinent to our subject, and on which I shall venture an opinion. The question is that of the preliminary approach to Ortega's philosophy as a whole. Huéscar, like Julián Marías, tends to regard it as a perfectly coherent body of thought which can be approached systematically. When an idea is not pursued fully in, say, text A, Huéscar proceeds not only to discuss text B for better comprehension —doubtless a legitimate step—but to suppose that the complete idea was implicit in text A. For example, in an early essay by Ortega, "Adán en el paraíso" (1910), the reader is likely to notice that the metaphor of perspective supports a *subjective* theory of values—a notion that will not reappear in later writings.[103] While Ortega states already in this essay that as many entities exist as there are points of view, and while it is remarkable that the metaphor should have been used by him so early in his career, what the metaphor actually signifies here seems very different from its later meanings. Yet Huéscar minimizes these differences, and even

[103] Cf. "Adán en el paraíso," *Obras completas* (Madrid, 1946), I, 495.

maintains that Ortega's subsequent idea is potentially present in "Adán en el paraíso."[104] On the other hand, there are readers of Ortega who regard his achievement primarily as a dynamic inquiry, a constant self-elaboration, an intellectual "narrative" of which no single phase can be said to contain fully what will follow.[105] This dramatic process, I think, is rather closer to the truth (and to Ortega's truth concerning human life). Thus, to return to our topic, Huéscar traces the term perspective from "Glosas" (1902) to *El hombre y la gente* (1949-1950). These uses cover a wide spectrum, ranging from the strictly philosophical to the notion of an artistic or intellectual "point of view" or even to the normal meaning of the word as found in ordinary Spanish speech. I am not qualified to offer here a full alternative to Huéscar's interpretation. The following may serve simply as an example of the different method.

Ortega recalls in this context Leibniz rather than Nietzsche,[106] as well as the work of, among others, Jakob von Uexküll (*Umwelt und Innenwelt der Tiere*, 1909), for whom the basic unit of biology is not the isolated organism but the functional whole including each body and its environment. In the *Meditaciones del Quijote* (1914) the idea is merely sketched, though with an interesting reference to a philosophy of objective values. There is a hierarchy of perspectives on the real, in agreement with the value attached to each. The individual, whose point of view is originally limited to

[104] Cf. *Perspectiva y verdad* (Madrid, 1966), p. 51.

[105] To a certain degree, and with important qualifications, this is the view of J. Ferrater Mora's brief but excellent *Ortega y Gasset: Etapas de una filosofía* (Barcelona, 1958).

[106] Cf. "Verdad y perspectiva," in *Obras completas*, ii, 18, note 1. After quoting the *Monadologie*, Ortega affirms that he follows neither Nietzsche nor Vaihinger. The latter had adapted the former's perspectivism to his own "fictionalism": cf. H. Vaihinger, *Die Philosophie des Als Ob* (Berlin, 1911), pp. 780ff. On Ortega's originality with respect to these philosophers, cf. J. Marías, *Ortega*, i, 391ff.

his *circunstancia* or environment, should develop a sense of relative position and distance in order to integrate his perceptions with the broad expanses of a larger reality.[107] While so doing, he must distinguish between what is near or present (for example, the trees he actually sees in a wood) and what is distant, latent, or copresent (the wood, which he never sees as a whole). This *teoría de la profundidad*, as applicable to art or to the structure of things, will remain an important feature of Ortega's thinking.[108]

But Ortega's ideas on the subject do not come to fruition until the first installment of *El espectador*, "Verdad y perspectiva" (1916), and especially *El tema de nuestro tiempo* (1923). On both occasions he insists that the concept of perspective permits one to avoid the twin poles of relativism (there are only individual opinions, hence truth does not exist) and dogmatism (a single body of truth does exist, hence individual opinions do not matter). Perspectives are like a bridge between the person seeking knowledge and reality. They are the dimension of man's apprehension of the real. This apprehension is selective and serves as a filter without leading necessarily into error. A "perspective" requires an individual "point of view" in order to be actualized and as such is not a subjective fallacy. An object offers to different persons different perspectives, all of which *can* be authentic, truthful, and, therefore, mutually complementary. One of Ortega's important contributions here is his presentation of the conditions that are needed for a point of view to be authentic and truthful. The opposites to be shunned are not only dogmatism and relativism. Man's knowledge is effective when he succeeds in not isolating "culture" from "life"—cultural aspirations from biological impulses, the imperatives of reason from those of living. The abstract exercise of reason fails to seize the mobility of existence, and a *razón vital* must

[107] Cf. *Meditaciones del Quijote*, in *Obras completas*, I, 321-322.
[108] Cf. Huéscar, *Perspectiva y verdad*, pp. 74-85.

be developed that is able to do so. A genuinely cognitive point of view must be spontaneous and rooted in experience —must be a vehicle of the *razón vital*. A point of view, in order to be illuminating, should be sincere—it cannot be feigned—while able to recognize its own limits: "La sola perspectiva falsa es ésa que pretende ser la única."[109] Let every man reason as forcefully as he can, instead of attempting to "see" with someone else's eyes, which is sterile, or with everybody's, which is impossible.[110] The relevance of this approach to humanistic studies is evident, and Ortega himself has skillfully applied the notion of the point of view to painting, literature, and music.[111]

Ortega's argument, however, is not quite clear or complete as he proceeds from a theory of knowledge and truth to perspectives as qualities of being, as ontology. "La perspectiva," he writes in *El tema de nuestro tiempo*, "es uno de los componentes de la realidad."[112] What is this reality that perspectives are components of? The objective conception of perspective is dangerously circular, since it implies an independent reality on which the point of view focuses, and then goes on to state that this reality consists in a combination of perspectives. Ortega is quite aware of this and holds that a perspective is an ontological predicate: "Cuando una realidad entra en choque con ese otro objeto que denominamos 'sujeto consciente,' la realidad responde *apareciéndole*. La apariencia es una cualidad objetiva de lo real, es su respuesta al sujeto." (When a certain reality collides with that other object we name "a conscious subject," the response of the reality consists in *appearing*. Appearance is an objective quality of

[109] *El tema de nuestro tiempo*, in *Obras completas*, III, 201.
[110] Cf. *ibid.*, III, 202.
[111] Especially in "Musicalia" (1921), *La deshumanización del arte* ("Una gota de fenomenología") (1925), "Don Juan y el resentimiento" (1921), "Sobre el punto de vista en las artes" (1924). For other texts, cf. Huéscar, *Perspectiva y verdad*, pp. 262-408.
[112] *Obras completas*, III, 199.

the real—its response to a subject.)[113] The implication, it seems to me, is unequivocal: perspectives are appearances, aspects, qualities of the real as perceived by individual subjects. Since Ortega has rejected previously any form of subjectivism or idealism, these appearances presuppose the reality they actualize or offer as a response to the subject. Unlike Nietzsche or Vaihinger, Ortega is not satisfied with perspectives as *mere* appearances, fictions, *subjective* values. Neither can he insert them into an equivalent of Leibniz's monadology. The reader remains anxious for a broader framework, a support for perspectives as objective appearances.

It can be argued that at this stage of Ortega's philosophy such a support in fact existed: his "circumstantial" theory, as formulated in the *Meditaciones del Quijote*. One can also add that his later insistence on a "filosofía de la vida" is a development of the earlier theory and may also serve as the needed framework. But I have promised to follow an alternate approach to Ortega's thought. It is also possible to indicate a dialectical tension not only between different ideas, but between different attitudes—aspects of the Spanish writer's personality as a philosopher. There is perhaps such a tension between the metaphor of perspective and the "idea de la vida."

"Yo soy yo y mi circunstancia" means that the self, instead of being ontologically independent, is inconceivable without its environment—and vice versa. (It is a unit, one might say, of human ecology.) The philosophical concept of *life*, likewise, signifies that the individual finds himself situated in a broader reality which is his life. "My life," to all intents and purposes, is the radical locus of the real. This radical foundation is not a thing, a substance, but a series of events, constantly renewed and changing, constantly reinvented by man.

[113] *Ibid.*, III, 236.

My life, Ortega insists in opposition to the idealists, is submerged in the world. But, on the other hand, perspectives are based on a *sujeto consciente* who apprehends the objects that are "out there" and seeks to pursue a dialogue, a kind of coexistence, with them. The metaphor of perspective is anthropocentric; and it normally implies the perception of objects—not of the nonobject which is the locus of the self and of its environment. It is true that Ortega was aware of the limits of visual analogies, and even wrote once that "no one has ever seen an orange."[114] While it is impossible to see an orange fully and simultaneously from all sides, it is not impossible to touch it or hold it three-dimensionally: "Es cosa clara que la forma decisiva de nuestro trato con las cosas es, efectivamente, el tacto. Y si esto es así, por fuerza tacto y contacto son el factor más perentorio en la estructuración de nuestro mundo." (It's very clear that the decisive form of our relationship with things is, actually, tactile. If this is so, touch and contact are perforce the most peremptory factor in the structuring of our world.)[115] Would a tactile analogy be more appropriate to the "idea de la vida"? Ortega, at any rate, held on to a metaphor in which a distinction between subject and object was implicit. The notion of perspective is not readily adaptable to a "life" that embraces both the perceiver and the perceived. How do I "see" my life, how do I alter it or reinvent it, without losing touch with its real status? The metaphor at best is partial, or relevant to knowledge and action rather than to reality itself. It corresponds to one attitude only in Ortega—that of the *espectador* whose intelligence is engaged in a form of intellectual vision, of meditation on the spectacle of existence.

In 1914, the year in which the *Meditaciones* appeared, Bertrand Russell's *Our Knowledge of the External World*

[114] "Nadie ha visto jamás una naranja" (*Meditaciones del Quijote*), quoted by Huéscar, *Perspectiva y verdad*, p. 76.
[115] *El hombre y la gente*, quoted by Huéscar, p. 389.

was also published. In this book Russell proposes to deal with the old doubts as to the reality of the world of the senses by applying the procedures of the new logic to the examination of ordinary experience. At one point in his argument, he suddenly suggests a hypothesis: each mind sees the world "from a point of view peculiar to itself" and perceives a private world which is a "perspective."[116] A little later, when he attempts to return from this metaphorical hypothesis to the central discourse of the book, Russell encounters serious difficulties. (Where is the intrapersonal mind that can construct from the various private worlds a public one? How can this logical construction be in itself anything but private? Etc.[117]) It should not be necessary, however, to analyze these difficulties in detail, as Russell himself, in an article entitled "How I Write," seems to have conceded the point: "The book was

---

[116] (London, 1952), p. 95. (A revised edition had been published in 1926).

[117] Certain sense data are primitive, Russell had begun, because they are not inferred from anything else, and others are derivative. The question is: Can the existence of anything other than our own hard or primitive data be inferred from them alone? As I walk around an object—say, a table—I find that my sensations are changing in a continuous way, not by sudden replacement but by the experience of a progressive correlation of muscular and other sensations with changes in visual data. After proposing the hypothesis that each mind thus sees a private world which is a perspective, Russell goes on to state that these private worlds do exist. By relating them, moreover, one *infers* a space that is not *in* any perspective, but is a system of relations between perspectives. The aspects of a thing seen from various perspectives are real, but the "thing itself" is a logical construction—which does not contradict our experience. My comments are: (1) The metaphor of perspective is not mobile or three-dimensional enough to deal with the progressive correlation of tactile or auditory data. (2) The notion of the single angle of vision is not a hard datum of experience: I may have to walk around a table to know that *it* exists, but I perceive immediately that the moving forms of a dancer correlate; the metaphor "freezes" both the subject and the object. (3) From a particular position what I see coincides with what another can see from the same place; in this sense the perspective is not "private." (4) and (5) The two questions asked in my text above.

very imperfect, and I now think that it contains serious errors."[118] In his case, as in Ortega's, the student of our subject is likely to observe above all the problems raised by the attempt to turn the metaphor of perspective into a full-fledged ontological concept. Solipsism threatens the effort of relating a multitude of perceiving entities to a single perceived reality by means of perspectives (without, like Leibniz, regarding these entities as substantial). There is also the reduction of the external world to aspects or qualities lacking any real foundation, as W. T. Stace indicates concerning this stage of Russell's philosophy: "The whole object of the theory, we understood at the beginning, was to get rid of hidden substrates, *Ding-an-sich*-like physical objects with unknowable intrinsic qualities. But now all this, which we were to get rid of, is back again on our hands. The only advance made on the theory of *The Problems of Philosophy* is that for the solid *Ding-an-sich*-like *thing* at the center with its intrinsic qualities, we have substituted *Ding-an-sich*-like *aspects*, with their intrinsic qualities, radiating from the center through space. This change in no way makes the theory more empirical."[119] One is tempted to think that the metaphor of perspective offers a way out of a serious philosophical problem. After Russell, Alfred North Whitehead in his later writings also speaks of perspectives, "perspectival feelings," "perspectival relatives."[120] He uses the term especially in *Modes of Thought* (1938), a series of lectures intended for an audience of nonspecialists.

Students of American philosophy will be familiar with the work of George H. Mead, Samuel Alexander, E. B. Mc-

---

[118] *The Basic Writings of Bertrand Russell*, eds. R. E. Egner and L. E. Denonn (New York, 1961), p. 64.

[119] "Russell's Neutral Monism," *The Philosophy of Bertrand Russell*, ed. P. A. Schilpp, 3rd edn. (New York, 1951), p. 370.

[120] Cf. V. Lowe, *Understanding Whitehead* (Baltimore, Md., 1966), pp. 54, 259, 279.

Gilvary, and the "perspective realists" and "objective relativists" whose work attracted attention before World War II. These different philosophers have in common an interest in the concept of perspective. In an article in a 1934 issue of the *Journal of Philosophy*, one finds a sentence indicative of a moment in the history of American thought: "in recent philosophy, the problem of perspectivity has become of the greatest importance."[121] Another article in the same journal for 1959, a respectful rejection by Arthur E. Murphy of McGilvary's posthumous *Toward a Perspective Realism*, spells out the change in the situation of philosophy over a twenty-five-year period.[122]

I can only mention in passing these philosophers, among whom important differences existed, and single out in particular Arthur O. Lovejoy's powerful critique in *The Revolt Against Dualism* (1930), which is broadly relevant to the notion of perspective. Although he refers to Mead, Whitehead, Donald A. Piatt, Edwin A. Burtt, and A. E. Murphy,[123] Lovejoy addresses himself to a general notion of perspectivity, along the following lines. Cognition is a direct relation between mind and object. Only certain aspects of the object enter into a relation of copresence with the mind. A perspective designates this relation, which makes the content of a given experience unlike the object as it appears in any other relation. The point of view or "standpoint"[124] is the set of con-

---

[121] P. L. DeLargy, "Perspectivity and Objectivity," *The Journal of Philosophy*, xxxi (1934), 29-38.

[122] "McGilvary's Perspective Realism," *The Journal of Philosophy*, lvi (1959), 148-165.

[123] Lovejoy associates the "perspective realists" and "objective relativists" with the scientific positivism of Mach and Petzoldt. Cf. *The Revolt Against Dualism* (Boston, 1930), p. 81.

[124] These writers often use "standpoint"—of German origin? Cf. J. Petzoldt, *Das Weltproblem vom Standpunkte des relativistichen Positivismus aus*, 2nd edn. (Leipzig, 1912), p. 142: "Wir können die Welt immer nur von dem Standpunkt aus denken, auf dem wir wirklich stehen, nicht von einem Standpunkt aus, auf dem wir überhaupt uns

ditions responsible for the perception of a certain aspect or appearance. The "face values" of things are seized by the mind as a "continuum of qualities" (Samuel Alexander's terms).[125] The mind is a focal point for perspectives—it does not create a synthesis. Perspectives are relative to the point of view but are not based on qualities existing independently from the perceiver (hence the "realist" in "perspective realist," and the "objective" in "objective relativist"). These ideas are supported by certain assumptions for which a satisfactory explanation is not always given. The assumption I have discussed earlier is that of a real foundation for perspectival appearances. But Lovejoy in this context criticizes also the concept of the point of view. Perspectivity, he stresses, does not simply suppose that a percept depends upon a conditioning relation with the percipient; it relies upon the *position* of the percipient. "The notion of a standpoint or point of view apparently implies, in the first place, a situation in which *some* element is initially taken as *not* relative to the percipient. . . . From my point of view the penny may appear elliptical, from yours, circular; but the phraseology implies that the same object, or at least the same region of space or space-time, is in some sense being viewed by both of us."[126] The point of view would be meaningless if one did not assume the previous existence of a region in space-time common to both the perceived object and the perceiving points of view. Lovejoy, further, is of the opinion that perspectivity brings about a subjective dissolution of *knowledge*. The professedly objective relativist emphasizes that all content is affected by perspectivity. This means that I can never know "things as they

---

gar nicht stehend denken können, oder von gar keinem Standpunkt aus. Es gibt keinen absoluten Standpunkt und es gibt keine Standpunktlosigkeit, es gibt allein relative Standpunkte, diese aber auch stets. . . ."

[125] Cf. B. D. Brettschneider, *The Philosophy of Samuel Alexander* (New York, 1964), pp. 82-83.

[126] Lovejoy, *The Revolt Against Dualism*, p. 120.

are" and am left with nothing more solid than my own point of view, which can only be the condition, not the goal, of knowledge. It all leads to "a general deliquescence of the notion of factual truth and falsity."[127]

The last objection turns, of course, on the definition of knowledge as the apprehension of "things as they are," and in this sense is circular. But there is an added factor in the equation which should be taken into consideration—what I called earlier the ultraindividual point of view. Let us not begin by asking that truth should exist independently of any experience of it. Let us rather question the quality of the experience. If closely related perspectives were *only* different from one another, objective knowledge would be in peril. Only when an individual receives an impression which others cannot receive, is the experience totally subjective.[128] If we notice or assert, furthermore, that the same point of view *can* be shared by several persons, that it can be ultraindividual, Lovejoy's objection loses part of its force. We have seen that according to Ortega the point of view has to be intensely personal.[129] On the other hand, some of the American perspectivists have defended the opposite conception—George Herbert Mead, for example. In the pragmatic philosophy of Mead (1863-1931), thought is a problem-solving activity, instrumental to behavior. The fundamentals of perception are a distant object and one's selection of that which is related to one's future action. In this pragmatic sense, then, "the perspective is the world in its relationship to the individual and the individual in its relationship to the world."[130] But perspectives are combined through action, and in action men

---

[127] *Ibid.*, p. 123.

[128] Cf. DeLargy, "Perspectivity and Objectivity," p. 32.

[129] Cf. Huéscar, *Perspectiva y verdad*, p. 101: "dos individuos situados sucesivamente . . . en el mismo lugar y mirando en la misma direcccción . . . representan, sin embargo, *dos puntos de vista diferentes* y, por consiguiente, *no ven lo mismo.*"

[130] G. H. Mead, *The Philosophy of the Act* (Chicago, 1938), p. 115.

function also as members of groups. The *location* underlying a perspective is a collective one,[131] as the "social individual is already in a perspective which belongs to the community within which his self has arisen. . . . This involves the assumption of the community attitudes where all speak with one voice in the organization of social conduct. The whole process of thinking is the inner conversation going on between the generalized other and the individual."[132] This is Mead's view of the locus of the standpoint. As for the question of the real basis for perspectival aspects, Mead thinks there is no absolute reality analogous to Newtonian absolute space and time, of which the perspectives would be but partial representations. The universe itself consists of perspectives, which exist not "on" an absolute behind the scenes, but "on" one another within a time-space continuum as revealed by Einstein's relativity.[133]

VIII

The notion of the ultraindividual point of view, then, is useful to the perspectivist insofar as it compensates for a considerable degree of subjectivism in his position. As an illustration of this, let us turn for a moment to literary theory. Let us suppose that a perspectivistic aesthetics exists in literary criticism and attempt to formulate briefly (and very imperfectly, I am afraid) what some of its principles might be. The work of art is a complex—one would begin—of potentialities, which criticism tries to actualize. There can be no actualization without the individual critic. A total, supraindividual

[131] Cf. *ibid.*, p. 64.

[132] *Ibid.*, p. 157. Cf. also E. B. McGilvary, *Toward a Perspective Realism*, ed. A. G. Ramsperger (La Salle, Ill., 1956). On uses by other thinkers of the metaphor of perspective (Merleau-Ponty, Sartre, A. P. Ushenko, C. F. Graumann, R. A. Tsanoff, F. M. Volpati), cf. especially Ferrater Mora, "Perspectivismo."

[133] Cf. Mead, *The Philosophy of the Act*, pp. 118-119.

realization is an abstraction inimical to the nature of the aesthetic experience, based as the latter is on perception. The literary work of art is a finite structure that is able to release infinite effects. As a structure, it presents objective forms to the critic, and as a work of art it multiplies itself endlessly through the aesthetic experience. Criticism consists of a temporal series of critical acts. No single critical act can encompass the wealth of the aesthetic experience, though it must proceed from it. This channeling or funneling of the experience into the act is the perspective. It is not an abstract method or a general approach, but an empirical relation between the one and the many. The work of art coincides solely with itself. Only certain aspects of its actualization by the aesthetic experience enter at any single moment into a relation of copresence with the critic's mind. This relation, or perspective, is the condition for the critic's reflective and verbal effort. It leads to his active apprehension of the work, to his own creative achievement. This achievement, if at all successful, brings us back to the work itself, in a kind of constant voyage between the finite structure and the endless critical perspectives. In this sense the existence of the work of art is not static or immutable, and the articulate discovery by the critic of real perspectives is irreversible. The perspective is relative, of course, to the critic's point of view, but this does not mean that either of the two are "his" alone. The point of view must be nourished by an individual sensibility, or no aesthetic experience would occur. At the same time, the point of view cannot be merely private, or criticism would be either illusory or sterile. The point of view assumes the existence of a public region where the critic's gifts and the objective structure of the work of art *can* meet. Although two different critics are unlikely ever to write identical essays, they are able to work with or from the same perspective—in the hope, besides, that their readers will follow suit. The genuine critical perspective combines precisely an *individual* creative effort with the actualization of a public truth through an *ultraindividual* point of view, so that it may be transferable to future readers or critics who are capable of occupying a similar position.

But it is not my purpose here to develop new perspectives. Broad though my topic has been, I have tried to confine myself in this survey to the conscious use of the term by painters, writers, and philosophers of past periods. It would be another matter, and a subject for another essay, to envisage the possible uses of the term as *our* own critical instrument—to study perspectives in, say, music or literature, as "symbolical forms." The idea of "seeing things in perspective," for example, has been applied particularly to history and to the individual's experience of it. This experience is relevant to those historical novels whose characters proceed with some difficulty from the hard truths of private life to the wider and more obscure ones of history. Nikolai Rostov at Austerlitz was no more aware of the larger patterns of the situation in which he found himself than Fabrice del Dongo had been at Waterloo; and the hedgehog—to borrow Isaiah Berlin's metaphorical terms concerning Tolstoy[134]—could be regarded as a fox who is able to see things in perspective (or the fox as an animal too involved in action to benefit from vision). In this connection, the notion of perspective has been applied to Manzoni's archetypal *I Promessi Sposi*, as far as I know, only in the most perfunctory fashion. I should like to suggest briefly the usefulness of such an approach.

In *I Promessi Sposi*, perspectives are introduced first of all by the illustrious description of Lake Como and the mountain called Resegone. This mountain towers over the novel, shifting and changing before the eyes of the various characters, as significantly as the steeples of Martinville will many years later for Proust. (Only when seen from the region of Milan does the Resegone look like a saw—hence its original name.)

[134] Cf. I. Berlin, *The Hedgehog and the Fox* (London, 1954).

The entire description of the landscape stresses mutability, especially in terms of the human eye and the innumerable vantage points it can occupy:

"E da qui la vista spazia per prospetti più o meno estesi, ma ricchi sempre e sempre qualcosa nuovi, secondo che i diversi punti piglian più o meno della vasta scena circostante, e secondo che questa o quella parte campeggia o si scorcia, spunta o sparisce a vicenda. Dove un pezzo, dove un altro, dove una lunga distesa di quel vasto e variato specchio dell' acqua; di qua lago, chiuso all' estremità o piuttosto smarrito in un gruppo, in un andirivieni di montagne, e di mano in mano più allargato tra altri monti che si spiegano, a uno a uno, allo sguardo, e che l'acqua riflette capovolti, co' paesetti posti sulle rive; di là braccio di fiume, poi lago, poi fiume ancora, che va a perdersi in lucido serpeggiamento pur tra'monti che l'accompagnano, degradando via via, e perdendosi quasi anch'essi nell'orizzonte." (Chap. 1)

("Thence the eye ranges over prospects of varying extent, always full of interest and always changing, as each point of vantage takes in different aspects of the vast landscape, and as one part or the other is foreshortened, or stands out, or disappears. One can see a piece here, another there, and then again a long stretch of that great varied sheet of water; on this side the lake is shut in at one end and almost lost among the ins and outs and groupings of the mountains, then spreads out again between more mountains, unfolding one by one, and reflected upside down in the water with the villages on the shores; on the other side is more river, then lake, then river again, losing itself in a shining coil among the mountains, which follow it, getting smaller and smaller until they too are almost merged in the horizon.")[135]

[135] *The Betrothed*, tr. Archibald Colquhoun (London and New York, 1959), p. 2. On perspective in Manzoni, see G. Zibordi, *Divulgazioni manzoniane,* 2nd edn. (Milan, 1934), p. 274.

Gina Alani has pointed out, concerning Manzoni's descriptions, the writer's fondness for the observation of linear contour, his fascination with distance and wide spaces: "Il suo sguardo è attratto dall'orizzonte."[136] Yet his concern with detail, with the insoluble riddles of the human heart—"questo guazzabuglio del cuore umano" (Chap. 10)—is just as evident. The private truth is the most enigmatic of all. How does the narrator reconcile this puzzled presentation of detail with his faith in God's overall design, with the long *prospettiva* of Providence? The possibility, at any rate, of such a reconciliation—or its impossibility for those persons whose viewpoint is all too human—is what Manzoni seeks to integrate into the form of the novel. The dimensions of time rejoin those of space. The constant movement from narrative incident to the large expanses of history underlines the necessity of a temporal perspective. In the conventional novel, time before and after the action—whatever its span, even beyond the plot— simply ceases to exist. Fictional time has a beginning and an end. But Manzoni needs endless time as the dimension of permanence or the revelation of design, or as a foil for transformation and mutability. In this manner the blending of novelistic action with real history becomes not just a means for reviving the past, or for pretending that the events in the story actually did happen, but the only method by which the reader can be supplied with temporal vistas that truly have an existence beyond the limits of the fictional plot. The historical novel becomes with Manzoni an instrument for placing the *complexities* of life on earth "in perspective"—in the temporal perspective of a philosophy of history. (This may be why visual metaphors are especially functional in the historical novel.)

Perspectivity in the novel was discovered and studied many years ago, particularly by Hispanic critics. In 1925

---

[136] *La struttura dei Promessi Sposi* (Zurich, 1948), p. 19.

Américo Castro singled it out as one of the achievements of Cervantes in *Don Quixote*: "El mundo en Cervantes se resuelve en puntos de vista."[137] This was one of the ideas to which Castro's influential *El pensamiento de Cervantes* gave currency: the external world in *Don Quixote* is a many-faceted "prism" that only subjectivity can interpret and endow with meaning; human situations, basically problematic, cannot be judged "from above," but rather from the points of view of individual lives. The concept of perspectivity in Cervantes was adopted by a number of critics, such as Jean Cassou and Manuel Durán,[138] and has found a traditional illustration in the famous discussion of Mambrino's helmet (Part I, Chap. 44), which to Don Quixote was a helmet, to Sancho Panza a barber's basin, and—Don Quixote added at a certain point—to other men could appear as other things as well. The fact that in such scenes Cervantes' actors take a stand on the basis of their *visual* interpretations of single objects lends special support to the use of the metaphor of perspective. Cervantes was able to combine subtly the narrative presentation of the problematic experience of truth with the contemporary fascination with visual trickery and optical fallacy—"el engaño a los ojos"—which I have discussed earlier with reference to Shakespeare's anamorphic simile in *Richard II*.[139]

Leo Spitzer, in a well-known article, associated this feature of Cervantes' art with what he called his "linguistic perspectivism," i.e., the instability in *Don Quixote* of proper names,

---

[137] *El pensamiento de Cervantes* (Madrid, 1925), p. 88.

[138] Cf. M. Durán, *La ambigüedad del Quijote* (Xalapa, 1960), pp. 184ff.

[139] The interpretation of visual enigmas in *Don Quixote* is not unrelated to those modern novels where a quest for truth culminates in vision: from Stendhal and Flaubert to, in the twentieth century, Kafka and Malraux; Proust's scrutiny of the hawthorn bush near Combray; Dos Passos' camera eye; the perspectives of Robbe-Grillet's heroes failing to penetrate opaque surfaces.

of certain common words, and of popular etymologies or styles, in each instance through a functional connection with the individuality of the speaker. The novelist is interested not in a monolithic world, not in a static language-in-itself, but in the copresence of both with singular minds on singular occasions. Dialect or slang words, for example, which to a Dante would have been inferior manifestations of an ideal or superior language, in Cervantes are modes of expression that respond to individual realities and as such are justified.[140]

Spitzer, unfortunately, believed that this aspect of *Don Quixote* was a form of "relativism," as well as an inherent characteristic of Christian thought.[141] A number of important Hispanic critics, on the contrary, regard it as an anticipation of the modern novel (in relation to an entire current of Spanish and Latin American literature, from *La Celestina* to a recent work like Carlos Fuentes' *La región más transparente*).[142] Whether an idea is right or wrong, such a critic might say, is not really the point in a novel, but how men confront, test, defy, neglect, are able to live with or from, ideas. To state that *Don Quixote* gives us a "relativistic" approach to ideas or beliefs is likewise beside the point, because it is wrongly assumed that these exist, like fixed stars, primarily outside the orbit of the novelistic action. The novelist does not ask what truth *is*; and if a character in a novel does, the center of gravity lies in his questioning, in his thought as an existential occurrence. This is radically different from the medieval debate (between a cleric and a layman, between water and wine, etc.) on a certain *issue*, around which the

[140] Cf. "Perspectivismo lingüístico en el *Quijote*," in *Lingüística e historia literaria* (Madrid, 1955), pp. 161ff.; or (in English), in *Linguistics and Literary History* (Princeton, 1948).

[141] Cf. *Linguistics and Literary History*, pp. 61, 73, 85 (note 37).

[142] Cf. *La región más transparente* (Mexico, 1958), p. 226; "porque las verdades están metidas en nuestros días y se quiebran en mil aristas a la luz de cada mirada, de cada golpe de corazón, de cada línea del azar...."

discussion revolves. The problem in the novel is not the diversity of human opinions—"quot homines, tot sententias," in the words of Terence—but the diversity of human lives under the banner of identical opinions and beliefs. A perspective, then, is a changing relation between the level of judgment and the level of existence. A novelistic perspective discloses a choice of values rooted not in the fixed character or status of the hero, but in his entire life, so that the process unfolded in the narrative is a constant manifestation and testing of a developing point of view.

This is normally distinct, I must add, from the varied use that Anglo-American critics make of Percy Lubbock's "point of view." In *The Craft of Fiction*, Lubbock (whose terms were often visual and well adapted to Flaubert and Henry James, to a period when artistic *correspondances* were fashionable) applied the notion of the point of view not so much to the character in the novel as to the relationship between the narrator and his material, or to the reader's participation in this relationship. From Henry James himself to Wayne C. Booth, the term has become a basic tool of formal analysis in Anglo-American criticism of the novel. It needs no further rehearsal here.

I should note, instead, still another usage, which one encounters in the later writings of Lukács. Generally speaking, Lukács has tended to employ "perspective" in the sense of "vista of the future"—or more precisely, as "a literary view of the historical future emerging from the present." We find this in *Der historische Roman* (first German edition, 1955) or in the discussion of Heine's ideas on the future of literature in *Deutsche Realisten des 19. Jahrhunderts* (1951). I have just singled out a similar conception of perspective as historical development beyond the limits of a fictional work in, strangely enough, Manzoni; but this should surprise no one, as what these two writers have in common is plain indeed: a dogmatic, unitarian philosophy of history.

The future is "distant" in a special manner, because the past, which for Lukács as for Hegel is the "necessary" prehistory of the present, has a concrete and precise shape which historiography and literature can bring to light and render very familiar to us; and because the revolutionary never loses sight of a goal in the future. Even in a socialist state, communism remains a further historical step and a task to be accomplished. In a communication written for the Fourth Congress of German Writers in January 1956, "Das Problem der Perspektive," Lukács applied the term more exactly to the novel and its historicity. A perspective, he explained, has three characteristics: it does not exist as yet; it is not utopian but a necessary consequence of an objective historical development; and it is not "fatalistic," for a perspective, of which we can only speak insofar as it has not yet been realized, depends on our continuing efforts and can assume unsuspected forms in the immediate future. What the Hungarian critic had in mind as far as the novel is concerned is that silent allusion to historical developments to come, with which certain novels are permeated. This allusion depends on an ending, as a meaningful silence does on the exercise of speech; but it also implies that everything in a novel builds and grows so as to allow the reader to extend the ending in his imagination. Lukács' main example is the Epilogue to Tolstoy's *War and Peace*. And his principal intent is to denounce two things: the inability of the bourgeois novelist to proffer historical perspectives for the future; and the error of those socialist writers who eulogize socialist societies so much that they thus forget that revolution is an uninterrupted process.[143]

[143] Cf. György Lukács, "Das Problem der Perspektive," in *Schriften zur Literatursoziologie*, ed. Peter Ludz (Neuwied, 1961), pp. 254-260. Before I take leave of perspective as an aesthetic term, I should recall that Karl Philipp Moritz had applied *Perspektive* and *Gesichtspunkt* to the literary work of art, meaning the search for a "center" on which the entire work converges. Cf. *Schriften zur Aesthetik und Poetik*,

The first of these points is not acceptable: it is disproved by the Providentialism of Manzoni, which I have just discussed; as well as—to pick a non-Catholic novelist whose qualifications as a bourgeois are beyond suspicion—by Thomas Mann's *The Magic Mountain*. Besides, it is a *petitio principii* to assume that the only authentic visions of the future are those which are based on an existing philosophy of history. Actually Lukács, with striking penetration and depth, struggles to come to terms with the very notion of "future" in a socialist society. How can there be a "perspective" or an imaginable future, i.e., something desirable and far removed, something not quite yet *known*, something unreal enough to fertilize the present as only the imagination can, if our philosophy of history has settled the matter and closed up shop once and for all? The answer, of course, for the "true" Marxist, should be that philosophies of history are themselves historical and must constantly be revised in the light of present developments and knowledge. Nevertheless, Lukács' insistence on the manner in which narrative fictions echo and reverberate in the reader's mind until they rejoin the movement and the conflicts of contemporary history is useful and very convincing. In my opinion, one needs critical techniques (if at all possible) with which to distinguish between allusive and nonallusive classes of literature. One might be startled to discover along the way that Tolstoy is no more allusive or prophetic, in the historical sense, than Virgil.

I shall soon discuss the disappearance of perspective in modern or avant-garde art (though not in commercial "art"). But the following questions must be asked before I close this section: Has perspectivity in the novel begun to vanish also

---

ed. H. J. Schrimpf (Tübingen, 1962), pp. 9-11, 16, 76-77, 120-124, and *passim*. Shortly before he died (in 1793), Moritz successfully engaged Caroline Herder and other ladies in Goethe's circle in the parlor game of asking, for example, "What is the *Mittelpunkt* in *Götz von Berlichingen*?" (Cf. pp. 345-347.)

in our century? Has this occurred only among the more original writers? To be sure, the analogy and the kinship between
the painter's and the poet's researches vis-à-vis the locus of
the real have been singularly operative since Mallarmé and
the Symbolists: the poetry of Wallace Stevens is an eminent
example of this research, and of the literal uses of perspective
("Thirteen Ways of Looking at a Blackbird"). Proust's *A la
recherche du temps perdu* is another. On the other hand,
there is mounting evidence too of a real diffidence or even
disbelief toward not only the novelist's "point of view" or
"perspective" but the validity of the individual psychic unit
in contemporary mass society. In this context, I think, Alain
Robbe-Grillet has fulfilled a central function; and 1957, the
year when *La Jalousie* was published, marks a crucial date in
the history of our subject.

Since Roland Barthes, the intensity of seeing in Robbe-
Grillet and the exact delineation of his characters' *regards*
have been interpreted as a sort of catharsis—the effort to
cleanse all objects of the values traditionally attached to them
and to look freshly at them, as if for the first time. To a certain degree this is true. And to that precise degree, one may
say that Robbe-Grillet is one of the first important writers
who has tried to divorce seeing from knowing, and vice
versa. Vision ceases to be cognitive. Yet it cannot be emphasized enough that Robbe-Grillet is engaging his readers—like
a good-humored Wittgenstein—in a sort of metaphysical
game. The rules change from moment to moment, the contest
is fluid and the stakes are high: Are the single objects (to
focus on *La Jalousie*) and situations no longer meaningful?
If there are no symbols left, what of A's obsession with clean-
liness, the spider, the violence, the repeated defloration, the
reiterated song? Are objects, paradoxically enough, affirmed
so much, as in a film, that they fascinate us with their consistency? Is there nothing at any moment beyond what one
sees (*esse est percipi*), and should time be inferred from the

data of space? Is it language that fails? Did Franck die? . . .
Obviously some of the answers to these questions contradict the
others. The metaphysical *Spieltrieb* cannot and does not play
itself out. And just as in Kafka meaning remains ever immi-
nent, what we experience in Robbe-Grillet is mostly the
imminence of meaninglessness—or of senseless vision.[144]

IX

Although only the very expert or the very adventurous
should be allowed to speak on the subject of modern painting, I will risk some observations with a principal purpose in
mind: that of discussing the different results which a single
concept may give rise to in different cultural areas. Many
years ago René Wellek warned us against the perils of par-
allel-hunting between the various arts, or between the arts
and intellectual history. His caveat has not lost its pertinence.
As far as literary history is concerned, we need only recall
the continuing tendency to totalitarian periodization, or the
aprioristic uses of shopworn sociological schemes by Marxist
critics. "Just as fallacious," Wellek wrote, "as the assumption
of a common social background of the arts at a given time
and place is the usual assumption that the intellectual background is necessarily identical and effective in all the arts."[145]
This is singularly relevant to the twentieth century and the
"modern" scene.

One welcomes the examination of concrete relations between poetry, painting, and ideas during the "banquet years"

[144] On the subject of perspectivity in Wallace Stevens, I have learned
from the essays of Michel Bénamou, such as "Sur le prétendu 'Sym-
bolisme' de Wallace Stevens," *Critique*, xvii (1961), 1029-1045. Concerning the "death of the point of view" in Joyce and contemporary
writing in general, I owe much to Fredric Jameson's recent "Seriality
in Modern Literature," *Bucknell Review*, xviii (1970), 63-80.

[145] "The Parallelism between Literature and the Arts," in *English
Institute Annual: 1941* (New York, 1942), p. 54. The substance of this
essay was incorporated into the *Theory of Literature*, iii, Chap. 11.

in Paris: for example, Herman Meyer's authoritative study of Rilke's early enthusiasm for Cézanne and later rejection of what Klee and Picasso stood for.[146] But the adoption by scholars of such comparisons as those proposed by Apollinaire in *Les Peintres cubistes* (1913), or the charting in a more than superficial way of a similar course for Cubism and atonal music,[147] has been far from persuasive. Generalizations of this sort usually become valid as soon as they cease being illuminating. Careful analysis reveals "an intricate pattern of coincidences and divergences"[148] at any given point in time, as each form of creative activity tends to find its own direction or its own rhythm within the larger "dialectics" of a period. That is to say, in a synchronic sense most cultural moments contain tensions and contradictions, stresses and strains, balances and counterbalances. Diachronically, "the various arts . . . have each their individual evolution, with a different tempo and a different internal structure of elements."[149] Thus the question is not simply one of—if I may say so—perspective, of distance or of proximity to the subject under study. A culture as a mobile combination of "stresses" is not easily explained by any *reductio ad unum*, or indeed by any reduction, by any single point of view. Those who fail to recognize this are perhaps not loyal enough to their own contemporary experience of culture as dialogue, confrontation, or struggle. Even in terms of a *modern* Marxist theory (a theory, that is, using modern socio-economic models instead of nineteenth-century ones), there are compelling rea-

---

[146] Cf. *Zarte Empirie* (Stuttgart, 1963), pp. 244-336.

[147] A. Neumeyer in *The Search for Meaning in Modern Art* (Englewood Cliffs, N.J., 1964), p. 121, indicates that Kandinsky's first non-representational pictures were created at the same time (1911-1912) that Schönberg was writing his first atonal compositions. But Greenberg, *Art and Culture*, p. 156, finds a correlation between Schönberg and the "all-over" picture (Pollock).

[148] Wellek, "The Parallelism between Literature and the Arts," p. 62.

[149] *Ibid.*, p. 61.

sons for regarding either the base or the superstructure of a society as forms of interaction rather than as instances of domination or homogeneity.

I am referring not to the inertia of the metaphor of perspective in everyday speech, but to philosophy. We saw that in 1914 Ortega y Gasset and Bertrand Russell sought support for their ideas in the figure or perspective, which Leibniz (on whom both wrote books) had first applied to metaphysics; and that numerous thinkers followed suit during the 1920's and 1930's. The year 1914 was one of the *anni mirabiles*— those years of the decade before World War I—that witnessed the emergence of radically new styles in painting. These would tend to dislodge or replace the convention of Florentine perspective, as well as the traditional conception of pictorial space. Furthermore, the "perspective realists" indicated their satisfaction with appearances, with a common-sense approach to ordinary experience, at a time when the plastic arts tended to do the opposite. I do not think that these contrasts reflect merely a distinction between traditionalism and avant-garde. Ortega and Russell were forward-looking thinkers, highly sensitive to the discoveries of their age. Only a student of modern philosophy, of its "internal structure" and itinerary and rhythm, is qualified to elucidate the situation I am describing. And whatever the appropriate comments must be, one should not be tempted (to recall our own caveat) by any single "reduction." Our contrast involves but a limited group of thinkers, and we are confronted with only one stress within a cluster of stresses. The origin of the tension may reside—this is my hypothesis—in changing attitudes toward vision as the possible instrument of knowledge and understanding. Renaissance perspective had applied to painting the laws of medieval optics. These laws were simplified into a practical representation of the facts of vision. Modern painting seeks alternatives not only to this simplification but to the absolute dependence of the work of art on everyday optics, against which Diderot had protested, in his own way, when he had written: "en un mot, la peinture est-elle l'art de parler aux yeux seulement? Ou celui de s'adresser au cœur et à l'esprit . . . , par l'entremise des yeux?"[150]

Any general consideration, naturally, must be empirically adapted to the serpentine course of the visual arts in our day. I have in mind two obvious features of the modern scene. The avant-garde is involved in skirmishes on a number of fronts at once and occupies extraordinarily varied, or even opposite, positions. The stresses and tensions of which I have spoken affect not only the particular arts but individual careers as well. This does not mean, moreover, that every style, every group, every "ism" is truly a fresh start or an independent achievement to be sealed off from the others. There are not as many significant styles in twentieth-century art as one might gather from the proliferation of movements and labels in which museum directors, art critics, and dealers have a more than sentimental interest. I find myself in sympathy with those historians who contend that the entire career of painting since Cézanne constitutes a single process and an unceasing, unbroken quest.[151] It seems to me that this is the most fitting approach, at any rate, to the question of perspective in modern art.

Some of the apparently boldest movements rely a great deal on conservative techniques like perspective. Recent "optical art" or "op art" (Vasarely, etc.) almost revives the assumptions of Cinquecento perspective. It proposes a return to the merely visual, to an *esprit de géométrie* as illusion-producing and as painstaking as that of the most Euclidian of Renaissance and Baroque theorists. It requires the spectator to be the extension of an eye, to *see* exclusively, intensely— from singular angles and points of view—and yet naïvely.

[150] "Salon de 1767," in *Oeuvres choisies de Diderot*, ed. F. Génin (Paris, 1886), p. 168.
[151] Cf. Francastel, *Peinture et Société*, pp. 173ff.

Like commercial art, of course, or an important sector of it, so-called "pop art" (Roy Lichtenstein, and others) cannot do without perspective (without the closeups, in fact, of comic strips) as an element of its ironic identification with the trivial and its attempt to stimulate the jaded palates of the over-sophisticated by means of a "low" style. Then there is the interesting case of Salvador Dalí. The liberation of pictorial content by surrealism led to either an analogous formal freedom (Ernst, Masson) or an exacerbated traditionalism (Dalí, Tanguy). The Catalan painter's remote horizons and vanishing vistas (in his surrealist phase, as in the work entitled *Perspectives,* ca. 1932)[152] have a Renaissance flavor in common with the "silent and infinite perspectives" of Giorgio De Chirico. But the chilling coherence of his pictorial dreams makes Dalí's academic hand curiously effective and functional.

Many of the outstanding achievements of twentieth-century art can be regarded as a development, a metamorphosis, or a destruction of the perspective scheme, rather than a full emancipation from it. An extreme instance is the naïve painter, whose rejection of conventional spatial relations implies—at least as far as most spectators are concerned —a reference to the past or the "cultured" in order to be fully significant. A similar observation would be valid to a certain extent for a series of antiperspective canvases by Matisse, such as *La Liseuse distraite* (1919), *Grand Intérieur—Nice* (1921), and several others in the same vein.[153] There the lovely Florentine ground plan or checkerboard is made to *look* rectangular, instead of converging on a vanishing point. (See Figure 5.) The geometrical pattern of Italian origin becomes an exotic arabesque—a most decorative effect. The ironic allusion to an old convention, besides, brings out the

[152] Reproduced in Neumeyer, *The Search for Meaning*, plate xxvi.
[153] Cf. Raymond Escholier, *Matisse* (New York, 1960), p. 96; and Alfred Barr, *Matisse* (New York, 1951), p. 435.

lack of unified space: these forlorn, daydreaming, absent-minded women (unlike the *liseuses attentives* of seventeenth-century Dutch painting) do not seem to belong to the radiant, light-filled rooms in which they happen to find themselves.

One could argue further that the Cubists themselves were still preoccupied with perspective when they combined shifting points of view to represent a simultaneity of vision (as the authors of dynamic montages and cinematic sequences obviously did—like Marcel Duchamp in the *Nude Descending a Staircase* [1912], and the Italian Futurists). But the formal arrangements of Cubism were also "real" in their own terms—autonomous and self-seeking. The possibility of an "abstract" space was one of its important contributions. This contribution would ultimately pose as many problems as it would solve. Is a fictional space to find some other principle of organization than perspective? How is it to be seen, to be approached by the beholder? I can only indicate here the pertinence of these questions—to Chagall and Kandinsky, for example. Chagall's spaces, to be sure, are mythical and unreal. Roosters and violins, clocks and bridal couples float in the atmosphere of a never-never land where the law of gravity does not exist. Yet this fabulous world is to be surveyed and seen *as if* it were real. One is allowed a bird's-eye view of it, by a kind of miraculous fairy-land dispensation. As for Kandinsky, his abstractions move in a not-so-abstract space about which Clement Greenberg has written: "The atmospheric space in which his images threaten to dissolve remains a reproduction of atmospheric space in nature, and the integrity of the picture depends on the integrity of an illusion."[154]

Though there have been other relevant departures (like the divided, afocal picture), the various styles of abstract

[154] *Art and Culture*, p. 112.

painting appear to have faced most boldly the consequences of the rejection of perspective. Let us consider these styles with one concern in mind: the relation between pictorial surface and pictorial depth. Art critics have discussed how Cézanne and the late Impressionists sought to coordinate the decorative surface of the canvas with the illusion in depth of the "inside"; and Clement Greenberg interprets in the same terms the discovery of collage by Braque and Picasso, who found that *trompe l'œil* could be used to undeceive as well as to deceive the eye. It could be used, that is, to declare as well as to deny the actual surface. If the actuality of the surface—its real, physical flatness—could be indicated explicitly enough in certain places, it would be distinguished and separated from everything else the surface contained."[155] The various "abstract" painters—*sensu lato*—have tended, similarly, to "declare" the surface of the picture at the expense of the illusion of coordinated three-dimensional space, or to subordinate the calligraphy of the surface to the suggestion of fictional depth, or to pursue intermediate directions. These are of course mere polarities. Generally speaking, there has been a tradition of the surface (from Mondrian and Klee to Tobey, Still, de Stäel, Tàpies), as well as a tradition of space (from Kandinsky, Tamayo, and Masson to Pollock, Riopelle). I do not mean to imply that the surface painters, who, like Tàpies, convert the surface into significant matter (or else tear and break it apart, like Burri and Millares), are not capable of producing fictional "worlds." They obviously are. But in their case the problem of perspective is solved simply by dispensing with the illusion of organized space. The pictorial surface has ceased to function as a window (Alberti's "finestra aperta"). The spectator's response, likewise, ceases to be merely visual. These works undeceive the eye so thoroughly that they seem above all to *exist*, to exist like objects—fragments or symbols of a larger reality.

[155] *Ibid.*, p. 72.

This trend manifests itself most forcefully in the work of the "space" painters, whose fictional structures transcend the perspective scheme. The entangled patterns of a Jackson Pollock, for example, provide us with uniform, unified spaces. But these are not unified by the act of seeing, either within the interior of the picture or with respect to the beholder. The surface, though open to inner space, is no mere open window, calling for the single glance or the appropriate point of view. The observer is asked not only to see but to *confront* the artist's created spaces. The act of seeing presupposes and maintains a fundamental gap between the order of reality which is the locus of the spectator and the order of the painting. Vision is an "introduction" to the painting. A fuller "confrontation" is now prompted by the fact that the picture begins to occupy the place of everyday reality, to dislodge it, to supplement it. The spectator is now invited to enter, to "find himself" in, the order of the work of art. This order (like Ortega's "idea of life," which I discussed earlier) becomes the radical enveloping condition of the observer's consciousness. The coordinates of perspective are superseded by the search for an illusion of life which uses and transcends the visual.

Contemporary painters, by the same token, strain against the limits of the single canvas. The abstract artist is again a central example (though there have been earlier ones, like Monet in his late *Water Lilies*). The dense tracery of the "all-over" picture, where every inch is charged with line and color (Tobey, Pollock, Riopelle), or the total metamorphosis of the surface into texture and matter (Tàpies), produces a work with no absolute beginning and end. The painter no longer needs the aesthetic function of the frame—or the reduced angle of vision of the spectator.[156]

This emergence of the picture from the frame requires a full collaborative effort on the part of the spectator. Here

[156] Cf. *ibid.*, p. 125.

contemporary painting—painting as confrontation and illusion of being—joins hands with the other arts. The enveloping effects of an art in the round, in which the spectator is asked to exist, to participate without reservations, are not only the province of "happenings," "environments," or the radical theater. They are also sought by the plastic arts. D.-H. Kahnweiler has related that Pablo Picasso in 1929 "was thinking of huge monuments which could be both houses for living in and enormous sculptures of women's heads, and which could be set up along the Mediterranean coast."[157] Similar monuments are being constructed today.[158] And to give a recent example from painting, Matta exhibited in Paris in the spring of 1966 a series of canvases assembled like the faces of a cube: "enfermant le spectateur dans le cube," a reviewer writes, "Roberto Matta veut, symboliquement, le plonger au centre d'un espace en extension: le spectateur occupe la place du peintre."[159]

A large section of contemporary art evidently tends toward the "conditions of architecture," i.e., toward the full involvement of men in environments which they help to model and inform. The probable future of twentieth-century painting

[157] As quoted by Greenberg, *Art and Culture*, p. 68.

[158] Like the huge, open figure of a recumbent woman built recently in the Stockholm Museum by Jean Tinguely, Niki de Saint-Phalle, and Per Olof Ultvedt.

[159] O. Hahn in *L'Express*, June 13-19, 1966, p. 90. What spectators, and how many? I can only mention here the evident but complex tensions between this search for existential three-dimensionality and the popular forms of our "image culture." The contradictions between the tradition of perspective and its modern replacements reflect only partially the relations in our time between mass art and avant-garde. The most sophisticated spectator is himself submitted to these tensions. His visual habits are also conditioned, not only by a film like Resnais' *L'Année dernière à Marienbad* (with its search for alternate solutions to the limits of cinematic montage, which can offer no more than one perspective at a time, since panoramic shots cannot be abused), but by photography, advertising, the cinemascopic screen, and even that most faithful replica of Alberti's pane of glass: the television set.

appears to be multidimensional, ecological, and—if at all possible—"metavisual." Our need, like Dante's in Canto xxx of *Paradiso*, is for a "novella vista": for a new response to the fields where vision fails.

X

Although little can be said in conclusion without oversimplifying the subject we have just surveyed, there remain some questions that need to be asked. We have seen that the metaphor of perspective has fulfilled a number of functions in different cultural areas. Is it valid to speak of *a* metaphor at all, in the singular? Does it "exist"? Or are we confronted with a row of particulars, beyond which only fruitless abstractions are possible? To a certain extent, it is true that every metaphor is a concrete particular that cannot be dissociated from its context. This applies not only to poetry, but to rational thought. Northrop Frye has pointed out the crucial role of single terms in the writings of important philosophers: "One often feels that a full understanding of such a word would be a key to the understanding of the whole system. If so, it would be a metaphorical key, as it would be a set of identifications made by the thinker with the word."[160] I think I have begun to show some of these identifications, with regard, for example, to Leibniz and Ortega.

On the other hand, every particular occurrence of a metaphor implies an origin, a *fundamentum analogiae,* which lies outside the single work and has a previous existence. If every metaphor is based on a "let A be B,"[161] and both B and the connection between A and B are uniquely related to the context, there are at least two elements the writer inherits and employs: A; and the "let A be . . . X"—the very possibility and momentum of the metaphor, in those cases where A has

[160] Northrop Frye, *Anatomy of Criticism* (Princeton, 1957), p. 335.
[161] Cf. *ibid.,* p. 123.

already been used figuratively. One would otherwise deny that there is any expressive contact between the product and the initial figuration on which it rests, that is, one would deny the existence of the metaphor not only in general but in singular instances. A metaphor "fades" both in everyday speech and in cultured writing when the force of its origin is no longer felt. Thus, although its use may be contextually unique, its nature implies an extrinsic relation. A metaphor, in this sense, is the transformation of an extrinsic relation into an intrinsic one. Furthermore, if we consider for an instant the former, we may be able to recognize the elements in the *fundamentum analogiae* which condition the final result. These elements compose a structure of possibilities. It should be feasible to point out, for example, that certain analogies are *not* likely to arise, or at least to occupy a central position in the overall area of the metaphor. For, as every good perspectivist knows, if the barber's headpiece looked like Mambrino's helmet to Don Quixote, and like a basin to Sancho, there are many things it could not have looked like to anyone.

These remarks are especially relevant to the figure of perspective, which is a "cultural" one. The metaphor was not latent in ordinary language, nor in a Christian symbol, nor in an ancient myth, nor in an archetypal image (though its cognitive uses were supported by the archetypal identification of vision with knowledge). It derived from a European, *historically* conditioned discovery in the visual arts, which was amenable to theory and as such could be called a cultural concept. It is probable that the metaphor will fade in the future, if not disappear altogether, as the framework of the concept and the *fundamentum analogiae*—namely, the close kinship of painting with optics and mathematics—loses its validity, just as it may reappear with the renewed vigor of this general assumption.

To analyze our metaphor as a *structure of possibilities* would extend this essay unduly. Briefly, its controlling elements could be found in the six assumptions which I described in my presentation of artistic perspective (pp. 291-293). I do not think that any of these assumptions were unequivocal or were proved incapable of producing contradictory results. Point two (the point of view) gave rise to a personal metaphor (Ortega) and an ultrapersonal one (Mead), both of which enter ordinary speech. Yet these polar uses retain a core in common—the connection between location and sight, percipient and knowledge. Similarly, the metaphor could lead to a stress on truthful appreciation (La Rochefoucauld, Ortega) or on problematic, subjective interpretation (Shakespeare, Baroque styles, Nietzsche). The concern with illusion or subjective value could be regarded as an emphasis on points one (painting as mimetic fiction) and two (the point of view, and its exaggeration by anamorphic pictures) at the expense of point five (structures are geometrically correct). Distance (point six) is stressed frequently both in everyday speech (perspective as mental outlook; seeing things in perspective) and in moral or philosophical writing (La Rochefoucauld, Ortega). Point four (perspectives are relational) is basic to Leibniz's use of the metaphor, together with points two and five; and also to its use by later thinkers (Mead). We have admired in Leibniz a particularly coherent utilization of the full structure of the metaphor.

This "structure" was, to be sure, present in the concept of perspective from the start, from the time when Brunelleschi and Uccello were active in Florence. But my concern in this essay has been with the historical process which gradually makes this structure not only accessible or comprehensible but real. To conceive of these historical events as "manifestations" (and of history as a dreary *Book of Changes*) is to be caught in a circular fallacy. It is too easy for the metahistorical scholar to dispense with history on the basis of historical information. The only solid reason for stressing the structure more than the historical process is to believe that the process was "necessary," that is, to possess a unitarian or aprioristic philosophy of history and thus doubly to commit a *petitio principii*. If single events were "contingent," then the process was contingent too; and our "structure of possibilities" must be honestly recognized as a precipitate of history.

Our glance at the idea of perspectivity in the twentieth century has shown, I think, that the second assumption, the *point of view*, has been most fruitful and adaptable to the intellectual circumstances of the modern age. This assumption meant that the structure and unity of the picture were dependent on the beholder; it also meant that several beholders, several points of view, could equally support the final result. The relevance of this notion to a certain intellectual attitude has been expressed most forcefully by Ortega, who called it a rejection of both dogmatism and relativism. The intermediate position is a methodological beginning rather than an end, though also in an undogmatic spirit—the only method that is certain to be wrong being (to paraphrase Ortega) the one pretending to be unique. I need not emphasize the kinship of this position with the procedures of modern science: the loyalty to the test of experience, the idea that knowledge is a continuing inquiry working within certain rules. As far as the humanities are concerned, I would like to quote some of the opening words from E. B. McGilvary's *Toward a Perspective Realism*:

"The perspective realist makes no claim that he can speak for the universe as it is for *itself*. He does not consider himself as an outsider looking on, a stranger, as it were, from some supernatural realm, passively contemplating a world of nature with whose goings-on he has no active business. On the contrary, he is a natural organism responding to natural stimulations and acquiring thereby such knowledge as nature thereupon puts at his disposal. This knowledge, as far as he can integrate it into a system, is his philosophy. As this knowledge and the integration of it develops, his philosophy develops. . . . A mature philosophy for him is an ideal never realized. He sees in part, he knows in part, he prophesies in part; and that which is perfect never comes, except as a goal that lies afar off before him."[162]

The immensity of the thinker's goal, which McGilvary brings out, goes hand in hand with the refusal to postulate, in the universe as it is "for *itself*," a systematic basis for our efforts to apprehend it. There is no need to visualize, in absolute contrast to our meager knowledge, a world that would yield a single key to the infinitely wise. Modern science, to recall a classic instance, no longer assumes that Newtonian laws, which are suited to the description of mechanical systems, are of use in the description of the atom. The philosophy of history tends to eschew the unitarian hypothesis, as "the problem of history," in Karl Löwith's words, "is unanswerable within its own perspective. Historical processes as such do not bear the least evidence of a comprehensive and ultimate meaning."[163] If this is so, and I honestly assume that it is, should one turn back to the broad expanses of theology or, rather, to those philosophies of history that offer comparable comforts in the sense that they maintain the "unitarian hypothesis" and lull us with unitarian solutions? Should one hold in abeyance the very hypothesis of a fully ordered cosmos, of a "universe" fully integrated in a more than physical or quantitative way? The modern scholar is obliged to confront three things: his own necessary limits as an interpreter; the huge diversity of a world that may not be a closed system; and the great complexity of his task. The cry for "perspective" often expresses, in fact, a desperate longing for

[162] P. 1.
[163] As quoted by H. Meyerhoff, *The Philosophy of History in Our Time* (Garden City, N.Y., 1959), p. 24.

order in a cluttered, helter-skelter world. It seems to me that in this context the metaphor of perspective has provided us with a modern version of Nicholas of Cusa's *docta ignorantia*. There is no plausible proportion between the individual mind and our "cultural world." Yet, in the words of the same theologian, "homo non potest iudicare nisi humaniter."[164] Our metaphor serves to underline the necessity of avoiding the individualistic chaos of knowledge while keeping in mind the endlessness of experience, the basic incongruity between man's limited capacity for understanding and the immense, expanding environment of which he is a part.

I have already discussed the limits of the perspectivistic figure—for example, the difficulties that were met in turning from epistemology to ontology, from a metaphor for knowledge to a metaphor for being (Ortega, Russell). The passage of time, besides, has reduced the cognitive force of the analogy. Generally speaking, Renaissance perspective was founded on a common-sense approach to the facts of vision, which under the scrutiny of modern psychologists, or of a philosopher like Wittgenstein,[165] appear increasingly complex and problematical. The environment of the post-Renaissance painter receded from him in all directions and underwent distortions which, as he looked at them, were compatible with a simple set of mathematical coordinates.[166] He lived in a geometrically organized world from which the human spirit considered itself distinct. *Distance* (our sixth assumption) was the premise of this basic distinction between nature and mind. It has become for the same reasons a stumbling block for modern artists. I have just said that the metaphor of perspective underlined the individual's limits in relation to the expanding universe of which he is a part. The inertia

---

[164] *De visione dei*, §6. Cf. E. Zellinger, *Cusanus-Konkordanz* (Munich, 1960), p. 57.

[165] Cf. *Philosophical Investigations* (Oxford, 1953), pp. 202, 213.

[166] Cf. J. White, *Perspective in Ancient Drawing and Painting*, p. 86.

of the metaphor also works against the feeling that he *is* a part—not simply a beholder. It sometimes seems necessary, in order to live and understand, to see things "out of perspective," to correct the foreshortenings and the vanishing convergences which impose their order of urgency on us. It seems desirable and unavoidable to act not merely in terms of what one *sees*. Curiously enough, it was a physicist, Niels Bohr, who stressed the truism that "we are both actors and spectators in the great drama of existence."[167] The reader who is familiar with Bohr's "complementarity" and Werner Heisenberg's "principle of uncertainty" will also recall the arguments among physicists concerning the extent to which the situation of the scientific observer affects the contents of his study: "natural science," Werner Heisenberg writes, "does not simply explain and describe nature; it is a part of the interplay between nature and ourselves; it describes nature as exposed to our method of questioning. This was a possibility of which Descartes could not have thought, but it makes the sharp separation between the world and the I impossible."[168] Similarly, the contemporary arts are no longer devoted to a description of nature based on a sharp separation between the world and the I. It may be that all sensory metaphors—including tactile ones—are insufficient to render the total experience of man's intimate involvement in his life and time.

[1966]

[167] As quoted by P. J. Doty, "Complementarity and Its Analogies," *The Journal of Philosophy*, LV (1958), 1100.
[168] *Physics and Philosophy* (New York, 1962), p. 81.

V

Literature as System

There are a number of reasons for thinking that literature constitutes systems, or that it manifests itself as system. Let us leave aside all nonhistorical acceptations of "literature," of the sort one is likely to encounter in aesthetics or in the theory of criticism. Let us assume that our concern is with the manifestation of systems in historical time. There are, then, several ways in which one can speak of literary systems. They correspond to the following areas of study (though additions and further subdivisions could of course be made): poetics, that is, mainly the theory of genres and the appearance of systems of genres; fundamental norms and materials, such as styles (the "three styles," etc.), rhetorical figures, themes, myths; structural relations existing among the parts of an actual configuration or whole, like a movement, a period, a national tradition, or the establishment of a canon by means of anthologies; and, finally, the individual reading experience.

My original interest, as I first approached the subject, was in the reading experience.[1] But it soon became clear to me that none of these categories could be treated independent of the others, and that it was necessary to confront the general problem of literary systematics. I found that this problem brought into focus, in turn, the need for a *structural* approach not merely to the single poem but to the basic units and terms of literary *history*. (It demanded, in fact, the elucidation of structures *in* history.) In the present essay I will attempt to show the significance and basic complexity of lit-

---

[1] The main idea in this essay goes back to the Saussurian model used in my article "Literatura como sistema (sobre fuentes, influencias y valores literarios)," *Filologia Romanza*, IV (1957), 1-29. The contents, however, are not the same.

erary systematics with regard especially to one area: poetics. I will begin to indicate how the different cognate systems shift, change, become superposed, and interact with one another. And I will suggest that the history of literature—as distinct from language or society—is characterized not so much by the operation of full systems as by a tendency toward system or structuration. Thus it appears that the historian is led to evaluate, for every century or phase in the history of his subject, the precise scope of a limited, persistent, profound "will to order" within the slowly but constantly changing domain of literature as a whole.

I

The poetics prevailing in any period of European literary history can be expected, though more or less explicitly, and with reference to various terminologies, to exhibit a tendency toward system. The first words of Aristotle's *Poetics*—"Concerning the poetic art as a whole and its species . . ."[2]—begin to formulate the dual purpose that would become traditional for literary theory: to elucidate the nature of the poetic art in itself or "as a whole," αὐτῆς (its goals, origins, validity); and to offer a theory of genres or "species." In Aristotle, the discussion of the genus "art of poetry" underlies the succeeding analyses of the more important poetic species (tragedy, epic, etc.)[3]—and this essential conjunction has remained traditional too. I do not allude here to the direct influence of Aristotle's *Poetics*, but to general aspects of Greco-Roman thinking on the subject of literature. The theory of genres to which an *ars poetica* leads, more often than not, is not a sim-

---

[2] I use Gerald F. Else's literal translation, where *autēs*, "in itself," is understood generically, in opposition to the species or forms mentioned immediately afterwards. Cf. *Aristotle's Poetics: The Argument* (Cambridge, Mass., 1957), pp. 1-3. (Translations of the *Poetics* below are quoted from Else or S. H. Butcher, as indicated.)

[3] Cf. Else, *Aristotle's Poetics*, pp. 4-5.

ple exercise in classification. It *is* a theory, insofar as it tries to organize the numerous facts at hand according to principles derived from an interpretation of the "poetic art as a whole," and beyond this, of its own place in a larger scheme of knowledge. Theory and the tendency toward system, then, go hand in hand. In the European tradition, poetic theory, far from being simply critical or descriptive, has tended to propose and establish genuine examples of intellectual order.[4] It is not necessary to face here the problems posed by the concept of genre itself (the extent to which genres, for example, were empirically adapted to actual differences existing between individual poems or plays). What matters in our context is the very existence, historically speaking, of such intellectual orders.

As a rule, the author of poetics does not provide the practicing writer with an endless spectrum of possibilities: he limits his options. To limit, subdivide, and distinguish is to make order and system possible. These, in turn, become "dwelling places" for the writer, that is, enveloping historical situations, though the poet may be as vaguely aware of them as he is of the other historical situations—the political, social, and economic systems—in which he lives from day to day. I should add that I do not deny that significant relations exist between these various structural situations. In fact, it seems to me that it is precisely the idea of literary system that makes cogent discourse possible on the subject of the relations between social or economic or political history, on the one hand, and literary history, on the other. I shall return to this question later. For the moment, let us take notice of the

---

[4] In his study of genre theory in China, James R. Hightower brings out the relationship between the broader aims of literary theory and the classifications of specific forms, with regard to the early Chinese theorists. Cf. "The Wen hsüan and Genre Theory," in *Studies in Chinese Literature*, ed. John L. Bishop (Cambridge, Mass., 1965), p. 513.

fact that a theory of genres supplies the writer, to use Ernst Robert Curtius' words, with a sort of "ideal space."[5] Wherever such spaces exist, the isolation of an individual genre is more apparent than real. Its delineation, its character will depend on the place and the purpose which other genres have been assigned, as well as on the connection existing between them.

What does one mean, in this context, by system? As far as the literary historian is concerned, a system is operative when no single element can be comprehended or evaluated correctly in isolation from the historical whole (or "conjuncture"—in Spanish, *conjunto* or *coyuntura*) of which it is a part. I assume that the term is to be used flexibly and dynamically, that it can refer to a stable order but also to a moment in a process of structuration. A system can be relatively open, loose, disjointed. We need have no "fearful symmetry" or other neatly proportioned arrangements in mind, for our model is neither mechanical nor visual. Our subject is a certain type of *mental* order, characterized by the functional importance of the relationships obtaining between its various parts. (In this sense, a system of poetics is like a linguistic code.) A system is more than a combination or a sum of its components. It implies a certain dependence of the parts on the whole, and a substantial impact of the basic interrelationships. Our principal models, then, are linguistic and social. We are essentially indebted, above all, to Ferdinand de Saussure's idea of linguistic system. System, not structure, as we know, was one of Saussure's favorite words —for example, on the subject of linguistic signs:

"C'est une grande illusion de considérer un terme simplement comme l'union d'un certain son avec un certain concept. Le

---

[5] Cf. *Europäische Literatur und lateinisches Mittelalter* (Bern, 1948), p. 16. I shall quote hereafter from the excellent translation by Willard R. Trask, *European Literature and the Latin Middle Ages* (New York, 1953).

définir ainsi, ce serait l'isoler du système dont il fait partie; ce serait croire qu'on peut commencer par les termes et construire le système en en faisant la somme, alors qu'au contraire c'est du tout solidaire qu'il faut partir pour obtenir par analyse les éléments qu'il renferme."[6]

Similarly, it seems like a "grande illusion" to isolate the components in a system of artistic forms. A considerable reliance of the parts on the whole, of individual definition on overall theory, has been operative in the area of poetics on a number of influential occasions, from Aristotle to Northrop Frye. But the analogy between linguistic and literary systems raises, to be sure, delicate and specialized questions, which ought not to be answered quickly. The social analogy, fortunately, is available and instructive in a less technical way. One need only recall ordinary notions of social class. "Middle class," "lower class," and such terms imply not only membership in a group but nonmembership in others. The number of classes that constitute a particular system does not affect this basic fact: class concepts are relative *within a system*; they signify a man's position and immersion *in* a society; whether a certain class is part of, say, a three-level or a five-level structure, or even of a relatively fluid pattern, it refers necessarily to the existence and importance of a system of class distinctions as a whole.

As far as literary "classes" are concerned, in the history of poetics, the impact of certain closely related branches of learning and forms of intellectual activity appears to have been crucial. I refer to the structures of grammar, philosophy, or education, with whose influence on the structures of literature we are familiar. Hermann Usener studied many years ago, in a useful article on the structural features of

---

[6] *Cours de linguistique générale*, 4th edn. (Paris, 1949), p. 157; see also p. 124: "la langue est un système dont toutes les parties peuvent et doivent être considérées dans leur solidarité synchronique."

ancient philology, the links between philosophical and grammatical systems in Greece and Rome: "the philosophical education which is the assumption of all systematics has preserved its original coloring in more than one place: it sprang from the Peripatetic school" ("die philosophische Bildung, welche die Voraussetzung aller Systematik ist, hat an mehr als einem Orte ihre ursprüngliche Farbe noch bewahrt; sie stammte aus der peripatetischen Schule").[7] During the Hellenistic period a fragmentation of philosophy had occurred, from which various branches of learning had arisen: grammar, rhetoric, poetics, philology, etc. Aristotle and his disciples had attempted to reconciliate rhetoric and poetics with the substantial goals and orderly procedures of metaphysics and logic. They showed that philosophy could validate the poetic "imitations" that Plato had denounced. "Aristotle's teaching on the art of poetry," E. R. Curtius affirms, "must, then, be seen in connection with his entire system: as a parallel discipline to ethics, politics, rhetoric, economics."[8] We also know that Quintilian's famous *Institutio oratoria* was actually a treatise on education. I do not think that the essential continuity of literature is a product of its pedagogical uses. But its systematization owes a great deal to pedagogy. As Curtius stresses in his indispensable book, the fact that literature has been a school subject for nearly twenty-five hundred years has a great deal to do with the emergence and the survival of a theoretical order: "wherever literature is a school subject, we have elements of a systematized study of literature. We have the science of literature, in a form suitable for beginners. Anyone who read Homer as a school text could not but learn that the *Iliad* is a poem in narrative verse (*epos*) and that verse is a form of discourse subject to

---

[7] "Ein altes Lehrgebäude der Philologie," in *Kleine Schriften* (Osnäbruck, 1965; reprint of 1912-1913 edn.), II, 303.

[8] *European Literature and the Latin Middle Ages*, p. 146.

rules."⁹ Education has not only tended to foster literary theory: it has traditionally built bridges between the sciences, or between the arts and the sciences, and promoted the application of methods of instruction developed in one field to cognate branches of learning. These academic contacts and cross-fertilizations have been steadily operative from late antiquity to the present day.

In the early Middle Ages, grammar, rhetoric, and dialectic (or logic) composed the pedagogical triad of the liberal arts. The range of rhetoric was flexible, but it most often subsumed instruction in the different poetic "styles" or levels—an obviously structural teaching—or the presentation, as in Quintilian (Bk. x, sec. 1), of a roster of great authors. Grammar was originally the foundation of the entire educational triad. Its study included instruction in both language and literature, in the grammatical rules as such and in their exemplary use by great writers. It could incorporate the figures of speech and metrics. In the thirteenth century Walter of Châtillon assigns poetry to grammar. Among the liberal arts named the *trivium*, he writes, "grammar takes a precedence as the first foundation; under her serves the troop of those who write in verse":

> Inter artes igitur, que dicuntur trivium,
> Fundatrix grammatica vendicat principium.
> Sub hac chorus militat metrice scribentium.¹⁰

In one of the thirteenth-century *artes poeticae* published by Edmond Faral, the *Laborintus* of Eberhard the German, when Poetry approaches, she is introduced as "Grammar's attendant":

> Grammaticae famulans subit ingeniosa Poesis.¹¹

---

⁹ *Ibid.*, p. 247.
¹⁰ Quoted by Curtius, *ibid.*, p. 45.
¹¹ Edmond Faral, *Les Arts poétiques du XIIe et du XIIIe siècle* (Paris, 1962), p. 345.

The "new Aristotle," Parisian scholasticism, the quarrel between the old system of the liberal arts and the proponents of philosophy and natural history, between men of letters and scholars, altered the propaedeutic role of grammar and rhetoric after the thirteenth century, but without canceling their impact on poetics. Similarly, the theorists of the Renaissance would take a fresh look at these changing relations without pretending to dissolve them. Giovanni Battista Pigna, for example, in *I romanzi* (1554), classified poetry, as well as rhetoric and dialectic, under logic. An innovator as a critic, Pigna the theorist had a great respect for logical procedures. Bernard Weinberg points out that there is throughout the Italian Cinquecento "a strong tradition that associates poetry with logic, grammar, rhetoric, and history as one of the discursive or instrumental sciences. Poetry belongs with the others as a discursive science because it uses words (or 'discourse') as its means."[12] Other critics would reserve a different place for poetry in the general scheme of the arts and sciences. But the desire to classify and coordinate was general among medieval and Renaissance theorists; and the tendency prevailed to make poetics, in conjunction with the other cultural activities of men, as systematic as possible.

The poetics of the Cinquecento, to be sure, did not coincide with the work or the impact of any single theorist or theory. The humanist's burden, like that of most eclectics, was *l'embarras du choix*. Bernard Weinberg's *History of Literary Criticism in the Italian Renaissance* charts the chronological course of three principal influences: Horace, Plato, and Aristotle. Renaissance theorists thus relied on widely differing principles of classification: poetry could be regarded as an ethical accomplishment, akin to moral philosophy; or it could be viewed as a verbal construction and a linguistic science.

[12] Bernard Weinberg, *A History of Literary Criticism in the Italian Renaissance* (Chicago, 1963), I, 13. On "Poetics among the Sciences," see I, 1-37.

Literary critics would attempt to relate their ideas to philosophical systems which they failed to comprehend fully, or which were not really amenable to artistic purposes. In short, the Italian sixteenth century, as Weinberg shows, yields no simple explanation: "it should be clear," he writes, "that the major theories exist simultaneously throughout the century."[13]

During this most characteristic and creative of periods in the history of European poetics, different systems indeed existed simultaneously—and it was their coincidence which made possible the famous theoretical quarrels of the second half of the century. It could be maintained that Minturno and Scaliger came close to being representative of the period, whereas Patrizi, for example, was an eccentric, and Campanella a reactionary. But Weinberg demonstrates that all these theorists (not merely the practical critics) should be seen against the polemical background of their time: "in a way the history of poetic theory of the Cinquecento might be organized as a series of quarrels or polemics, similar to those so prominent in practical criticism."[14] Cinquecento literary theory, in sum, *tended* to be highly systematic. As a result of this tendency, and of the submission to different influences and constantly shifting principles of classification, it became an unceasing quarrel among competing intellectual orders.

To what extent, we could now ask, have theories of genres been systems? In what ways have they functioned as systems? At this point in our inquiry, I should like to propose the following observations.

1. The history of poetics as a whole exhibits the tendency not merely to enumerate but to arrange and coordinate norms. Literary works have been submitted, especially, to philosophical, grammatical, and sociological principles; or also, principal characteristics have been inferred from these works and then turned into principles, alternatives, and polarities.

[13] *Ibid.*, I, 37. [14] *Ibid.*, II, 809.

2. The history of poetics offers, on the other hand, many instances of the failure to organize poetic models into systems of norms. Often the attempt falls short and one is left with a half-way stage in a process of structuration. One may also encounter simple enumeration (as in Horace, perhaps, or Sir Philip Sidney's "sundry more special denominations"), while the tendency toward system manifests itself on other levels of artistic theory and practical criticism.

3. An evident but essential fact must be stressed: the extraordinary persistence through the centuries, in European literature, of a limited number of generic models (it might be advanced that the most persistent have been comedy and the short lyric forms)—and of the places which these models occupied within generic systems. Although changes and additions have been made constantly, a general awareness has existed of the unusual continuity of literary norms. (For centuries, one might say, a relative stability prevailed in the realms of culture. The social analogy comes to mind, of course, as we know full well that an awareness of the relative continuity of social conditions was for a long time one of the psychological bases for class distinctions and a reason for their perpetuation.)

4. The relationship between the norm (or model) and the system to which it belongs is one of the conditions for the continuity of both. Thus the concept of tragedy can survive a period in which a single dramatic genre, such as comedy, keeps the idea of the theater alive (perhaps in Rome, where few good tragedies were written; yet tragedy occupied a prominent place in Horace's *Ars poetica*). In such cases, the system will retain the class which has traditionally belonged to it. On other occasions, a system will absorb a new work and legitimate it as a normative model on the strength of some structural connection between the new model and the existing classes. (The Byzantine philologist Photius, ca. 820-897, regarded the late Greek romances by Heliodorus

and Achilles Tatius as examples of *dramatikon*.)[15] It happens rather often that a new work or an eccentric author is forced by the system into an inappropriate category. Or conversely, a generic term will be "carried" by a system long after its original meaning has been forgotten. (Wilhelm Cloetta pointed out long ago that a number of the most authoritative writers of the Middle Ages, beginning with Saint Isidore of Seville, had no idea of what a theatrical performance really was: so that Averroës' misreading of "tragedy," which Renan and Menéndez Pelayo commented upon, and which inspired Borges to write one of the best stories in *El Aleph*, was far from exceptional.) Genre and system, in other words, reinforce and perpetuate each other.

5. Systems will tend, generally speaking, to absorb change and assimilate innovation. On the other hand, assimilation becomes a small step in a larger process of change. (The classic example is the famous sixteenth-century quarrel concerning Ariosto. Several things could happen: the *romanzo* might be absorbed by the epic; the system, or rather its proponents, might "reject" it; a special niche might be found for a *favola mista*, etc. Ultimately, the assimilation of the *romanzo* caused a jarring and loosening of the system; and this became one of the conditions for the rise of the novel.) In this connection, the roles of the critic and the reader are important. Most critics (or writers functioning as critics) view a new work "through" a system: they perceive, judge, and decide, for better or for worse, within the coordinates of an available critical scheme. The critical intelligence "assimilates" and "accommodates" nearly in the sense that the psychologist Jean Piaget gives to these terms.[16]

[15] Cf. Irene Behrens, *Die Lehre von der Einteilung der Dichtkunst* (Halle and Saale, 1940), p. 38.

[16] Assimilation takes place whenever the individual incorporates the data of experience into a previous logical framework. Piaget distinguishes between three kinds of *assimilation*, of which the third is more pertinent to our subject ("l'assimilation généralisatrice, la plus

6. Not all literary classes or groupings, of course, constitute systems of *genres*. But it is often difficult for the modern historian to discover whether a certain class used in the past is at all comparable to what he would today consider a genre. Yet he must try to distinguish between systems of genres and other cognate systems, not only because they are closely related but because one of the latter could have influenced, shaped, or even displaced the former. I will limit myself to recalling three fundamental kinds of classes: (a) Literary genres themselves—or what modern criticism recognizes as genres (my own approach here being primarily historical). For a long time these were thought of as "species" of a wider "genus," and for a very good and obvious reason: because a generic model, tautologically enough, should be susceptible of "imitation." The genre Z, in the modern view, should not be so comprehensive that it could not be said of a particular work, in the singular: this is *a* Z. For instance: this is a comedy, an elegy, a novel. A genre is not a mere aspect of a work but one of its principles of unity. Practically speaking, it makes possible literary composition—the actual assemblage of the work as a whole. In this sense, it is broad enough. Yet it should not be so vague that it serves more as a premise than as a model. A genre endures (and not to endure, not to become, in Fernand Braudel's words, a *longue durée*, is not to emerge fully as a genre) insofar as it continues to be a problem-solving model, a standing invitation to the matching of matter and form. (b) Works classified with respect to

---

féconde sans doute puisqu'elle conduit à élargir le domaine d'un schème donné et par là même à élargir la classe des objets pouvant lui être assimilés"). Cf. Yvette Hatwell, "Propos des notions d'assimilation et d'accommodation dans les processus cognitifs," in *Psychologie et épistémologie génétiques . . . Hommage à Jean Piaget* (Paris, 1966), p. 128. Assimilation alone brings no effective knowledge of the object and is countered constantly by *accommodation*, through which the subject actively participates in the refinement of cognitive schemes.

versification alone: the Greek iambics, the elegy, etc. That prosody and "external form" are not a satisfactory basis for classification (we need only think of modern studies of the ode or the sonnet, regarded not solely as verse forms),[17] most critics have known since the beginning of the nineteenth century. But the point is historically important: despite the example of Aristotle (*Poetics*, 1447b), who pointed out that Homer and Empedocles had nothing in common save meter, it has been a central tradition of Greco-Roman literary theory to identify poetic form with metrical structure. Diomedes (fourth century), whose *Ars grammatica* was highly influential during the Middle Ages, maintained that the essence of poetry was to be found in versification.[18] This confusion between meter and form postponed the emergence (until at least the Renaissance) of an effective idea of the lyric, which one could not differentiate from dramatic or narrative verse on the basis of meter alone. (c) Presentational *modes*, like "narrative" and "dramatic." (There are of course other modes or so-called "universals," such as satire or allegory, that cut across the differences between historical genres.) I am referring here to what Northrop Frye calls "radicals of presentation." "We have to speak of the *radical* of presentation," he proposes, "if the distinctions of acted, spoken and written word are to mean anything in the age of the printed press."[19] Frye's system is the tetrad "epos," "prose," "drama," and "lyric." He then goes on to subdivide these modes into "specific forms," which are like the older "species" of the *artes poeticae* and our own genres. Unlike Frye, I do not think that these modes constitute the central principle of all generic differentiation, and that the specific genres are forms

---

[17] Cf. Karl Viëtor, "Die Geschichte literarischer Gattungen," in *Geist und Form* (Bern, 1952), pp. 291-309.

[18] Cf. Curtius, *European Literature and the Latin Middle Ages*, p. 439.

[19] *Anatomy of Criticism* (Princeton, 1957), p. 247.

or instances *of* these modes. But I shall not argue my case here. My concern is with the history of poetics, which shows that modes and genres have composed different systems and that one of the tasks of the historian is to observe the changing relations between the two. It seems to me that modes have lent themselves to systematization, or have resulted from it, much more readily or frequently than genres have. We have known systems of modes; but in the area of genre, perhaps because of the proximity of "specific forms" to the literary works themselves, what we often meet is a mere "will to structure."

7. The history of poetics reveals at first glance, strikingly enough, the recurrence of the number three as a simple principle of systematization. Further study shows, besides, on a still more fundamental level, an underlying combination or articulation of two kinds of scheme: dyads and triads; or to be more explicit, "natural" dualisms (natural insofar as they are based on "opposition" models) and cultural triads (based on "construction" or "reconciliation" models). The "ideal space" that writers have confronted has been, more often than not, dualistic on a certain level and triadic on another.

I realize full well that these seven points (or working hypotheses) should be supported and illustrated as objectively as possible. Before I begin to do so, however, there are some misunderstandings to be forestalled; and I should like to clarify certain implications of two of the points—the third and the seventh—that are most likely to cause difficulty.

I am stressing here the recurrences, or the continuity, in the career of European poetics; as well as one of the characteristics—the articulation of dyads and triads—that renders this continuity most visible. Now, one would expect the following objection to be raised. These principles of systematization, these schemes and structures, one might say, are meager evidence for the claims that have been made; they are formal, fleshless abstractions, far removed from either poetics or poetry; and no theory should forget that literary goals, programs, or manifestos, including systems of genres, are formulated not by triadic spaces but by human beings living in historical societies.

My answer to this (for the moment) would be fourfold. Let it be clear, first of all, that the systems we are studying are not metatemporal or metahistorical; they are not hidden structures, "manifestations," or merely formal relations inferred or extracted a posteriori by the computing mind. These systems, on the contrary, have *happened*. They have, moreover—and this is my concern—continued to happen. A triadic scheme B occurs at one point and is followed by a triad C and a triad D, and so on. In other words, I am speaking of attitudes and recurrences that are or have been as historically real—within the order of literature, "culture," or the arts—as certain long-lasting political, social, or legal institutions. No one denies, secondly, that each individual instance (each particular *ars poetica* or literary system) should be thoroughly described and interpreted in all its singularity. But this is only a part of the truth. And it remains one of the tasks of literary history (despite the critic's usual satisfaction with the study of the isolated work or the single writer) to confront that section or province of the poetic imagination which is (indubitably so in the area of poetics) as repetitive, established, and enduring as a social institution. I have already indicated, thirdly, the extent to which these systematic recurrences involve not only the realm of poetics but such other cultural orders as grammar, philosophy, and pedagogy. The relevance of a scheme to more than one of these classes is surely an important condition for its durability. My feeling is that the effectiveness of such links derives largely from the fact that they help to make "order" possible, to serve as principles of organization and structuration. A principle as basic as these becomes part and parcel of the minds of men (of human beings living in historical societies) and of their reason-

ing and decisions. In fact, the broad diffusion of certain structures brings to light one of the ways in which human minds
are submitted not to aprioristic universal categories, as in
Kant, but to "designs" and "pictures" of *historical* origin.

What I am beginning, fourthly, to propose is that the theoretical orders of poetics should be viewed, at any moment in
their history, as essentially mental codes—with which the practicing writer (the writer as individual, as *hombre de carne y
hueso*) comes to terms through his writing. The structures of
this order are no more alien to the poems he produces than
the linguistic code is to the actual utterances in his speech.

The now famous division into three genres—"narrative"
(or "epic"), "dramatic," "lyrical"—was fully presented and
defended for the first time, according to Irene Behrens,[20]
by Francisco Cascales in his *Tablas poéticas* (1617). (One
is puzzled by the apparent neglect of Antonio Minturno, who
sketched a similar view in his *De poeta* [1559];[21] as well as
by the possible motives for Cascales' spirited advocacy of this
system. In Spain as in no other country during the sixteenth
and seventeenth centuries, to be sure, poetry, the drama, and
the novel prospered simultaneously: Góngora, Lope de Vega,
and Cervantes were near-contemporaries.) An obscure humanist of the period, Pedro González de Sepúlveda, who
taught rhetoric in Alcalá, objected in a learned epistle to
Cascales' idea. (The objections were published in the latter's
Cartas filológicas in 1634.) Are there only three "species of
poetry"? "If there are no more," Sepúlveda wrote, "I am on
your Grace's side; but unless my reason deceives me, they are
not so few; if one looks at the matter carefully, these are different *modes* used by poets in their narrations rather than
different *species* of imitation. Who will say that comedy and
tragedy are a single species? Do they perchance differ from

[20] Cf. *Die Lehre von der Einteilung der Dichtkunst*, pp. 128-129.
[21] Irene Behrens is of the opinion that Minturno's notion "bleibt . . .
stehen" (p. 86), and so remains undeveloped.

each other only in the choice of meter? Is the difference not greater between a comedy and a tragedy than between two comedies? Is it also not greater between a lyric and a dithyramb than between two lyrics? But the use of meter differentiates the latter; therefore the distinction among the former must be one of species; and thus the species of poetry must be more than three." ("Si no son más, de su bando me tiene v. m.; pero si no me engaña mi juicio, no son tan pocas; porque ésas, si bien se mira, más son diversos *modos* de que el poeta usa en sus narraciones, que diversas *especies* de imitación. ¿Quién dirá que la comedia y tragedia son una especie? ¿Por ventura no se diferencian más que en número? ¿No hay mayor diferencia entre una comedia y tragedia que entre dos comedias? ¿No la hay también mayor entre una lírica y ditirámbica que entre dos líricas? Pues éstas se diferencian en número; luego la distinción de aquéllas habrá de ser especie; por donde las especies de poesía más habrán de ser de tres.")[22]

To which Cascales responded that according to his division there are no more than three species (*épica, lírica,* and *escénica*), "and though, rigorously speaking, tragedy and comedy are different, because both are dramatic and are *represented on the stage,* one speaks of them as of one species. And should we call them different, as they are, to the ends that your Grace seeks, that does not matter. As for the epigram and the sonnet, they cannot be reduced to comedy or tragedy, because they do not coincide in anything, I mean, in anything essential; either because these are totally dramatic, and the sonnet is not; or because they have an action to celebrate and the sonnet does not. For the fable of a sonnet is a *concept* only, not an action, so that it cannot, for the same reason, be reduced to the epic. As the sonnet, then, has

[22] "El maestro Pedro González de Sepúlveda al Licenciado Francisco Cascales," in Cascales, *Cartas filológicas,* ed. Justo García Soriano (Madrid, 1951), III, 217 (italics mine).

as the soul of its poetry a concept, as lyrics do, but does not comprise an action, as heroic, tragic and comic writings do, to what, beside the lyric, could we apply the sonnet?" ("Y según esta división, no hay más que tres especies, que son épica, lírica y scénica; que si bien la tragedia y comedia son en rigor diferentes, pero porque la una y la otra es dramática, y se *representan en el tablado*, se habla de ellas como de una especie. Y cuando las digamos, como lo son, distintas, al propósito y fin que v. m. lleva, no importa. Pues el epigrama o soneto no se puede reducir a la comedia ni a la tragedia, porque en nada, digo, esencialmente, convienen entre sí, ya porque estas son dramáticas totalmente, y el soneto no lo es, ya porque tienen acción que celebrar, y el soneto no la tiene; pues la fábula del soneto es un *concepto* no más, y no una acción, y por las mismas causas tampoco se puede reducir a la épica. Teniendo, pues, el soneto por alma de su poesía un concepto, como la lírica, y no comprendiendo acción, como la heroica ni como la trágica ni como la cómica comprehende. ¿a quién, sino a la lírica, podemos aplicar el soneto?")[23]

Sepúlveda, the more conservative of the two and the better Aristotelian, considers tragedy and comedy to be *especies* (as our modern "genres" were then called). And he proposes to retain the traditional distinction between genres and modes. He recognizes, actually, in keeping with the Aristotelians, that different though tragedies and comedies are as specific genres, they have in common what Aristotle had described in the *Poetics* (1447a, 1448a) as a mode of imitation. The various kinds of poetry, Aristotle had said, differ from one another in three respects: the medium employed, the object of imitation, and the manner or mode of imitation. Concerning the latter, he had written (1448a): "there is still a third difference—the manner in which each of these objects is imitated. For the medium being the same, and the objects the

---

[23] *Cartas filológicas*, III, p. 239 ("Epístola X").

same, the poet may imitate by narration—in which case he can take another personality as Homer does, or speak in his own person, unchanged—or he may present all his characters as living and moving before us."[24] This is one of the more obscure and disputed passages in the *Poetics,* but it may be safely said that whatever the basic principles at work may exactly signify—narration, direct speech, representation— they are not relevant to the other two *differentiae* of the poetic art (the medium employed and the object of imitation). Sepúlveda does not allow himself to overlook this, so as not to confuse the Aristotelian modes of imitation with the actual poetic species or genres. Today Gerald F. Else makes the point quite clear:

"Hence one cannot simply identify the *dramatic mode* with the *drama,* since the former may appear outside of the latter, or the mixed mode with either epic or lyric, since it may appear in either. The *differentiae* do not simply run with the established genre-divisions or with each other; they cut across each other and so bring out significant differences. From one point of view, therefore, one might say that 'drama' is anything that uses the dramatic method; but a more correct definition will draw on the *differentia* of medium as well and distinguish two actual dramatic genres, tragedy and comedy."[25]

The "dramatic mode" and the "drama" did not coincide, further, insofar as the former implied not the conditions of staging or of performance but rather "direct" speech and dialogue. Much emphasis was placed on the poet's presentation or representation of a character or a voice other than his own. Thus it would become possible for certain theorists in the Platonic-Aristotelian tradition to reduce the dramatic

[24] S. H. Butcher, *Aristotle's Theory of Poetry and Fine Arts,* 4th edn. (London, 1911), p. 13.
[25] *Aristotle's Poetics,* p. 91.

mode to imitation in the sense of impersonation, to *mimesis* as mimicry: the attempt to speak for, or even as, someone else.[26] During the Middle Ages it was often held that several of Virgil's *Eclogues* (offering dialogue only) were among the purest instances of the dramatic mode.

These traditional concepts are echoed by Sepúlveda, and they retain one advantage: a fairly free and loose relationship between the system of modes and the roster of specific forms or genres. Cascales, the innovator (much though he owed to Antonio Minturno), takes two decisive steps: he transfers the triadic "ideal space" to a system of *genres*; and he basically applies but one principle of definition to the drama and another to the lyric. He visualizes the stage, the scenic factor, as the essence of drama, whether tragic or comic. And he tests the validity of a fresh category as the proper basis for a definition of the lyric. Aristotle had written that the object of all poetic imitation was "men in action" (1448a). Cascales maintains that the main argument (or "fable") of a sonnet is not an action but a *concepto*; and he suggests that this is the distinctive feature of all lyrics. (Covarrubias' *Tesoro de la lengua castellana,* a dictionary published in 1611, defines *concepto* as a discourse born in the mind and executed later by either the tongue or the pen: "el discurso hecho en el entendimiento, y después ejecutado, o con la lengua o con la pluma.") The prestige of Petrarch and of the Italian lyric in general had led the theorists of the sixteenth and seventeenth centuries to seek a particular "object" for lyrical poetry that would be clearly distinct from the "action" found in either narrative or dramatic verse. The poet's

---

[26] *Mimeisthai* in the larger sense "means to make or do something which has a resemblance to something else" (cf. Aristotle, *Poetics*, ed. D. W. Lucas [Oxford, 1968], p. 55). The more restricted "impersonation" became confused with the other (or with the *imitatio* of great authors or poetic models) in the minds, for example, of Renaissance theorists; cf. Weinberg, *Literary Criticism in the Italian Renaissance*, 1, 60-63.

thoughts could be such an object. Insofar as they were *his own* thoughts, the category used was fresh but not completely non-Aristotelian. It was extracted from Aristotle's system of modes: the lyrical poet was the poet fully speaking for and as himself, needing to impersonate no one and to "imitate" no action. Cascales, in his *Tablas poéticas*, maintains the three "modes of imitation," which he calls *exegemático, dramático*, and *mixto* (the first of these going back probably to Diomedes' *Ars grammatica*, where *exegematikon* was an equivalent of *enarrativum*, meaning "the poet speaks alone"), but the tendency to identify the genres with the modes and to apply to them a common tripartite order is clear. In this connection, one should also reread one of Cascales' *Cartas filológicas* (Carta vi, "Sobre el número ternario"), an extensive, scholarly encomium of the number three. Why, he asks at one point, with respect to the recondite meaning of the Three Wise Kings, so many "triplicities"? "These Wise Kings were three, according to Saint Augustine, Saint Leon, Rupert, and others: they were called Melchior, Gaspar, Balthazar. Three were the regions whence they came: Arabia, Sheba, Tarsus; three were the gifts they offered Jesus: gold, myrrh, and incense. But why so many triplicities? Because in adoring Christ, and through Him by way of concomitance the Father and the Holy Ghost, they adored intrinsically the Holy Trinity; because it was not possible that all three should have come together except as a *symbol of the divine Triad,* which God was willing to signify in a thousand ways and places" ("Pues ¿por qué tantas triplicidades? Porque adorando a Cristo, con quien por vía de concomitancia asistían al Padre y el Espíritu Santo, adoraban intrínsecamente la Santísima Trinidad; que no es posible que hubiesen venido tres para menos que para *símbolo de la divina Tríada,* la cual quiso Dios significar de mil maneras y en mil lugares.")[27]

[27] *Cartas filológicas*, i, 115. On the three modes ("exegemático, dramático, y mixto") in Cascales, see his *Tablas poéticas* (Murcia, 1617),

The debate between Cascales and González de Sepúlveda is a brief chapter in the gradual shift in European poetics from a triad of modes to a triad of genres. I shall add some comments and raise some questions concerning this topic, with regard particularly to the relationship between poetics and other systems. Aristotle's system of modes is usually attributed to the influence of Plato, though others prefer to stress its original features. Among recent commentators, D. W. Lucas assumes its Platonic origin,[28] while Gerald F. Else writes: "we must recognize that this long and tenacious tradition [i.e., the three modes] is jointly Platonic-Aristotelian, fed partly by the *Republic* and partly by an Aristotelian work (almost certainly the dialogue *On Poets*), but that it has been shaped more decisively by Aristotle than by Plato."[29] Plato had introduced in the *Republic* (392d-394d) an apparently original arrangement of the "radicals of presentation." Socrates singles out three poetic modes: the dramatic, or, to use his own words, the "kind of poetry and tale-telling which works wholly through imitation, [like] tragedy and comedy"; another which uses "the recital of the poet himself, best exemplified, I presume, in the dithyramb"; and a combination of both, as "in epic poetry and many other places."[30] A small number of actual genres is mentioned, merely as instances of the practice of these modes, and it seems clear that this distinction should be understood in the light of the main philosophical and pedagogical objectives of the *Republic*. Else-

---

p. 30; on the three genres, p. 38; see also p. 30: "el lírico casi siempre habla en el modo exegemático, pues hace su imitación hablando él propio, como se ve en las obras de Horacio, y del Petrarca, poetas líricos." Though first published in 1617, it seems that the *Tablas poéticas* were already written in 1604. As for the sixth *Carta*, Cascales may have known Ausonius' *Gryphus ternarii numeri*.

[28] See his edition of the *Poetics*, pp. 66-67.

[29] Else, *Aristotle's Poetics*, p. 99.

[30] I quote here and below from *The Republic*, tr. Paul Shorey (Cambridge and London, 1935), I, 231.

where, of course, Plato calls in question the social and moral
validity of poetry. Is the practice of impersonation and tale-
telling an invitation to mutability, formlessness, dispersion of
character? (It seems interesting that Plato should object explicitly to stories about the transformations of Proteus [381];
as ". . . God is altogether simple and true in deed and word,
and neither changes himself nor deceives others by visions or
words or the sending of signs in waking or in dreams"
[382e].) Why do we have a triad of modes? Such questions
must be left to Hellenists and experts in Platonic philosophy,
who can determine whether the system of poetic modes is
significantly affected by the sociological and psychological
structures which the *Republic* proposes. Socrates explains at
length, to be sure, that the three elements of the soul—the
appetitive, spirited, and rational—correspond to the three social groupings of the ideal state: the economic, auxiliary, and
guardian classes.[31] The triad of modes may not be quite independent of the broad analogy between the social and the
ethical—between the city and the soul—that Socrates recom-
mends as a fundamental method of inquiry (434e-435a):

"But now let us work out the inquiry in which we supposed
that, if we found some larger thing that contained justice and
viewed it there, we should more easily discover its nature in
the individual man. And we agreed that this larger thing is
the city, and so we constructed the best city in our power,
well knowing that in the good city it would of course be
found. What, then, we thought we saw there we must refer
back to the individual and, if it is confirmed, all will be well.
But if something different manifests itself in the individual,
we will return again to the state and test it there and it may
be that, by examining them side by side and rubbing them
against one another, as it were from the fire-sticks, we may

[31] See R. C. Cross and A. D. Woozley, *Plato's Republic: A Philosophical Commentary* (New York, 1964), pp. 112-115.

cause the spark of justice to flash forth, and when it is thus revealed confirm it in our own minds.

"Well, he said, that seems a sound method and that is what we must do."

The Platonic-Aristotelian triad returns in the writings of the grammarians, rhetoricians, and scholiasts of later antiquity. The same division into "narrative" or "repertorial" (*diēgēmatikon, apangeltikon*), "dramatic" or "imitative" (*dramatikon, mimētikon*), "common" or "mixed" (*koinon, mikton*) occurs in Probus or Servius (fourth century), Proclus (fifth century), the anonymous prolegomena to Hesiod, and elsewhere.[32] Proclus' scheme enters his highly influential *Chrestomathia* or grammatical textbook based on literary excerpts and selections; and this is not, I think, a chance encounter. "Having grown up under the aegis of Greek philosophy, literary science came of age in the form of Hellenistic philology," Curtius sums up at one point. "It was called upon to classify the matter of literature—'studiorum materia,' as Quintilian puts it (x,1,128)—in accordance with two different principles: by genres and by authors. The selection of authors presupposes a classification of genres."[33] This observation is surely pertinent to our subject. Doubtless the normative systems or "ideal spaces" of literature were often formed around a cluster of "great authors," each of whom would occupy the position that was ordinarily assigned to a particular genre. A history of anthologies—of *how* the canons of authors and authorities arose and coalesced through the centuries of late antiquity and the Middle Ages—would contribute a great deal to our understanding of systematics. It would probably begin with the consideration of the most elementary questions: What did anthologists build upon? How

[32] Cf. Else, *Aristotle's Poetics*, p. 98; Behrens, *Die Lehre von der Einteilung der Dichtkunst*, pp. 25-32.

[33] Curtius, *European Literature and the Latin Middle Ages*, p. 248.

coherent were the "classifications of genres" mentioned by Curtius? What other orders or systems did they reflect? No doubt a certain kind of anthology offered a mere succession, a serial choice. In other cases, a process of selection was derived from orderly criteria, thus facilitating a restricted roster of "representative works," fragments of works, or (as in ancient grammars) brief quotations. I have already mentioned that although the Platonic-Aristotelian triad remained predominant, no widely valid system of *genres* emerged from the literary theory of Greece and Rome. Under the circumstances, two positions appear to have been characteristic. First, there was the example of Aristotle: genres were referred to other orderly arrangements, while at the same time none was considered in isolation—so that the epic was confronted with tragedy (1449b, 1459b) and the *Poetics* ended with a final comparison of the merits of the two. Secondly, a number of grammarians, rhetoricians, and theorists merely enumerated and described the different genres and forms one by one. There were such series in the authoritative grammar of Dionysius Thrax (second century B.C.), the rhetorical works of Cicero (*De optimo genere oratorum,* §1), or the *Ars poetica* of Horace, who glided over the epic, the elegy, and the iambic (largely in terms of meter) and then went on to expatiate at length upon the three theatrical genres (tragedy, comedy, and the satirical play). The tone and method of an epistle like the *Ars poetica,* of course, had to be informal; but Horace indicated along the way that he was familiar with the traditional division into dramatic and narrative modes (1. 179: "aut agitur res in scaenis aut acta refertur").

The status of the lyric, in this connection, clarifies the influence that the anthologist exerted on the theorist. If the association with the lyre was not to be taken too literally, and was mostly symbolical of a poetic "quality," one often wonders whether either a genre or a mode was being denoted at all. Horace clearly alluded to the great lyrical *poets* in a number of his compositions. "He wrote poems," C. M. Bowra states, "to be read in the study and not to be sung in company, but in obedience to his Greek models he assumed a convention that they should be sung to the lyre. He did not mean this to be taken literally; his purpose was rather to claim his spiritual and artistic descent from Alcaeus, Sappho, and Pindar."[34] This last remark is important: Horace never did elucidate what he meant by a lyrical poem. Like other ancient theorists, he was deterred from framing a clear conception of the lyric by several factors: the stress on meter; the modal system based on events and actions ("aut res . . . aut acta"); the wavering relationships between the different "melic" and "lyrical" forms and music. The poems regarded as either melic or lyrical by Alexandrian philology composed a heterogeneous group. The lyrical was not simply the nondramatic and the nonnarrative. There were narrative passages in the odes of Pindar. The dithyramb was originally choral and half-dramatic—yet Simonides and other lyricists wrote dithyrambs. The distinction between choral song and monody was not absolute: "a *hymnos*, or hymn to the gods, could be sung by a choir, as in Pindar's Hymns, or by a single person, as it must have been in some Hymns of Alcaeus and Sappho."[35] The elegiac poem was composed for the flute, rather than the lyre. Archilocus of Paros was a highly personal poet; but being an author of elegiac and iambic verse, he was not accepted as one of the lyrical poets by the Alexandrian critics: "he put the self into poetry," Bowra comments, "but he himself preferred an art which was closer to speech than to song."[36] No doubt there was a difference between a poem actually sung and one merely written for musical accompaniment: the latter was spoken or recited, though the tune might force a metrical pattern on the poem. Demetrius (first cen-

[34] C. M. Bowra, *Greek Lyric Poetry,* 2nd edn. (Oxford, 1961), p. 1.
[35] *Ibid.*, p. 6.
[36] *Ibid.*, p. 14.

tury A.D.), the author of *De elocutione*, was a passionate admirer of the "divine Sappho"; but he did not think all her works were lyrical; and he wrote about some of her wedding songs: "these poems of hers are . . . better suited for use in conversation than for singing. They are by no means adapted for a chorus or a lyre—unless indeed there is such a thing as a conversational chorus."[37]

Rather than to poems, the term "lyrical" became most clearly attached to an elite of poets. The appearance of a lyrical mode is an outstanding example of the impact that a system of authors can have on the other systems of poetics. Alexandrian criticism refined a "classical" conception of literature, consisting of the great writers from Homer to Menander, for the use of grammarians and philologists in the classroom. These very few poets were the select, the aristocracy, "the admitted" (*egkrinomenoi*). (Curtius brings out sharply the analogy between social elite and anthology.)[38] Aristophanes of Byzantium (ca. 257-180 B.C.) and Aristarchus of Samothrace (ca. 220-145 B.C.) drew up a list of model authors of various kinds. There were nine lyric poets (Alcman, Alcaeus, Sappho, Stesichorus, Ibycus, Anacreon, Simonides, Pindar, Bacchylides). (Irene Behrens remarks that the word *melikos* was applied in Alexandria to the noncanonical poets, while *lyrikos* was used almost exclusively of the Nine.)[39] These would be the *novem lyrici* whom Horace would strive to emulate and join (*Carmina*, I, 35-36)—and with every success, according to Quintilian, who felt also that Pindar was the first, by far, of the nine lyric poets (Bk. X, sec. 1: "novem vero lyricorum longe Pindarus princeps"). Later, pantheons and *pléiades* of selected lyric poets would follow.

[37] Aristotle, Longinus, Demetrius, *The Poetics. On the Sublime. On Style,* ed. W. Hamilton Fyfe and W. Rhys Roberts (Cambridge and London, 1932), p. 407.
[38] Cf. Curtius, *European Literature and the Latin Middle Ages,* p. 249.
[39] Cf. Behrens, *Die Lehre von der Einteilung der Dichtkunst,* p. 7.

There is certainly a difference between a canon of great writers—like the *novem lyrici*—and an actual anthology of poems. The former implies an adjectival sort of comment—*lyricus* as quality or mode. The latter often presupposes the additional choice of, and limitation to, a genre or a subgenre. Meleager's famous *Garland* (first century B.C.),[40] on which the *Greek Anthology* was built, was a collection of epigrams —the lightest and briefest of poetic forms. Some of the writers picked by Meleager were second-rate—or at least subordinate to the genre, the occasion, the anthology as a whole. One would wish to ask: Is it a fact that the selection of classical canons and anthologies played a central role in the rise of the lyrical modes in general? But this is a question which (like many of the interesting questions of literary theory) only comparatists trained in the Oriental literatures can possibly answer. For the purposes of this essay, I will briefly cite the following.

The oldest of Chinese poetic monuments was a vast collection, the *Shih Ching* (or *Shih King*), or *Classic of Songs*, containing 305 poems composed and sung between 1000 and 700 B.C. In the words of James R. Hightower: "the *Classic of Songs* is after all an anthology of poetry, and its four-fold division into *Feng*, Big and Little *Ya*, and *Sung*, may have been an attempt by its compiler to establish different categories of song."[41] Another ancient collection was the *Ch'u tz'u*, which preserved the special elegiac verse known as *sao*. But a more precise attempt on the part of anthologists to delimit the various provinces of poetry took place much later: from the days of Chih Yü, who compiled "the first known anthology of diverse genres,"[42] and died around A.D. 310, to the sixth-century

[40] On Meleager's possible predecessors, cf. *The Greek Anthology*, ed. A.S.F. Gow and D. L. Page (Cambridge, Eng., 1965), I, xvi.

[41] "The Wen hsüan and Genre Theory," p. 515, note 7. (See above, note 4.)

[42] *Ibid.*, p. 515.

Wen hsüan, with its 37 different types of writing. "The development of genre theory in China," Professor Hightower summarizes, "has been closely associated with anthology making."[43] As for the area of Islam, the influence of anthologists and philologists, like Abū Tammām and al-Buḥturī, was considerable during the Golden Age of Arabic literature, from the eighth to at least the eleventh century.[44] "The report that al-Walīd II (d. 744) caused to be made a collection of 'the *dīwān* of the Arabs . . .' is thought to be quite plausible."[45] Since the eighteenth century and Sir William Jones's translation (1783), European readers have known of the *Mu'allaqāt* or "Seven Suspended Odes"—the illustrious poems chosen in the eighth century by Ḥammad al-Rāwiya, "the Transmitter," and regarded for hundreds of years as models of the all-important art of the *qasida*.[46]

I spoke earlier of the effects on poetic theory of the grammarian's turn of mind, which was schematic and normative: a language was divided, or shattered, into parts of speech, and then put back together again by means of orderly rules. These structures were bequeathed to the European Middle Ages by the scholars of imperial Rome. Among these, the *grammaticus* Diomedes (fourth century) was influential; and he had something to say on the subject of poetics. His grammar proposes the usual modes: a *genus activum vel imitativum*, in which the poet does not intervene and the characters act "alone"; a *genus enarrativum*, where the "poet himself" speaks; and a *genus commune*, mixing the other two. Moreover, Diomedes decides to assign to the traditional triad a number of subordinate "species" or genres. In other words,

[43] *Ibid.*, p. 512.
[44] Cf. Francesco Gabrieli, *Storia della letteratura araba* (Milan, 1962), pp. 29, 165-166, and *passim*.
[45] A. J. Arberry, *The Seven Odes* (London and New York, 1957), p. 17.
[46] See Arberry's detailed account, in *The Seven Odes*, of the diffusion and translations of these poems.

genres become—a crucial step—submodes. There are, for example, four species of the first mode: *tragica, comica, satyrica, mimica*. (Though these appear to be theatrical forms, including mimes and satyr plays, the emphasis is on direct speech: the First and Ninth Eclogues of Virgil are inserted in this category.) The second mode embraces, *inter alia*, didactic writing (Empedocles, Lucretius), which Aristotle had considered alien to poetry (1447b). Lucretius is placed among the poets who speak "for themselves," but not Horace, since lyric poetry is subsumed under the third mode. There are two species of the *genus commune*: *heroica species* (Homer) and *lyrica species* (Archilocus, Horace).[47] Diomedes' scheme includes three modes and nine species. (A moment ago I spoke of the *novem lyrici*.) His contribution to the history of poetics was far from negligible, for he was one of the first to suggest a system of genres. This was the strained but tidy solution which would begin to prevail during the Renaissance and thus make possible the modern generic triads.

The old system of modes, Platonic and Aristotelian, retained its position for many centuries still. Julius Caesar Scaliger had no other division to recommend in his highly respected *Poetices libri septem* (1561);[48] but of course Scaliger could not have cared less for the great vernacular writers: he did not attempt to adjust traditional systems to the masterpieces of his own age. Other theorists were more sensitive to the need for different models and ideal spaces. I have already mentioned Antonio Minturno and Francisco Cascales. Minturno attended the Council of Trent, and became Bishop of Ugento and Cretone. His Latin treatise, *De poeta*

---

[47] On Diomedes, cf. Curtius, *European Literature and the Latin Middle Ages*, pp. 439-441; Behrens, *Die Lehre von der Einteilung der Dichtkunst*, pp. 25-30.

[48] Cf. Bk. 1, Chap. 3, "Poematum per modos divisio, et eorum ordo"; p. 6 of the facsimile edition by August Buck (Stuttgart and Bad Cannstatt, 1964).

(1559), was followed by *L'arte poetica* (1563), a rather more didactic dialogue in Italian.[49] Both books proposed explicitly the new triad: "*Vespasiano*: Quante adunque sono le parti della poesia? *Minturno*: Tre generali: l'una si chiama Epica, l'altra Scenica, la terza Melica, o Lirica, che dir vi piaccia."[50] This arrangement was buttressed with numerous other triads: there were three kinds of imitation, three types of character, three species of the epic, three "causes of poetry," three forms of drama, and so on.[51] Bishop Minturno did not make clear, as his Spanish successor would, that the principal types were "species" rather than "modes." But he was as zealous a believer in *la divina Tríada*. So were other Christian humanists of the sixteenth and seventeenth centuries. In her very useful book, Irene Behrens has told the rest of the story—the gradual diffusion of the tripartite system in poetics from the seventeenth to the nineteenth centuries: through Gravina (1708), the Abbé Batteux (1746), the rise of a comprehensive idea of the lyric (despite the weakness and delaying effects on that score of the French neoclassical theorists), and the triumph in Germany around 1800 of the *Dreiteilung der Dichtkunst*, the threefold division of the poetic art. It would be tempting to view the systematic itinerary of our subject as the secularization of the number three. But even on the simplest levels of systematization, as I suggested earlier in this essay, there are other dimensions to be studied.

II

More than forty years ago Roman Jakobson and Nikolai S. Trubetzkoy began to develop a structural conception of language as a set of binary oppositions, especially from a phono-

---

[49] Cf. Bernard Weinberg, "The Poetic Theories of Minturno," in *Studies in Honor of Frederick W. Shipley* (Freeport, N.Y., 1968; reprint), pp. 101-129.

[50] *L'arte poetica del signor Minturno* (Naples, 1725), p. 3. A marginal note reads: "tre maniere di Poesia."

[51] Cf. *L'arte poetica*, pp. 2-8.

logical point of view: the phonetic events themselves were not to be defined in isolation from the system of oppositions and correlations which they manifested. This was incorporated later into Jakobson's "distinctive feature system," where all features evidence binary structures ("voiced-unvoiced," "tense-lax," "strident-mellow," "continuant-interrupted," etc.). In the *Fundamentals of Language* these structures were reduced to twelve oppositions, "out of which each language makes its own selection."[52] In the social sciences also, the British anthropologist A.-R. Radcliffe-Brown explored the variety of forms of primitive social life in order to infer, by means of the comparative method, certain universal structural principles, such as the union of opposites: Heraclitus had said that "strife is king, and rules all things"; and the Yin-Yang systems of ancient China (the union of male and female, day and night, summer and winter, producing the organized totality or *tao*: the couple, the day, the year) corresponded probably to social customs like the pairing of rival clans by marriage.[53] Radcliffe-Brown, however, abstracted his "structural forms" *from* the variations of particular instances, or from the proven continuity of certain social structures in historical time.[54] Claude Lévi-Strauss, in an exceptionally thought-provoking series of studies, went on to postulate logical models in anthropology on the strength of

[52] Cf. Roman Jakobson and Morris Halle, *Fundamentals of Language* (The Hague, 1956), p. 29; Jakobson, "Retrospect," in *Selected Writings* (The Hague, 1962), I, 631-658; Nikolai S. Trubetzkoy, "Essai d'une théorie des oppositions phonologiques," *Journal de Psychologie Normale et Pathologique*, XXXIII (1936), 5-18; and Eugen Pauliny, "The Principle of Binary Structure in Phonology," *Travaux Linguistiques de Prague*, II (1966), 121-126.

[53] Cf. A.-R. Radcliffe-Brown, "The Comparative Method in Social Anthropology," in *Method in Social Anthropology* (Bombay, 1960), pp. 91-108.

[54] Cf. Meyer Fortes, "Time and Social Structure: An Ashanti Case Study," in *Social Structure. Studies Presented to A.-R. Radcliffe-Brown*, ed. M. Fortes (New York, 1963), p. 54.

structural analogies between the human mind and the world it interprets and organizes. In *Le Totémisme aujourd'hui* (1965), for example, each group of relations is treated as a single instance of a broader system of thought that is either real or potential, so that all instances may be derived or explained through the appropriate rules of transformation; thus the so-called totemism of "primitive" tribes is but a particular way of expressing the basic oppositions that are also manifested in myths, customs, beliefs.

Turning to poetics again and our historical inquiry (though not historical in a merely inductive way, as in Radcliffe-Brown: the historian of literary systems must be permitted to submit his array of facts to theoretical hypotheses and openings), we might ask: Have ternary systems functioned on all basic levels? When the ideal spaces of poetics are tripartite (at least on the explicit level of genre theory, where doubtless, *tertium datur*), are there underlying dichotomies at work too? Surely a principle as essential to most conscious or unconscious frameworks as opposition (logical, psychological, formal) plays a role in the shaping of the imaginary choices and alternatives of which poetic systems are made. One can readily discover in these systems the joint operation of binary and ternary forces—both tending, simultaneously or on different strata, toward systematization.

I shall only propose some examples and topics for further study. First of all, it would be useful to return to what we know concerning the earliest intellectual systems of our civilization and the relationships existing among them. I cited earlier the investigations of Hermann Usener, who documented the impact of the orders of grammar on the other branches of culture in Greece and Rome. The basic grammatical form was the tetrad (*lectio, enarratio, emendatio, iudicium*). A tetrad, of course, may unfold or resolve an original set of polarities, as in the "natural" dualism of winter and summer, barrenness and fertility, spreading out in the four seasons of the year. (In our day the "natural tetrad" reappears in Northrop Frye's *Anatomy of Criticism*.) Aristotle had referred in several of his works to the "table of opposites" of the Pythagoreans (*Metaphysics* 986a: Limit-Unlimited, Odd-Even, Unity-Plurality, Right-Left, Male-Female, Rest-Motion, Straight-Crooked, Light-Darkness, Good-Evil, Square-Oblong). In the *Physics* he explained that the notion of opposites was characteristic not only of the Pythagoreans but of their predecessors: "for they all, even when they assumed them without due process of reasoning, nevertheless taught that the elements and what they called first principles were opposites, as if under the compulsion of the truth itself" (188b). The allusion was to Empedocles, Heraclitus, and the search on the part of the pre-Socratics for interacting *archai* or first principles.[55] Usener himself stressed the prevalence of both triads and tetrads in Greece: among the grammarians, Asclepiades of Myrleia employed a ternary system, in the manner of the writers on medicine, architecture, or city-planning; of the tragedian and philosopher Ion of Chios (fifth century, B.C.), reputed to have written a *Triagmos* or disquisition on the number three;[56] of Plato's *Republic*,[57] and the various followers of Aristotle—who praised the number three in his *De caelo* with regard to the motion and the dimensions of natural bodies:

"Magnitude divisible in one direction is a line, in two directions a surface, in three directions a body. There is no magnitude not included in these; for three are all, and 'in three ways' is the same as 'in all ways.' It is just as the Pythagoreans

---

[55] On the Pythagorean opposites, cf. J. A. Philip, *Pythagoras and Early Pythagoreanism* (Toronto, 1966), pp. 44-59.

[56] Cf. Usener, "Ein altes Lehrgebäude der Philologie," pp. 272-276; Ernest Barker, *Greek Political Theory*, 3rd edn. (London, 1947), p. 81; and Pauly-Wissowa, *Real-Encyclopädie* . . . (Stuttgart, 1916), I, 1864-1865.

[57] Cf. Barker, *Greek Political Theory*, pp. 215, 263.

say, the whole world and all things in it are summed up in the number three; for end, middle, and beginning give the number of the whole, and their number is the triad. Hence it is that we have taken this number from nature, as it were one of her laws, and make use of it even for the worship of the gods."[58]

Aristotle singled out the three parts of the syllogism and, above all, the idea that virtue is a mean between opposite excesses. In his *Politics* the same doctrine of the mean (a good example, I think, of an assumption capable of pervading men's minds) was applied to the three classes of society: "now in all states there are three elements: one class is very rich, another very poor, and a third is a mean" (1295b).

Usener goes on to illustrate the increasing diffusion of the tetrad in Rome (especially through the impact of Varro's linguistics).[59] This point is confirmed by Curtius in his study of the different "levels of style." He sees a transition, in this area, from a Hellenistic trichotomy to a tetrad and other systems in classical and late Rome. The earliest evidence we have of the notion of the "three styles" is in the *Rhetorica ad Herennium* (ca. 86-82 B.C.) and in Cicero. But Quintilian admitted that intermediate styles were legitimate too; and the tetrad of styles was proposed by Hermogenes and Demetrius (first century A.D.).[60] Curtius extends this observation (in partial refutation of Erich Auerbach) to the Middle Ages, a period, in his opinion, when the boundaries not only between the styles but between poetry and prose were most fluid: "the division of the *ars dictaminis* [into meter, rhythmical prose, and regular prose] had as a result the replacement of the

---

[58] *On the Heavens*, tr. W.K.C. Guthrie (Cambridge and London, 1939), p. 5.

[59] Cf. Usener, "Ein altes Lehrgebäude der Philologie," pp. 303-307.

[60] Cf. Demetrius, *On Style*, ii, xxxvi, 323; and E. R. Curtius, "Die Lehre von den drei Stilen in Altertum und Mittelalter (zu Auerbachs *Mimesis*)," *Romanische Forschungen*, lxiv (1952), 57-70.

dyad poetry-prose by a triad or a tetrad. The boundaries between poetry and prose thus became more and more blurred."[61]

The doctrine of the mean obviously implied the existence of binary oppositions—in ethics, society, literature. "In Aristotle's own ethical theory the aim of ethical conduct," writes J. A. Philip, "is presented as some point that is median, but not necessarily the middle, in the whole locus or area lying between contraries."[62] Similarly, the median term in the old triad of styles implies the polarity that logically precedes it (the style called *mediocre* in Saint Isidore is only meaningful with respect to the opposites *grandiloquum* and *humile*), even as the rhythmical prose of the Middle Ages is dependent on a much broader framework (and the prose poem in the nineteenth century, on Baudelaire's regular prose and regular poems).

Does the "natural" binary opposition yield, for different historical reasons in various societies, in connection with linguistic and social systems, to more complex "cultural" structures—of which the most important in the field of poetics has been the triad? The mixed effects of binary and ternary systems are palpably present in the history of art theory, for example: the *Poetics* of Aristotle; J. J. Winckelmann; and the conflicting claims within the systems of Romanticism. Gerald F. Else has shown that the procedures of *diaeresis* (Plato, *Phaedrus* 265d-266a: concepts are split into two until true classes are discerned) are applied by Aristotle in the *Poetics*, though to the parts of a triad: "within the tripartite division . . . Aristotle does proceed diaeretically."[63] For example, the three *differentiae* of poetry are defined (medium,

---

[61] *European Literature and the Latin Middle Ages*, p. 149.

[62] *Pythagoras and Early Pythagoreanism*, p. 49.

[63] Else, *Aristotle's Poetics*, p. 16; see also pp. 67-68, 91-101, and *passim*; and among Plato's other dialogues, *Philebus* 16-18, *Sophist* 253d.

object, and mode); under the heading of each, then, a dichotomy is introduced. The resulting oppositions stand out most visibly in the historical remarks on the origins of poetry (1448b-1449a): poetry originally "split up" according to the characters belonging to it, either superior or worthless men; it produced either invectives or heroic hymns and encomia; but as time passed, invective gave way to comedy, and heroic verse to tragedy: "the lampooners became writers of comedy, and the epic poets were succeeded by tragedians, since the drama was a larger and higher form of art."[64] Though forms and genres may change, a basic polarity remains; and the central genres—tragedy, epic, comedy—have their places in a continuing system of binary oppositions.[65]

In modern times, the superseding or transcending of elementary oppositions by means of the triad has usually been significant in a more than literal way. The number three—standing not just for itself or for a kind of number but, rather, *for this transcending of oppositions as a whole*—has often coincided with the introduction, broadly speaking, of constructive schemes. It is difficult to think of a historical imagination that could thrive within the strict restraints of oppositions and polarities, or without that "other," that "third person" (not merely in the grammatical sense), through which an experience of diversity becomes possible. An illuminating case in point is the celebrated Johann Joachim Winckelmann, whose *Geschichte der Kunst des Altertums* (1764) was the first of the great historical monuments in the field of the

[64] Butcher, *Aristotle's Theory of Poetry and Fine Arts*, p. 17.

[65] Averroës' confusion of tragedy with panegyric, which Menéndez Pelayo ridiculed—see his *Historia de las ideas estéticas en España* (Madrid, 1909-1912), II, 137—preserved the basic polarity in Aristotle, so central also in the rhetorical tradition (*topoi* conveying the ideal of the perfect man, the idyllic landscape, etc.) with which Averroës was in sympathy. On Antonio Viperano's Renaissance poetics of satire and eulogy, cf. Weinberg, *Literary Criticism in the Italian Renaissance*, I ,209.

arts. Winckelmann was able to submit the bric-a-brac of eighteenth-century classical scholarship, and of his own immense erudition, to a few distinct and powerful conceptions. Like many of his contemporaries, though more intensely so, he was conscious above all of the inescapable confrontation between the civilization of Greece and that of his own day: it was always "they" against "us"; it was Phidias against Bernini and his successors; it was Apelles against Antonio Raphael Mengs. A mind both normative and historical, however, Winckelmann hesitated between this essential, urgent polarity and the claims of a more far-sighted, wide-ranging periodization of history. For he was also very proud of his ambitious attempt as a writer to erect a system (*Lehrgebäude*) of a historical nature. At one point in his *History*, Winckelmann indicates the wish to develop a five-part periodization that would be comparable to the division into five acts of the neo-classical play: as every action has five stages, namely, beginning, progress, state of rest, decrease, and end, so it is—he writes in Book VII, Ch. 1, 4—with the succession of time in art. But in the arts the beginning and the end of a process are inferior; thus Winckelmann must concentrate in practice on the three principal periods of Egyptian, Etruscan, and Greek art—in keeping with the praise of the triad with which his study of the human form opens: "The structure of the human body consists of triads. Three is the first uneven number, and the first number of relation, for it contains in itself the first even number, and another which unites the two together. Two things, as Plato said, cannot exist without a third. The best band is that which binds together most securely itself and the thing bound, in such a manner that the first is related to the second as the second is to the intermediate. Hence the number three contains in itself beginning, middle, and end. It was regarded as the most complete of all numbers, and by it, according to the doctrines of the Pythagoreans, all things were determined" (*History of Ancient Art*, tr. G. Henry Lodge [London, 1881],

1, p. 372). Of special interest to us here is not only Winckelmann's vacillation between oppositions and more complex orders (between the authority of the norm and the freedom of historicism) but the extent to which these orders were dependent in his mind upon such previous designs as the five-act division of French drama and Pythagorean numerology.

"Woe to the cognoscenti who love their systems more than beauty!" Friedrich Schlegel warned his brother August Wilhelm in a letter of 1796—or to the theorist forced to "destroy history" in order to further his system![66] It was characteristic enough of the Romantics at once to detest and pursue all kinds of intellectual order. Friedrich Schlegel himself elaborated the idea that the history of Greek literature was exemplary insofar as it comprised three stages (first epic, then lyric, and finally dramatic)—a triadic periodization reflecting the rise of the three genres. This was a decisive attempt to reconciliate the newfound sense of history with the traditional sense of system. It involved a temporal unfolding, as it were, of the timeless, archetypal "ideal space."[67] August Wilhelm Schlegel, in his lectures of 1801 (*Vorlesungen über schöne Literatur und Kunst*), went a bit further: he applied the recent Fichtean scheme of "thesis-antithesis-synthesis" to the triad of principal literary genres. Plato's original division (of modes) was not valid, Schlegel's notes began; and he proceeded to blend a contemporary philosophical system with poetic theory and its usual tripar-

[66] *Friedrich Schlegels Briefe an seinen Bruder August Wilhelm*, ed. Oskar F. Walzel (Berlin, 1890), p. 263: "Wehe dem Kenner, der sein System mehr liebt als die Schönheit, wehe dem Theoristen, dessen System so unvollständig und schlecht ist, dass er die Geschichte zerstören muss, um es aufrecht zu erhalten!"

[67] Which goes back to the beginnings of historical periodization, to be sure: to the triad "ancient-medieval-modern" in Cellarius (1634-1707) and its origins in the Renaissance. Cf. Ernst Bernheim, *Lehrbuch der historischen Methode und der Geschichtsphilosophie*, 5th edn. (Leipzig, 1908), p. 78. (See p. 423, n. 6, of this volume.)

tite arrangement: "Division of genres in Plato . . . Not valid. No real poetic principle of division.—Epic, lyric, dramatic; thesis, antithesis, synthesis. Light density, powerful singularity, harmonic completeness and wholeness . . . The epic, the purely objective in the human spirit. The lyric, the purely subjective. The dramatic, the interpenetration of both." ("Einteilung der Gattungen beim Plato . . . Ungültig. Kein poetischer Einteilungsgrund.—Episch, lyrisch, dramatisch; These, Antithese, Synthese. Leichte Fülle, energische Einzelheit, harmonische Vollständigkeit und Ganzheit . . . Das Epische, das rein Objektive im menschlichen Geiste. Das Lyrische, das rein Subjektive. Das Dramatische, die Durchdringung von beiden.")[68]

A rather more profound and influential step in the "temporalization" of the archetypal triad was taken, of course, by Hegel. In his useful 1951 essay on "The Aesthetics of Hegel," Lukács lays much stress on the passage from the first edition of the *Encyklopädie* to the second (1827), in which Hegel really comes to terms for the first time with the validity of the history of the arts *before* and *after* classical Greece and is thus able to delineate, by means of a simple periodization—a symbolical (Oriental) period, a classical period, and a romantic (medieval and modern) period—a truly tripartite historical evolution both of society and the arts.[69]

The success of such triadic periodizations (in Auguste Comte and Karl Marx, for example) coincided with a decidedly dualistic and polemical view of literary history, of which a famous seminal expression was Schiller's essay on "naïve" and "sentimental" poetry (1795). Poets, playwrights, critics fought and lived for a radical distinction between two attitudes and traditions—the "classical" and their own—while

[68] A. W. Schlegel, *Kritische Schriften und Briefe*, ed. Edgar Lohner (Stuttgart, 1963), II, 305-306.
[69] Cf. Lukács, "Hegels Ästhetik," in *Probleme der Ästhetik* (Neuwied, 1969), p. 114.

the martial metaphor of the "avant-garde" came into its own. The tendency of the true Romantic was to polarize not only writers or writings but ideas and attitudes into opposite camps, as Francesco De Sanctis remarked long ago: "study all Romantic conceptions, and you will find at bottom an antithesis" ("studiate tutte le concezioni romantiche, e vi troverete in fondo un'antitesi").[70]

The nineteenth century, generally speaking, would witness the coexistence of binary and ternary systems (from Hegel and Marx to Taine and Freud).[71] In the area of poetics the best example I know is Victor Hugo's Preface to *Cromwell*. "Mettons le marteau," Hugo demands, "dans les théories, les poétiques et les systèmes." Elsewhere in the same manifesto, nevertheless, he erects a theory and a system. He expatiates upon the three ages of poetry, "dont chacun correspond à une époque de la société: l'ode, l'épopée, le drame."[72] Beyond this historical triad, Hugo proclaims and acclaims an

[70] "Triboulet," in *Saggi critici*, ed. Luigi Russo (Bari, 1952), I, 263.
[71] There is an interesting alternation in Marx between a nonbinary descriptive approach (as in *The Class Struggle in France from 1848 to 1850* [1850]) to a class system consisting of more than two classes, and the revolutionary vision of a two-class society, composed of the object of revolution (the bourgeoisie) and the agent of revolution (the proletariat). On class systems, see the important book by the Polish sociologist Stanislaw Ossowski, *Class Structure in the Social Consciousness* (New York, 1963), as well as his earlier "La vision dichotomique de la stratification sociale," *Cahiers Internationaux de Sociologie*, XX (1956), 15-29. In Taine, there are, besides the three primordial forces (*race, milieu, moment*), essential cause and effect polarities; see the *Introduction à l'Historie de la littérature anglaise*, ed. Gilbert Chinard (Princeton, 1944), VII, 25: "il y a ici des couples dans le monde moral, comme il y en a dans le monde physique, aussi rigoureusement enchaînés et aussi universellement répandus dans l'un que dans l'autre. Tout ce qui dans un des ces couples produit, altère ou supprime le premier terme, produit, altère ou supprime le second par contrecoup." I allude in Freud to the passage from the tripartite conception of personality to the later conflict between Eros and the death instinct.
[72] *Théâtre complet*, ed. R. Purnal, J.-J. Thierry, and J. Mélèze (Paris, 1963), I, 434, 422.

ultimate or "natural" polarity between the grotesque and the sublime in literature. Poetry will advance and thrive in the future, if only the ideas of a *critique philosophique* can make themselves understood: "Elle [la poésie] se mettra à faire comme la nature, à mêler dans ses créations, sans pourtant les confondre, l'ombre à la lumière, le grotesque au sublime, en d'autres, termes, le corps à l'âme, la bête à l'esprit; car le point de départ de la religion est toujours le point de départ de la poésie. Tout se tient."[73]

Tout se tient. These words, and the conception they imply, have been applied to the study of language by modern linguists since Saussure with conspicuous success. It remains to be seen whether they are equally relevant to literary history. I have tried to show that on the level of poetics, systematization has been remarkably explicit and self-perpetuating. (For the Marxist critic some of these structures might appear as signs of an *Überbau* or "superstructure." But their durability across several historical periods, their status, in Braudel's terms, as *longues durées*, comparable not to economic events but to long-lasting social or political institutions, has been my principal concern here.) We may remember that Baudelaire wrote, as any true poet might: "un système est une espèce de damnation qui nous pousse à une abjuration perpétuelle."[74] How does a poet confront the fact that he is no solitary inventor, that he writes and exists as a writer within a system of signs and a network of forms that are as traditional or perhaps more "conservative" than the community in which he lives? In what ways is literature for him a potential, enveloping system? A grammar of models? Not merely a *musée imaginaire*, but an imaginary city? Or rather, his own personal version of that "city," which is like a secondary system? For the moment, I think, we would need to clarify the terms

[73] *Ibid.*, I, 416.
[74] *Oeuvres*, ed. Y.-G. Le Dantec (Paris, 1961), p. 995.

of the problem. The systematics of genre theory offer one of several points of departure. But there are of course others. I have glanced in this essay at the historical interaction between genre theories and other orders, such as the systems of "great authors" and the "three styles." Regarding the latter, we have the exceptional example of Erich Auerbach's *Mimesis*, which is based on a simplified and highly effective model of the relationship between systems of genres and systems of styles. Much information is available concerning their connections with rhetorical classes (the five divisions of rhetoric, the three kinds of eloquence) or with the schemes of ancient psychology and ethics.[75] I have only begun to mention the influence of social systems (social conditions as mediated by the minds of men). Historians of literature are reasonably well acquainted with such systems as the medieval "Virgil's wheel" and its application to poetic themes and forms of a triadic social space (symbolized through a circle divided by three radii);[76] the framework of ternary relations

[75] Cf. Curtius, *European Literature and the Latin Middle Ages*, pp. 68-69; Charles S. Baldwin, *Medieval Rhetoric and Poetic* (Gloucester, Mass., 1959), p. 64; Behrens, *Die Lehre von der Einteilung der Dichtkunst*, pp. 124, 174. Cf. Friedrich Schlegel, "Gespräch über die Poesie," in *Charakteristiken und Kritiken I*, ed. Hans Eichner (Munich, Paderborn, and Vienna, 1967), p. 356. Cicero thought (*Orator*, 20-21) that the three styles corresponded to the three kinds of eloquence—the three functions of oratory being *docere, delectare, movere*. It was also traditional to mention analogies between the three modes of poetry and the three psychic faculties of man (memory, reason, imagination), as well as the three parts of man in the Christian view (spirit, soul, body). Armand Nivelle has shown that the rise of an aesthetic science in the eighteenth century coincided with the recognition of a third or aesthetic faculty in man's inner being, dealing with "taste," "feeling," or "judgment." On the tripartite division of the spirit in J. G. Sulzer, M. Mendelssohn, and Kant, see A. Nivelle, *Les Théories esthétiques en Allemagne de Baumgarten à Kant* (Paris, 1955), pp. 96, 103, 109, 293.

[76] The *rota Vergilii* is described in the *Poetria* of John of Garland (thirteenth century); cf. Faral, *Les arts poétiques* . . . , p. 87; the full text is in Giovanni Mari, "Poetria magistri Johannis anglici de arte pro-

in Dante's *De vulgari eloquentia*;[77] the hardening of social analogies in the literary theories and hierarchies, markedly "monarchical," of the Renaissance and Baroque; the division of poetic modes in Hobbes according to "the three regions of mankind, court, city, and country."[78] We have also seen that Aristotle's three social classes owe much to his doctrine of the mean, and to the logical and ethical roots of this doctrine. It is *itself* a theory. For often the thinking mind, in Wittgenstein's words, "is held captive by a picture."[79] The idea that the modern novel is a product of the bourgeoisie rests on a notoriously convincing analogy not between two sets of hard data, but between two "pictures" and two systems. Class distinctions, like theories of genre, mediate between the events themselves and the consciousness of individuals and groups.

There are two ways of confronting the problems of literary history with which I cannot concur. The first consists in dissolving the processes of literature into "general history." The immediate aim becomes a succession of totalities, each of which assumes absolutely the unitary principle: not only *tout se tient* but *tout est un*. But can the historian record more

---

sayca metrica et rithmica," *Romanische Forschungen*, xiii (1902), 900. The three sections of the circle correspond to Virgil's *Aeneid, Eclogues*, and *Georgics*. The *Aeneid*, for example, stands for the "grave" style, the soldier as a type, Hector and Ajax as heroes, the horse as animal, the sword, the city or war camp, the laurel and cedar trees, etc.

[77] To the *ydioma triphiarum*, i.e., the languages of *oc, oïl*, and *sì* (reflecting the three classical languages) correspond the three social classes of Sicily (Bk. i, sec. xiii), the three sorts of being (angels, men, beasts), the three parts of man, the three kinds of action (Bk. ii, sec. iii), the three styles, the three parts of the *canzone*. I refer to the divisions as given in *De vulgari eloquentia*, ed. Aristide Marigo and Pier Giorgio Ricci (Florence, 1957).

[78] "The Answer of Mr. Hobbes to Sir William Davenant's Preface before Gondibert," in *The English Works of Thomas Hobbes* (London, 1840), iv, 443.

[79] Cited by Avrum Stroll, "Statements," in *Epistemology. New Essays on the Theory of Knowledge*, ed. A. Stroll (New York, 1967), p. 192.

than the efforts of men to devise and establish, vis-à-vis the oneness of the physical world around them, comparably interrelated and coherent orders? "One may suspect," Jorge Luis Borges writes briefly, "that there is no universe in the organic, unitary sense of this ambitious word" ("Cabe sospechar que no hay universo en el sentido orgánico, unificador, que tiene esa ambiciosa palabra").[80] The second method consists in seeking meaningful connections between the single literary work and entire social, economic, or intellectual systems. The incongruity is obvious and the problem thus posed nearly as absurd as the attempt to relate an isolated economic fact to an entire artistic period. My interests (to propose one more triad) lie somewhere between these two opposites. Literary systems, like social or linguistic ones, exist; whereas the "universe," as Borges quietly suspects, may not. Our task, I think, is to identify the careers of these different systems in historical time, to discover those that prevailed, and to listen to the dialogue between them.

[1969]

[80] "El idioma analítico de John Wilkins," in *Otras inquisiciones* (Buenos Aires, 1960), p. 143.

Second Thoughts on Literary Periods

I

To explore the idea of literary history may very well be the main theoretical task confronting the student of literature today. Where criticism is concerned, no one will deny that the work of theorists in recent years has been spectacular and influential. The most subtle command of terms and methods can be encountered in the writings of countless scholar-critics. Metaphors have been applied to the concept of metaphor, symbols to the symbol, and myths to myth. But the situation is remarkably different in the area of literary history, where the understanding of basic terms and methods seems oddly limited or relatively stationary. One of the features of the present moment in literary studies is this strange imbalance between a fast-growing body of practical criticism, well grounded in theory, and the reluctance to translate individual insights into persuasive historical constructions, in alliance also with adequate theory.

A great deal of useful thinking has been devoted to "interrelationships," first of all to those between literature and general history—the history, one might say, of non-art. Despite the abusive, or rather, the one-sided character of certain exercises in formal analysis, the relevance of various aspects of the history of societies and civilizations to the illumination of literary texts has been widely recognized and demonstrated during the last twenty or thirty years. Most often, however, these connections are not a contribution to *literary* history. They involve, on the one hand, the poetic text in its supratemporal dimension (as it emerged initially from the flow of historical time), and, on the other, the history of non-art. These contacts usually subsume, or tend merely to predict, a history *of* literature itself—the attempt to recapture and interpret the process of literature in historical time.

The mutual dependence of criticism, theory, and literary history, which has been a cornerstone of René Wellek's teaching and writing,[1] is of course the condition, or the indicator, of the imbalance I am commenting upon. And the study of the relationships between literary criticism and literary history is likely to remain an ungrateful task as long as our conception of the latter is so much more obscure and less robust than our idea of the former.

Let us take the metaphor of "current," for example, which, as applied to literature, is frequent enough. Like many of the terms composing the vocabulary of literary history, we use it easily and most often without second thoughts. One associates it readily with some sort of dynamic or continuous process, more or less akin to the notion of development. "But the concept of the development of a series of works of art," Professor Wellek has remarked, "seems an extraordinarily difficult one."[2] Upon scrutiny, the notion of current, like the entire conceptual framework of literary history, perhaps, poses serious problems, which the following pages propose to identify.

One might begin by observing that the idea of "literary current" appears to complement that of "literary period." This alliance seems more than empirical. There is, as it were,

---

[1] The present essay was first published, under the title "Second Thoughts on Currents and Periods," in *The Disciplines of Criticism: Essays in Literary Theory, Interpretation, and History Honoring René Wellek on the Occasion of his Sixty-fifth Birthday,* ed. Peter Demetz, Thomas Greene, and Lowry Nelson, Jr. (New Haven and London, 1968), pp. 477-509. On the mutual dependence of criticism, theory, and literary history, cf. "Literary Theory, Criticism, and History," in René Wellek, *Concepts of Criticism* (New Haven and London, 1963), pp. 1-20, items B4, B6, B54, and C12 of the bibliography; and Chaps. 4 and 19 of René Wellek and Austin Warren, *Theory of Literature,* 3rd edn. (New York, 1956).

[2] Wellek and Warren, *Theory of Literature,* p. 255.

a limit in each of the concepts that calls for complementation by the other (or by the dimension it represents). At first glance, they could respond or correspond to the two principal aspirations which H.-I. Marrou, in his recent summary for the *Encyclopédie de la Pléiade*, thinks are essential for historians: *reconstitution d'un devenir* and *récupération de valeurs*.[3] Literary currents would suggest a reconstruction of past processes of change, while literary periods would imply values revisited. Our initial hypothesis might then be: currents are diachrony, and periods, synchrony (of values).

But one discovers immediately the difficulties such a scheme raises. Do literary periods generally fail to be dynamic or diachronic, and, if so, is this understood? Is it possible that in the particular branch of history which is literary history, a process of change or of becoming should exclude the recapturing of values, such as those present in the literary works themselves? How can this experience of values based on artistic forms be, on the other hand, a sensitive instrument for the apprehension of time? Are periods and currents but different methods for the conceptual grasp of an identical chronology? If history, as Lucien Febvre said, is "the science of man in time," how can any reflection on the history of literature find pride in independence from diachrony?

II

It would be impractical to review here the complex question of periodization as it has been understood by various modern schools of historiography. But I can witness to the shock of the literary critic when he first approaches the subject and notices that it is common among general historians to think of epochs, eras, and periods with freedom, open-mindedness, or even skepticism. I know no better example of

[3] Cf. H.-I. Marrou, "Comment comprendre le métier d'historien," in *L'Histoire et ses méthodes*, ed. C. Samaran (Paris, 1961), pp. 1475, 1481.

the severely critical position toward periods than J. Hui-zinga's deservedly famous essay on the idea of the Renais-sance.[4] Somewhat less bold is the widespread tendency among historians of non-art to use periods as a temporal backdrop of neutral, conventional content—almost as a simple chronology or quantifying device—to which more in-teresting constructions can be referred, or to consider them as necessarily provisional, biased, or pedagogical. One need only recall, among the lively discussions in which German historians took part, the debate between Karl Heussi (who had challenged the notion of a generally valid periodization) and Georg von Below in the early 1920's;[5] and, in our day, the remarkably flexible and creative attitude of Fernand Braudel and his collaborators toward the never-ending organization of the past: "le bornage, toujours à reprendre, du temps perdu."[6]

[4] Cf. Johan Huizinga, "Het probleem der Renaissance" (1920), re-printed in *Tien Studiën* (Haarlem, 1926) and in *Verzamelde Werken* (Haarlem, 1949), IV; quoted hereafter from *Wege der Kulturgeschichte*, tr. W. Kaegi (Munich, 1930).

[5] Cf. K. Heussi, *Altertum, Mittelalter und Neuzeit in der Kirchenge-schichte. Ein Beitrag zum Problem der historischen Periodisierung* (Tübingen, 1921), and G. von Below, *Ueber historische Periodisierun-gen* (Berlin, 1925), as well as the earlier "Ueber historische Periodi-sierungen," *Archiv für Politik und Geschichte*, IV (1925), 1-29, 170-214; and the review by P. Joachimsen, *Historische Zeitschrift*, CXXXIV (1926), 369-373; H. Spangenberg, "Die Perioden der Weltgeschichte," *His-torische Zeitschrift*, CXXVII (1923), 1-49; K. Brandi, "Ueber historische Perioden," *Vergangenheit und Gegenwart*, 4th suppl. (1924), 10-17; also, W. Schneider, *Wesen und Formen der Epoche* (Munich, 1926).

[6] F. Braudel, "Qu'est-ce que le XVIe siècle?" *Annales E.S.C.*, VIII (1953), 73. On the general problem of the history of periodization (the Renaissance discovery both of itself and of the Middle Ages; the com-mon division into ancient, medieval, and modern history since the late seventeenth century and Christopher Cellarius; the perpetuations of the older schemes of the "four monarchies" and the "seven ages of man"; the many additions to Cellarius' triad during the nineteenth century and its transformation into other triads, etc.), which is itself an aspect of the history of historiography, there is a large bibliography. Cf. Ernst Bernheim, *Lehrbuch der historischen Methode und der*

The German debate of the 1920's did not, by and large, uncover any new issues, nor was it necessary to do so. Even during the nineteenth century, which marked the heyday of periodization among historians of non-art, there were more than a few vocal dissenters. Though Luigi Settembrini (with evident loyalty to his name and to the old notion of the seven ages of man) had divided Italian literature into seven parts, in his *Lezioni di letteratura italiana* (1866-1872), Francesco De Sanctis, a much greater student of the same subject, paid little heed to periods or epochs in his critical practice. A contemporary of both, the English historian Edward A. Freeman, affirmed in *The Unity of History* (1872) that the traditional separation of the past into periods should be abandoned, as being detrimental to a unified vision of man's historical achievement. More significant, the intensification of the debate during and after World War I indicated a change of emotional approach toward the issues: a substantial, fervent response, through one's interpretation of the past, to the experience of contemporary history.

Those crucial years, which produced not only Spengler's famous *Untergang des Abendlandes* (1918, 1922) but Theodor Lessing's confrontation with the possible "meaninglessness" of history in his prophetic *Geschichte als Sinngebung des Sinnlosen* (1916), have sometimes been associated with the new "crisis of historicism" (*Krise des Historismus*). The experience of total war (to put it much too simply) had precipitated a separation between the proper study of history, on

Geschichtsphilosophie, 5th edn. (Leipzig, 1908), pp. 70ff.; Paul Lehmann, "Mittelalter und Küchenlatein," *Historische Zeitschrift,* cxxxvii (1928), 197-213; Giogio Falco, *La polemica sul Medioevo* (Turin, 1933); Wallace K. Ferguson, *The Renaissance in Historical Thought* (Cambridge, Mass., 1948); Alberto Tenenti, "La storiografia in Europa dal Quattro al Seicento," in A. Tenenti et al., *Nuove questioni di storia moderna* (Milan, 1964), ii, 995-1045; and George Huppert, "The Renaissance Background of Historicism," *History and Theory,* v (1966), 48-60.

the one hand, and, on the other, systematic philosophy based on rationalism. Hegel's grandiose attempt to find logical forms in history, and its numerous successors, were no longer persuasive to a number of minds for whom the twentieth century had failed to prove the rationality of the real. The dualism of reason and history, which had been characteristic of the eighteenth century, and against which the Hegelians had fought, was thus revived, for good or ill, in our time. (Contemporary "structuralism" in French anthropology could be regarded as a further step in the same split, and another chapter in the *Krise des Historismus*.) A number of historians felt the need to pry their subject apart from any conceptual postulate, any faith in history as development, purpose, progress. The most obvious of these orderly schemes, particularly since Hegel, was periodization. The nineteenth century had inherited the triadic division of the historical past into ancient, medieval, and modern (which one could regard, in a sense, as a chronological unfolding of the fundamental triads of Greek thought and Christian theology), and had then gone on to further subdivide the post-medieval or modern centuries. Periodization became a dynamic and unceasing striving for order. Though every single scheme pretended to be orderly, the overall effects of periodization in historiography were highly complex and fluid.

The fact that literary historians, on the contrary, almost always defended a broad and stationary pattern of periodization, is rather puzzling. The reasons that come to mind are very basic, and they can only be sketched here in summary fashion. A literary work of art, as we know, is a response to experience, and it cannot be grasped properly, in social or historical terms, without reference to that experience. It is also a construction, in the final analysis, of forms transcending, or emerging from, the flow of time which had surrounded the response. This is the difficult, self-denying historicity with which the literary scholar has to deal. When an economic historian, in contrast, isolates a list of prices, a balance of payments, or an index of production, he is defining events firmly embedded in temporal change except insofar as he is able to place them in a significant whole. The individual fact must be integrated by the historian into a structure, or inserted in a larger pattern of facts, such as an economic cycle. No single economic event can possibly coincide with the cycle, the *conjoncture*, or any similar economic period-concept. The single events and the total pattern are fundamentally different.

In contrast, the literary historian is structuring structures. His starting point is already charged with significance. Were we to turn to the modern (yet basically theological) vocabulary of those structuralist discussions in the manner of Lévi-Strauss and Barthes, where single events are deemed "contingent" and only the larger pattern is gifted with significance, one would immediately need to point out that in the world of art the situation is quite the opposite: nothing is less contingent than the individual phenomenon (the work of art), or less necessary than the total process.[7] It is useless, at any rate, to isolate any radical difference in kind between the literary scholar's reflections on the style of an individual work and his thoughts on the style of a group of works. The economic historian proceeds from event to structure while remaining timebound. The literary historian moves from one structure to another while maintaining all the way an ambiguous attitude toward historical time.

The group of works just mentioned as the object of a literary scholar's thoughts can also be regarded as characteristic of a certain *period*. In this case, the literary historian may develop broad generalizations about a series of works associ-

---

[7] In *La Pensée sauvage* (Paris, 1962), p. 37, C. Lévi-Strauss states that the work of art functions halfway "entre l'ordre de la structure et l'ordre de l'événement"; cf. also p. 99; and R. Barthes, *Critique et vérité* (Paris, 1966), p. 51.

ated with a period without abandoning the level of stylistics, or without returning for an instant to the flow of historical becoming. He has made the transition from the work to the series and from the series to the period-concept, that is to say, from criticism to so-called literary history, without re-entering history. I am not saying that I condone this; I simply note that stylistics *can* entertain the illusion of history by merely proceeding from the work to the series. In the final chapter of the *Theory of Literature,* dealing with literary history, René Wellek and Austin Warren stress that the individual work of art is not an instance of a class or a type, but a part of the concept of a given period and its process of definition. Nevertheless, literary norms, standards, styles will tend to form static clusters. They do not, like economic cycles, have periodization of change as a primary goal. It is not uncommon for a critic to confuse his typology of stylistic responses with the section of time to which they responded, and to conclude that a style *is* a period or a concept fully coincident with it. As the critic can become a historian without modifying his principal target—literary forms—it seems natural that he should develop in the process an inclination for the kind of period-concept that is as solid and as "timeless" as his definition of a style.

For this he can hardly be blamed. His task is particularly arduous. Universals based on artistic forms are not readily reconciled with history. It may be that no generalization concerning a group of works can possibly provide us with a dynamic organization of historical change comparable to, say, economic cycles, unless it focuses on a subject that, unlike style, does not transcend time in the first place. The difficulty may reside not merely in relating art to the history of non-art, or structures to events, but in studying literary systems—particularly collective ones, shared by entire generations of writers—*as* events.

III

We are all familiar with a conception of literary epochs that is less monolithic. In 1961, to mention but one instance, Jean Rousset summarized his experience as a critic of the Baroque in such words as these:

"Bien entendu, nous devons être conscients qu'il s'agit d'une espèce de grille, construite par nous, historiens du XXe siècle, non par le artistes du XVIIe. On évitera de confondre la grille et les artistes, le schéma interprétatif et les oeuvres soumises à l'interprétation. Les catégories ne sont qu'un moyen d'investigation de ces faits que sont les oeuvres, on les considérera comme des hypothèses de travail et des instruments d'expérience, comparables à des échafaudages qui perdent leur utilité une fois la construction édifiée."[8]

The concept of period serves here to interpret a style which reached its peak during a certain section of time. But this dominant style in no way coincides with all the valuable artistic work of the moment. Homogeneity is neither the goal nor the premise of such a critical position, for, as Rousset also makes clear, "en histoire de l'art comme en histoire littéraire, c'est la diversité des tendances qui frappe autant que les similitudes, et les résistances au Baroque presque autant que les consentements." It will not do to underestimate the "dominated" style, any more than a true critic will neglect a minor poem. There is no simple equivalence between the Baroque and the seventeenth century: "Si le principe baroque est peut-être le plus actif, occupant dans l'époque une position centrale, il y a toutes sortes de courants parallèles ou latéraux, toutes sortes de solutions individuelles pos-

---

[8] J. Rousset, "La définition du terme 'baroque,'" in *Actes du IIIe Congrès de l'Association Internationale de Littérature Comparée* (The Hague, 1962), p. 167.

sibles; et les grands artistes sont précisément ceux qui réussissent des solutions singulières."[9]

Rousset's approach may be compared to those interpretations, too substantial to be reviewed here, which succeed in making room for both Classicism and Baroque, or even Mannerism, Classicism, and Baroque, within the *same* section of time. I am reminded, for example, of E.B.O. Borgerhoff and Lowry Nelson, Victor L. Tapié and Pierre Francastel, on the subject of the seventeenth century.[10] Or of Huizinga's refusal to consider the Renaissance as more than one aspect of the culture of the sixteenth century.[11] Or of Ortega y Gasset's insistence on the interplay of generations in history, where the (I think very arguable) theory of generations had the advantage of bringing out the extent to which any historical situation, if only we try to visualize it as a "today," is a "drama," a "dynamic system" of attractions, polarities, and polemics.[12] The earlier notion of period as harmony or singleness of style, so characteristic of *Geistesgeschichte,* yields in these cases to an emphasis on competition, confrontation, dialectics.

The dialectics of literary history tend to blend, naturally, with those of general history. Literary controversies will evoke class struggles, and, beyond these, the economic and political fabric of societies. While the static or synchronic conception of periods usually depends on stylistic harmonies,

---

[9] *Ibid.*, pp. 173, 174.

[10] Cf. E.B.O. Borgerhoff, "Mannerism and Baroque: A Simple Plea," *Comparative Literature*, v (1963), 323-331; L. Nelson, Jr., *Baroque Lyric Poetry* (New Haven and London, 1961), p. 166; V. L. Tapié, *Baroque et Classicisme* (Paris, 1957); and P. Francastel, "Baroque et Classicisme: histoire ou typologie des civilisations," *Annales E.S.C.*, xiv (1959), 142-151.

[11] Cf. Huizinga, *Wege der Kulturgeschichte*, p. 119.

[12] Cf. J. Ortega y Gasset, *En torno a Galileo* (1933), in *Obras completas*, 6th edn. (Madrid, 1964), v, 40.

the dynamic or diachronic view draws upon social tensions. Time, moreover, is involved again. Insofar as we restore the polemics of time past, we are likely to rejoin the perspective of time passing. A system of generations such as Ortega's will require a trajectory of events, a series of triumphs and reversals. Francastel, who practices with great tact the joint study of painting and society, does not surprise us when he likewise demands a diachronic idea of the Baroque: "le Baroque ne s'est pas défini entièrement au départ. Ce n'est pas une formule qu'on applique. C'est un bilan que nous dressons après épuisement d'une veine longtemps créatrice."[13]

But these views create a number of difficulties that can only be handled with respect to an appropriate conceptual framework for periodization. However briefly, it will be necessary to pose here one or two of the questions that are basic for an understanding of the subject.

The first, unavoidably, concerns method. By this I mean a method for relating period-concepts to single works of art. It has long been assumed that the idea of a Baroque or a Romantic period was reached by means of induction. In practice it appears that this was often not the case, although one is not surprised to find a prevailing loyalty to "facts" in a field —literary history—where the integrity of an occurrence like *Macbeth* can hardly be denied or regarded as an assumption of some kind. It is, however, the relationship between the single work of art and a period that is often seen as dependent, in Jean Rousset's previously quoted words, on "hypothèses de travail." I need not enter into the reservations with which modern logic discusses inductive procedures. More important for us here, contemporary developments in linguistics and anthropology have shown that generalizations in the humanities and in the social sciences are attained most effectively not by the pretended reasonableness of an inductive

---

[13] Francastel, "Baroque et classicisme," p. 146.

approach to facts, but rather, as in the natural sciences, by the choice of certain rules in order to explain certain results, or, as this is often termed now, by establishing hypothetical "models of description" which are later referred to all empirical instances at hand.[14] In practice, periods have sometimes been hypothetical models of description of the dominant products of a given section of time in artistic history. But it is not uncharacteristic of the literary critic, so proud of the fine edge of his sensibilities, to deride in principle the kind of speculative daring Ortega portrayed so well thirty years ago:

"Para des-cubrir la realidad es preciso que retiremos por un momento los hechos de en torno nuestro y nos quedemos solos con nuestra mente. Entonces, por nuestra propia cuenta y riesgo, imaginamos una realidad, fabricamos una realidad imaginaria, puro invento nuestro; luego, siguiendo en la soledad de nuestro íntimo imaginar, hallamos qué aspecto, qué figuras visibles, en suma, qué hechos produciría esa realidad imaginaria. Entonces es cuando salimos de nuestra soledad imaginativa, de nuestra mente pura y aislada, y comparamos esos hechos que la realidad imaginada por nosotros produciría con los hechos efectivos que nos rodean."

(In order to dis-cover reality, it is necessary to blot out for a moment the facts around us and remain alone with our minds. Then, at our own pleasure and risk, we imagine a reality, we devise an imaginary reality which is our pure invention; then, while alone still with our intimate imaginings, we find what aspect, what visible figures, in brief, what facts

---

[14] Cf. Barthes, *Critique et vérité*, p. 58; M. Barbut, "Sur le mot et le concept de 'modèle,'" *Annales E.S.C.*, xvii (1963), 383-386; also Morris Halle, "In Defense of the Number Two," in *Studies Presented to Joshua Whatmough*, ed. E. Pulgram (The Hague, 1957), pp. 65-72; and Noam Chomsky, "Explanatory Models in Linguistics," in E. Nagel, P. Suppes, and A. Tarski (eds.), *Logic, Methodology and Philosophy of Science* (Stanford, 1962), pp. 528-550.

this imaginary reality would produce. At that point we emerge from our imaginary solitude, from our pure and isolated minds, and compare those facts which the reality imagined by us would produce with the facts which in effect surround us.)[15]

There are, of course, differences between the general mode of thought to which Ortega refers and the scientific use of descriptive models by Noam Chomsky or Claude Lévi-Strauss. Chomsky tests logical or mechanical analogues (in *Syntactic Structures*) for the complex process of language generation. In Lévi-Strauss the model signifies not so much the terms of the subject to be interpreted (or the output of a process) as the structural relations between these terms, and, as a result, not only a real but a potential subject.[16] To what extent such procedures have actually been used in periodization, or could be used, is a question that can only be posed here, though I would add that there seems to be much promise in Umberto Eco's study of models in terms of "transactional" psychology.[17]

The "system of literary norms, standards, and conventions"[18] that, according to René Wellek, is the core of a literary period, does not have to be isolated, then, only or exclusively by the direct contemplation of single works, followed by a cautious or laborious passage from the particular to the general. An alternate conception posits a number of generalities founded not only on facts but on hypotheses, i.e., on structures and assumptions deriving to a large degree from the observer. Corrections and connections are then made, in the opposite direction, between generalities and particular events. My point here is that no system of norms,

---

[15] *En torno a Galileo*, in *Obras completas*, v, 16.

[16] Cf., for example, Lévi-Strauss, *Le Totémisme aujourd'hui* (Paris, 1961), p. 23.

[17] Cf. U. Eco, "Modelli e strutture," *Il Verri*, no. 20 (1966), 11-28.

[18] Wellek and Warren, *Theory of Literature*, p. 265.

standards, or conventions is merely given to us. A complex of this kind proceeds from the questions that we choose to direct to the single works; from the theory of genres which we decide, either consciously or in routine fashion, to accept; from our attitude toward the appropriate poetics. Historians and philosophers of history normally recognize today that there is no such thing as a ready-made subject matter of history. It exists only insofar as the historians have selected it and shaped it for us. "Objectivity" in history is as much of a misnomer or *petitio principii* as "realism" in the novel (if one assumes in both cases an honest search for truth). The same certainly applies to the order of *literary* history (and perhaps also to poetics and certain general categories of criticism, our outstanding contemporary "model" being Northrop Frye's *Anatomy of Criticism*). At any rate, the isolation of a period must rely on the previous choice of pertinent criteria. It is only a *certain* set of criteria which makes it at all possible to distinguish between the Middle Ages and the Renaissance in the history of literature. As H.P.H. Teesing makes clear in his valuable book, the unity of a period is inseparable from that of the examples one has chosen to interpret.[19] Any periodization, while sufficiently "objective" or "real," is partial and does not preclude, as we shall see later, other principles of organization of historical time. In each case a certain objectivity resides in the coherence between the criteria initially chosen and the facts to which they are supposed to apply.

IV

A mere discussion of method has taken us fairly far afield. But the question of the relationship between periods and historical time must also be looked into. It might be useful, as a start, to turn back to the ideas of Bogumil Jasinowski in a

[19] Cf. H.P.H. Teesing, *Das Problem der Perioden in der Literaturgeschichte* (Groningen, 1948), Chap. 1.

suggestive article on the logical foundations of history published in 1937. In the Polish philosopher's view, periods are not entirely discrete entities. They do not exclude one another like objects existing simultaneously in space, or like the parts resulting from the division of a single entity. They are different moments in a temporal continuum: "Les époques consécutives ne s'excluent donc pas, comme s'excluent les membres d'une division en classes, car les unités périodologiques ne sont pas fondées sur la disjonction des caractères et ne relèvent pas du principe de contradiction dont toute la discrimination dans le domaine du discontinu (*entia discreta* d'une classification) reste inséparable."[20] It is not only because "transitions" occur between one period and another, as is often said, or because one gradually gives way to another for a limited interval, that periods cannot simply be placed side by side, or juxtaposed. Within the continuous flow of a culture, there are no islands, but only qualitative differences. For example, in the history of Spain, according to Américo Castro's interpretation, what is most important periodologically is the break between culture and culture at the time of the Islamic invasions of the eighth century, and on a certain level all subsequent periods overlap totally. Jasinowski's own example is Dante, whom he regards not only as the heir of Virgil and the climax of the Middle Ages, but as the beginning of the Renaissance. Huizinga once stressed the fact that medieval culture runs into, or beneath, the Reformation of the sixteenth century, and even recommended that the Middle Ages and the Renaissance be considered not only as severed by a vertical line but as flowing horizontally together.[21]

[20] B. Jasinowski, "Sur les fondements logiques de l'histoire," in *Travaux du IXe Congrès International de Philosophie* (Paris, 1937), p. 44.
[21] Cf. "Het probleem der Renaissance," in *Verzamelde Werken*, IV, 257: "Liep ónder de Renaissance de middeleeuwsche cultuur inderdaad

Periods do happen *after* one another—but the meaning of "after" is not fixed. How much diversity does temporal succession imply? Do we tend to visualize it spatially, as a separation, a complete break? If "after" connotes difference, it denotes above all succession and perhaps even *continuity*. The question with regard to Jasinowski's view, then, is whether a period can adapt itself to the trajectory of time as intimately as such a view assumes. In other words, the distinction between an absolute and a relative periodization is not simply a matter of logical stress—as if, for example, we were saying: when we focus on the dominant features of a period, differences tend to come out sharply; but if, on the other hand, we stress dialectics, and keep in mind the "dominated" traits, which are likely to recur in another period, we tend to obtain a mixture of differences and similarities. Jasinowski's basic concern, essentially, was with *temporal* (as against merely spatial) typologies, and with their peculiar nature. Our own concern should be with the extent to which periods are supposed to reflect becoming or to parallel the course of time. To understand the degree of their diachrony, to measure their proximity to time, is to be in a position to know what "after" and "before" mean in this area of discourse. In fact, every period-concept gives away something, loses something, on the level of diachrony, but the degree of the loss in each case is important.

In the last chapter of *La Pensée sauvage*, Claude Lévi-Strauss brings up the same question, that is to say, the distinction between time as continuity and time as succession of discontinuous parts, in the following terms: "le codage chronologique dissimule une nature beaucoup plus complexe qu'on ne l'imagine, quand on conçoit les dates de l'histoire sous la

---

door in de Hervorming, dan was de grenslijn tusschen Middeleeuwen en Renaissance niet alleen verticaal te trekken, maar nog horizontal bovendien"; and in *Wege der Kulturgeschichte*, p. 119.

forme d'une simple série linéaire. En premier lieu, une date dénote un *moment* dans une succession: *d2* est après *d1*, avant *d3*; de ce point de vue, la date fait seulement fonction de nombre ordinal. Mais chaque date est aussi un nombre cardinal, et, en tant que tel, exprime une *distance* par rapport aux dates les plus voisines.''[22] The problem is whether history can recapture the process of change in men and societies—whether it is able to render or reflect *becoming* so genuinely, so entirely "from within," that it offers a particularly intimate and faithful knowledge of human existence.

But Lévi-Strauss points out, time is one thing, and chronology, which is a "code," a conventional system, a patterned approach to time, is another. All historical narrative is anchored in chronology, in the quantified system. Chronology is composed of a number of classes, each instance of which refers basically to another member of the *same* class: 1685 has meaning with regard only to 1610, 1648, 1715, and other members of this particular class; the same applies to the class seventeenth century, second century, etc.; or to the class January 18, September 24, and so forth. Thus, the vaunted reconstitution of becoming takes the form not of an uninterrupted and homogeneous series but of a constant leap from one order to another:

"Il n'est donc pas seulement illusoire, mais contradictoire, de concevoir le devenir historique comme un déroulement continu, commençant par une préhistoire codée en dizaines ou en centaines de millénaires, se poursuivant a l'échelle des millénaires à partir du 4e ou du 3e, et continuant ensuite sous la forme d'une histoire séculaire entrelardée, au gré de chaque auteur, de tranches d'histoire annuelle au sein du siècle, ou journalière au sein de l'année, sinon même horaire au sein d'une journée. Toutes ces dates ne forment pas une série: elles relèvent d'espèces différentes. . . Les événements

---

[22] *La Pensée sauvage*, p. 342.

qui sont significatifs pour un code ne le restent pas pour un autre. Codés dans le système de la préhistoire, les épisodes les plus fameux de l'histoire moderne et contemporaine cessent d'être pertinents; sauf peut-être (et encore, nous n'en savons rien) certains aspects massifs de l'évolution démographique envisagée à l'échelle du globe, l'invention de la machine à vapeur, celle de l'électricité et celle de l'énergie nucléaire."[23]

My comment on these words will be twofold. They lead us, in the first place, to visualize more clearly the distance existing between periods and the flow of events to which they refer. It is obvious that periods do not compose a class of chronology (though the frequent need to equate them with centuries—particularly in Italy—indicates a tendency to confuse them with chronological classes), not only because they can span a century, or three centuries, or thirty years, or a millennium, and therefore would not, according to Lévi-Strauss, make sense as chronology vis-à-vis one another, but because they do not respond to quantification at all. A system of periodization is a criticism of becoming. It attempts to make time intelligible or meaningful by creating an order, a parallel level, that is more or less removed from temporality itself. As I suggested earlier, it acts like a series of temporal "models." The historical presentation of events in their detailed trajectory (*histoire événementielle*) alludes to chronology as to a fundamental framework for narrative. In this sense, it is twice removed from time. The concept of a given period, thrice removed, looks back to both chronology and the tale of events in order to work out its own structural goals. We should therefore expect periods most often to form a series of discontinuous parts, as separate from one another as cardinal numbers are. Periods, existing somewhere between the order of chronology and that of an atemporal

[23] *Ibid.*, p. 344.

typology, between diachrony and synchrony, are thus a good example of "le caractère discontinu et classificatoire de la connaissance historique,"[24] though only more so than the chronological classes of which Lévi-Strauss was speaking.

It seems to me, secondly, that Lévi-Strauss has underestimated on this occasion the functional advantages of that very leap from one class of chronology to another which is so characteristic of historical writing; and the extent to which this reflects a human being's experience of historical time. One need only imagine such leaps (or indeed read the admirable paragraph Lévi-Strauss writes about them) to see how near they come to that flow of becoming, intimately reconstituted from within, which *La Pensée sauvage* was willing to concede to history. And why is this so? The obvious must first be reiterated: history is necessarily selective and constructive. That it must surrender a certain portion of the topic, of its concrete abundance, in order to become intelligible, is a predicament on which the historical disciplines have no monopoly. Lévi-Strauss knows full well that after a social scientist's subject has been analyzed in its individual richness, a second step forces him to move away and measure the distance between his subject and the intellectual means that he has at his disposal (cf. *La Pensée sauvage*, pp. 334-335). This being granted, one can only admire the extraordinary wealth and complexity of chronology as an approach to time, on the one hand, and on the other, the appropriateness of switching from one level of chronology to another—say, from brief sections of time like hours to huge expanses like millennia— while being forced to *speak* of only one class at once.

Although it is certainly true that, as Lévi-Strauss explains, a century followed by an hour and a week does not compose a series, it is also reasonable to presume that none of the series to which each belongs is ever "interrupted," that is,

---

[24] *Ibid.*, p. 345.

that these codes or structures are such that they are potentially available at any moment: the levels of the weeks, of the days, of the centuries, *can* go on, *can* flow by, simultaneously, whenever we choose to imagine them jointly; and it is only a matter of intellectual montage that persuades us to refer *explicitly* to one and then to another. In fact, though one level of chronology may be uppermost in our conscious mind at a given moment, we are also dimly aware of the others and constantly led to reshuffle this tacit hierarchy of chronological classes. It is as if there were not simply *one* flow of time to which *various* classes of chronology refer, but a multiplicity of both code and coded subject, signifying and signified. What is reflected so well by the richness, the variety, even the contradictions or the absurdity of chronology is precisely the diversity and the multivalence of time as experienced by persons and groups. And I think this is important for periodization from the point of view of diachrony and historical becoming.

Personally speaking, and with only a slight measure of exaggeration, I realize as I write these lines that I can experience this moment in my life, after an effort of consciousness, as embracing simultaneously, or participating in, various levels of chronology and history. I can recognize the late hour of the day, the heat and the last phases of summer, the start of a new week, the imminence of a new academic year, as distinct of course from a calendar year or a fiscal year, the proximity of a birthday, or of middle age, or (in a more collective and periodological sense) a period of accelerated social change, another of political stagnation, the continuation of an old tradition of nationalism, the persistence of so many different institutions (born in a number of historical epochs), or even the survival of such ancient institutionalized crimes as capital punishment (can *l'âge des lumières* be simply a thing of the past?), a certain rhythm in the process of contemporary music, reminiscent of that in the plastic arts thirty years ago, another rhythm in painting and poetry, and still another in sculpture; as well as the technological age stressed by Lévi-Strauss in the quotation above, going back to the industrial revolution, yet constantly starting anew, and the dawn of that electronic or "tactile" era of which Marshall McLuhan is the prophet. I can imagine that a day could come in certain countries, a day of extreme political convulsion, during which one might witness within a few hours the end of a historical millennium. (We know that a revolution can be regarded as the fruit of an extended process.) In other words, chronological classes and historical periods mingle, touch, or overlap in one's most immediate awareness of change. Their variety renders faithfully the multiplicity of temporal processes which surround the lives of men and societies, and which historians are called upon to recapture. And there is nothing a posteriori about Jasinowski's remark that Dante (though this could not have been Dante's vocabulary) was the heir of Virgil, the beginning of the Renaissance, and the culmination of the Middle Ages.

V

What I have just described is merely a single person's sense of participation and involvement in the cluster of "durations" of which his time is made. I should acknowledge at this point my debt (in this and in other essays) to one of Fernand Braudel's fundamental contributions, namely the distinction between *courtes durées* and *longues durées*. (These are also named *temps brefs* and *temps longs*; yet *durée*, not in the Bergsonian but in the traditional sense, is the more informative term: how something lasts, *endures*, before it ceases to exist.) The historiography of the school of Braudel involves the interplay of a number of durations and, it seems to me, a recognition of "the multiplicity of time." (Gaston Bachelard had written earlier on "la dialectique de la durée," and the sociologist Georges Gurvitch on "la multiplicité des temps sociaux." Do men exist in a single, unitary process of time any more than they do in a homogeneous Newtonian space?) Brief durations, extended durations, as well as a number of intermediate processes, occur or "flow" together within the limits of a unit of chronology. At one end, there is the *courte durée* of so-called "events" ("histoire événementielle"), particularly those that are of interest to the political or the military historian. At the opposite end, there are the *longues durées* of, especially, social and axiological history—the near-permanence of certain social structures and systems of values through the centuries. Now, it seems clear that literary history portrays a great deal more than a succession of short-lived events. The first performance (like any performance) of *Hamlet* may have been a *courte durée*: its persistent appeal to the imagination of spectators, readers, and critics is, for the historian, a *longue durée*. A poetic school (gathering a number of individual writers around a teacher and a norm), an academy, an avant-garde movement, may also be "brief durations." As for rhetorical devices, systems of genres, recurrent themes or types, extensive though their life-span is, their status is not metatemporal. I think it is very useful to consider them, as Braudel and Erich Hassinger have suggested, and Ernst Robert Curtius has shown in historical practice, as characteristic "long durations."[25]

It is in the context of historical "becoming" (considered not as the contrary of "being" but as one of its forms) and the multiplicity of time that the problem of periodization, as well as the dialectics of "period" and "current," takes on full force.

[25] Cf. Fernand Braudel, "Histoire et Sciences sociales: La longue durée," *Annales E.S.C.*, xiii (July-Dec. 1958), 725-753; "Qu'est-ce que le XVIe siècle?"; and E. Hassinger, "Die Weltgeschichtliche Stellung des 16. Jahrhunderts," *Geschichte in Wissenschaft und Unterricht*, ii (1951), 708.

Before turning to the notion of current, I will add a few more comments and examples with regard to periodization.

One of the more familiar facts of periodization is the "international time-lag." The Renaissance did not reach country A quite at the same time it did country B, and so forth. The splendid synchrony of the many Baroque churches, palaces, fountains, and monuments that brighten the cities of the West from South America to Eastern Europe, for instance, must be painstakingly restored by scholars to the slow temporal process of growth and propagation, conflict and ascendancy through which history comes to life. In his *Baroque et Classicisme* (1957), Victor L. Tapié retraces the stages of this development in the plastic arts, from the origins in Italy to the Rome of Maderna, Borromini, and Bernini; from Longhena in Venice, later in the seventeenth century, to Fischer von Erlach and the countries of the Danube, culminating in Prague and spreading as far as orthodox Russia; from the triumph of the *retablo* or altarpiece (moving out to become the façade of the church) in Salamanca or Seville to the full flowering of the Iberian Baroque in Mexico, Ecuador, Peru, and Brazil. Tapié praises highly the architectural and sculptural works of the last of the great Baroque artists, António Francisco Lisboa, called Aleijadinho, who carved the twelve prophets below the church of Bom Jesus de Matozinhos in Brazil. Aleijadinho died in 1814—some thirteen years after Novalis.

These temporal *décalages* from one country to another are obvious enough; but what is more important is their existence within the boundaries of a single culture. Tapié shows how sixteenth-century French art admitted both the Italianate Renaissance styles of the court of François I and the medieval flamboyant style which had survived in the provinces or in the hands of *craftsmen*: not merely the passage of time but the collaboration of workers, masons, image-makers whose cultural and social origins did not coincide with the architect's explains the encounter of several styles in so many significant buildings. (Does this occur in other works of art? Should we recognize more often the simultaneous presence of different styles—in the normative, collective sense—in individual plays or novels? May this not apply to a Cervantes, a James Joyce, a Dante?) The altarpieces of the French seventeenth century brought together or blended Flemish practices, Renaissance forms from Fontainebleau, twisted columns and other new shapes borrowed not directly from Italy but from the etchings available in contemporary treatises on domestic architecture. As Tapié indicates, for example, with respect to Czechoslovakia in the same period— ravaged by the Thirty Years' War, limited in rural districts to two classes, the nobles and the peasants—the visual, sumptuous consolations of the Baroque were accepted fervently by the poor in strictly hierarchical societies where ecclesiastical rituals played a central role. The career of the Baroque, in any case, cannot be severed from the dialectics of the city and the countryside, the nobility and the bourgeoisie, the planners and the craftsmen.

These dialectics, oddly enough, are often overlooked by Marxist critics (who are furious periodizers). The virtue of the approach of which Tapié's book is an example, it seems to me, is a special proximity to the diachronic texture of history, made possible by a constant awareness of conflict and confrontation; this is what I call, in the temporal terms of this essay, the "multiplicity of time." Now, one of the crucial and most persuasive tenets of Marxism is the idea that "it is not man's consciousness which determines his being but, on the contrary, his social being [or existence] which determines his consciousness" (Preface to the *Contribution to the Critique of Political Economy* [1859]). Let us take a hypothetical case: a German poet of lower middle-class origin, living in a small provincial town toward the middle of the nineteenth century. Let us suppose also that (in keeping with our historical "dialectique de la durée") the conditions of industrial revolution, in the hands of the prevailing bourgeoisie, have not yet reached the poet's immediate surroundings: the economic production of the town is still limited to that of small craftsmen, pursuing their individual labors. Were we interested today in discovering the sources of the poet's "consciousness," would we not trace it back to his concrete "existence"? If our poet moved or went on to study in another town, or in a large city, thereby encountering the general circumstances of capitalism, as well as the intermediate phases of manufacturing, would we not record the contrasts experienced by the poet as he passed from one process to another, i.e., not just the "contradictions of capitalism" but the contradictions between capitalism and noncapitalism or precapitalism? Nevertheless, György Lukács, in more than one essay on Schiller, ascribes the thinking of the great poet and theorist, born not in the middle of the nineteenth century but in 1759, to an unqualified periodological condition: *the division of labor* (responsible for Schiller's insight into the divisions and lacerations of modern man, etc.). The poet's personal experiences, his individual life as distinct from that of some of his contemporaries, are not considered. At no point does Lukács derive Schiller's consciousness from his "concrete existence" (or from that of his class). (See Lukács' *Beiträge zur Geschichte der Aesthetik* [1954].) If anything, the work of Marxist critics should be reproached for not introducing *enough* economic facts of pertinence to the topic under consideration. One is startled by this profound vacillation between an avowed concern with "hard" historical developments and the submission of all particulars to secondhand concepts, ready-made labels, stale aprioristic schemes. Hence the strange abstractionism, the air of unreality, with which the efforts of Marxist literary critics are often surrounded.

These are of course problems that would require, as a foundation for further study, a historical and practical survey of past schemes of periodization, and of how these schemes differ from one national literature to another. I will only offer a sketch, in closing this section, of two limit-concepts, two poles, toward which most systems of periodization are likely to tend.

At one end, the emphasis is on discontinuous structures. These structures of norms and values are static enough to be comparable to "dwelling places" (Américo Castro's *moradas vitales*) in history. The historian "settles" his imagination in a portion of the past, after having traversed time backwards, as it were, and moved into a period where, as in a safe haven, time no longer flows visibly. Intervals, smaller units, contradictions are overlooked. At this pole, the sense of "before" and "after" as qualitative distinctions is very strong. Basically, by singling out the predominant traits of a period, we subsume change and underemphasize continuity. Time is used as the condition or the support for a certain kind of otherness, and the period emerges from it in order to gain full significance. In other words, though this form of periodization, like any other, seeks an organization of historical time, it does so by providing us with eternal "presents" in the past. Highly structured and intelligible in terms of values, these periods, from our point of view, are instances of pseudodiachrony (as they do not render processes of becoming) and of pseudosynchrony (insofar as they cover many years at once and do not really intersect time). They reflect the antinomies of chronology of which Lévi-Strauss wrote: "pour autant que l'histoire aspire à la signification, elle se condamne à choisir des régions, des époques, des groupes d'hommes et des individus dans ces groupes, et à les faire ressortir, comme des figures discontinues, sur un continu tout juste bon à servir de toile de fond."[26]

The outstanding and most influential example of period

[26] Lévi-Strauss, *La Pensée sauvage*, p. 341.

as axiological cosmos is probably Jakob Burckhardt's idea of the Renaissance. While Michelet, and other predecessors, had associated the Renaissance with the Enlightenment and the concept of progress, with emphasis on dynamic development, Burckhardt would isolate it and view it as a cultural ideal *sui generis*. But the purest examples of static periodization can be found in *Geistesgeschichte*, whose roots are a romantic belief in the homogeneous spirit of ages and a love of local color in time, which are like a synchronic counterpart of the diachronic myth of national character. Concerning this pole or limit-concept, finally, I should like to touch upon two topics that might be worthy of further consideration. One is a Marxist comment, taking into account the prevalence of periodization in the nineteenth century and the thought of Marx in such writings as the postscript to the second edition of *Das Kapital*:[27] periods, one might say, domesticate historical change and insert revolutions into a reassuring pattern; the dialectical stress on history as ceaseless change through negation frightens the bourgeois class and threatens the stability which they wish for themselves and which they also value in the life of past epochs. Secondly, I have not discussed the ways in which a system of periodization can *assume* a theory of history: either explicitly—whenever the concept of history as coherent development domi-

---

[27] Cf. Karl Marx and Friedrich Engels, *Werke* (Berlin, 1962), XXIII, 27: "In ihrer rationellen Gestalt ist sie [die Dialektik] dem Bürgertum und seinen doktrinären Wortführern ein Aergernis und ein Greuel, weil sie in dem positiven Verständnis des Bestehenden zugleich auch das Verständnis seiner Negation, seines notwendigen Untergangs einschliesst, jede gewordne Form im Flusse der Bewegung, also auch nach ihrer vergänglichen Seite auffasst, sie durch nichts imponieren lässt, ihrem Wesen nach kritisch und revolutionär ist." Cf. F. Martini, *Deutsche Literatur im bürgerlichen Realismus, 1848-1898* (Stuttgart, 1962), p. 15: "Das bürgerliche Bewusstsein . . . suchte, gegenüber der bewegten Zeitlichkeit des Lebens und seinen Veränderungen, das Humane als etwas Zeitloses zu bewahren."

nates[28]—or unconsciously. This is a dimension that would require a historical survey of our subject. But a minimal form of such a philosophy might be this: the meaning of a period justifies those components that otherwise might offer some resistance to design; each part, each detail of a period "spreads out" and rejoins the meaning of the whole; a single event, such as a literary movement, could appear *contingent* or accidental alone and by itself; but if it falls within the bounds of a period, it did not simply happen, but has its place in a larger pattern; even when a periodized history pretends to delay an explanation, it offers a constant vindication of itself.

At the opposite end of the polarity, a dynamic periodology is often found among reformers and liberal personalities, such as Georg Brandes, whom I will discuss presently, and generally in the twentieth century, so conscious of its own experience of accelerated change. Yet Francesco De Sanctis wrote during the nineteenth century a history of a national literature that is hailed by all today as the masterpiece of the genre, and which sought to recreate the development of literature without any serious reliance on a conventional scheme of literary epochs: "al nostro scopo," in his own words, "è più utile seguire il cammino del pensiero e della forma nel suo sviluppo, senza violare le grandi divisioni cronologiche, ma senza cercare una precisione di date che ci farebbe sciupare il tempo in conietture e supposizioni di poco interesse" (for our own purposes, it is most useful to follow the course of thought and of form in its development, without violating the great chronological divisions, but without seeking, either, a precision in dating which would fritter away our time on conjectures and suppositions of little interest).[29] Turning to recent years, I will mention two studies

[28] Cf. E. Cione, *Dal De Sanctis al Novecento* (Milan, 1945), Chap. 8: "Il periodizzamento storico ed i concetti funzionali."

[29] F. De Sanctis, *Storia della letteratura italiana*, ed. Benedetto Croce (Bari, 1939), I, 107. Cf. also G. Getto, *Storia delle storie letterarie*

in which periods are presented and understood through a constant preoccupation with duration and change. In 1957 Michael Seidlmayer published *Weltbild und Kultur Deutschlands im Mittelalter*, which contradicts the idea of the medieval period as the most unanimous and homogeneous in the history of Europe. Seidlmayer, instead, portrays a restless and vital world, charged with tensions and energies. The "unity" of the Middle Ages was not simply destroyed by conflicting forces after a certain date. It was always questionable. Underlying stresses, strains, and contradictions—between empire and papacy, between monasticism and the secular spirit in education or in the knightly life—were at work as early as the ninth century.[30] The slow emancipation of earthly attributes from a clerical design is compared by Seidlmayer to a mighty process of breathing in and breathing out, where the breathing organ was the religious system. With these tensions in mind, he is able to distinguish between four subperiods, all dynamically defined.[31]

My second example deals with an epoch, the second half of the nineteenth century, where the unorthodox, the deviant, the individual are expected to play a central role. In an admirable history, *Deutsche Literatur im bürgerlichen Realismus, 1848-1898* (1962), Fritz Martini refuses to impose an artificial unity, either stylistically or historically, on a period characterized by a sense of crisis. During those years of change and inquiry, German literature presented a series of different "strata" (*Schichten*). Although the concept of "bourgeois realism" is used as an organizing principle, Mar-

---

(Milan, 1942), p. 32: "Il De Sanctis rifugge in effetti da ogni catalogazione di epoche definite, e tenta invece di rendere dinamica la storia letteraria segnando, più che le divisioni, i passaggi."

[30] Cf. M. Seidlmayer, *Weltbild und Kultur Deutschlands im Mittelalter* (Darmstadt, 1957), p. 12. (An English translation can be found in the series "Studies in Medieval History," edited by G. Barraclough.)

[31] Cf. *ibid.*, p. 19.

tini does not claim that it is a period style, a diffuse aesthetic presence; for the decades he proposes to study, he writes, made room above all for antinomies, original temperaments, and "centrifugal tendencies."[32] The problem is not one of logic but of critical pertinence and tact. The capacity to "see" one's own time was a gift certain German authors of "bourgeois realism" had in common with Flaubert, but also with Marx and Nietzsche, their contemporaries. The best work of the narrators in the group, from Stifter to Meyer, disclosed consistently the nineteenth-century writer's ability to challenge both social and artistic conventions, and to draw strength from a solitary, relentless dialogue with the epoch in which he lived.

In addition to these internal dialectics of periodization, I will now glance at the broader polarity with the notion of "current," of which Georg Brandes was the most spontaneous and forceful proponent.

V I

"The course of history can be likened to the flow of a great stream as it runs down to the ocean. There are places where the swift current will break its force against hidden rocks. When the winter snows have melted, the river may burst its dikes and flood the countryside. During the summer drought the flow can be sluggish and great sand bars will appear above the surface. But also over long distances the river will flow peacefully and majestically toward an unknown sea."[33]

The words are familiar, the simile has endless possibilities, and the passage appears in a book called *Historical Change*. Jorge Luis Borges holds that though metaphors are potentially infinite, only a few have shown that they are enduringly significant, like the pairing of dreams and death, stars and

---

[32] Cf. Martini, *Deutsche Literatur*, pp. 4, 13, and 3.
[33] Lewis Einstein, *Historical Change* (Cambridge, Mass., 1946), p. 6.

eyes, women and flowers, old age and the setting of the sun, time and water.[34] Time and water, time and the river have alluded together to the destinies of individual men, but also (Heraclitus spoke for all philosophers, and the death of Jorge Manrique's father for the death of all fathers) to the eternity, the faith, or the mutability of all men. In a collective way also, the metaphor, fatally enough, was called on to qualify history during the history-conscious nineteenth century, and to assume many forms. That of "current" has been frequent in literary history. We have already seen, in an earlier quotation, that Jean Rousset used it in the midst of a discussion of the Baroque period ("si le principe baroque est le plus actif, occupant dans l'époque une position centrale, il y a toutes sortes de courants parallèles ou latéraux . . ."), and this compensating function is rather characteristic of the term. In a brief essay on Romanticism, Benedetto Croce speaks of *correnti* in a similar frame of mind:

"Ma poiché 'romanticismo' non è semplice equivalente della partizione cronologica 'prima metà del secolo decimonono,' né della partizione etnica 'civiltà germanica,' tanto vero che in quello stesso limite di tempo e in quello stesso limite nazionale si distinguono correnti romantiche e correnti non romantiche, correnti dominanti e correnti d'opposizione, e si parla di un romanticismo francese e di uno italiano, e anche di un preromanticismo e di un protoromanticismo;—giova determinare quali fatti e quali disposizioni spirituali si richiamino o si dovrebbero richiamare alla memoria con quella parola."

(But since "Romanticism" is not a simple equivalent of the chronological partition "first half of the nineteenth century,"

---

[34] Cf. J. L. Borges, "La metáfora," in *Historia de la eternidad*, 4th edn. (Buenos Aires, 1966), p. 71. The point is made by Borges often, also in fictional form: cf. "La busca de Averroes," in *El Aleph*, 6th edn. (Buenos Aires, 1966), p. 98.

nor of the ethnic partition "Germanic civilization," particularly when we notice that people distinguish, within that same limit of time and within those same national limits, between Romantic currents and non-Romantic currents, dominating currents and opposing currents, and people speak of a French Romanticism and an Italian one, and also of a pre-Romanticism and a proto-Romanticism;—it is useful to determine what facts and what spiritual dispositions should be brought to mind by means of that word.)[35]

Usually the metaphor, though it may have completely "faded," is rather complex, and can be subdivided into "undercurrents," "crosscurrents," and so forth. Some argue, we read in Lewis Einstein, that historical change is caused by the clash of opposites or "crosscurrents."[36] Musing on a splendid landscape, Brandes explored the literal level of the term in a description of the southern end of Lake Geneva: "The spot is one of the loveliest in the world. Pass the island and cross another bridge and you see the Rhone rush, impetuous and foaming white, out of the lake. A few steps further and you can see its white stream joined by the grey slow waters of the Arve. The rivers flow side by side, each retaining its colour."[37] In contrast with such combinations and clashes, or because of them, others prefer to single out "main currents," "major currents," and the like. One recalls that currents and rivers have a direction—or a goal, or even a purpose—and that one of the meanings for "current" in the *Oxford English Dictionary* is "course of progress in a definite direction: tendency, tenor, drift (of opinions, writings,

---

[35] B. Croce, "Le definizioni del Romanticismo" (1906), in *Problemi di estetica*, 5th edn. (Bari, 1954), p. 293.

[36] Einstein, *Historical Change*, p. 3.

[37] G. Brandes, *Main Currents in Nineteenth Century Literature* (London and New York, 1906), I, 17. On the notion of literary current as a "vital," "intuitive," or "unconscious" trend, see Renato Poggioli, *Teoria dell'arte d'avanguardia* (Bologna, 1962), p. 32.

etc.)."[38] Thus, Marcel Raymond, writing about the period of French poetry that was to be the subject of *De Baudelaire au Surréalisme,* could state: "il est nécessaire de considérer les choses dans leur durée, et en profondeur, pour apercevoir le courant majeur qui anime la poésie, l'idée qui s'incarne en elle, souvent à l'insu des poètes, et qui commande son développement"; even as Cleanth Brooks, a comparable critic of the modern poetic tradition, would offer this comment on one of the meanings of the word: "we can speak of *the* tradition, whereby we mean the essential line of development coming to us out of the past, the main current as distinguished from the accidental or the peripheral."[39]

T. S. Eliot, in "Tradition and the Individual Talent," stressed at one point that he did not really have in mind "the whole of the literature of Europe from Homer," but, rather, only what (most untraditionally) *he* thought was the best in it: "the poet must be very conscious," he wrote, "of the main current, which does not at all flow invariably through the most distinguished reputations."[40] It would subsequently become possible to speak of "traditions" as if they were "main currents," and vice versa. One could also use the term, of course, to depreciate time. A tradition thus *may* signify a main current to which a very real value is attached; and it is interesting to note in passing the dogmatism that lurks in diachrony as it does in synchrony. An emphasis on historical becoming does not by any means imply an absence of belief.

[38] *The Oxford English Dictionary* (1961 edn.), II, 1270. An example is given from Locke, *Toleration* (1692): "in your first paper, as the whole current of it would make one believe. . . ."
[39] M. Raymond, "Les étapes récentes de la poésie française" [Second International Congress of Literary History, Amsterdam, 1935], *Bulletin of the International Committee of Historical Sciences,* IX (1937), 385; C. Brooks, "Tradition," in *Dictionary of Literature,* ed. J. Shipley (New York, 1953), p. 418.
[40] T. S. Eliot, "Tradition and the Individual Talent" (1917), in *Selected Essays, 1917-1932* (New York, 1932), p. 5.

Traditions isolate continuities and unify the timeless in time, as periods do within the limits of a section of history. For period-concepts are historical in a way traditions are not. Tradition connotes history, but does not denote it. Traditionalists (like some aristocrats) would rather praise than investigate the past. Or to make my point more clearly: whenever I speak of the "tradition of X," I formulate my awareness not exactly *of* a historical continuity, but, rather, of the mere *fact that it exists*. I color the present with a legitimacy rooted in the past. Thus, literary traditions are oriented to the present and to synchrony. They are only vaguely, or sentimentally, historical.

Because the notion of "main currents" is selective, it lends itself to the abuses of ideologists such as V. L. Parrington in his *Main Currents in American Thought* (1927-1930), whose principal concern was political, sociological, extraliterary. These are the pitfalls, to which I shall return later, of a metaphor that is commodious indeed: it suggests continuity; change, too, or increase; and, within such change, the clashes of different elements, the rhythm of diminution and growth. It also implies, very easily, development, evolution, plan. My purpose here, however, is to discuss a term that has been advantageous in the past, mainly because it filled a void in the restricted vocabulary of literary history.

The notion of literary currents is frankly diachronic, dynamic, open-ended, and suggestive of relations with historical and social developments. I need not dwell on its diachronic aspect. I have already mentioned, apropos of a very similar kind of period, that this quality is often associated with the image of history in the making, of the evolution of society, by means of an understanding, as in Ortega and Francastel, of contradictions, alternatives, confrontations. This coloring is present even in as old-fashioned a book as Frederick E. Pierce's *Currents and Eddies in the English Romantic*

Generation (1918).[41] Clearly what matters is the plural, "currents," and the image of their simultaneous process, their coexistence in time, within a single section of history, a single period. Finally, there is the aspect I have termed "dynamic." I have in mind those historians who call forth a picture of the vitality of man, of his capacity for creation and progress. For them, the diachrony of "currents"—or of kindred terms—is complemented by an awareness of the continuity of man's artistic and intellectual achievement. Writing simply as a humanist and a literary historian, Wladyslaw Folkierski once complained that literary periods were unpersuasive abstractions and that it would be preferable to develop different concepts that might be more amenable to the flow of cultural history:

"Laissons à nouveau couler le flot ininterrompu de la vitalité europénne depuis l'Occitanie jusqu'à Pétrarque et Desportes, depuis Arnaut Daniel jusqu'a Marini, depuis Joachim de Flore jusqu'aux rêves millénaires de certains illuminés du XVIIe et du XVIIIe siècles . . . Il est à présumer, dès maintenant, que de la sorte on n'aboutirait guère à des coupures brusques qui veulent arrêter sur une année ou même sur un quart de siècle tel mouvement puissant, tel flot de la pensée européenne, mais que bien plutôt on arriverait à noter la courbe d'une vague plus ou moins rythmée avec ses flux et ses reflux, ses hauts et ses bas."[42]

---

[41] Published in New Haven in 1918. Pierce describes the different literary camps, the cleavages, the polemics, the interplay of various movements, i.e., the picture from the point of view of the original readers of Romantic and non-Romantic poetry. He writes about "the Eddy around Bristol," the "Spanish Current" (Southey, Landor, Byron, Mrs. Felicia Hemans), the relationship between the different social strata of the reading public and the literature that was available to them (Chap. 2, p. 93 and *passim*).

[42] W. Folkierski, "Renaissance et Romantisme ou les sables mouvants dans l'histoire littéraire" [Second International Congress of Literary

VII

It is difficult to speak fairly of Georg Brandes. Though some may have overrated him as a literary critic, others have underestimated him as a literary historian. The history of criticism and the theory of history can be, of course, melancholy disciplines unless one approaches the critics and historians of the past with some of the sympathy we willingly grant poets and novelists when we begin to read them. The practical judgments of these critics will seem today, more often than not, obsolete and mistaken, but there are three other aspects of their achievement one cannot neglect: their quality as writers; the nature of their method; and their ability as historians, that is to say, as builders of large compositions. In the case of Brandes, even for those readers who have no Danish, the lucid, burning intensity of his writing is such (I am told) that it tolerates translation. The point of view, particularly in the *Main Currents in Nineteenth-Century Literature*, is that of the liberal reformer and believer in scientific progress—a position common enough in the nineteenth century, or even in our own. In Italy, for example, one recalls the histories of Italian literature by P. Emiliani-Giudici (1844) and Luigi Settembrini (1866-1872), with their emphasis on the old battle between Guelphs and Ghibellines.[43] Among historians, a Michelet in France or a Lelewel in Poland, and of course many others, are not often reproached for defending the idea of progress or the concept of freedom. Yet on the part of Brandes this is sometimes considered naïve or obnoxious. Finally, his *Main Currents*, and some of the later books as well, evidence a vigorous capacity for historical construction—our principal interest here. We must grant Brandes, writes René Wellek, "an original, effer-

---

History, Amsterdam, 1935], *Bulletin of the International Committee of Historical Sciences*, ix (1937), 333 and 332.

[43] Cf. Getto, *Storia delle storie letterarie*, pp. 233, 290, and *passim*.

vescent sensibility, an insight into psychology, and a power of marshaling currents or movements, which, as he knew very well, is an art."[44]

Professor Wellek explains that Brandes, in the six-volume work originally entitled *Hovedstrømninger i det 19de Aarhundredes Literatur* (1872-1890), is actually writing a history of "national minds" in the romantic sense.[45] This is certainly an important part of his achievement. Brandes himself promises his readers, in starting, a history of the "psychology" or the "soul" of Europe during the first half of the nineteenth century. In fact he presents us with an eclectic combination of approaches. He doubtless enjoys formulating his ideas on national character, particularly in the fourth volume on England and Ireland. In the same volume, too, he stresses more than once the notion of period. Just as often, however, Brandes singles out international Romantic themes, like childhood, incest, or suicide, or a particular idea of poetry, or an international "current" like the revival of the ballad after Bürger and Sir Walter Scott.[46] His real gift, as René Wellek also points out, may be for portraiture, à la Sainte-Beuve, and there are numerous chapters in which writers like Friedrich Schlegel are treated biographically. Brandes is even capable of textual commentary, as in the pages on Heine and, particularly, the *bravura* passage on the translations of Shakespeare by August Wilhelm Schlegel, which he studies genetically.[47] Nevertheless, given such variety, what holds the entire work together is the image of literature in the making, of work in progress—the whole powerful stream of events that imparts a common impulse and movement to all instants

[44] René Wellek, *A History of Modern Criticism: 1750-1950* (New Haven and London, 1965), IV, 368. Chap. 16 is devoted to Brandes.

[45] Cf. *ibid.*, p. 358.

[46] Cf. Brandes, *Main Currents*, IV, Chap. 2 (also, I, 135, or II, Chap. 8); IV, Chap. 1; and IV, pp. 3ff.

[47] Cf. *ibid.*, II, Chap. 3.

and components in the narrative. That Brandes is actually dealing with *events* and telling a story, is corroborated by the fluency of his pure narrative writing, as in the sequence on the Irish rebellions against English rule.[48]

The "currents," then, are made up mostly of single portraits and critical pieces, and of the unifying effect of a mighty historical élan. The subject is the period of 1800-1848, but Brandes perceives it dynamically as a great movement—essentially, as a passage from the constructive forces of the Enlightenment, through the French Revolution, the decades of reaction, the setbacks of 1848, to the synthesis of liberalism and scientific creativity in the second half of the century. His strategy is the study of a succession of representative writers. By treating one writer at a time, as exemplified usually by a single book, which often emerges as a type (for instance, *Adolphe, Obermann, Werther, Lucinde*), he is able to stress the linear nature of the currents at hand. It is not an exhaustive but a highly selective history (he limits himself to France, England, and Germany, with the addition of frequent digressions on Denmark but with few references to Italy, Russia, or Spain), though so wide-ranging that the total effect is that of a great flow along a few fundamental lines.[49]

Fortunately, though Brandes' currents may augur an identical goal in the future, they can, at any moment in the narrative, confront each other and clash. This is made possible by the dialectics of progress and reaction. Brandes' individual analyses are often surprising and far from one-sided, not because a doctrinaire mind is being tempered by tact, but because his interest in the dynamics of history elicits the contradictions of the past. The principal paradox is that the nineteenth century had upset the eighteenth while perfecting the ideals of the Enlightenment. Romanticism overthrew neo-

[48] Cf. *ibid.*, iv, Chap. 12.
[49] On these points, cf. Wellek, *A History of Modern Criticism*, iv, Chap. 16.

classicism while returning to Rousseau. And similar oppositions, of course, had filled the eighteenth century itself:
"Frenchmen had instituted a Republic and overturned Christianity," Brandes writes, "before it occurred to them to dispute the authority of Boileau." One might say, in the terms
of this paper, that Brandes is aware of the superposition of
periods, or of the fact that they are not discrete entities.
These contradictions have effects of varying scope. The literature of exile, for example, typically shows a dual character ("whatever the nature of the compound, a double current
is discernible in emigrant literature") and Brandes underlines the dualism of individual writers like Novalis, or Benjamin Constant ("no truth, he was accustomed to observe, is
complete unless it includes its antithesis. He succeeded in
completing many truths"), or even of single works such as
Chateaubriand's *René* or Kierkegaard's *Enten-Eller*.[50]

Harry Levin has appropriately remarked that for Georg
Brandes a book is a force, a "continuing force," and, within
the causal relation existing between literature and society, a
cause rather than an effect.[51] Obsessed with the need for forward movement, Brandes admires those literary works that
are vital enough to be new, that is, to start anew, as each generation must on the basis of its own vitality and capacity for
creation. Madame de Staël's *De l'Allemagne*, he says, was
epoch-making "because, not accidentally but on principle, it
broke with all antiquated literary traditions and indicated
new sources of life." (Unfortunately, he was not able to recognize the novelty of Novalis or Hölderlin, for whose sensibilities he had no understanding.) Brandes the battler, the
militant critic, was *engagé* in the past exactly as if it were the
present. He practiced in criticism the commitment he sought
and appreciated in literature: "for a nation has a literature

[50] Brandes, *Main Currents*, I, 31; IV, 71; cf. II, 188; I, 39.
[51] Cf. H. Levin, *The Gates of Horn* (New York, 1963), pp. 13-14.

in order that its horizon may be widened and its theories of life confronted with life."[52]

The character of such an *engagement* is inseparable from Brandes' position on our topic, i.e., his subordination of periods to currents. Brandes studies the passage from the Enlightenment to the first half of the nineteenth century. He is also profoundly aware of the relationship between that time and his own. Brandes could very well have regarded the first half of the nineteenth century *as a period,* and then, in counterposition to it, individualized his own as well. This is precisely what certain historians of the first half of the century had done vis-à-vis both (and simultaneously) the Renaissance and the eighteenth century.[53] This had been made possible by the French Revolution and the collapse of the previous political and social systems. Brandes (it would be interesting to compare his views with those of other literary historians writing in the 1870's and 1880's about the beginning of the century, like Emile Faguet and De Sanctis) could have *individualized* his period and the preceding one if only he had been able to rejoice over the failure of the 1848 liberal revolutions and to consider them a cleavage as substantial as that of the French Revolution. He preferred, instead, to regard the nineteenth century as a single, dynamic, unfinished movement emerging from the eighteenth, marked by tensions and ambiguities from the start, and still engaged in an indecisive battle. He thus preserved his feelings of solidarity with the spirit of the Revolution, and his hopes that Scandinavia might yet take its proper place or play a larger role in the general liberation of Europe from reaction, hypocrisy, and oppression.

Brandes writes somewhere that the horses in Fouqué's *Zauberring* are the only creatures in the book whose psy-

---

[52] Brandes, *Main Currents,* I, 107, 101.

[53] On this point, cf. Jasinowski, "Sur les fondements logiques de l'histoire," pp. 42-43.

chology the author has fully mastered. Yet despite his bias, and even with regard to writers he does not esteem, or fails to understand, Brandes lacks spite, and maintains a sort of serenity. Perhaps this was due to the fact that his century had known so many setbacks, and that he received at first so little recognition in Copenhagen. He was not a utopian, and did not expect the realization of his ideals in his own day. In fact, he judged it indispensable, like Unamuno (who shared his "fire," and discovered Kierkegaard through him), to shock and irritate his contemporaries.[54] As a person, he was the opposite of the man Taine advised him to be in a letter of July 23, 1873, after having read *Main Currents*: "Permettez-moi de vous conseiller, en un sujet si brûlant, l'attitude du spectateur abstrait: vos coups seront d'autant plus perçants que vous paraîtrez au-dessus de toute polémique; il faut partir de ce principe que vos adversaires n'existent pas, ou mieux encore, que votre domicile est dans une autre planète."[55] But Brandes, so committed to his planet, had never gotten over the impression he had received as a youth from reading the *Ethics* of Spinoza, which he recounts in his memoirs: "A love of humanity came over me, and watered and fertilised the fields of my inner world which had been lying fallow, and this love of humanity vented itself in a vast compassion."[56]

In later years, Spinoza would be replaced by Darwin, and still later by Nietzsche, and Brandes would continue to suffer, as Oskar Seidlin explains, from the conflict between his vitalism, or his philosophy of the individual will, and his scientific

[54] Cf. M. de Unamuno, "Ibsen y Kierkegaard" (1907), in *Ensayos* (Madrid, 1951), II, 415 (I am grateful to Juan Marichal for this reference); cf. Brandes, *Main Currents*, IV, 124.

[55] *Correspondance de Georg Brandes*, ed. P. Krüger (Copenhagen, 1952), I, 13.

[56] Brandes, *Reminiscences of My Childhood and Youth* (New York, 1906), p. 102.

positivism.[57] Yet it seems to me that at all moments Brandes was inspired by a religious or a metaphysical need, despite his doubts concerning a God, and that his feelings of solidarity with other men (harsh though their expression could be), his awareness of continuity, if only within an earthly order, his desire to participate in the main historical currents of his century responded to such a need. How can one bear being simply *nailed* to life—"cloué à la vie"?—he asked his good friend Georges Noufflard in a letter of April 1875; and his advice to Noufflard was: "il faut regarder la chose individuelle d'une manière symbolique, la chérir, y voir une image du grand tout et s'y attacher le plus sérieusement que l'on peut. Ainsi on peut dire avec une certaine raison que l'on a participé à la grande vie, n'ayant vécu qu'un court temps dans un espace circonscrit."[58]

VIII

In my discussion of periods and currents, a number of the points I have touched upon obviously brought to mind some of the subjects that fall under the jurisdiction of the theory of history. This is an affinity I can only note in passing, not because of any lack of space, but because of a matter of method and priorities. Let us grant that any instrument, any term, any metaphor for the interpretation of literary diachrony begs, echoes, or assumes a philosophy of history. Do literary currents, for example, imply some version of evolution or of development—the fulfillment of a law, or of a purpose? Literary currents would have to be associated with a linear, basically Judeo-Christian view of history. But as a nineteenth-century term, despite these theologies, a current

[57] Cf. O. Seidlin, "Georg Brandes, 1842-1927," *Journal of the History of Ideas*, III (1942), 428.
[58] *Correspondance de Georg Brandes*, I, 75.

is normally open-ended and inconclusive. It seems that most of us can agree on a minimal notion of continuity as being basic to the historical existence of literature and characteristic of its nature.[59] Consequently, it seems difficult to yield to any *historical* pessimism in our field, to the melancholy, for example, with which anthropologists view the slow death of the "savage mind." The Brazils and the New Guineas, the Ashantis and the Nambukwaras of the poetry of the past will long remain available in our libraries, with the peculiar freshness of poetry, insofar as they have been recorded and printed. But how does this continuity withstand the constant additions to our literary heritage? How are we to conceive of the accretions of time?

One could go on, in a more rigorous fashion, to investigate these issues. But the matter that I am considering is one of preliminary approach or method. The idea of literary history, to which this essay alludes, would seem to require the application to the literary field (this being a principal task for comparative literature) of recent gains and accomplishments in the philosophy of history. But it is also true that a philosophy of the history *of literature* must build on its own premises and learn above all from its own investigations and achievements. It should, first of all, study and understand itself. It is simple and practical enough to continue to speak of "development," "tradition," "unity," or "national literature" without conscious intent; and some sort of cathartic liberation from routine and *idées reçues* would be welcome in this area. But it is also a facile procedure automatically to adapt to literary studies a set of systematic ideas from general history, politics, economics, science. It cannot be assumed that a theory of literary history will coincide in all essentials with a comprehensive philosophy of history (and thus lack any specificity and justification). Neither can it be supposed that

[59] On the idea of continuity in history, cf. K. Löwith's discussion of Jakob Burckhardt in *Meaning in History* (Chicago, 1957), pp. 21-22.

it will not. For the moment one can demand that literary scholars, in order to make such confrontations and cross-fertilizations possible, look after their own affairs with a fair measure of independence.

Toward this end, the growing dialogue today between American or Western European critics and the historians of Eastern Europe should be particularly fruitful for all concerned. One must doubtless be grateful to György Lukács and his more thoughtful followers for asking the great questions, for discussing themes and opening vistas to which too many Western critics are indifferent. Marxism, in this sense, has brought about the beginning of a *rapprochement* between literary theory and the philosophy of history. To these difficult and important problems, however, Marxists often offer ready-made solutions. It is curious that some should be so slow with the questions, and others so fast with the answers. It is to be hoped that many scholars will pursue the theory of literary history in a spirit of confidence and freedom from preconceptions.

In this essay, I have discussed some of the difficulties raised by periodization, especially with regard to diachrony and the organization of historical time. My purpose was not to further any form of nominalism, of surrender to flux and mutability, of indifference to generalizations.[60] An attitude of this kind would be, as it were, "colonial," for it would mean that in practice one would rely, for reference and clarity, on the periodological *points de repère* laid down by others. In fact, I have tried to discuss those forms of periodization that provide us not only with an access to styles and

---

[60] Cf. Wölfflin, *Kunstgeschichtliche Grundbegriffe*, as quoted by Teesing, *Das Problem der Perioden*, p. 38: "Alles ist Uebergang, und wer die Geschichte als ein unendliches Fliessen betrachtet, dem ist schwer zu entgegnen. Fuer uns ist eine Forderung intellektueller Selbsterhaltung, die Unbegrenztheit des Geschehens nach ein paar Zielpunkten zu ordnen."

values, but with a sensitive and genuine vision of history, and hence can serve as foundations for an idea of literary history.

I was led by the analysis of a paragraph from Lévi-Strauss to support a multiple-process descriptive model that would accommodate the realization that men apparently live in more than one "period" at once. I went on to say that there is not simply *one* current of time to which various classes of chronology and periodization refer, but a multiplicity of both code and coded object, signifying and signified. Our critical vocabulary presents some problems here, of course, and it would be necessary to define and refine one's terms much more fully. Let us accept for the moment that we do not mean by period simply a section of time. We mean a critical concept that is applicable to a section of historical time and to its dominant structures and values. My hypothesis is that a section of historical time—the goal, that is, of the concept of period—should not be monistically understood as an undivided entity, a bloc, a unit, but as a plural number or cluster of temporal processes, "currents," "durations," rhythms or sequences—flowing, like the Arve and the Rhone so vividly portrayed by Georg Brandes, simultaneously and side by side. If we conceive of the diachronic object of periodization as being multiple in the first place, it is then not so difficult to accept the idea of multiple periodization, either in terms of dynamic, dialectical periods or of separate "durations," "currents," processes, and other terms comparably diachronic in character.

Thus we took notice of the fact that the seventeenth century has already been studied most convincingly not as a Baroque period but as a blending of Baroque, Classical, and Mannerist "currents." I have repeatedly recalled Huizinga's suggestion that the Renaissance should not be approached as a monolith (the only possible solution to that tiresome riddle). It seems obvious, as a final example, that the literature of the turn of the last century should not be interpreted as a single Symbolist *period*, but as a strong Symbolist "process" in poetry, in aesthetics, in the novel, coincident and diachronically contemporaneous with a continuing realistic or naturalistic vein in the novel, various forms of decadentism, aestheticism, or art nouveau; with the final stages of certain Romantic styles, such as the political "poetry of ideas"; with the final phases of the Parnasse, a brief interval of neoclassic or idyllic poetry, and the first emergence of experiments that would ultimately flow into Surrealism and other avant-garde movements of the twenties—each of these "durations" having its own rhythm, speed, intensity, and particular life-span. It is only in such terms, certainly, that one can approach periodologically the work of poets writing, like Rubén Darío, far from Paris, and the situation of authors in the next section of time, so as not to overestimate the participation in an exclusive "Symbolist heritage" of post-World War I poets like Lorca or Montale.

IX

A special obstacle lies in the way of an idea of literary history, and I should like to indicate its seriousness as I finish this exploratory essay: the obstacle is the absence of an appropriate terminology. This lack brings out most eloquently the fact that literary history has been until now, by and large, an *ens ab alio* or "dependent" discipline, i.e., that it has possessed no mature idea of history of its own to build upon. Our vocabulary in the area of literary history is extremely limited. Any current glossary of literary terms will demonstrate this. Nine-tenths of the critic-historian's lexicon is of use to the critic but not to the historian. One of the better dictionaries we have, the *Dictionary of World Literature* edited by Joseph T. Shipley (New York, 1943, 1953), does not carry such terms as "movement," "school," "current," "generation," "avant-garde"—although it includes the words "period" and "tradition." "Period" has been the topic of this essay. "Tradition," I have also begun to show, is only apparently—or even fraudulently—holistic, and is of little use to the historian. Shipley admitted also "taste" and "style," which are pliant notions of some pertinence to history. Nevertheless, the old-fashioned concept of taste (despite Lionello Venturi's attempts to revive it in *Il gusto dei primitivi*)[61] fails to meet our need, not only because it denotes an aesthetic faculty but because it is monistic and vague. The idea of style, even when it is—very properly—normative and collective, and defines a set of verbal conventions shared by a group of writers, singles out alternatives rather than confrontations. It cannot be made too comprehensive without becoming critically ineffective, that is, as vague and monistic as taste. Shipley does not admit "school," "movement," or "avant-garde," which have been admirably delineated by Renato Poggioli in his *Teoria dell'arte d'avanguardia* (Bologna, 1962).[62] The truth is that

[61] (Bologna, 1926). The title is ambiguous, as it refers to both a taste *for* the primitive, on the part of critics and artists since the Renaissance, and the taste *of* primitive artists. Still, Venturi was primarily preoccupied with the taste of groups and schools: "dichiaro che intendo per gusto l'insieme delle preferenze nel mondo dell'arte da parte di un artista o di un gruppo di artisti" (p. 15). These are really artistic assumptions, comparable to Wölfflin's *Grundbegriffe* in his *Kunstgeschichtliche Grundbegriffe* (1915).

[62] Poggioli gathers all groupings of the past (Provençal troubadours, *Dolce stil nuovo, Minnesang, Pléiade*, and so forth, until the Enlightenment) into "schools." A school implies traditions to be respected, skills to be learned, a master to teach them, and a pupil who regards his future experience as insufficient: *ars longa, vita brevis*. Since Romanticism, on the other hand, movements have flourished whose aims are immanent. Each movement attempts to elaborate or proclaim its own conception of the possibilities of art. It regards culture not as increment but as creation. The spirit and the characteristics of movements are displayed most purely by the avant-garde. These are, it seems to me, definitive distinctions. But Poggioli's purpose must not be misunderstood. He reflects on self-conscious, self-styled events and groupings of the past. The literary historian, or the theorist of literary history, whom I have in mind, is primarily concerned with a posteriori con-

our vocabulary supplies us with a wealth of advice on the level of critical classification, interpretation, and analysis, but not on that of literary history. It derives basically from classical poetics and rhetoric and is generally ahistorical.

A terminology is not necessarily a jargon (intended to exclude a certain *class* of readers). Neither does it manifest only the fact—discussed by T. W. Adorno in a brilliant essay—that foreign borrowings and technical innovations, awkward though they may seem, help to break down routine, *idées reçues*, conventional barriers between disciplines.[63] The terminological advances that one looks forward to in the field of literary history would show above all the ability to elaborate principles of construction in accordance with the particular nature of literary historical experience. To organize and conceptualize process, rather than to eliminate or dis-

---

structions of the past. From the vantage point of our time, literary developments previous to the Romantic years cannot always be described as a series or a combination of schools. Critics have tried to classify, for example, the principal poets of the second half of the sixteenth century in Spain into a "school of Salamanca" and a "school of Seville." The results have been unconvincing. (The history of painting, a more practical craft, may lend itself better to this view.) In Seville, Fernando de Herrera was the acknowledged master of a poetic school, while Don Juan de Arguijo presided over an academy. But there were writers in Seville who belonged to neither: Miguel de Cervantes, a struggling young poet and playwright, and Mateo Alemán, who translated Horace and planned a large picaresque novel. The artists who revolutionized the visual arts in France before and after World War I have been labeled the "school of Paris" (particularly in Paris), and Poggioli mentions that the label is superficial. What accepted term could possibly do justice to the interplay of movements, manifestos, exhibitions, and little magazines during the "banquet years" in Paris? Nearly all partook of the spirit of the avant-garde. The future historian, obliged to chart his own itinerary and refine his own categories, will in all probability neither restrict himself to a mere summary of all the self-appointed movements of the time, nor extend indefinitely the range of Surrealism, as some historians and period-hunters are tempted to do.

[63] Cf. T. W. Adorno, "Wörter aus der Fremde," in *Noten zur Literatur II* (Frankfurt, 1961), p. 115.

solve it, is of course what one needs. We have seen the extent to which the idea of period accomplishes this. We have also observed that the notion of current has been brought in to compensate for the failure of periods to render diachrony. It seems to me that the literary historian actually seeks words with which to define a sort of literary *conjuncture*, or equivalent thereof, without postulating the identity of poetic processes with economic processes—a constructive configuration which, like economic conjunctures or cycles, implies change, absorbs the vicissitudes of time, and evokes the profile of history in the making.

"Conjuncture" is holistic and all-embracing but not monistic. It implies the articulation or junction of *various* parts. It has become clearly associated, through its uses in economic history, with mutability and the flow of time, while singling out dominant moments and trends. The economic historian Pierre Chaunu explicitly identifies "conjuncture" with movement, and "structure" with immobility. Thus a conjunctural narrative ("récitatif conjoncturel") is able to deal with shorter fluctuations and cycles, "temps brefs" as well as "temps longs."[64] Jan Marczewski defines an economic conjuncture as a set of variations within an interval of time: "l'ensemble des variations non saisonières de l'activité économique d'un espace géographique, pendant une période de temps."[65] It must be understood that the definition of a certain conjuncture is not the starting point but the final result of the researches of an economic historian: it is the final theoretical design that he proposes on the basis of those researches. Moreover, such factors as total national income, index of employment, index of prices, and balance of payments are not, according to Jean Prudhomme, the components but

---

[64] Cf. Fernand Braudel, "Pour une histoire sérielle: Séville et l'Atlantique (1504-1650)," *Annales E.S.C.*, xviii (1963), 542.

[65] Marczewski, *L'Europe dans la conjoncture mondiale* ("Cahiers de l'I.S.E.A."; Series AC, April-May 1963), p. 3.

rather "les indicateurs de la conjoncture."[66] Thus, in our own field, schools and movements, systems of styles and genres, conventions and institutions would all serve as "indicators" of the literary conjuncture, or of the equivalent of the conjuncture, which the historian proposes to interpret.

Until such a terminology is developed, the example of De Sanctis and of a growing number of contemporary critics has made quite clear the nature of a workable alternative to periodization and the shattering of literary history into discrete units. The alternative is simple enough. It relies on the use of a noninterpretative chronology (in Italy, Trecento, Quattrocento, etc.).[67] It stresses essentially the confrontation, within such chronological units, of a plurality of durations, movements, systems, schools, institutions, and other temporal processes. The historian's task, writes Fernand Braudel, consists in grasping a hierarchy of forces, currents, or movements, and then in perceiving once more "constellations" and vast wholes: "qu'on se place en 1558 ou en l'an de grâce 1958, il s'agit, pour qui veut saisir le monde, de définir une hiérarchie de forces, de courants, de mouvements particuliers, puis de ressaisir une constellation d'ensemble."[68]

[1967]

[66] J. Prudhomme, "Un apport de J. Marczewski à l'étude de la conjoncture," *Annales E.S.C.*, xx (July-Dec. 1965), 337-340.

[67] Sometimes pure chronology becomes colored with significance, as in Italy, where a derogatory meaning was long attached to Seicento and secentismo—Alfieri's "il Seicento delirava": cf. Vittorio Santoli, *Fra Germania e Italia* (Florence, 1963), p. 274.

[68] "Histoire et Sciences sociales: La longue durée," p. 735.

ESSAY 11

On the Object of Literary Change

I

One often hopes that theory might benefit from the imminence of practice. The theoretical questions that are posed by the organization of literary history are seldom simple and never superficial. Today we are reminded of these questions by the "History of European Literature" which the Hungarian Academy of Sciences is planning in cooperation with the International Comparative Literature Association. This project fully deserves the support and collaboration of comparatists everywhere. In the initial stages, our support may well take the form of theoretical discussions concerning the basic problems of literary historiology.[1]

That the leading role is being assumed by the Hungarian Academy is a fortunate circumstance. The very remarkable contribution of Hungarian scientists, humanists, and artists to the intellectual life of this century is evident to all. Hungary's central position in Europe, its contacts with the most varied trends of thought, its independence from those chauvinistic or ethnocentric instincts which weigh so heavily in the balance when either Western or Eastern Europeans contemplate their past are all conditions that augur well for the future of this enterprise.

Two general features of the plan are most attractive. The first is very obvious, and the other slightly less so. We are promised a genuinely comparative history of European lit-

---

[1] The core of this paper was read at the third meeting of the American Comparative Literature Association, held in Bloomington, Indiana on April 18-20, 1968. The topic of the panel discussion for which it was written was "A Literary History of Europe: Approaches and Problems." The paper appeared in expanded form in *Yearbook of Comparative and General Literature*, XVIII (1969), 19-35. Section II has been added here.

erature, first of all, in the sense that the readers will not be provided merely with a row of so-called national literatures, neatly contiguous, with the addition of remarks on influences, borrowings, and translations. What is at stake is the kind of historical category or strategy capable of generating a comprehensive view of European literature. Secondly, it seems that the principal instrument of historical organization across national boundaries will not be the notion of literary period. This could initiate a salutary reaction against the widespread tendency in comparative studies to replace the traditional emphasis on national literatures, as they appear "horizontally" or diachronically, with a renewed stress on the synchrony, or rather the pseudosynchrony, of international periods, eras, or epochs.[2] We have been told that the proposed "History of European Literature" will be based on "courants littéraires" or "literary movements." These terms, as Tudor Vianu pointed out in the 1962 Budapest conference,[3] are very much in need of clarification. Nevertheless, they imply an awareness of the fact that currents or movements coexist and clash within a single section of time. They suggest a sensitive perception of historical becoming, that is to say, of the processes and confrontations of the past.

We have also been told that a substantial question remains unanswered: that of the limits of what is meant by European literature. The problem, it is suggested, is not so much temporal as it is spatial or "geographical":[4] Should one include all literatures or significant literary works written in Euro-

[2] I refer to the conception of literary periods as a sequence of time sections. See "Second Thoughts on Literary Periods," pp. 420-469 of this volume.

[3] Cf. T. Vianu, "Formation et transformation des termes littéraires," in *La Littérature Comparée en Europe Orientale* (Budapest Conference, October 26-29, 1962), ed. I. Sötér (Budapest, 1963), pp. 59-60.

[4] Cf. the 1967 "Report on the Project for a History of Literature in European Languages" (mimeographed and circulated to members of the I.C.L.A. before the 5th Congress in Belgrade), pp. 7-10.

pean languages across the world, from Manila eastwards to Vladivostok? Some who answer this question in the affirmative go so far as to maintain, with Mihály Babits,[5] that European literature, in the broadest sense, ought to be defined typologically. A literary class or set of classes would constitute its real identity.

I am inclined to support the position of the "little Europeans." The proposed field of study should be qualified and circumscribed for the following reasons. A typological definition may be the final product of a survey, but it does not coincide with it. The survey itself, the narrative of European literature in the making, unfolds a sequence of events, not a class beyond time. Keeping in mind that we are dealing with a process of change, the fundamental question that arises is one of the relationship between the narrative of literary events and the itinerary of the peoples and societies from which these emerged. Who were the agents of such a history? Who made the events possible? To whom did they happen? Such queries can scarcely be avoided, and it would seem odd for the literary critic to appoint himself a historian while showing an utter disregard for the *identity* of his historical subject. This does not mean that I am prejudging the nature of the relationship between what the Russian formalists called the "literary series" and the "historical series." Though the two series may be far from equivalent, or even parallel, an unequivocal connection should exist between the spatial-temporal limits of the one and the corresponding limits of the other. And we are thus led to rely on the way in which the concept of Europe itself is isolated by the social or the political historian.[6]

---

[5] Cf. M. Babits, *Az európai irodalom története, 1760-1925*, 2 vols. (Budapest, 1934). I have seen the translation *Geschichte der europäischen Literatur* (Zurich, 1949). Babits' aristocratic position is such that he equates European literature with *Weltliteratur*; while he scorns "die orientalisch-exotischen Kulturen" (p. 5 and *passim*).

[6] An alternative consists in dealing with literatures "written in European languages." This is a retreat from the historical problem I

With this further question in mind, I am substantially persuaded by the conclusions of Oskar Halecki in *The Limits and Divisions of European History* (1950). European civilization, with its basic Germanic, Scandinavian, and Slavic components, develops in an area and in a section of time that are distinct from those of its Greco-Roman predecessor, whose center was the Mediterranean. Ernst Robert Curtius' bias in his *Europäische Literatur und lateinisches Mittelalter* is that, while stressing the continuity of a literary series, he neglects the profound changes that took place in the historical series from one civilization to another. This passage takes the form not of a transition from "period" to "period," but of a thousand-year-long process of cultural change. It coincides with Christianization, and it begins much before the fall of the Roman empire. As Alfons Dopsch and Christopher Dawson have shown, it continues until at least the year 1000—or perhaps up to the conversion of the Lithuanians in 1387, or of the Spanish New Christians during the sixteenth and seventeenth centuries. The imposition of Christian unity on the Iberian peninsula represents, for good or ill, the final Europeanization of Spain and Portugal, while making possible at the same time, through the creations of Cervantes and other Spanish artists, the injection of Semitic-Oriental elements into the bloodstream of European civilization.[7] The

---

am discussing, rather than a solution. I do not underestimate the use of language as a unitary principle for the organization of literary studies. In fact, it is a more satisfactory principle than nationality. But a plurality of languages (i.e., a multiplicity of media) makes little sense. It brings us right back to the need for a definition of the adjective "European," and of the spatial and temporal limits of Europe itself, which I mention below.

[7] I accept, and deeply admire, the main trend of Américo Castro's interpretation in *La realidad histórica de España*, 3rd edn. (Mexico, 1962). Castro has gathered the facts to prove his contentions—such as the stress on the "pluricultural" and profoundly Semitic nature of Spanish civilization and history. On the Semitic aspects of Cervantes' "discovery" of the novel, cf. particularly "La palabra escrita y el 'Quijote,'" in Castro's *Hacia Cervantes* (Madrid, 1957), pp. 267-299.

example of Spain is methodologically central because it visibly indicates that history is composed not of a sequence of periods but of the coexistence and confrontation of processes and "durations." While Europeanization was still taking place in the Iberian peninsula, the discovery and conquest of America marked the beginning of the most creative of all processes of dissolution. Europe as a self-centered, distinct civilization ceases to exist even as it expands and begets and exports its works across the planet. I suspect that these observations apply also to the limits and configurations of European literature, which can be distinguished from a broader "Western literature." The transformation of Europe into a Western or an Atlantic community may be reaching its crucial stages today, even though the themes and the procedures of Greco-Roman poetry can reappear in Manila or in Vladivostok. It might be pointed out that there is usually a time-lag between the temporal boundaries of a civilization and those of its literature, since continuity and conservatism are such strong factors in the literary field. But ultimately one is led to recognize that Europe does not coincide with the West,

---

My point is that though the peculiarity of Spanish civilization is undeniable, its impact on European history is irrefutable too, so that no definition of European civilization, and especially, of European literature, which excludes Spain or fails to take into account the impact of Islamic and Hebrew history on Europe is at all viable. Perhaps an analogy could be made with the impossibility of drawing absolute frontiers between neighboring languages. Cf. Louis Hjelmslev, "The Content Form of Language as a Social Factor," in *Essais linguistiques* (Copenhagen, 1959), p. 93: "it has long been realized that however widely languages may differ, they may come to resemble each other if there is cultural communication between them. Kristian Sanfeld has shown how the Balkan languages, which are of widely different origin, have drawn very close to each other. . . . Cases of this kind are known to linguists as linguistic associations: thus there is a Balkan linguistic association, and a European or more specially a West European association." (The reference is to *Sprachbünde*, as discussed by R. Jakobson and N. Trubetzkoy, cf. Hjelmslev, p. 16, note 1.)

and that its proper dimensions have been smaller and more fine-grained—the coordinates of differentiation that made us so aware of the distinctions between Florentines and Neapolitans, Czechs and Slovaks, Catalans and Andalusians. To restrict Europe in space and time is to stress this essential texture, and to perceive how different it is from the dimensions of Western civilization today.

Yet there are even larger questions that call for preliminary discussion. Had we no longer any doubts concerning the "practical" limits of our topic, certain decisions would still have to be made with regard to not only the character but the very objectives of literary history. For the basic principles of literary *history* as an intellectual discipline continue—to tell the truth—to appear unclear. Surely, the same does not apply to literary *criticism*. The efforts and procedures of criticism, at the very least, tend to converge on individual objects. These objects are works of art. It is always possible for the critic to rely on the unity or "form" of the literary work, and to expect that his own responses will evidence a minimum of integrity. But what holds a particular history of literature together? No historian limits himself to holding up a mirror to a past "reality" previously sorted out and arranged for him; today we know that historiography is unavoidably "constructive." As the student of literature moves away from the single work of art and approaches the wider expanses of historiography, the choice of a "constructive" principle becomes increasingly necessary.

There can be no objective without an object, no history without a core that may serve as the protagonist of the historian's narrative, or at least as an occasion for the perception of change. A row of single poems, stories, and plays arranged against the background and the drama of political or social history, like a string of corks bobbing on the ocean, does not offer us a picture of the change—and therefore the history—*of* literature. It is not the predicates but the subjects of the historian's discourse which stand in need of initial clarification. "No science is possible which does not have its distinct object,"[8] writes René Wellek concerning Kant's identification of an "aesthetic realm" in the *Critique of Judgment*. The main question concerning the "science" of literary history is what the nature of its *object* is.

The concept of Europe will not come to our rescue now, as it did a moment ago when spatial boundaries were being discussed. The question remains, vis-à-vis such a broad area, of what the province of the literary historian actually is. What is the object of his investigations, and how does it differ from that of *other* historians? We know, to be sure, that to ask a question, to identify a problem, constitutes the beginning of an approach toward the field under study. It may be that the guileless question I have just raised implies such an approach: the attempt to regard the student of literature from the start as a historian *among historians*.

A negative check might confirm this point. Let us notice in passing what is *not* being asked: the age-old question of the relationship between "literature" and "history." Aristotle laid down a famous distinction between the two in his *Poetics* (1451b): history presents what has happened, literature (or poetry) what may happen; literature tends to express the universal, history the particular, etc. Aristotle's topic was the nature of poetry, and its different "species" (these two, the nature of poetry and the division into species, being closely interconnected); so that he naturally found it useful to emphasize the contrast between the achievement of the poet and that of the historian. His concern was not with the theory or with the various species of *history* (though he began to practice literary history in the *Poetics*: 1448b, for example). The modern theorist's is. For his task begins where the aesthetician's ends—or where the "philosopher of poetry" is re-

[8] *A History of Modern Criticism: 1750-1950* (New Haven, 1955), I, 230.

placed by the philosopher of history. We do not doubt that an authentic corpus of poetry exists—for example, a number of sixteenth-century Spanish poems. We assume that these poems have already "happened," and have already been differentiated from the accomplishment of those other sixteenth-century Spaniards who conducted scientific experiments, carved statues of saints, waged wars, built cities, destroyed civilizations. The question concerning the connections that could have existed between the efforts of these men and the works of the poets is not that of the relationship between "literature and history": it is entirely dependent, instead, on the skills of the modern historian and the ways in which he organizes the scattered data he possesses—military, social, political, or whatever. We are dealing basically with the relations between *literary history* itself and *social history, political history, economic history,* etc.

The theory of history that one might support, then, would postulate (as Aristotle did with regard to literature in the *Poetics*) that there are several "species" of history. *Literary* history would exhibit, whatever its aim or its character, some measure of "specificity." Now, I quite understand that autonomy and specificity are two very different things; and I am not for a moment suggesting that the history of literature be considered in glorious isolation from that of societies, economies, or dominant values. I am concerned here so much with historicity, in fact, that I assume literature is not exempt from it. I assume that it is not fruitful to continue to speak of "literature" in a purely aesthetic, rhetorical, nonhistorical manner, on the one hand, and of "history" on the other, and then, having severed the two so neatly, to struggle for meaningful "relations" between them. It is preferable to discuss the connections between literature and either society or language from a radically historical point of view, that is, while regarding each of these systems as intrinsically (at least in part) diachronic and changeable. Thus our question seeks to identify the goal which makes of the discipline under consideration both a "specific" enterprise and a genuine province of history. This means, most probably, that the object of literary history must itself admit of change. The working hypothesis of the historian is that historical change does not flow *around* his topic; but, rather, that the careers of society, language, and literature all compose processes—flowing, as it were, simultaneously and side by side, though with different speeds or rhythms. Surely, as far as historical discourse is concerned, one is likely to admit Alfred North Whitehead's idea that the notions of process and existence, or of process and individuality, presuppose each other. As Whitehead writes in *Modes of Thought*, "process and individuality require each other. In separation all meaning evaporates. The form of process . . . derives its character from the individuals involved, and the characters of the individuals can only be understood in terms of the process in which they are implicated."[9] With regard to the study of literature in historical time, "specificity" and "historicity" are two inseparable requirements. And their union reflects within our discipline the interlocking of what Whitehead calls in his metaphysics "process" and "individuality."

I should add that I do not propose to confuse these "individuals" of literary history (the specific objects of literary change) with the isolated works of art. Critics have often tried to link entire historical periods, in the broad sense, with single literary works. Critics of style have gone further: having analyzed a particular style, they have then attempted— for example, in the manner of Leo Spitzer—to identify in a single verbal device the microcosm of contemporary *Geistesgeschichte*. From a historian's point of view, these are implausible endeavors. Let us suppose for a moment that the

⁹ Alfred North Whitehead, *An Anthology*, ed. F.S.C. Northrop and Mason W. Gross (New York, 1953), p. 869. Cf. Ivor Leclerc, *Whitehead's Metaphysics* (London and New York, 1958), pp. 63-80.

opposite were being attempted. Let us return to those sixteenth-century men I mentioned a while ago—Spaniards who waged wars, conquered civilizations, built churches and cities. One would pick a single action: the construction, say, of one of the 365 churches in Cholula and its vicinity. What would the analogous procedure be? One would go on to show a satisfactory and sufficient relationship between this individual occurrence and the entire design of the literature of the *Siglo de Oro*. Doubtless no sane scholar would waste his time on such a hypothesis. It would be disingenuous to pretend that the building of even all the churches in Mexico could be discussed seriously without the previous insertion of the subject into the appropriate economic, political, or religious frameworks. Where historical facts of this sort are concerned, one does not ordinarily suppose that an isolated event is fully representative, "emblematic," or "symbolical" of entire economic conjunctures or processes of social change. Yet a similar notion, to go back to the individual poetic work, has been maintained by many a literary critic.

A reason for this is that the verbal work of art has long been regarded as essentially emblematic or symbolical, and artistic "form," or expressive form, as a kind of mediation between the One and the Many. In Aristotle's opinion, as we just recalled, literature tended to express the universal, while history related the particular. Among the Romantics, especially, it was believed that the poet, like a prophet or a seer, was a pursuer of the absolute. Schelling affirmed that only symbolism in art, as distinguished from abstract thought or allegory, was capable of presenting the general through the particular. Coleridge found in the imagination the means to "make the changeful God be felt in the river, the lion and the flame. . . ;"[10] etc. An interesting instance, because of its apparently structural terminology, is one of Friedrich Schle-

[10] Cf. Wellek, *A History of Modern Criticism*, ii, 76, 163, and *passim*.

gel's longer aphorisms from the *Athenäum*. Schlegel praises the feeling of the ancient Greek poets for both "individuals" and "systems"; and he asks whether any systems, or "real unities," exist that are not historical:

"Kann man etwas andres charakterisieren als Individuen? Ist, was sich auf einem gewissen gegebnen Standpunkte nicht weiter multiplizieren lässt, nicht ebenso gut eine historische Einheit, als was sich nicht weiter dividieren lässt? Sind nicht alle Systeme Individuen, wie alle Individuen auch wenigstens im Keime und der Tendenz nach Systeme? Ist nicht alle reale Einheit historisch? Gibt es nicht Individuen, die ganze Systeme von Individuen in sich enthalten?"

(Can one characterize anything else than individuals? Is there not just as much historical unity in what cannot be multiplied from a given point of view as in what cannot be further divided? Are not all systems individuals, even as all individuals, at least in the bud and according to the tendency of each, are systems? Is not all real unity historical? Are there not individuals that contain whole systems of individuals?)[11]

It would be possible to show that these Romantic ideas underlie Benedetto Croce's well-known invitation to discover in the individual work of art a concentrated, meaningful expression of "history." Having granted that universal history unfolds, in post-Hegelian terms, the career of the Spirit, one can find no better access to this necessary evolution than the appreciation of art. The single work of art, Croce writes in "La riforma della storia artistica e letteraria" (1917), encloses the entire world and all of history in a single form: "tutto l'universo e tutta la storia in una forma singola."[12] This form being only available to the kind of literary criti-

[11] Friedrich Schlegel, *Charakteristiken und Kritiken I* (1796-1801), ed. Hans Eichner (Munich, Paderborn, and Vienna, 1967), no. 242, p. 205.

[12] "La riforma della storia artistica e letteraria," in *Nuovi saggi di estetica*, 4th edn. (Bari, 1958), p. 177.

cism which is oriented toward the "individual" ("critica individualizzante"), literary history must therefore consist of a series of monographs or single essays. This idea was well received by some of the more distinguished critics in Italy. Francesco Flora has stated that the history of literature "absorbs" all the other materials of history, which only art can transform into "content."[13] Luigi Russo exacerbates Croce's thought and goes so far as to write that literary history is a task for "retarded minds" ("una fatica di menti arretrate").[14] Apropos of Karl Vossler's study of the *Divina Commedia*, Russo writes that world history has become "incarnated" in the great poet's spiritual vision:

"Bisogna giungere al concetto che la poesia è, sì, fantasma, sogno, lirica visione; ma fantasma, sogno, lirica visione che nasce nella storia. Non nella storia presa nella sua esistenza obiettiva, come qualche cosa che esista lì, di fronte al poeta, e con la quale egli debba fare i conti, ma nella storia che si è incarnata, si è contratta in lui, e in cui consiste e di cui irrequietamente si fa tutto il suo spirito. . . . Così si può dire che l'artista, generando la sua poesia, genera al tempo stesso tutta una storia del mondo, da cui pur quella poesia nasce. Ebbene: indagare quella storia del mondo contratta in lui, e da lui attualmente generata, val quanto spiegare il nascimento della poesia stessa."

(We should finally come to the idea that poetry is, by all means, a phantom, a dream, a lyrical vision; but a phantom, a dream, a lyrical vision born in history. Not in history re-

---

[13] Cf. Francesco Flora, "Storia letteraria," in "Occasioni e aperture," *Letterature Moderne*, xi (1961), 434: "una storia delle lettere assorbe tutta l'altra storia che, diversa da quella, o materia da cui soltanto l'arte potrà formare un contenuto, la cinge per l'ora presente e per la evocata memoria del passato. Non c'è altro storicismo."

[14] Cf. "Il Croce e la storia della letteratura," in *La critica letteraria contemporanea* (Florence, 1967; rev. edn.), p. 157: "ma una *Storia*, se non nella forma del manuale scolastico, come lavoro strettamente scientifico appare a tutti gli intendimenti una fatica di menti arretrate."

garded in its objective existence, like a thing out there, in front of the poet, with which he must come to terms, but in history as it has become incarnated, contracted, in him, and by which his spirit is restlessly nourished. . . . Thus one can say that the artist, while giving birth to his poetry, brings forth at the same time a whole history of the world, from which such poetry is born. To investigate, then, that history of the world contained in him, and later turned into poetry by him, amounts to explaining the birth of poetry itself.)[15]

The obvious circularity of this oft-encountered notion is difficult to discuss, for a rebuttal would require a thoroughgoing discussion of the postulates involved. For example, I have assumed that there are several "species" of history, whereas Russo implies that there is only one. But if even such questions were to be left aside, this difficulty would remain: that historians cannot dispense with time. The product or culmination *of* history which Russo perceives in an isolated poem cannot possibly coincide with the process, the sequence, the *narrative* of history *itself*. The historian arranges diachronically a series of "particulars," to use the Aristotelian term— whatever the scope of the particulars may be. Even though Russo's ideal critic may deal with the genesis of the poem (as in the poetics of Walter Binni), he goes on to focus on the ways in which a narrative of events "contracts" into timelessness. He is, in short, a spurious historian. To be sure, it cannot be denied that it has been fruitful to define the "spiritual unity" of singular historical periods or epochs, like the Middle Ages and the Renaissance. But the Renaissance is *not* "tutta la storia in una forma singola." In this sense, as a "particular" of history, it is comparable to the concept of national literature. Croce argued most persuasively that the unitary idea of national literature—as when certain critics speak of the "genius," the "character," or the "sense" of Italian litera-

---

[15] *Ibid.*, p. 254.

ture—is not a valid critical category.[16] Luigi Russo followed suit in a long essay entitled "Ritorni ed esaurimento di vecchie ideologie romantiche."[17] Croce's point was that art expresses both the individual and the generally human, but not that halfway house called the nation: "essendo l'arte in quanto arte sempre individuale e sempre universale, e perciò sempre sopranazionale."[18] National literatures, that is, are neither particulars nor universals. The same applies to whatever portion of history a single poem may symbolize.

We saw earlier that the diachronic study of literature implied two requirements: "historicity" and "specificity." A third requirement, then, would be "structure," or "system," or "integration." I shall soon return to these terms, with which the linguist and the social scientist are familiar. Essentially, the literary historian cannot be satisfied with an atomistic approach to literature (though the critic may). Insofar as history demands interpretation, and interpretation rests upon constructive principles, it is not sufficient to enumerate —to arrange a row of individual objects. This seems evident enough when the subject is European literature. But even if the topic were less ambitious, literary history would still presuppose the existence of extensive processes and configurations, rather than of merely partial or isolated events. In practice, this is what the better literary historians have achieved. In theory, there is much that remains to be done, and it is generally thought today that the most useful analogies can be drawn from linguistics and the social sciences— especially from the latter.

Louis Hjelmslev, in the essay titled "An Introduction to Linguistics" (1937), discussed the differences between the broad view of linguistic systems and the regional study of lin-

---

[16] Cf. "Storie nazionalistiche e modernistiche della letteratura," in *Nuovi saggi di estetica*, pp. 181ff.

[17] Cf. *La critica letteraria contemporanea*, pp. 376-392.

[18] Croce, *Nuovi saggi di estetica*, p. 271.

guistic change: the latter he called "idiodiachrony," as opposed to "pandiachrony."[19] Similarly, the concern of the historian of European literature is with "pandiachronic" objects of study, such as movements and currents. At the same time, the peculiar "complexity" of his task is such that the relationships between these different currents or processes, on the one hand, and between literary history and what I have been calling the other "species" of history, on the other, are continuing problems. These problems, as far as I know, are comparable to those that the anthropologist is called upon to confront. The limits of "language"—i.e., what language is *not*— are much clearer than the contours of the social scientist's "culture." Language, consequently, provides us with the better structural model, though at the expense of the intersystematic considerations that arise when the various levels or parts of complex cultures are being differentiated.

Forty years ago Edward Sapir regarded this as an advantage: "linguistics would seem to have a very peculiar value for configurative studies," he wrote, with reference to configurative or Gestalt psychology, "because the patterning of language is to a very appreciable extent self-contained and not significantly at the mercy of inter-crossing patterns of a non-linguistic type."[20] Today, it is the inter-crossing of patterns that attracts our attention. A culture embraces a plurality of levels or orders (material practices, group values, religions, etc.) which are roughly the counterparts of the various species of history. Now, there obviously is more than simply a difference of breadth between an investigation of blanket-weaving among the Navahos and a study of their social organization as a totality. It has been one of the principal tasks of anthropological theory during the last thirty

---

[19] Cf. Hjelmslev, *Essais linguistiques*, pp. 18-20.

[20] "The Status of Linguistics as a Science," in *Culture, Language and Personality*, ed. David G. Mandelbaum (Berkeley and Los Angeles, 1956), p. 74.

years to refine the terms which make possible a total or "holistic" interpretation of cultures. "Societies," Pierre van den Berghe summed up recently, "must be looked at holistically as systems of interrelated parts."[21] In order to describe this congruity among the parts of a society, a number of terms have been used: "values," or "grammars of values," for example. In their study of *The Navaho* (1947), Clyde Kluckhohn and Dorothea Leighton singled out nine "basic convictions" or "premises"; earlier, Ruth Benedict had studied "psychological sets" and "patterns"; A.-R. Radcliffe-Brown, a "system of sentiments," with regard to the Andaman islanders; Ralph Linton, "universals," "specialties," and "alternatives"; Morris Opler, "themes"; John Gillin, "objectives"; J. A. Barnes, apropos of complex societies, "networks."[22] Of course, these various terms respond to different criteria and stresses. I shall discuss presently the need to distinguish between "domination models" and "interaction models" with respect to the structural study of history. For the moment, I should reiterate that literary history as a genuine "species" or "genre" of history implies a structural object of study. The essential choice is between chronological or serial enumeration, based on the principles of construction which the other genres of history have supplied, and a systematic description postulating that the literary scholar is capable of making his own contribution to historical knowledge. This last point has been forcefully expressed by Louis Hjelmslev:

[21] "Dialectic and Functionalism: Toward a Theoretical Synthesis," *American Sociological Review*, xxviii (1963), 696.

[22] Cf. Morris E. Opler, "Some Recently Developed Concepts Relating to Culture," *Southwestern Journal of Anthropology*, iv (1948), 107-122; Robert L. Carneiro, "The Culture Process," in *Essays in the Science of Culture. In honor of Leslie A. White*, ed. Gertrude E. Dale and R. L. Carneiro (New York, 1960), pp. 145-161; and S. N. Eisenstadt, "Anthropological Studies of Complex Societies," *Current Anthropology*, ii (1961), 201-222. (One might add M. J. Herskovits' "cultural focus.")

"Toute description scientifique présuppose que l'objet de la description soit conçu comme une structure (donc, *analysé* selon une méthode structurale qui permet de reconnaître des rapports entre les parties qui le constituent) ou comme faisant partie d'une structure (donc *synthetisé* avec d'autres objets avec lesquels il contracte des rapports qui rendent possible d'établir et de reconnaître un objet plus étendu dont ces objets, avec l'objet considéré, sont des parties)."[23]

In the literary field, what I have been saying is that the historical view (necessarily comprehensive and constructive) requires a systematic object of study: an object, in Hjelmslev's terms, which is not merely synthesized with other intelligible objects, but can itself be structurally considered.

II

I have been using the words "structure" and "system," and should clarify at this point my understanding of these terms. Doubtless they both denote sets of constituent units in which the interrelations between the units are meaningful. Beyond this, the scope of each term varies, and should remain flexible. Within the context of this essay, i.e., of the problem of literary history, I think that the following distinctions are advisable.

The literary historian is interested in structures and systems as *historical occurrences*. There are, of course, linguists and anthropologists who will interpret these—somewhat derogatorily—as mere "surface structures" or one-shot "manifestations"; and they are just as entitled to this view as they are to the construction of potential models from which one may deduce, through the appropriate transformational rules,

[23] "Pour une sémantique structurale" (1957), in *Essais linguistiques*, p. 101. Hjelmslev's point of departure in this context is the thought of Rudolf Carnap in *Der logische Aufbau der Welt* (1928) (cf. p. 32).

real phenomena. But the concern of the *historian*, very legitimately too, is with those systems which really "happened," those structures that in actual fact connected the various interacting parts of a historical configuration, those antagonisms, refutations, or struggles for order in which human beings were directly involved. It has been traditionally thought, to return to Aristotle once more, that history arranges "particulars" (or sets of particulars), while poetry expresses universals. Today eminent anthropologists add: history deals with "contingents," anthropology with universals. With respect to either thought, *literary* systems and structures are, to be sure, particulars and contingents. Let us suppose that the shape of a certain succession of events appears to have been contingent, or to make very little sense: it is then the duty of the historian to show an understanding of contingency rather than a nostalgia for sense. (This does not mean that a system actually occurring on a year X does not include "potential" components that may develop in later years. A theory of genres published in 1795 was both one of the events of that year and a potential framework for creative writing. Historians will record the ways in which that theory gradually gave way to accomplishments, even though—or because—this was a contingent development.)

There is, secondly, a useful distinction between "structure" and "system" which one may wish to retain. "Structures," according to this conception, designate especially the interrelations (of mutual and meaningful dependence) between constituent units. "System" denotes either the set which is "held together" by these relations or the larger configuration which embraces one set after another in historical time. Thus system is the broader term; structure, the more precise one. Among social scientists, A.-R. Radcliffe-Brown conceived a structure to be "the set of actually existing relations, at a given moment in time, which link together certain human beings."[24] A system always encloses a structure, but the opposite is not true, as Lein Geschiere points out with regard to language. A single sentence, responding to an individual situation, does not coincide with the broader system or subsystem. In "Je l'ai vue hier," *hier* belongs to the subsystem *hier-aujourd'hui-demain*, and the other words to other subsystems belonging to a larger linguistic system. Geschiere proposes an analogy with the regulation of traffic through red, orange, and green lights: as a system, this arrangement is intended to meet certain needs and contingencies, while the exact relations between the various lights at a given moment constitute the structure.[25]

In the context of literary history, I should repeat that a system is meaningful only when it is known to have endured over a certain period of time, and to have made individual occurrences possible. "Poetry-prose-prose poem" is a subsystem, while the relation between the three is a structure. This subsystem was effective in France for several decades after Aloysius Bertrand and Baudelaire; and it connoted a passage from a binary structure based on a "conflict model" (poetry versus prose) to the more complex triad, which has often evidenced in the career of poetics a structure (a "reconciliation model") more akin to "history" than to "nature." In the area of rhetoric, the notion of the "three styles" is a structure within an enduring rhetorical system. In the history of mod-

[24] Meyer Fortes, "Time and Social Structure: An Ashanti Case Study," in *Social Structure. Studies presented to A.-R. Radcliffe-Brown*, ed. M. Fortes (New York, 1963), p. 54. For a social scientist's definition of system, cf. Robert L. Carneiro, "The Culture Process," in *Essays in the Science of Culture*, p. 146: "we may define a *system* as a set of structurally and functionally related elements articulated into a working whole."

[25] Cf. Geschiere, "Fonction des structures de la phrase française," in Sem Dresden, Lein Geschiere, and Bernard Bray, *La Notion de structure* (The Hague, 1961), pp. 12-13.

ern literature since the sixteenth century, the novel is an important subsystem, while the opposition "symbolism-naturalism" has been one of its leading structures since the end of the nineteenth century. Within the subsystem of Spanish literature (whose temporal span I shall discuss later), the opposition "popular-cultured" has traditionally been regarded as a structure; even as Góngora was the protagonist of a famous polarity in seventeenth-century poetry, and the neoclassical form of Cervantes' *Numancia,* the counterpart of Lope de Vega's increasingly popular pattern. The Romantic movement is a system whose structure has been repeatedly analyzed. In cases such as these, the concern of the historian is with the fact that these structures and systems, of which the actually existing relations between a Cervantes and a Lope de Vega are an instance, actually did last or endure for a considerable number of years.

It seems necessary to distinguish, further, between systems and structures, on the one hand, and, on the other, the intrinsic *formal* relations that are characteristic of the verbal work of art (though this is an arduous question, blurred by terminological confusions). To be sure, the single work of art, the great poem, is an extraordinarily coherent network of reciprocal relations, going far beyond the structures of ordinary language, and can or should be considered a special sort of system. This quality of the poetic artifact, often identified with the concept of structure, though not in the latest sense, has been associated with literary criticism since its inception. Aristotle recognized in his *Poetics* the unity of the poetic work and the interrelationship of the parts in a dramatic plot. His "structural analysis of the tragic plot" was carefully interpreted by Gerald F. Else not long ago: "recognition" in tragedy (*anagnorisis*) implies not only that the tragic hero attains a higher level of knowledge but that the play itself discloses the necessity and the impact of its internal structure.[26] This insight, so long forgotten, was not truly regained until the eighteenth century, as René Wellek points out in his *History of Modern Criticism*. The unitary qualities of the work of art make their reappearance in the "organic metaphor" of Herder, Goethe, the German Romantics, and later Coleridge and Victor Hugo; and in the notion that the work of art represents a gathering of tensions and balances: "T. S. Eliot and after him I. A. Richards constantly quote the key passage in Coleridge's *Biographia Literaria* describing imagination as the balance of opposite or discordant qualities."[27] This idea, Professor Wellek shows, Coleridge owed largely to Schelling. In *Die Lehre vom Gegensatz* (1804) Adam Müller had derived from Schelling and Fichte the idea that literature is the locus of the reconciliation of opposites. In our time John Crowe Ransom, Allen Tate, and Cleanth Brooks have stressed the tensions and the interplay of contraries underlying the uses of paradox, irony, and wit.

I merely wish to suggest that the recent advances in the concept of structure—in the social sciences, in literary history, and in other areas—should not be allowed to clash, or to ambiguously fuse, with this traditional recognition of the formal virtues of the work of art. It strikes me that history, including literary history, is *not* the locus of the reconciliation of opposites. The structural opposition between two writers and two schools may remain in fact an unresolved, though fruitful, conflict. Literary history may reveal a dialectical interplay of contraries in the Hegelian sense, as stages in a process of growth, but not the timeless harmony which the "reconciliation of opposites" connotes in aesthetics. One does not expect the *history* of the pastoral novel (and its interplay with various kinds of satirical or realistic fiction) to exhibit the union of opposites, because it is not *like* a pastoral novel.

---

[26] Cf. Gerald F. Else, *Aristotle's Poetics: The Argument* (Cambridge, Mass., 1957), pp. 349ff.

[27] Cf. *A History of Modern Criticism*, I, 2.

We suppose that it will draw us closer, instead, to the discordance of historical experience.

Thus it seems advisable to reserve the terms "structure" and "system" for the extrinsic relations existing between works of art, schools, styles, etc., and the word "form" for the intrinsic principles of unity at work in the single work of art as a result principally of the efforts of the individual creator, man the maker, the "poet"; in other words, to apply the former to literary history, and the latter to literary criticism. I am well aware of the fact that these two kinds of order are intimately linked; but the nature of their connection is still another problem.

Without our going any further, however, the terminological distinctions I have just made allow us to see a little more clearly into the special character of our subject. We have seen this: that the *systems* and *structures* of literary history admit in certain cases (when the single parts are works of art) constituent elements which are *forms*. This peculiar combination of distinct kinds of relations means in turn two things: first, that the processes of literary history embrace both contingency and necessity (the "structures," which might have been different, were contingent, whereas the artistic "forms" reveal an exceptional degree of necessity); and second, that they blend in a particular manner (hence the originality and specificity of literary history as a genre of history) the apprehension of the past with the presentness of the aesthetic experience.

The first of these points, regarding the manner in which contingent historical structures (as defined in this essay) envelop and admit necessary poetic forms, requires no advocate in the circles of literary criticism. Today it might be most useful to formulate it within the framework proposed by Roman Jakobson in "Linguistics and Poetics," in *Style in Language*, ed. Thomas A. Sebeok (Cambridge, Mass., 1960), p. 358: "the poetic function projects the principle of equiva-

lence from the axis of selection into the axis of combination."
I have stated elsewhere, following Jakobson, that the poem
projects the qualities of system (one of which is equivalence)
from the axis of selection into the axis of combination. I might
then add in the present context: this projection is also the kind
of informing process or of informing effort through which
the various components and *moments* of the temporal axis of
combination become uniquely interrelated and irreplaceable
and are therefore vindicated and individually justified. The
informing energy involved in the poetic function of language
so orders the linear and temporal succession of verbal events
as to endow these events (*événements*) with the values of
"necessity." As for my second point, dealing with the apprehension of the past in connection with the present aesthetic
experience, it calls for some additional words of explanation.

In the Introduction to his lectures on *The Philosophy of
History,* Hegel differentiated between what he called "original history," which can be found in the works of Thucydides
and other writers dealing with events on which they had first-
hand information or whose "spirit" they shared, and "reflective" (or "philosophical") history, where temporal as well as
axiological distance is assumed and imaginative constructions
are required from the writer. We all know that this distinction is only partly relevant to the history of literature, painting, or music. All artistic criticism is, to repeat an expression
used in Italy with respect to the visual arts, *critica in pre-
senza.* Benedetto Croce tried to deny this peculiarity of literary history: the presence of the work of art before us, he
thought, is only physical; while as a mental event its status is
not different from that of other historical materials.[28] One
must recognize with him that the difference is not absolute:
surely the "presence" of a work by Euripides or Dante or
Tintoretto must be the fruit of a great deal of effort and prep-

---

[28] Cf. "Alcune massime critiche e il loro vero intendimento" (1919),
in Croce, *Nuovi saggi di estetica,* pp. 219-221.

aration on the part of the reader or the spectator. Yet the distinction between what has only entered the lives of others and what *we*, in a certain degree, have ourselves been able to experience is crucial.

Croce's view is the exception; and it has normally been felt that, on the contrary, the presentness of the artistic object is a hindrance to the perception of its historicity. Literary history is a paradoxical endeavor, in the words of Roland Barthes, because the poem or the play is both "signe d'une histoire, et résistance à cette histoire."[29] The problem, in fact, could be stated negatively: the literary work of art is not ephemeral enough; it endures, or at least its form tends and is intended to endure; and insofar as it does (and the ways in which it perseveres need of course to be qualified), it is not a proper object of historical change. Indeed one is reminded of that chilling sentence in which Auguste Comte credits the mortality of man—the passing of the generations —with being an essential condition of social progress: "en principe, il ne faut point se dissimuler que notre progression sociale," he wrote in the *Cours de philosophie positive*, "repose essentiellement sur la mort."[30] The very opposite, to be sure, would have to be predicated of the poetic *word* and recognized as an essential condition not only of the "institutional" aspects of literature but of the mode of existence and the character of literary systems.

While this mode of existence contains a singular degree of continuity, it remains, in the historical view, temporal. (In one of the more old-fashioned and yet widely read rhetorical treatises of the last third of the nineteenth century, A.-E. Chaignet rejected literary history, like Benedetto Croce some years later, but for another reason: "je comprends mal une

[29] "Histoire ou Littérature," in *Sur Racine* (Paris, 1963), p. 149.

[30] *Cours de philosophie positive* (Paris, 1830-1842), IV, 635; cited in Julián Marías, *El método histórico de las generaciones*, 3rd edn. (Madrid, 1961), p. 34.

histoire des lettres. L'histoire a pour objet ce qui passe, ce qui change, ce qui est mort, et par conséquent ce qui était mortel. . . . Les lettres, comme les arts, n'ont pas besoin de cette évocation magique; elles ne sont pas mortes; dans leur beauté, qui est leur essence, elles sont immortelles.")[31] Our framework is not "immortality," but varied and numerous kinds of process, becoming, permanence in time. I have tried elsewhere to designate literary systems as systems of "durations," or "clusters of durations." Systems and structures are durations spanning particular intervals of historical time, lasting, growing, or changing from decade to decade. The same applies to such constituent units as collective styles or themes. The individual "form" or work of art is a duration too, but it is the only one which can "last" until the present day with the special immediacy and availability to the reader's subjectivity we have just described.

I realize that I have just begun to articulate the problem. Does literary history, regarded as a specific branch of history, provide us with a privileged region of experience where presentness intersects with historicity? Does it accomplish this not merely through the aesthetic perception of single forms but by way of that "structural object of description" which Hjelmslev, as we saw a moment ago, required as the goal of every genuine effort of cognition? Following Rudolf Carnap, Hjelmslev also mentioned that "a scientific statement must always be a statement about relations without involving a knowledge or a description of the relata themselves."[32] (Thus linguistics becomes "a metalanguage of the first degree.") We might say that literary history proposes statements about relations involving an immediate knowledge of the relata themselves in such a manner that the intrinsic historicity of the statement resides not in the latter but in the re-

[31] A.-E. Chaignet, *La Rhétorique et son histoire* (Paris, 1888), p. x.
[32] "Structural Analysis of Language," in Hjelmslev, *Essais linguistiques,* p. 32.

lations. To suggest a simple example: if I read a sonnet by Quevedo (with the necessary historical or philological preparation, but only in an instrumental or propaedeutic fashion), I dwell in an area of aesthetic presentness; when I read a sonnet by Góngora, the same occurs; but the comprehension that may follow of the relationship existing and having existed between the two, i.e., of a *structure*, is, to a limited but very characteristic extent, a *historical experience*. Structural relations, rather than individual events, permit the critic-historian to replace the poem in the past without seeing its artistic substance vanish completely in the distance.

I should add that the word "system" has been used with effectiveness a number of times in the context of literary theory. I quoted earlier in this essay one of the several aphorisms in which Friedrich Schlegel, like other Romantics, weighed *Systeme* against *Individuen*. The Polish scholar Wladyslaw Folkierski, speaking at the second International Congress of Literary History (1935), stressed the need to place the literary work within a "système de coordonnées."[33] But the word, of course, is common enough; and we recognize a more precise application of the idea to literary history in René Wellek and Austin Warren's *Theory of Literature* (1949): "we must conceive rather of literature as a whole system of works which is, with the accretion of new ones, constantly changing its relationships, growing as a changing whole."[34] The Saussurian model on which my own conception is based (since the essay "Literatura como sistema," written in Spanish in 1956)[35] had been brought to bear on the problems of literary history, before Professor Wellek, by the

[33] Cf. "Renaissance et Romantisme ou les sables mouvants dans l'histoire littéraire," *Bulletin of the International Committee of Historical Sciences*, IX (1937), 332.

[34] René Wellek and Austin Warren, *Theory of Literature*, 3rd edn. (New York, 1956), p. 255.

[35] Cf. note 45, p. 52 of this volume.

Russian formalists. The first truly significant instance of this conscious parallel between structural linguistics and the theory of literary history is to be found in a brief article by Roman Jakobson and Yuriy Tynyanov, published in *Novyj Lef* in 1928.[36] I was only able a short while ago to read Tynyanov's own longer essay "On Literary Evolution" (1928), where the idea is fully developed, though with an unfortunate emphasis on three points: the notion of national literature, a strict antithesis between synchrony and diachrony, and a serial view of literary history.[37] In the footsteps of these older masters of formalism, Tzvetan Todorov is now confronting with considerable sophistication the questions raised by the literary uses of this linguistic model.[38]

In recent years also, Vittorio Santoli, in an article on Cesare De Lollis in which the concept of institution, dear to Italian linguistic and literary studies, is briefly mentioned, praises most highly the kind of critic "che studia la cultura letteraria di un dato tempo e spazio come un sistema espressivo articolato negli 'istituti' che lo compongono, con i loro contrasti e le loro tensioni, ascese e decadenze" (who studies the literary culture of a given time and space as an expressive system articulated into the "institutes" which compose it).[39] And not long ago, in an article published in English, Santoli spoke of literary systems in the following way: "in a historical judgment . . . , everything is polarized in establishing the place and the role of a work (or of many works

[36] For a recent translation, see "Les problèmes des études littéraires et linguistiques," in *Théorie de la littérature*, tr. Tzvetan Todorov (Paris, 1965), pp. 138-140. See also René Wellek, *Concepts of Criticism*, ed. Stephen G. Nichols, Jr. (New Haven and London, 1963), p. 50.

[37] Cf. "De l'évolution littéraire," in *Théorie de la littérature*, pp. 120-137.

[38] Cf. Tzvetan Todorov, "L'héritage méthodologique du formalisme," *L'Homme*, v (1965), 64-83.

[39] "De Lollis e la stilistica letteraria," in *Fra Germania e Italia* (Florence, 1962), p. 269.

of an author) in the system of the linguistic-literary and artistic culture to which it belongs. . . . The distinctions among literary genres date back to ancient poetics and stylistics, whose schemes do not fit in with the modern concept of literary system which, even though synchronic, is still historical and not abstractly morphological, which is dynamic and not static."[40] I could not agree more with Professor Santoli.

III

Let us now glance back at some of the ground we have covered. In the main, we have observed three essential qualities of literary history. Ideally, the object of literary history is: 1. "specific"; 2. "historical" (in the internal sense); 3. "systematic." But the theory and the practice of literary history are, of course, two very different things. The "model" I have started to delineate is markedly distinct from some of the principal procedures which have been followed in the past. I shall offer some comments on four of these types of literary history.

A common procedure, first of all, consists in presenting exercises in individual literary criticism one after another—a succession, that is, of relatively short critical monographs held together either by chronology alone or by a combination of chronology and occasional references to social, political, or intellectual history. As history, this is an *ens ab alio*: it seeks a principle of coherence beyond the poetic works themselves, as well as beyond styles, genres, themes. In some cases, an internal evolutionary principle is shown to be operative, even though its outline may be blurred when more than one form or theme is being studied. Croce thought that a chronological sequence of critical essays, brought together by the history of non-art, was not *literary* history, and I of

[40] Santoli, "Literary History and Literary Criticism in Twentieth-Century Italy," *Comparative Literature Studies*, II (1965), 74, 77.

course agree—though Croce meant it as a compliment. Basically, the reader is provided with a diachronic montage of critical readings. These readings are superposed on a film of social and political history. Of the three conditions I have just stressed, this kind of history fulfills only the first—that the object be specifically literary; otherwise, its goals are neither intrinsically historical nor systematic; and it thus fails to render forcefully either continuity or change.

This first type of literary history reveals still another failing which deserves some comment. One notices that the so-called historian of literature often considers the proper object of his study to be a series of *new* works. This is profoundly characteristic of his discipline. (Even the formalist Yuriy Tynyanov, as I have just noted, elaborated a serial conception of literature.) The "literary series" which the historian describes becomes a succession of "discoveries" and freshly written works, a tale of modernity in the making and artistic originality at work. Unfortunately, the itinerary of literature in historical time is a much more complicated affair. To repeat René Wellek's words: "we must conceive rather of literature as a whole system of works which is, with the accretion of new ones, constantly changing its relationships, growing as a changing whole." This is the process of cultural development which a social scientist like Julian H. Steward would call "additive" or "accumulative," rather than merely "substitutive."[41] As far as literature is concerned, the historian must always be alert to the interplay between the "already living," in Eliot's words, and the new struggling to live—or between the need for each generation to "start anew" (which is not the same as to innovate) and the essential continuity of the written word. Each period, moment, or "conjuncture" is marked by the places occupied in the more significant contemporary systems by the old together with the recent; and

[41] Cf. Julian H. Steward, "Evolution and Process," in *Anthropology Today*, ed. A. L. Kroeber (Chicago, 1953), p. 314.

I allude not only to writers but to conventions, genres, theories. The situation of the theater in Madrid in 1960 would have to be portrayed in terms of the new plays that were written and also of the classics that were *not* produced. The situation of poetry in Paris at the same time would have to be evaluated in terms not only of Char, Ponge, and Bonnefoy, but of the Baroque poets who had just been rediscovered and reedited. (In this connection, the bibliographer and the historian of the *book* have important contributions to make.) The situation of poetry and poetic systems in eighteenth-century Paris could be defined through the status of the ode or of the lyric genres in general—as well as of Marot and Du Bellay—in the neoclassical treatises of the day, etc.

This notion, I suspect, is most persuasive when one thinks of architecture and the fine arts. There one can speak not of "imaginary" but of real museums; and, especially, of cities. A city such as Paris or Seville represents the most visible and palpable of artistic "systems" or "structures," in which the various styles of the past are blended and continue to come to life. The first of the great Baroque cities doubtless was Rome. But Rubens, Velázquez, and Poussin did not visit Rome exclusively in order to admire the so-called Mannerist and Baroque artists. (Venice, rife with recent glories, had no classical past.) In a sense, the idea of literary system, which I have begun to outline, may be regarded as a verbal equivalent of the authentic, living, growing *city*.[42]

A second type of literary history, dealing with national literatures, might appear to meet all three of the requirements mentioned above. Actually, it does not—for a curious reason: because the extensive object whose career it delineates is a

---

[42] Literary systems, of course, are not only additive but selective; certain authors and forms will be *omitted* by each, etc. May this be comparable to what is neglected and left unseen in a city? It is not difficult to imagine what Boileau must have felt, or rather, failed to feel, as he walked in the vicinity of Notre Dame.

spurious institution. Literary works are rooted in language and experience, not in nations (or races). Literary history and cultural nationalism were both products of the nineteenth century. Consequently, the concept of national literature—as a specifically *literary* category—became a retroactive illusion which nineteenth-century critics foisted on the writers of the Middle Ages and the Renaissance. On some occasions, it has led to determinism, ethnomania, and various reactionary attitudes. On others, it has been a notoriously effective and fruitful concept. Even the Russian formalists used it, for reasons I ignore, though one notices that they dealt with poets and novelists of a period, the nineteenth century, when national literatures were genuinely operative frames of reference.

My point is that this is a notion which should itself be approached historically. Its origins are obviously not artistic. How—one should ask—did the "myth" of national literature fulfill certain social or political functions? In the hands of a number of governments during the nineteenth and twentieth centuries, classroom study of the great national authors was one of the main instruments employed to shape the young citizen in the official image of the community. (This could not quite happen in the United States, whose national language was not exclusively their own: Was this a favorable condition for the development of literary criticism in America?) In what ways, further, did the "myth" of national literature compensate—in the psychological sense of the term—for injured pride, for the oppression of the individual, for the submission of the intellectual to the state? In Europe, the idea of a national literature first arose in Italy, from the days of Francesco Saverio Quadrio and Giacinto Gimma (*Idea della storia dell'Italia letterata*, 1723) to those of Paolo Emiliani-Guidici and Luigi Settembrini. To what extent was this a response to the economic and political decline of the Italian states? Besides: have we not underestimated the extent to

which the all-embracing awareness of being a Frenchman, a
Spaniard, a German, not so much in the minds of the unedu-
cated as among the middle class and the intellectuals, functioned as a *substitute* for vanishing faiths? Questions such as
these would deserve, I think, careful study. The rise of national *canons*—of systems of authors, generally valued and
recommended as authorities—should be fully described and
accounted for, in the manner so splendidly outlined by Ernst
Robert Curtius.[43] In the case of Spain, where such research
has scarcely begun, I should propose this working hypothesis: Spanish literature has been a valid *system* for approximately two hundred years, between sometime in the
eighteenth century and sometime in the twentieth. It is only
after 1750, *grosso modo*, that the tendency to liberate poetry
from the domination of unitary, unchanging norms (from an
absolute poetics), and to place it under the tutelage of national history, gained wide momentum. Before this, one could
encounter, to be sure, much pride in the Spanish *poets*. It was
understood that there were worthy representatives of Spain
on Mount Parnassus. But there was, so to speak, only one
Parnassus. As the sixteenth century drew to a close, Fernando
de Herrera sang the praises of Garcilaso, who had proved not
only his mastery of the eclogue but his ability to rival the ar-
rogant Italian poets. (No Italian doubted, he added, the military prowess of the Spaniards.)[44] But Herrera was every inch
the humanist, always mindful of the Latin origins of his native Seville. It could not cross his mind that there was such
a thing as Spanish *poetry*, or that Garcilaso had cultivated a
Spanish *form*, a Spanish *genre*, or a Spanish *style*. These no-

---

[43] Cf. *Europäische Literatur und lateinisches Mittelalter* (Bern,
1948), Chap. 14, pp. 267-274; and the section "Französisches und
spanisches Literatursystem," in *Gesammelte Aufsätze zur romanischen
Philologie* (Bern and Munich, 1960), pp. 20-22.

[44] Cf. *Obras de Garci Lasso de la Vega con anotaciones de Fernando
de Herrera* . . . (Seville, 1580), pp. 612-613.

tions, which were in conflict with classical poetics, would arise much later.

Their emergence can be studied in connection with the publication of the first national anthologies: from the nine-volume *Parnaso español* by López de Sedano (1768-1779) to Quintana's *Tesoro del Parnaso español* (Perpignan, 1817), the collections published in France by émigrés like Pablo Mendíbil and the Abate Marchena (1819, 1820), Don Alberto Lista's *Colección de trozos escogidos de los mejores hablistas castellanos* (1821), and others. An interesting aspect of this development was the gradual emancipation of anthologies from the schemes of poetics and especially of rhetoric—i.e., from the display of the kinds of "eloquence" to be imitated by the readers, as in Mendíbil's *Biblioteca selecta de Literatura Española, o Modelos de Elocuencia y Poesía* (Bordeaux, 1819)—and, at the same time, the elaboration of historical selections arranged serially and chronologically. Now, as far as the present is concerned, I will risk a comment. Since 1960, approximately, it has been noticeable that the "national" idea of Spanish literature, as an enveloping situation and an operative framework for the writer, has begun to be dislodged by two other categories: by an increasing interest in all literary works written in Spanish, be it in Europe or in America; and by a quickened awareness of the fact that Spain, as a state, is "pluricultural" and encloses at least three literary languages—Castilian, Catalan, and Galician. The roots of the Catalan language have proved to be profound. Will Catalan writing continue to flourish in the future? Will the die-hard chauvinists and theologians permit what might be viewed as a belated but auspicious revival of the original pluriculturalism of Spain? I doubt very much that events of this nature can be foreseen or predicted. But on a European scale, the direction of change can be discerned. One is inclined at times to visualize the temporal profile of European literature in the shape of an hourglass: broad and unitary from the

Middle Ages to the seventeenth century, slimming down to the idea of literary nationality in the eighteenth and the nineteenth, and broadening out again, in the form of increasingly complex systems, during the nineteenth and particularly the twentieth centuries.

There is little need to comment at length upon the third type of literary history, whose purpose is to interpret the itinerary of a single genre (like comedy, or a lyric form, or the historical novel), of a mode (like irony or satire), of a theme, or an aspect of rhetoric or a device of style. By and large, this has been the most satisfactory kind. Within the terms of this essay, its validity (from a theoretical standpoint —I am not dealing with success or failure in practice) arises from the fact that it meets not only the first of the conditions I mentioned earlier—literary specificity—but the second as well: the historicity of an object admitting of change. It is the continuity of the object of study, of course, that allows the perception of change. This is a story, as it were, with a growing hero and a developing point of view. In this context, the title of one of the more recent histories is very appropriate: Roy Harvey Pearce's *The Continuity of American Poetry* (1961). The reader is given a clear and powerful principle of construction. But what of our third condition? Is it not implicit in the other two? Do these studies fail to offer an integrated picture of literary history? In some cases, they do. But in others they do not, and the dividing line cannot be drawn too sharply. The object of study may be regarded as a sign, a model, a heuristic phase in an open-ended process of inquiry. How legitimate is the comparative "perspective," Pearce wonders as he starts, when we have scarcely begun to ask what American poetry "actually is"? And he adds:

"There is yet a larger reason for holding in abeyance such comparatist questions. We have not yet sufficiently realized the degree to which the history of American poetry is a sort of model, an initial if not initiating test-case, for the recent history of all Anglo-European poetry. Almost from the beginning, the American poet's world has been the one we know everywhere around us: where the very role and function of poetry as a valid human act is in question; where the creative sensibility struggles not just to express itself, assured that such expression has a place, some place, in the world, but merely to survive."[45]

It is society, then, which isolates the poet; and this situation is itself a socio-historical circumstance. But one wonders too: Does the critic, in turn, isolate the poet from *other writers,* artists, intellectuals? Theoretically speaking, the problem is one of the extent to which the critic wishes to recognize that a genre belongs to a structure of genres, and beyond it, to a system of literary options. Though the poetic series may be presented as a dialogue with society at large, the fact remains that we are being provided, as far as literature itself is concerned, with a kind of synecdoche; and that the part may be symbolical of the whole (as we said apropos of Luigi Russo) but not representative of the historical structure (which is basically relational). Other stages in the complex inquiry of the literary historian could be described as the attempt to test and extend the insights derived from the interpretation of genres and modes, by means of a decisive passage from the literary component to the literary system, and *consequently,* to a further understanding (following Pearce himself) of the relationships of mutual dependence existing between "cultural" systems and social or economic configurations.

Some schools of criticism maintain, fourthly, that the evolution of society, which economic or social history describes, supplies the student of literature with a sufficient principle

[45] Roy Harvey Pearce, *The Continuity of American Poetry*, 3rd edn. (Princeton, 1965), p. 8.

of construction. The career of literature is viewed as an aspect of the total history of man, and the activity of the poetic imagination as a response to that history. This monistic approach—curiously enough, like the attitudes of certain formalists and idealists—implies the immediate dissolution of literary history as an intelligible process. It fails to account for any of the particular requirements I singled out earlier. (It does not grant specificity to the itinerary of literature, nor any intrinsic historical content; and it does not pretend to discover relevant structures beyond the pale of social and economic systems.) Such an approach seems most distant, therefore, from our "model." And yet it presents a real challenge, which, I suspect, one cannot meet without examining certain assumptions and postulates that do not lie within the purview of this discussion. I shall outline, if not elaborate, my own position—i.e., the assumptions underlying our working model—as briefly as I can.

To be sure, it is absurd to conceive of the history of literature as a kind of separate "current," while social institutions and economic conditions run their own "parallel" but distinct courses. The impact of the latter on the workings of the poetic imagination is constant as well as crucial. On the other hand, it is equally absurd to overlook the extraordinary continuity of literary forms—to assume that every year poetry is reborn, like the Phoenix, from its ashes. (This essential continuity, as I said earlier, is what a history of *new* works only, instead of systems, fails to render impressively enough.) A writer's response to his social experiences and origins, which I do not underestimate, but which I assume implies a contact between intelligible processes, may take the form of the revolutionary use of an inherited medium such as the novel, and thus be simultaneously (Robbe-Grillet is a good example) an answer to fresh social conditions and a link within the internal history of the literary system to which the novel be-

506 ▪ On the Object of Literary Change

longs. As Madame de Staël suggested long ago, and Harry Levin has decisively shown for us,[46] literature is an "institution." This does not mean that it should be confused with other institutions. The very opposite is intended—and left-wing critics can ill afford to forget that literature has been one of the most formidable, durable, and self-perpetuating of all historical institutions.

As a child in European schools, I was introduced at an early age to the traditions of Spanish and French literatures, even as I was to other institutions. I did not turn away from the social or the external world, I did not flee "reality" as I learned poems by heart for the classroom or began to read longer novels: I was being exposed to a singularly well-formed arrangement of experience. I had entered an ancient "city," an order of signs as forceful as any other, for it proffered meanings, enthusiasms, values, even privileged moments of happiness and faith. In short: while studying literary history we are confronted, as in life itself, with an unceasing interplay between evolving orders and competing institutions. Consequently, our theoretical problems are comparable to the social scientist's, though with a special stress on process and historical time.

"Integration," or "cultural integration," is a characteristic

[46] Cf. Harry Levin, *The Gates of Horn* (New York, 1963), pp. 16-23. In article form, "Literature as Institution" first appeared in *Accent*, VI (1946), 159-168. I mentioned earlier in this essay that there is an Italian tradition, too, of interest in the institutionality of language and literature; cf. *Epistolario di Renato Serra*, ed. Luigi Ambrosini, Giuseppe De Robertis, and Alfredo Grilli (Florence, 1953), pp. 290-292, 303; Giovanni Nencioni, *Idealismo e realismo nella scienza del linguaggio* (Florence, 1946), pp. 155-170 (see Nencioni, p. 41, for a bibliography of the metaphor of institution in Croce); Giacomo Devoto, *I fondamenti della storia linguistica* (Florence, 1951), p. 26, and *Nuovi studi di stilistica* (Florence, 1962), pp. 8, 10, 218; Giovanni Getto, "Francesco Flora e le istituzioni letterarie," in *Poeti, critici, e cose varie del Novecento* (Florence, 1953), p. 121; and Luciano Anceschi, *Le istituzioni della poesia* (Milan, 1968).

term used by some anthropologists to designate the forces working for order and coherence in a culture otherwise based on a certain structural differentiation. It has the merit of implying the passage of time. Though "pattern," for example, is a merely structural term, integration has the added meaning of "process behind structure."[47] These are instructive concepts for us, insofar as our task consists, I think, in retaining recent advances in the idea of structure while rewinding, so to speak, the clock of historical time. Our ideal literary historian, like the student of cultures, is a "structural diachronicist."[48] This being said, the further and more arduous question arises of whether structural relations are, as it were, reciprocal; or as I suggested earlier, of whether we have in mind for literary history a "domination model" or an "interaction model." Marxist literary critics, for example, who often are structural diachronicists, may postulate that all correlations between economic or technological structures and literary structures follow the same direction, and thus manifest a kind of instrumentality on the part of the verbal imagination. This is a pure instance of the domination model. On the other hand, Marxists are also interested in "ideology," in the disparity between theory and practice, values and behavior. They show that these disparities can be acknowledged, "healed," or contradicted by the artist, so that a process of clarification or even of *liberation* may begin, through the constraints of artistic form.[49] As a militant old liberal, Georg

---

[47] Cf. Elizabeth E. Hoyt, "Integration of Culture: A Review of Concepts," *Current Anthropology*, II (1961), 407-426.

[48] The term is used by André Martinet, "Structural Linguistics," in *Anthropology Today*, pp. 574-586.

[49] Cf. Herbert Marcuse, "Repressive Tolerance," in Robert Paul Wolff, Barrington Moore, Jr., and Herbert Marcuse, *A Critique of Pure Tolerance* (Boston, 1965), p. 89: "art stands against history, withstands history which has been the history of oppression, for art subjects reality to laws other than the established ones: to the laws of the Form which creates a different reality—negation of the established one even where art depicts the established reality."

Brandes, said a century ago, "a nation has a literature in order that its horizon may be widened and its theories of life confronted with life."[50]

I have tried to show elsewhere that the literary imagination is able to contradict history and social fact, to challenge our complacency and force us to recognize the distance separating values from acts.[51] For the social scientist or the philosopher, none of this is surprising. The former is familiar with the interplay between the different parts or levels of cultures (ideals and material conditions, challenges and compensations, antidotes, etc.), with internal conflicts and incongruities. Although societies exhibit a tendency toward stability and consensus, they "simultaneously generate within themselves the opposite of these."[52] The participation of people in a common cultural system can take the form of fulfilling separate, inimical, and yet interlocking functions—just like "the relationship between mathematics, engineering, and mechanical skills that makes a factory possible."[53] In a synthetic article, Fred W. Voget points out that anthropology has passed from a homogeneous idea of culture and its evolution (functionalism, evolution by interaction among cultures) to a looser conception of culture as itself being constant interaction. This principle of interaction, he affirms, is now paramount in our sense of reality.[54] And Eric R. Wolf agrees with

[50] *Main Currents in Nineteenth Century Literature* (London and New York, 1906), I, 101.

[51] Cf. my article "Individuo y ejemplaridad en el *Abencerraje*," *Collected Studies in Honour of Américo Castro's 80th Year*, ed. M. P. Hornik (Oxford, 1965), pp. 175-197; and essay 6 of this volume.

[52] P. L. van den Berghe, "Dialectic and Functionalism," p. 697.

[53] David F. Aberle, "The Influence of Linguistics on Early Culture and Personality Theory," in *Essays in the Science of Culture. In Honor of Leslie A. White*, p. 15.

[54] Cf. Fred W. Voget, "Man and Culture: An Essay in Changing Anthropological Interpretation," *American Anthropologist*, LXII (1960), 943-965.

this conclusion in his book-length presentation of current anthropological theory:

"For the first time in the history of anthropology, as in the development of human thought about man, we stand upon the threshold of a scientifically informed conception of the human career as a universal process. It differs from previous formulations in its understanding that the universal human process is not unitary, but an articulation of many diverse parts and forces, which are yet interconnected and directional."[55]

As far as philosophical models are concerned, and their possible relevance to our subject, the central question is perhaps whether a "total" reality exists (beyond or within the regularities confronted by the natural sciences) with which a "total" historiography may deal. My own assumptions in this essay are akin to Alfred North Whitehead's in a passage of *Modes of Thought* which I should also like to quote:

"Epoch gives way to epoch. If we insist on construing the new epoch in terms of the forms of order in its predecessor we see mere confusion. Also there is no sharp division. There are always forms of order partially dominant, and partially frustrated. Order is never complete; frustration is never complete. . . . The essence of life is to be found in the frustrations of established order. The Universe refuses the deadening influence of complete conformity. And yet in its refusal, it passes towards novel order as a primary requisite for important experience."[56]

The literary scholar, as a "structural diachronicist," or to put it more simply, as a structural historian, whose goal is the itinerary of poetic systems, makes a significant contribution to our understanding of the human process as an "articula-

---

[55] Eric R. Wolf, *Anthropology* (Englewood Cliffs, N.J., 1964), p. 94.
[56] Whitehead, *An Anthology*, ed. Northrop and Gross, p. 862.

tion" of diverse parts and interacting forces, as the unending creation of "order" in the face of the material cosmos whose oneness the scientist's laws try to seize. In this sense, insofar as the literary scholar strives to recapture the structures available in the tumultuous and partially chaotic course of history, in the apparently linear sequence of events, his is a very human—perhaps a humanist's—occupation. Should there exist, beyond this, an ultimate "structure of structures," historically real, it would seem most fruitful to consider the object of literary change—the ancient city of literature, *civitas verbi,* expanding and yet enduring as a living order through the centuries—as one of its terms.

[1968]

INDEX

43